Cultures of Antimilitarism

Cultures of Antimilitarism

National Security in
Germany and Japan

Thomas U. Berger

The Johns Hopkins University Press

Baltimore and London

This book has been brought to publication
with the generous assistance of the Karl and Edith Pribram Fund.

The Johns Hopkins University Press
2715 North Charles Street
Baltimore, Maryland 21218-4363
The Johns Hopkins Press Ltd., London

Library of Congress Cataloging-in-Publication Data

Berger, Thomas U.
    Cultures of Antimilitarism : national security in Germany and Japan /
Thomas U. Berger.
        p.   cm.
        Includes bibliographical references and index.
        ISBN 0-8018-5820-8
        1. Germany—Defenses. 2. Militarism—Germany—History—20th century.
3. Germany—Politics and government—20th century. 4. Japan—Defenses.
5. Militarism—Japan—History—20th century. 6. Japan—Politics and
government—20th century. I. Title.
UA710.B494   1998
355'.033043—dc21   97-48479
                                CIP

Contents

Tables

Preface

In THE MID-1980s, when I began my research on post–World War II German and Japanese security policy, I took it for granted that these two nations were on the verge of assuming political and military responsibilities commensurate with their status as burgeoning global economic powers. At the time, this assumption was widely shared by most students of international relations and security. For over forty years Germany and Japan had pursued largely passive approaches to defense and foreign policy. Having come to eschew the use of military force as a tool of foreign policy, they relied largely upon an outside power, the United States, for their security needs. Given the extreme suspicion with which these two former enemy nations were regarded by the rest of the world, it appeared for a long time that such a subordinate role in international affairs was the only rational course of action open to them.

With the winding down of the Cold War, however, circumstances changed. Germany and Japan emerged as the economic powerhouses of their respective regions, and with their new economic power came increased self-confidence at home and political influence abroad. As a result, many observers argued that it was only a matter of time until Germany and Japan would begin to behave again like great powers, seeking to carve out their own spheres of political-military influence and preparing to resort to force whenever it was in their national interest to do so.

By beginning my research before the two nations actually had made the transition from their status as Cold War allies of the United States to world leaders in their own right, I hoped to be in the privileged position to closely observe the development of the two nations' post–Cold War foreign and security policies and trace their impact on the international political order. Subsequent events, however, proved these more or less unquestioned assumptions wrong. Instead of assuming the kind of great power role I and so many others had expected them to aspire to, Germany and Japan have gone out of their way to preserve their subordinate status in the international system. Rather than taking on new security responsibilities, they have actively avoided involvement in actions that included the use of military force, even when pressured to do so by the United

Preface

States and other allies. Instead of building up and modernizing their defense forces, they have reduced them. And rather than reaching a new national consensus on defense and foreign policy, the domestic political debates in both countries have continued to display much the same hesitancy and deep political divisions over the use of the military as a tool of foreign policy that has characterized their politics for the past fifty years.

Confronted with an empirical reality at odds with my original theoretical premises, I was compelled to recast my research questions substantially. Rather than becoming the chronicler of Germany's and Japan's entry into the great power league, I searched for the factors behind their refusal to take this role. This now became the central empirical focus of my research. I felt like Sherlock Holmes in *The Hound of the Baskervilles:* The puzzle was not that the dog barked, but rather that it did *not.*

The solution to this puzzle, as I shall show, lies in the strong antimilitarist sentiments that emerged in Germany and Japan in the wake of their catastrophic defeat in World War II. These sentiments were starkly at odds with the two nations' martial traditions. They not only fundamentally reshaped the military and security policies of the two nations during the immediate postwar period, but over time they were institutionalized and became constitutive components of Germany and Japan's broader postwar political cultures. Antimilitary sentiments and values played a decisive role in the construction of the two nations' new national identities in subsequent years, and to this day, fifty years after the end of World War II, they continue to be characteristic of the political systems of both nations. While these cultures of antimilitarism have evolved over time, their core principles have remained much the same as they were in the 1950s and 1960s when the two nations found themselves in international contexts very different from those with which they are confronted today. These cultures of antimilitarism continue to play a decisive role in present-day German and Japanese domestic political debates, and all signs indicate that their security and foreign policies will continue to be driven by them for years to come.

These findings have a number of important practical and theoretical implications. On the practical side they suggest that German and Japanese antimilitarism has far deeper roots than is commonly assumed by American critics who argue that the two nations are merely free riders on the international security order underwritten by the United States. As a result, an American withdrawal—or threatened withdrawal—from regional security is not likely to have the kinds of salutary effects that these critics maintain. Rather than producing a more equitable sharing of the burden of maintaining order in the international system, Germany and Japan are unlikely to quickly take up the slack left in the wake of a U.S. pullout. Such actions are thus much more likely to result in increased regional, if not worldwide, instability.

This does not imply that the United States should remain content with the status quo. On the contrary, if major new military security threats should emerge in the post–Cold War world, greater German and Japanese participation in security affairs is essential. The task of getting these two nations to assume such enhanced security roles, however, will be far more difficult than is usually postulated and will require a far-reaching resocialization of the German and Japanese publics and their elites. While such a process of building a new domestic consensus is already under way, it is far from complete, and in the interim the United States will need to remain intimately involved in Eastern Asian and Western European regional security affairs if destabilizing power vacuums are to be avoided.

The findings of this research also have broad theoretical implications for the study of defense and foreign policy–making in general. First and foremost, my findings lead me to take issue with two of the prevailing orthodoxies in international relations: system determinism and material rationalism. To be sure, pressures emanating from the international system clearly have an important impact on the foreign policy–making process of any state. Yet the way states perceive the international system and the ways in which they choose to respond to external pressures and opportunities are profoundly influenced by domestic political forces and institutions. Beyond that, it is of some importance to appreciate that, although the calculation of material interest and power most certainly influences the decisions of political actors, other nonmaterial interests weigh heavily as well. Moreover, an actor's understanding of his or her material environment is conditioned by the cognitive lenses provided by society, most importantly by socially negotiated understandings of past historical events. To put it simply, nations with different cultural-institutional structures are likely to behave differently even when they are placed in the same material-structural situation.

The writing of this book has been something of an intellectual odyssey, with many ports of call, storms, and even shipwrecks along the way. Throughout this intellectual journey I have been fortunate enough to encounter many individuals willing to give me advice and assistance, and, when necessary, to help put me back on course. First and foremost, I wish to thank my thesis supervisors at the Massachusetts Institute of Technology, Lucian Pye, Dick Samuels, and Bill Griffith. In Japan, I am particularly indebted to Sato Seizburo, who served as my host at Tokyo University, and in Germany I received similar assistance from Wolfgang Bergsdorf of the University of Bonn. I also owe special thanks to Michael Stürmer and Uwe Nerlich as well as to all members of the staff at the Stiftung Wissenschaft und Politik at Ebenhausen who graciously made available to me the wonderful facilities and resources there.

A large number of individuals found time to talk to me about the evolution of the defense debate and defense policy in their respective countries. In Japan, I particularly benefitted from discussions with Raymond Aka of the U.S. Embassy in Tokyo, Chuma Kiyofuku of the *Asahi* newspaper, General Goda Yutaka, Hata Ikuhiko, Inoguchi Takahashi, Inoki Masamichi of the Research Institute of Peace Studies, Itō Keiichi of Mitsubishi Heavy Industry, Itō Kobun of the National Institute for Defense Studies, Kaihara Osamu formerly of the JDA, Kondoh Keichi of the Ministry of Foreign Affairs, Kumagai Akira of the Defense Research Institute, Maruyama Katsuhiku of the 21st Century Institute, Moroi Kem of Keizaidōyūkai, Nishihara Masashi of the National Defense University, Colonel Nishimura Shigeki, Ambassador Okazaki Hisahiko, Onodera Ryūji of the Defense Agency, Ōtake Hideo of Kyoto University, Sakanaka Tomohisa of Aoyama University, Admiral Sakonjō Naotoshi, Satō Yukio of the Foreign Ministry, Major General Taguchi Hatsuyuki, Takahara Akio of the Sasakawa Peace Foundation, Watanabe Akio of Aoyama University, Yamauchi Chisato of the JDA, and Yasue Ryosuke of Iwanami Publishing. A number of members of the Japanese House of Representatives—Eda Satsuki, Hiranuma Takeo, Horie Masao, Kamei Shizuka, Kujiraoka Hiyōsuke, Mori Kiyoshi, Nakao Eiichi, and Takazawa Torao—also generously took time to speak to a young foreign researcher. Special thanks are owed to Matsuura Ryosuke for teaching me about the other side of Japanese politics. Back in Washington, D.C., Funabashi Yōichi of *Asahi* helped me keep abreast of developments in Japan.

In Germany, I also was fortunate to talk to a large number of knowledgeable individuals who helped explain to me the realities of the German defense debate. I would in particular like to express my thanks to Dr. Jörg Baldauf, Dr. Christoph Bertram of *Die Zeit,* Dr. Hans Dieter Brauch, Dr. Wilhelm Bruns, Ernst Czempiel, Major Thomas Enders, Dr. Joachim Fest of *Die Frankfurter Allgemeine,* Christian Hacke, Ambassador Wilhelm Grewe, Josef Joffe of the *Süddeutsche Zeitung,* Mathias Joppe, Thomas Kielinger of the *Rheinischer Merkur,* Evald von Kleist of *Wehrkunde,* General Christian von Krause, Gert Krell,

Dr. Ekkehard Lippert, Dr. Lübkemeyer of the Friedrich Ebert Stiftung, Dr. Dieter Lutz, Dr. Berthold Maier, Dr. Wolfgang Pfeiler of the Konrad Adenauer Institute, Heinrich Rentmeister, Erwin Scheuch, Hans Jochen Veen, Lieutenant General Jörg Schönbohm, Dr. Hans Ruhle, and Dr. Hans Heinrich Weise. Bundestag Deputies Hans Apel, Peter Petersen, Willi Weiskirch, and Willi Wimmer went beyond the demands of maintaining our transatlantic relationship in finding the time to answer my questions.

In the United States, I have benefitted from the assistance of Catherine Kelleher, Kosaka Masataka, and Terry McDougal of Stanford University and representative Shiina Motō. I am also grateful for friendship and shared interests with Yamaguchi Noboru GSDF, Michael Green, Peter Rudolf, Joseph Keddell, Kumazawa Hiroshi, Thomas Risse-Kappen, Sheila Smith, Soeya Yoshihide, Tachibana Masaru, Ushio Masato of the ASDF, and Yutaka Iimura.

Without the time and cooperation of these individuals, as well as help from many others I have been unable to list here, it would have been simply impossible to write this book. The errors and misinterpretations that remain do so despite their best efforts.

Financial support for my research in Japan was provided first by the Fulbright Commission and then by the Japan Foundation. The generous support of the German Academic Exchange Service helped make the German side of the research possible. The MacArthur Foundation supported the initial write-up of my findings. The Olin Institute at the Center for International Affairs under the sage leadership of Sam Huntington made possible a year of postdoctoral studies which allowed me to further refine my ideas and polish the manuscript.

Cultures of Antimilitarism

1

The Cultural Context of Defense Policy Formation

MORE THAN fifty years after the end of World War II, Germany and Japan have rejoined the ranks of the world's leading nations. Economically, they are, after the United States, the world's second and third most powerful nations. Politically, they have succeeded in establishing stable democracies and have achieved notable successes in the areas of industrial policy, the provision of welfare to their citizens, and the maintenance of social order. Internationally, Germany and Japan, long considered pariah states by the rest of the world for much of the postwar period, have come to play central roles in the politics of their respective regions. Today they are increasingly called upon to exercise leadership in world affairs.

In one crucial respect, however, Germany and Japan differ sharply from other great powers: Among comparable advanced industrial nations they stand out for their extraordinary reluctance to become actively involved in international military security affairs. While it would be inaccurate to describe either nation as pacifist, the German and Japanese approaches to national security can be fairly called antimilitarist. Although both have built up formidable military establishments, they have gone to great lengths to minimize the size of their armed forces and, whenever possible, they have placed stringent limitations on the kinds of weapons their militaries may acquire and the missions they may perform. In this respect, Japan and Germany represent historical anomalies. They contradict a large body of literature that suggests great powers inevitably seek to develop military capabilities commensurate with their economic strength and overall political status in the international community.[1] This pronounced aversion to military power is all the more striking in that it represents a radical departure from the militaristic values and patterns of behavior that characterized Germany and Japan before 1945.

In recent years no event has demonstrated more dramatically the continued resilience of these antimilitary sentiments than the two nations' response or, to be more accurate, their *lack of* response, to the Persian Gulf War. Prior to Iraqi leader Saddam Hussein's invasion of Kuwait, it had been widely anticipated that Germany and Japan would emerge as major political actors on the global stage. Moreover, given their high degree of dependence on oil from the region, it can be argued that Germany and Japan had more at stake in the conflict than any of the other major Western powers. Yet, instead of responding forcefully to the challenge to international order posed by Saddam Hussein, Germany and Japan fell into a state of policy paralysis. Whereas virtually every other Western nation—including recently democratized Czechoslovakia—dispatched at least a small contingent of forces to demonstrate their solidarity, Germany and Japan, torn by internal dissention, were unable to make even a minimal contribution of personnel, military or nonmilitary.

In Japan, widespread antimilitary sentiments—both on the popular and elite levels—prevented the Kaifu government from dispatching even small, nonmilitary support teams to the Persian Gulf. And although Helmut Kohl's conservative government in Germany desperately sought to find ways to rise above checkbook diplomacy and express solidarity with its Western allies, antimilitary sentiments similar to those in Japan also ruled the day in Germany. In the end, only a single squadron of Bundeswehr jets was dispatched to Turkey, the only Middle Eastern member of NATO, to be used only in the highly unlikely event that the Iraqi government would chose to attack its giant neighbor to the north.[2]

Despite the provision of substantial financial assistance to the allied war effort in the gulf, the failure to become directly involved posed significant risks to long-term German and Japanese national interests. Criticism of the two countries was fierce, particularly in the United States, where Germany and Japan were accused in editorials and cartoons of practicing "ostrich politik" and public resentment flew high over the perception that American troops had become little more than mercenaries ensuring the continued flow of oil to Japan and Western Europe. At one point the House of Representatives even debated a resolution demanding that U.S. forces stationed in Japan be reduced at the rate of five thousand men per year unless Japan began to bear a fair share of the military burden of maintaining the international security order.[3]

Ultimately these anti-German and anti-Japanese sentiments faded away in the wake of the American military triumph over Iraq. Yet, if U.S. forces had sustained the number of casualties that a broad range of military experts, including the former heads of the Joint Chiefs of Staff, among others, had predicted, criticism of Germany and Japan undoubtedly would have become even more virulent and, by feeding American isolationist sentiments, could well have had long-lasting political consequences. Such an outcome would have represented a severe blow to German and Japanese national interests, for it would have undermined the security arrangements upon which they have come to depend. In other words, it is possible to view Germany's and Japan's general unwillingness to participate in international military actions as part of a perfectly rational strategy of "free riding" on the international security order underwritten by the United States.

However, if the two nations wished to preserve that free ride, they should have dispatched at least token forces to the region, if not on the same scale as Britain or France, then at least on a level comparable to the contingents sent by Italy, Holland, or Belgium. Such a gesture, while ardently desired by the United States and many of the two nations' leading defense and foreign policy experts, was impossible in light of virulent domestic political opposition. The German defense minister, Volker Rühe, is reported to have sadly observed that, after forty years of antimilitary indoctrination, you can't expect the German people to change their minds overnight.

A number of explanations have been proffered to account for the two countries' exceptional antimilitarism. One set of arguments explains their peculiar brand of antimilitarism through reference to some unique feature of either country's historical experiences or geopolitical circumstances. So, for instance, Japan's reluctance to contemplate the use of military force is frequently attributed to the trauma of the atomic bombs dropped on Hiroshima and Nagasaki during World War II. Others maintain that Japan's status as an island nation relatively isolated from the conflicts of the Cold War and the turmoil that afflicted the rest of Asia have inclined it to stay aloof from military security affairs.[4]

In the case of Germany, many contend that the legacy of the Holocaust and other Nazi atrocities has inflicted such deep wounds on the German psyche that large sections of the population are unwilling to once again sanction the use of force in the name of the nation and the state.[5] Others attribute post–World War II German pacifism and antimilitarism to Germany's long-time status as a divided country and its geopolitical location on the front line of any potential Cold War conflict. Yet others assert that Germany places relatively little emphasis on military power because it is embedded in a dense network of multilateral economic and security institutions that anchor the country in Western Europe and make it unnecessary, even counterproductive, for it to develop an independent defense agenda.[6]

While many of these explanations may at first appear plausible, they become less credible when the two countries are compared with one another. There can be little doubt that feelings of guilt over the crimes committed in the name of the German nation under Adolf Hitler have weighed heavily on contemporary German discussions of defense and security. Yet Japan has been at least as inhibited as Germany in the making of its defense policies, despite the fact that Japan as a nation appears to suffer from a form of collective amnesia regarding the atrocities committed by the Japanese Imperial Army during the 1930s and 1940s. Similarly, although the bombings of Hiroshima and Nagasaki have made the Japanese unusually sensitive to the potential horrors of modern warfare, Germans as well exhibit a pronounced aversion to the use of force without having had any comparable experiences. Clearly each country's unique circumstances have colored in distinct ways its views of war and the military. Nonetheless, on a more general level, both countries share similar inhibitions regarding war, the military, and the use of force.

A second set of explanations attributes the origins of German and Japanese antimilitarism to common features in their geostrategic positions. A considerable number of analysts emphasize the two nations' reliance on trade and access to foreign markets for their economic prosperity. As a result, it is maintained, both are highly vulnerable to disruptions in international commerce. In the past Germany and Japan sought to remedy this vulnerability through the creation of autarchic empires. The spectacular failure of those efforts has led them to rely instead on diplomacy and cooperation in the postwar period.[7]

A related line of reasoning points to the role of the United States in the creation of an international security environment that provides Germany and Japan with few incentives to adopt more active military postures. Having helped defeat Germany and Japan in World War II, the argument goes, the United States disarmed and occupied the two countries and imposed an elaborate system of domestic institutional safeguards and external alliances designed to prevent their reemergence as military threats. As the Cold War gained momentum, however, the Western nations were compelled to shift gears. Under the leadership of the United States, Germany and Japan, the despised villains of World War II, were rebuilt and transformed into key regional allies in the campaign to contain communism. Despite their transformation from defeated foes to valued allies, neither the United States nor other countries were ready to accept full German and Japanese rearmament. Consequently, the United States retained primary responsibility for German and Japanese military security, most importantly in the crucial area of nuclear deterrence. Freed from the burden of having to fend for themselves, Germany and Japan were able to concentrate their energies on the development of their economies. In a few short years they achieved two of the most remarkable economic recoveries in history. Under the aegis of the United States, the German and the Japanese people realized levels of prosperity that previous generations could only dream of. With the reunification of Germany in 1989 and the expansion of both German and Japanese political and economic influence in their respective regions, the two nations achieved by peaceable means the power and influence they failed to attain by force prior to 1945. Under such circumstances, it is argued, there existed little reason and little opportunity for either nation to assume a greater military role in international affairs.

While these arguments identify some important structural determinants of the German and Japanese approaches to national security, they fail to adequately explain the strength of German and Japanese aversion to the use of force. To be sure, it can be maintained that interdependence, together with democracy and high levels of prosperity, have made many nations—including Germany and Japan—less belligerent and more willing to resolve their differences through nonmilitary means. Yet this line of argument is unable to explain why German and Japanese antimilitarism have become so much more pronounced and persistent over time than similar sentiments expressed in other countries comparably dependent on outside sources of raw materials and equally oriented toward international trade. Not only are Great Britain and France far more willing to contemplate the use of force to achieve their ends, but even much smaller, more externally dependent trading states such as Sweden, Switzerland, and Singapore are demonstrably less antimilitaristic than either Germany or Japan.

Similarly, the impact of the security order created by the United States explains to a great extent why the German and Japanese approaches to military security evolved in the ways they did. Without the security guarantees provided by the United States, in all likelihood Germany and Japan would have had little choice but to develop more powerful military capabilities, including independent nuclear deterrent forces. Yet the American factor by itself cannot account for the strength of German and Japanese antimilitarism. A more careful analysis of the history of German and Japanese national security in the postwar era reveals that their latitude for action was considerably greater than the American security order line of argument suggests. Although shortly after 1945 the two countries had little choice but to disarm and demilitarize, at various junctures thereafter powerful domestic and international political pressures emerged that could have permitted their respective governments to adopt quite different approaches to national security. Internationally, while the United States is certainly intimately connected with the two nations' renunciation of war and military aggression, the United States also on numerous occasions has urged both countries to expand their defense efforts in order to achieve a more equitable distribution of the burdens of defense and containing communism. Domestically, at various points in time there have been powerful leaders in both Germany and Japan who believed that it was in the national, and in their own political, interests that such enhanced defense efforts be made. Yet, as subsequent chapters will show, in each instance efforts to significantly expand the German and Japanese defense establishments and their international roles foundered on the shoals of domestic opposition. In the end, Germany and Japan opted to make only limited, incremental changes to their defense policies, and the overall antimilitary bias of their underlying approaches to defense has remained unshaken.

Events since the end of the Cold War have further accentuated the two countries' profound antimilitarism. The termination of the East-West conflict and the former superpowers' preoccupation with domestic affairs made for a dramatic increase in the range of options open to German and Japanese policymakers. Yet despite this profound shift in the international system, Germany and Japan have hewed closely to their established low-profile policies. In short, while American hegemony may have been a *necessary* condition for the emergence of German and Japanese antimilitarism, it almost certainly was not the *sufficient* cause of the phenomenon.

What then accounts for German and Japanese antimilitarism? The answer to this question can be found neither in any feature peculiar to either country, nor in commonalities in their positions in the international system. In the final analysis, German and Japanese antimilitarism can best be explained by each nation's struggle to draw lessons from its troubled past. In both cases these lessons were shaped by the fierce political debates of the early postwar years, which took different routes in each country and provided the resulting antimilitary sentiments of each with decidedly distinct flavors. The confrontation with the unspeakable atrocities of Germany's Nazi past raised traumatic questions of collective guilt and drove a whole nation to a fundamental reappraisal of what it means to be German. In Japan, by contrast, the dominant perception was one of dual victimization. On the one hand, the Japanese felt they had been victimized by the blind ambition of Japan's wartime military leadership. On the other hand, they also felt victimized by the United States and other foreign nations which, in the Japanese view, had conducted a ruthless campaign of conquest in order to increase their own power.

Despite dramatic differences in their perceptions of the war, the two countries developed similar aversions to power politics, and both shared an iron determination to avoid a repetition of past mistakes. When they were ultimately compelled by external forces to rearm, their political leaders were forced to negotiate carefully crafted compromises between these widespread antimilitaristic domestic sentiments and the exigencies of a hostile international system. These compromises were institutionalized on two related levels. On the policy-making level, they led to the institutionalization of elaborate systems of rules and regulations designed to curtail the size and scope of the new German and Japanese military establishments. On the level of collective memory they led to the perpetuation of political struggles over the meaning of recent history for many years to come.

In certain respects this argument may appear self-evident. Anyone familiar with contemporary Germany or Japan is well aware of the extent to which memories of the past continue to weigh heavily on the present. Yet there exists a general tendency on the part of analysts to underestimate the extent to which such seemingly intangible social and psychological forces actually influence the policy-making process. Political scientists in particular are inclined to look for explanations based on the material interests of political actors. This tendency may in part be attributed to the intrinsic character of political science as a social scientific discipline. If economists can be called practitioners of the "dismal science," then surely political scientists, as heirs of Machiavelli, deserve to be labeled followers of the "cynical science." They tend to trust only tangible facts and overt events, and typically discount whatever sense and meaning those facts and events may have for the actors involved. Politics, as Harold Lasswell once said, is about who gets what, or as Lenin put it, more ominously, who does what to whom. In addition, the modern political scientist's quest for theoretical propositions that can be generalized induces him or her to belittle or ignore the extent to which human behavior may be the product of unique, not easily generalizable, features.

Beyond the fundamental prejudices of the discipline, however, there are other more substantive reasons why contemporary political scientists are often reluctant to rely on cultural and ideological factors as categories of explanation. For one, the term *culture* is extraordinarily broad and has been used in many different ways. For another, it is exceedingly difficult to identify all the elements that go to make up the culture of a given group or society. By definition, the analyst is forced to abstract from the multitude of elements available those germane to the argument, and thus is left open to accusations of prejudice and whim.[8] Even if the researcher does succeed in defining the broad parameters of a particular culture at a particular point of time, he or she frequently discovers that cultures can and do change, often in very substantial ways within remarkably short periods of time. Because of these difficulties, there exists a strong tendency for "culture" to be seen as a residual category of explanation, prone to tautology and essentially immune to falsification.

Such conceptual and methodological shortcomings, needless to say, are not unique to culture-based approaches and *mutatis mutandis* can be applied to any theoretical enterprise. Yet, because of the intangible nature of the phenomenon of culture, many of these methodological difficulties are compounded. For this reason it is incumbent upon the analyst who makes use of culture as a category of explanation to provide a short overview of how the concept is defined and used for the purposes of the analysis.

This book directly confronts these central dilemmas of cultural analysis. It sets out to provide a more stringent definition of the concept of culture and, with the introduction of the concept of "political-military culture," it abstracts those elements of the larger culture that shape defense and security policy formation. The two cases that have been selected for analysis here further compel us to examine directly the issues of cultural shift and transformation.

The authoritarian and militaristic cultures of Germany and Japan responsible for World War II were of such a profound and pervasive nature that early postwar observers expressed considerable skepticism as to whether either country could ever become a peaceable democracy. Martial values have deep roots in German and Japanese history, and by the second half of the nineteenth century the military as an institution had come to dominate the social and political lives of both countries. In Japan, the motto of the Meiji Restoration of 1868, "Rich Country, Strong Army" *(fukoku-kyōhei)*, reflected that country's peculiar blend of militarism with aggressive notions of national destiny, while the Germany of the Wilhelmine period beginning in 1871 was arguably the most militaristic industrial society of the time. Despite civilian attempts to steer a more moderate course—during the Weimar Republic in the case of Germany and the liberal Taisho period of the 1920s and 1930s in Japan—by the outbreak of World War II the bellicose spirit of both nations and their formidable war machines posed a threat to the rest of the world.

Yet, as the record shows, a profound cultural transformation took place after 1945. To many skeptics this suggests that culture is merely an epiphenomenon that masks the working out of concrete interests. That is to say, when it appears to be in the interest of a given group or nation to be aggressive and belligerent, that group will develop a militaristic culture to legitimate that behavior; when circumstances change and appear to favor peaceful coexistence, then once again the group or nation will adopt a corresponding ideological and cultural stance. Hence, critics contend, culture-based explanations are inherently tautological as they seek to deduce a cause from its effects.[9] It is possible, however, to formulate a concept of political culture that can withstand these criticisms.

The Concept of Political Culture and its Study

The term *culture*, as used in the social sciences, refers to the ideas, beliefs, and values that are held by a specific group and transmitted from one generation to the next through mechanisms of socialization. Political scientists have used the concept of "political culture" to refer to that subset of beliefs and values of a society that relate to the political system.[10] While these cultural beliefs and values are influenced by forces and events external to the culture itself, they profoundly influence how such forces are perceived and shape the way in which a given society responds to them. In this sense cultures enjoy a certain degree of autonomy and are not merely subjective reflections of concrete "objective" reality. Consequently, individuals or groups with different cultural backgrounds are likely to respond quite differently even when confronted with objectively identical situations. For example, if German and Japanese policymakers had the same cultural attitudes toward defense and national security as, say, French policymakers do, it is safe to assume that they would pursue policies very different from those that they have in fact pursued.

Within the broad parameters of the foregoing definition it is possible to identify two general approaches to the study of culture, each with a different conception of the origins of culture and of the way in which it is embedded in society. The first can be called the *anthropological* approach, which sees culture as rooted in the deeper structures of a given society, such as its personality, religion, language, and primary socialization—that is to say, precisely those structures that have been the traditional focus of anthropological and sociological investigation. In this view culture is typically seen as bubbling up from below. For a given political culture to change there first must occur changes at this deep structural level. For example, if a society is to support a stable democracy, it is expected that congruent democratic orientations must first develop on the microsocial level, including those of the family, the workplace, as well as in day-to-day interactions between ordinary people.[11] Culture thus understood typically has an indirect impact on political attitudes and is therefore difficult to identify and to manipulate.

Not all forms of culture, however, are merely a function of such deep social structures. Political orientations are also born of historical events and experiences and the debates that seek to interpret and give meaning to these experiences. Such interpretations can be institutionalized in a society and thus become constitutive elements of a new culture. While not the product of deep social structures, they nonetheless exhibit the chief characteristics associated with the concept of culture. That is to say, they shape and give direction to political action; they are not merely subjective reflections of objective reality but enjoy a fairly high degree of autonomy; they are transmitted through socialization; and by providing individuals with cognitive maps, they serve as filters through which subsequent events and experiences are apprehended. Change on this level of political culture is not the result of shifts in the underlying social structure, but rather is the product of new events and efforts to interpret them. The effects of this type of culture on political behavior are comparatively direct and easy to observe and, at least at the nascent stage, are relatively open to manipulation. Once formed, however, these new cultural orientations can be institutionalized. They then develop dynamics of their own and cannot be readily changed. This second approach to culture can be termed the *historical-cultural approach.*

At the same time, the two forms of culture are all too often held to be identical to one another, sometimes leading to erroneous judgments. For instance, because everyday life in Japanese firms remains highly regimented, it is often assumed that some deeply rooted militaristic impulse lies buried in Japanese society, waiting to emerge when the time is right. Likewise, the continued obsession in everyday German life with following clearly delineated rules and regulations has led many observers to conclude that the authoritarian streak in the German national character has not yet died out and that hence German democracy is inherently unstable. What such analyses overlook is the extent to which people are able to operate in seemingly incompatible ways in different areas of their lives. It is perfectly possible for a Japanese white-collar worker in a major electronics firm to slavishly obey his superiors and fiercely defend his company interests, and still take to the streets to protest government defense policies, as hundreds of thousands of white-collar workers did in the 1950s, 1960s, and 1970s. The two levels of behavior, and the types of culture that inform them, are only indirectly linked and should not be equated with one another.

It is important to appreciate that these two approaches are not mutually exclusive. In fact, they can be seen as being complementary to one another. Each looks at different levels of the larger phenomenon of culture and may account for different levels of political behavior. The anthropological approach to the study of political culture appears to be particularly well-suited to the study of patterns of political communication, relations among political leaders, and the ties that form between leaders and their followers. On the other hand, the historical-cultural approach offers useful insights into institutional dynamics such as those pertaining to the development of organizational structures, the formation of group identities and, of particular relevance to the present discussion, to the evolution of policy preferences such as defense and national security.[12]

It is important to appreciate that the analysis of historical culture not only involves an investigation of behavior and attitudes as reflected in opinion polls and political documents, but also requires the careful investigation of political institutions. In the literature, the studies of culture and political institutions are often treated as two separate and mutually exclusive enterprises. According to Peter Hall's widely accepted definition, institutions are those "formal rules, compliance procedures, and standard operating practices that structure the relationship between individuals in various units of the polity and economy."[13] While some scholars working within the institutionalist research program include informal institutions (that is, not yet codified norms, beliefs, and practices), many prefer to focus exclusively on readily identifiable, codified institutions such as laws, political organizations, and administrative structures.[14] The distinction between formal and informal institutions, however, presents a false dichotomy. The debates over which comes first—whether it is formal institutions that create culture or culture that shapes institutions—are as sterile as the proverbial debate over the chicken and the egg.[15] Institutions and culture exist in an interdependent relationship, each relying upon the other in an ongoing way. Formal institutions play a key role in anchoring broader societal beliefs and values and provide continuity and permanency to them. Cultural forces, in turn, influence the shapes institutions take and provide them with legitimacy and meaning. The interaction between formal institutions and the beliefs and values prevalent in a given society becomes particularly relevant in periods when the political system is undergoing change. An approach that combines the analysis of formal institutions with those of a more informal nature allows the researcher to provide a better account of how both change in response to historical events.

The Genesis of Historical-Political Cultures

One of the central problems in the study of political culture is how to explain shifts in culture if and when they occur. The transformation of German and Japanese attitudes toward defense and national security poses this central problem in a particularly dramatic way. As indicated, historical culture is the product of events and experiences, such as revolutions, wars, economic and natural catastrophes, and, at times, the impact of intellectual movements. In this sense historical events and ideas are the primary forces that drive cultural change. Historical experiences may become anchored in the collective memory of a given society and shape and support the population's orientations toward politics. Each subsequent experience, in turn, is filtered through the lens of the existing political culture, although shock experiences may force a reinterpretation of the prevailing patterns of thought. Every episode in a nation's history, however, can be interpreted in a number of different ways. In the mind's eye every military setback can be redefined as a victory and every successful feat of arms can become a defeat. In other words, it is interpretation that determines the ultimate impact of a given political event and the kinds of lessons that are drawn from it.

Various groups participate in the process of interpretation and reinterpretation of events in a particular culture, guided by a combination of self-interest and ideology. Through their participation in the political process, however, each group comes under pressure to accommodate itself to the overall constellation of forces dominating the political arena. While a particular group may reject the prevailing political reality for some time, ultimately it is forced to either make compromises or it runs the risk of becoming politically marginalized. Even those groups fortunate enough to achieve their immediate objectives in the policy-making process have a strong incentive to make compromises in order to shore up wider political support.

Compromises, in turn, need to be legitimated both internally, within the group, and externally, to the larger public. A group's leaders may choose to claim that a compromise has been made for purely tactical reasons, saying, in effect, that they bowed to the superior power of the other side. In the long run, however, such halfhearted legitimations are inherently unstable. They reduce the likelihood that the group's membership will rally behind the compromise for long or that opposing groups will accept them as genuine. Once compromises have been reached, there exist strong pressures for the group to justify them through reference to higher principles. When a compromise has been negotiated and legitimated in this manner, it becomes difficult for a group to abandon it. In this sense, historical-political culture can be understood as a form of *negotiated reality*. What is at stake in any particular policy debate is not merely the policy itself, but the version of reality and the norms and values used in its legitimation.

Once the main participants in the political system have accepted the legitimacy of such compromises, it becomes increasingly difficult to challenge the policies born out of the political bargaining process. With time, these policies gain in stability, especially when a new generation of political leaders comes to the fore who did not take part in the original policy-making process and hence is less aware of their negotiated nature. For the new generation the legitimacy of these policy outcomes is taken for granted. Over time such experiences and interpretations of reality accumulate. They are sedimented in overlapping layers to form a more or less stable political culture, one that typically is reinforced by the agents of secondary socialization such as schools, the media, and literature.

Not all elements of a given culture change with equal ease or speed. Following Talcott Parsons's approach to the cultural system, analysts in the historical-cultural tradition see political culture as having a core comprised of its interpretive codes.[16] The most basic of these interpretive codes is language, but they also can include various other deeply embedded beliefs and values—for instance, a belief in the efficacy of democracy or in the futility of war. So, for instance, it is a characteristic of a country like the United States, which defines itself as a democratic society, to interpret the rest of the world through democratic lenses—to automatically see progress wherever democratic behavior is identified and to believe that authoritarian, antidemocratic behavior has a broad range of negative consequences, even though in reality the relationship between, say, democracy and economic growth is far from straightforward. This belief in the efficacy of democracy, however, is deeply embedded in American political culture and cannot be easily changed or resisted. It is closely associated with such grand events as the American Revolution, the Civil War, and World War II. It is linked to other core American values such as freedom and equality. And finally, it is anchored in various formal political institutions, beginning with the Constitution. In other words, culturally derived codes determine how reality is perceived and interpreted and provide meaning to political action. This feature of political culture provides it with continuity and prevents it from being a merely ephemeral or dependent variable without any explanatory power of its own.

This view of political culture bears a close similarity to Imre Lakatos's view of how theories evolve in the natural sciences. Lakatos contends that there are theoretical research programs with a core set of beliefs composed of positive and negative heuristic elements regarding the fundamental nature of reality. This core generates a "belt" of hypotheses which use these heuristics to explain empirical reality. Individual hypotheses may be disproved, but as long as the core remains vital, it will generate hypotheses to account for new data while leaving the core beliefs intact.[17]

In a similar way, the core of a given culture includes a central set of beliefs about the nature of reality which, in turn, produce various auxiliary hypotheses to explain empirical reality and guide behavior. Harry Eckstein refers to these core beliefs as orientations that produce attitudes toward specific objects.[18] By way of illustration one may posit that Russian culture has a core belief, or orientation, that political authority should be both centralized and absolute. This core orientation toward authority shaped the Russian peoples' attitudes toward both the autocratic government of the tsar and that of the Communist regime, leading in both instances to similar patterns of obedience.[19]

The analogy between the development of scientific theories and the evolution of political culture also suggests under what circumstances cultural change is likely to occur. Eventually, Lakatos argues, even core beliefs will change if they are unable to generate hypotheses with sufficient explanatory power to cope with new phenomena or the discovery of new evidence concerning old ones. Research programs then enter a period of "degenerative decay" leading to their ultimate replacement. Similarly, as Thompson, Ellis, and Wildavsky recently noted, cultures remain vital only if their core principles continue to generate solutions that satisfy human needs and make sense of the world. When cultures cease to provide such solutions, when they cease to make sense, their members begin to doubt them, and, if plausible alternatives are available, members ultimately defect.[20]

Cultures, however, are even more resistant to change than are research programs. In addition to core beliefs about the nature of reality, which tell members how the world is, cultures also have normative beliefs that tell them how the world ought to be. For obvious reasons it is more difficult to falsify the latter. In contrast to research programs, cultures exercise a powerful emotional hold on their adherents and supply, at least in part, the criteria for measuring their own success.

The historical-cultural approach assumes that over time the cultural core will respond to historical pressures, but holds that change usually occurs incrementally and that new institutions are not invented de novo, but are likely to follow previously established patterns. Occasionally more rapid changes in core beliefs and values take place, but only after they have been thoroughly discredited and society is under great strain. Such rapid and fundamental change in a given culture tends to be accompanied by psychological distress and in many ways fits Thomas Kuhn's description of paradigm shifts in the natural sciences.[21]

Political-Military Culture

To explore the links between political culture and security policy formation it is useful to introduce a new analytical concept, that of *political-military culture*. Political-military culture can be defined as that subset of the larger historical-political culture that encompasses orientations related to defense, security, the military as an institution, and the use of force in international affairs.

Political-military culture as defined here resembles the concept of "strategic culture" as developed by Jack Snyder, Colin Gray, Yitzak Klein, and others.[22] Both concepts rely on the notion that a semiautonomous realm of ideas and beliefs shapes how states approach national security. The strategic culture literature, however, has been largely informed by the research efforts of cognitive psychologists, and consequently has been less sensitive to the impact that larger societal and cultural shifts may have on attitudes toward national defense. In contrast, the political-military culture approach as defined here draws on the political culture literature that addresses the problem of cultural change more directly.

Cultures of Antimilitarism

The political-military culture of a nation influences defense and security policy in a number of ways: (1) it supplies the fundamental goals and norms of political actors; (2) it determines how political actors perceive the existing domestic political environment; (3) it influences the actors' assessment of the international situation; and (4) it strongly conditions their ability to mobilize the national resources for military purposes.

Utilizing the concept of political-military culture, we can construct a security policy–making model that allows us to see how culture interacts with other variables (see Figure 1.1). This culturally bounded model differs from the rational actor model commonly used for the analysis of foreign and defense policy making. The following diagram highlights the differences between these two analytical approaches.

Both the rational actor model and the cultural model of policy making see defense policy as shaped by a combination of domestic and external forces. States seek to maximize their national interests as constrained by their domestic resources and by their international environments. When the outcomes generated by existing foreign policies fail to fulfill their national interest, states are compelled to revise either their security policies or to redefine their national goals. Despite their differences, both approaches envision the state as being engaged in an ongoing process of learning and adaptation. The key difference between the cultural and rational actor models lies in the way the national interest is defined and how learning is assumed to take place. Rational actor approaches are based on the assumption that the national interests of all states are fundamentally similar and are rooted in universal human needs and desires, including on the most basic level the desires for security, prosperity, and status. Various schools of thought within the rational actor paradigm attach different levels of importance to such goals. The cultural model, on the other hand, proposes that the goals a nation pursues cannot be assumed as given, but have to be investigated separately in each case. In other words, the "national interest" is a construct emerging out of contingent historical, social, and rational processes that can vary considerably across different states at different points in time.[23]

Moreover, the rational actor school assumes that learning from the international system occurs in a relatively direct and straightforward manner. An approach that factors in culture, on the other hand, maintains that learning is filtered through the cognitive lenses of the cultural system. In other words, whereas the rational actor evaluates each event in the international system in

Figure 1.1
Contrasting Models of Foreign Policy Formation

I. Rational Actor Model

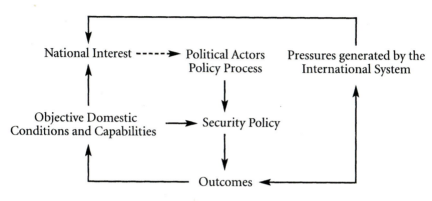

II. Culturally Bound Actor Model

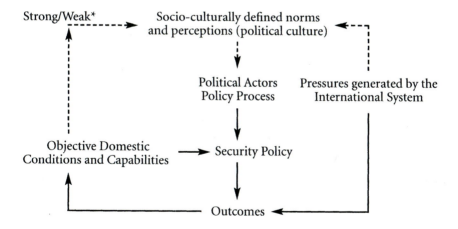

*The causal relationship between objective national capabilities and political culture is relatively strong in the view of the historical culture school; it is relatively weak from the perspective of the anthropological culture school.

- - - - Causes changes in (direct causal relationship)

———— Shapes perceptions, provides goals (mediated, indirect causal relationship) terms of its potential impact on what can be done to maximize utility, the culturally bound actor interprets such developments in terms of culturally constructed concepts and categories. In addition, the mode of response itself is likely to be influenced by culturally accepted norms and values. Changes in the objective condition of any given country may trigger changes in its cultural system, leading to shifts in the normative and interpretative schemes of its political actors. Such alteration of the cultural system, however, can be expected to be neither rapid nor easy. In this sense, culture frequently serves as a source of inertia in policy making, and the response to pressures from the international system is likely to be far slower and more unpredictable than is assumed by the rational actor models.

The argument in favor of a cultural model becomes clear if one looks at the post–World War II West German and Japanese cases of defense policy–making which constitute the subject of this book. It should be emphasized again that these two models of interpretation are not contradictory. However, looking at the cultural context allows for a much more comprehensive and detailed understanding of what actually happened.

Rational actor models, such as realism or neoliberalism, highlight some of the factors which at different points in time weighed on the decision making of German and Japanese leaders. For instance, the perceived increase in Soviet military power during the 1970s clearly was an important factor shaping the two nations' security policies in the 1970s and early 1980s. To the extent to which rational actor models correspond to the way a given group of decision makers actually view the international environment, they yield powerful, parsimonious explanations of the policies nations chose to pursue. However, as we shall see, in reality, it is rare that a political system is dominated by a single understanding of how the world works. In Germany and Japan in the 1970s and 1980s, different political actors interpreted changes in the international environment in very different ways. A wide range of solutions were proposed—ranging from accommodation with the Soviet Union all the way to acquisition of an independent military capability—each one based on supposedly highly rational calculations of the national interest. Under such conditions, where a number of different solutions may apply (what rational choice theorists refer to as "multiple equilibria games"), or where there exists no clear political consensus on how to proceed, policy proposals that are consistent with existing beliefs and values are naturally privileged and likely to win out in policy-making battles.[24]

In short, rational actor models may be highly parsimonious and attractive by virtue of their elegance. Yet they tell only part of the story, and often create a false impression of certainty in situations that are in fact indeterminate and in flux. Introducing cultural factors gives the appearance of producing a more cluttered explanation. Yet, as the discussion of the West German and Japanese cases in this book suggests, this is a price well worth paying for the purpose of understanding actual events.

In real life it is impossible to find either a pure rational actor or a pure culturally bound actor; both modes of cognition exist side by side in every individual or group. Arguably the two complement one another, for rationality by itself cannot define the goals which it seeks to achieve, while culture without rationality would be static and prone to paralysis. The goals rationality seeks to fulfill can only be provided by genetically determined instincts or by some outside agency, such as culture. Even the most cold-blooded practitioner of realpolitik, the epitome of the rational actor in international relations, operates implicitly on the basis of an ethical code that places the interest of the nation-state above all other goals.

In other words, realpolitik itself is anchored in a cultural system whose guiding principles have been stripped down to a minimum. In modern times that minimum is the survival of the nation-state and the expansion of its power. In older times the basic guiding principle may have been loyalty to the tribe, the city-state, or the individual ruler, as in Kautilya's *Arthashastra* or Machiavelli's *The Prince,* although already in Machiavelli one can observe the tension between loyalty to the state and to the ruler. Even if one were to maintain that people are born with an instinct for survival, and perhaps a lust for power as well, and that all other norms and values are fundamentally subordinate to these instincts, it remains an empirical fact that human beings also have other innate, but less clearly defined, needs. Primary among them are the basic needs for community, meaning, and identity. How that community (family, region, religion, or nation) and the individual's relationship to that community are defined is in large measure determined by culture.

Testing the Model

This book applies this new model of political-military culture to post–World War II Germany and Japan. Such an enterprise requires a detailed, multilayered research strategy that encompasses three central empirical tasks.

First, it is necessary to investigate the original set of historical experiences that determined the post–World War II German and Japanese views of the military, national security, and the use of force. To this end, careful attention will be paid to the ways in which different groups in these two societies interpreted the traumatic events of the 1930s and 1940s. Second, the political processes by which actual security policies were made and subsequently legitimated need to be examined. In this context it is important to define the core features of both the political-military culture of each country and the security policy associated with it at particular points in time. Chapters 2 and 3 will do so by exploring the origins of the German and Japanese political-military cultures in the early postwar period. Third, it is necessary to trace the evolution of both the new political-military cultures and the defense policies associated with them, monitoring how they evolved in response to domestic and international pressures. Chapters 4, 5, and 6 undertake such an analysis, tracing developments through the Cold War period into the mid-1990s. Chapter 7 returns to theoretical issues and offers projections for the future of German and Japanese security policies.

Such a longitudinal analysis allows us to escape the trap of deriving culture from behavior that leads to the kind of tautological, ad hoc reasoning of which cultural analysis is often accused.[25] While in practice it is nearly impossible to separate culture from behavior, for analytical purposes it is possible to disaggregate policy behavior from the meanings that political actors and the general public attach to such policies. These meanings can be discerned through the systematic examination of public opinion polls, parliamentary debates, books and articles written by opinion leaders, newspaper editorials, and so forth. This differentiation between action and meaning allows us to judge the degree of consistency between behavior and expressed beliefs and values over time. If culture, in this case political-military culture, changes without any corresponding shift in behavior, there are grounds to question the posited relationship between the two. Likewise, if behavior changes without any corresponding shift in the expressed beliefs and values that have been associated with earlier policies, then again we have reason to doubt that the two factors influence one another. In other words, expressed cultural beliefs and values should develop in tandem with behavior—in this case, with defense and national security policy.

According to the model of cultural change followed in this book, under normal circumstances culture should change only incrementally in response to ordinary historical events such as shifts in the balance of power or the formation of international institutions. When major new policy initiatives violating existing norms and values are proposed, resistance in the form of demonstrations, inter- and intraparty confrontations, and virulent political polemics in general should be observable. If major changes occur without generating such resistance, then the presumed relationship between political-military culture and defense policy can be considered to have been falsified, or at least considerably weakened and made less plausible.

Through such a systematic analysis of the evolution of German and Japanese security policies and the political debates surrounding them, we will be able to identify the core features of their new cultures of antimilitarism and the forces that led to their formation in the first place. Inasmuch as these norms, values, and understandings that emerged in the post–Cold War era continue to shape the behavior of these countries in the international system today, such an exercise will give us important clues about how these two nations are likely to behave in the future.

2

From Swords into Plowshares and Back

WORLD WAR II shattered the German and Japanese martial nationalist ideologies of the prewar period and toppled the aggressive political regimes that had actively propagated them. Their supposedly invincible war machines had been crushed, and the Allied powers, fearful of a repetition of the unsuccessful effort to tame Germany after World War I, occupied the two countries and instituted far-reaching programs of political reform. The military defeats of 1945 represented massive shocks to the old German and Japanese cultures of militarism and created conditions in which new ways of thinking about the military institution and the problems of defense and national security could be devised and institutionalized. During this period, which was characterized by an extraordinary degree of political conflict and uncertainty, the German and Japanese attitudes toward defense and national security were highly malleable, and a combination of historical forces, both domestic and international, combined to bring about the emergence of new political-military cultures that were as profoundly antimilitaristic as the old ones had been militaristic.

Although the German and Japanese experiences of defeat and occupation were broadly comparable, there existed important differences in how the Pacific and European conflicts had ended, in the kinds of political regimes that came to power in the two countries, and in their respective geopolitical environments. These dissimilarities led the two nations to implement defense policies that were strikingly different in a number of respects and contributed to the development of new military institutions and political-military cultures that, although superficially similar, in actuality were based on very different ideas and principles.

The Dimensions of Defeat

In order to understand the dynamics behind the emergence of Germany's and Japan's new cultures of antimilitarism, it is first necessary to appreciate the magnitude of the two countries' defeat in World War II and the enormous material and psychological damage that had been inflicted upon them. Because the Germans, unlike the Japanese, had decided to fight to the bitter end, thereby turning much of their country into a war zone, the level of physical destruction there was much greater. Altogether, six and a half million Germans are estimated to have died in the war, approximately half of whom were civilians. Virtually all military personnel, nearly eleven million in all, were imprisoned by the Allied forces, and many were transported as slave laborers to the Soviet Union, where they were to remain for many years. The intense aerial bombardment of the final stages of the war transformed most large German cities into hollow, burned-out shells, and terrible shortages of food, clothing, and other necessities developed.

In Japan, the number of casualties, although fewer than those in Germany, were still appalling—altogether three million Japanese lost their lives in the war, and the total number of killed and wounded exceeded a staggering eight million. Japan's cities, like Germany's, were subjected to an intense bombing campaign, culminating in the atomic bombings of Hiroshima and Nagasaki, and the country's economy was paralyzed by a highly successful American submarine blockade. In both countries industrial production was reduced to a mere fraction of its prewar level and, were it not for the infusion of massive doses of American humanitarian assistance, thousands more soon would have died of starvation.

In addition to the human and economic costs, Germany and Japan lost large tracts of territory. The Soviet Union took advantage of its position of strength in Eastern Europe to shift its borders westward, annexing most of eastern Prussia and gobbling up large chunks of Poland and Czechoslovakia. To compensate the Poles and the Czechs, the Soviet Union shifted their borders, in turn, to the West, stripping Germany of much of its pre-1938 territory. In all, Germany lost more than 20 percent of its total territory, and what remained was divided into four occupation zones, each controlled by a different Allied power—Britain, France, the Soviet Union, and the United States. Soon it became evident that the Soviet zone, encompassing approximately one-third of Germany, was increasingly isolated from the parts controlled by the Western powers. While the final separation of the two Germanys was not completed until the erection of the Berlin Wall in 1961, Germany had been de facto partitioned into two countries by 1946.

Japan, by comparison, lost far less of its territory after the war. Soviet forces advanced only as far as the sparsely populated northern territories, and the American President Harry Truman turned down Soviet requests for control of Hokkaido and the Northern tip of Honshu. Nonetheless, Japan lost control of Okinawa and the southern Ryukyu Islands, and it was stripped of its extensive overseas territories, including Korea and Taiwan, which in the prewar era had been formally annexed and whose populations had been, at least in principle, citizens of the Japanese empire.

One immediate consequence of this redrawing of national boundaries was a vast influx of refugees. An estimated sixteen and a half million Germans were displaced during the war and its immediate aftermath, of whom as many as two million perished, three and a half million settled in East Germany, and ten million settled in the West. In Asia, nearly six million Japanese soldiers and civilians were repatriated to the Japanese home islands, further straining the resources of an already overcrowded and impoverished nation.

At least as important as these human, economic, and territorial losses, defeat also exacted a great psychological and symbolic toll. The outcome of the war discredited not only the Nazi and Japanese militarist regimes, but on a more fundamental level, it put into question the grand achievements upon which the legitimacy of the modern German and Japanese states had been based. In the case of Germany, not only had Hitler's murderous schemes for the expansion of the lebensraum of the Aryan race been dashed, but the unity of the German people in a single political state—the dream of German nationalists since the Napoleonic war and the crowning achievement of the old German Reich—had been effectively undone.

For Japan, the defeat not only signified the end of the militarist vision of a united Asia under Japanese tutelage, but the Allied occupation of Japan implied that the military had failed to fulfill the overarching imperative of securing national independence, which had been the driving force behind the Meiji Restoration of 1868 and the subsequent creation of the Japanese empire. Even worse, the emperor, the temporal and spiritual head of the Japanese nation, the living god upon whom the legitimacy of the imperial state rested, was now cast on the mercy of the victorious Americans, most of whom were determined to put him on trial as a war criminal.

In short, by the end of the war in 1945, Japan and Germany had been shaken to the core both physically and psychologically. The old nationalist dreams of power and empire were no longer able to inspire the war-weary and disillusioned populations of Germany and Japan, and, for a time at least, simple survival and reconstruction became the top priorities of both nations. With their wartime leaderships imprisoned and the legitimacy of their nations' old political orders severely damaged, German and Japanese elites were compelled to reexamine the definitions of their national identity and to find new moral visions and goals to guide their nations. What the new national purpose for either country could be, however, remained vague. For some time after the war, many observers, both in Germany and Japan and abroad, continued to believe that some of the traditional themes could reemerge, perhaps even in a radicalized form. That such revanchist movements failed to materialize can be attributed to a variety of factors, primary among which was the domestic and international political environments created by the American occupations in both Germany and Japan.

The American Occupation and the Origins of Antimilitarism

From the beginning, the Allies were determined to transform Germany and Japan. First and foremost, the occupation sought to dismantle the two countries' still-vast military machines. The physical aspect of this enterprise was achieved relatively easily. Within a few months after their surrender, most of their military arsenals were destroyed or confiscated, their military manpower demobilized, and tight restrictions imposed on their capacity to produce warfighting materials. Aside from preventing Germany and Japan from soon reemerging as military threats to their neighbors, the physical disarmament had two further, far-reaching effects. First, disarmament removed the military as a political force during the crucial period when postwar Germany's and Japan's new political systems were created. This allowed the postwar leaders of both countries to put into place a level of civilian control over their future armed forces unprecedented in their history. Secondly, by taking control of the two nations' domestic and foreign affairs, the occupation made them militarily dependent on the United States, a state of affairs that was to last far longer than anyone could have foretold.

Disarmament, however, was only one part of the American occupation's much greater design. Unlike most conquering powers in history, the United States was determined not only to defeat its enemies, but to remake them—in its own image, if possible—and ensure that they would never again become a threat to world peace. These goals were enshrined in the "four Ds"—denazification, demilitarization, decartelization, and disarmament—and were agreed upon, at least verbally, by the Allied powers at their summit meeting in Potsdam. Yet, despite the similarity of the occupiers' goals for Germany and Japan, the ways in which they were implemented differed considerably in each country, a fact that was to have important long-term consequences for the character of the two countries' postwar political orders and their approaches to national security. Three sets of factors deserve particular attention in this context: the conditions under which the two countries surrendered; the way in which denazification and issues of war guilt were handled; and finally, the process through which their new political institutions were established.

Although both countries, in principle, had surrendered unconditionally, in actuality Japan's defeat proved far less total than Germany's. A much greater degree of continuity existed between Japan's administrations during the presurrender and postsurrender periods than was the case in Germany. The chief reason may be attributed to the fact that moderate elements in the Japanese leadership managed to engineer a more or less orderly surrender that left much of the apparatus of government in place when American occupation began. The Germans, in contrast, fought to the bitter end, and by the summer of 1945 civil order had virtually collapsed. As a result, from the beginning of the occupation, the Allied military governments were compelled to become deeply involved in the direct administration of Germany, aided by the Germans who appeared trustworthy and by exiles and former prisoners of the Nazi regimes. In Japan, on the other hand, occupation authorities were confronted with an entrenched bureaucracy upon which they had to rely to implement their decisions. In addition, linguistic and cultural barriers made occupation authorities in Japan far more dependent on the local bureaucracy than those in Germany.

The relatively smooth transition from conquest to military occupation in Japan had some obvious benefits, above all in terms of saving lives and minimizing human misery. Yet there was a price to be paid as well. The old elites' hold on state and society was not decisively shaken, and many former wartime leaders were able to stage political comebacks in the postwar era. Most importantly from the Japanese point of view, the imperial institution was preserved, even though it was stripped of much of its formal political authority. In contrast, large numbers of West Germany's old political elite, particularly those whose involvement with the Nazi Party was more than nominal, were evicted from their positions of power. Some of Hitler's bitterest enemies, men like Theodor Heuss and Kurt Schumacher, who had strong personal interests in the fundamental reform of the German political system, emerged as powerful leaders, supporting the Allies in their decision to pursue vigorously the issue of war guilt in Germany.

The segment of the old Japanese elite that was hardest hit by the American occupation was its armed forces, which became the main targets of the occupiers' efforts to purge the government of those implicated in the misdeeds of the wartime regime. In all, over 117,000 former military men were barred from taking up positions of political authority. In contrast, only 2,000 Japanese businessmen were purged, while merely 2 percent of the hundreds of thousands of bureaucrats screened were ultimately affected. In Germany, on the other hand, the U.S. occupation authorities primarily investigated former members of the Nazi Party in positions of administrative responsibility as well as members of the SS, who were held responsible for wartime atrocities. Thus, the manner in which the purges were conducted in Japan helped to further stigmatize the armed forces, while in Germany blame was focused on the extreme nationalism embodied by the Nazis.

A central element in the Allied reeducation plan was to convince Germans and Japanese that not only had they lost the war militarily but, more importantly, that they bore moral responsibility for the war and the way it was conducted. The chief instruments chosen to make these points were the war crime trials, in particular those of German and Japanese wartime leaders conducted at Nuremberg and Tokyo.

At first glance, the task of convincing the Germans and Japanese of their guilt would not appear to have been difficult. In both cases, hostilities clearly had been initiated by the Axis powers, in Europe through the German invasion of Poland and in Asia by the Japanese attack on Pearl Harbor. Before these events, Japan and Germany had created hostile international environments by pursuing territorial expansion and embarking on massive armaments programs. The evidence of atrocities was even more compelling. During the war Allied authorities had collected testimonials from witnesses of German and Japanese atrocities, and thousands of former victims were ready to testify in court. In addition, vast amounts of physical evidence were available in the forms of mass graves, films, and photographs, as well as internal military and police documents that detailed what had transpired in German and Japanese concentration camps. The chief problem faced by the Allied prosecutors was not a shortage of evidence, but its mind-numbing superabundance.

Yet from the start, the war crimes trials were beset with difficulties. The chief charges on which the defendants had been arraigned—crimes against peace, conspiracy against peace, and crimes against humanity—had to be created for the purpose of the trials, giving them an *ex post hoc* character that undermined the air of impartiality the Allied authorities sought to create. Furthermore, it was often difficult to prove that individual leaders were responsible for the acts that had been carried out by their subordinates, and the concept of collective guilt, whereby the defendants were tried not as individuals but as representatives of criminal organizations, was a dubious one from a legal point of view. Finally, many of the crimes of which the Germans and Japanese were accused—indiscriminate bombing, unrestricted submarine warfare, and mass expulsions of peoples—could be plausibly leveled against the Allies, especially the Soviets, as well.

In Japan, the trials confronted a number of additional obstacles. Unlike Germany, which had been governed under a single regime since 1933, Japan had had no fewer than seventeen different cabinets since 1928, making it difficult to prove that any one set of decision makers had plotted the expansion of the empire that led to the war in the Pacific. More importantly, SCAP (the Supreme Commander Allied Powers, the official name of the American military government in Japan) chose not only to exempt the emperor from prosecution, but even barred his being called to testify for fear of provoking domestic turmoil. By removing the emperor, who under the terms of the Meiji Constitution was the supreme head of state and whose formal approval was required for all major policy decisions, SCAP crippled the investigations before they began and made the political character of the trials plainly evident. Moreover, the Japanese leaders who were placed on trial often refused to give evidence whenever the questioning turned to matters concerning the role of the emperor, even when doing so hurt their own chances for acquittal. Although by the end of the war Japan's wartime leaders had enjoyed little popularity among the broader Japanese populace, this self-sacrificing display attracted much public sympathy. As the trials progressed, many Japanese came to view the defendants as martyrs and the trials as an exercise in victor's justice.

Ultimately the prosecution won its case in both Nuremberg and Tokyo, and most of the accused were sentenced either to death or to life imprisonment. Yet, on the balance, it was widely felt that the trials had been inadequate as means of bringing to justice those responsible for the wartime atrocities, and there were also doubts concerning their effectiveness in reeducating the German and

Japanese peoples. Even the U.S. military governor of Germany, General Lucius Clay, is said to have privately viewed the Nuremberg proceedings as a disaster.[1]

Despite their many shortcomings, the trials and other reeducation efforts appear to have enjoyed a modicum of success, at least in Germany. Many Germans were genuinely appalled by the revelations of Nazi atrocities, and a good number expressed the conviction that the trials had not gone far enough. Politically powerful groups, most notably the Social Democratic Party (SPD) as well as the Protestant and, to a lesser extent, Catholic churches, took a leading role in condemning both the Nazis and the so-called *Mitläufer*—those Germans who had gone along with the Nazis' immoral policies, whether out of convenience or a misguided sense of duty. The German intelligentsia and the media contributed to a bitter mood of self-recrimination that swept the country. In the years immediately following the Nuremberg trials the German populace, absorbed with the task of reconstruction, did not dwell further on the Nazi past, the media and the many Germans who had suffered at the hands of the Hitler regime helped keep the war guilt issue alive even after the occupation had ended. As a result, throughout the 1950s and 1960s German courts continued to prosecute war criminals, and association with the Nazis became an indelible stigma whose discovery could bring down high officials as late as the 1970s. Conversely, an anti-Nazi record became an invaluable asset for many of West Germany's postwar leaders.

The contrast with Japan could not be greater. While many on the Japanese Left, especially among the intelligentsia, strongly condemned Japanese atrocities in Asia, they tacitly agreed with conservative defenders of the war in criticizing the West for its racist colonial policies and the atomic bombings of Hiroshima and Nagasaki. The Left's efforts to confront the past were further stymied by a population that was more concerned with the task of rebuilding the economy than dwelling on the past, and by an entrenched political establishment that was hostile to efforts to keep the war guilt issue alive. While some of Japan's postwar leaders, including Prime Ministers Yoshida Shigeru and Ishibashi Tanzan, had at least to a limited degree been involved in antiwar activities (and even they had not suffered the level of prosecution that many prominent German leaders such as Heuss and Schumacher had), others had been active supporters of the war effort. Perhaps the best example was Kishi Nobosuke, munitions minister under General Hideki Tōjō and one of the signatories of the declaration of war, who in 1958, a mere thirteen years after the end of the war, became prime minister of Japan. Such a rehabilitation would have been unthinkable in the German context—it would have been as if Albert Speer had sauntered out of Spandau prison to become the chancellor of the Federal Republic.

Once back in power, leaders like Kishi sought to prevent the spread of a view of history that would undermine their political legitimacy. As soon as the occupation of Japan came to an end in 1951, the war crimes trials were suspended and the government began to release former war criminals who had been imprisoned by the Allied authorities. In addition, the government used its control over the contents of the textbooks used in Japan's highly centralized school system to present children with a sanitized version of their country's history, and pressure was brought to bear on the media by right-wing groups to avoid raising issues that might be interpreted as an affront to the honor of the emperor or the nation.

The only people who were effectively barred from holding positions of political power in postwar Japan were members of the old military elite, many of whom had a difficult time even making a living during the occupation period. In Japanese historiography, the military was usually singled out as the chief villain responsible for leading Japan into the disastrous war against the West, conveniently ignoring the role played by civilian leaders.

The new institutions of the postwar German and Japanese states further reinforced the fractured relationship between the military and democracy in these two countries. Both the new Japanese constitution and the German Basic Law (Grundgesetz) emphasized their nations' commitment to a peaceful world order and included special provisions renouncing war. These antimilitary passages were to act as important constraints on future German and Japanese military policy.

Strong pacifist sentiments permeated the newly drafted Japanese constitution, beginning with the first paragraph which emphasized Japan's dedication to the goals of peaceful international cooperation and its resolve never again to suffer the horrors of war. This pacifist rhetoric received further substance in Article 9, which proclaimed that the Japanese people forever renounced their sovereign right as a nation to settle international disputes through force, and that to this end Japan would never maintain military forces or produce warfighting materials. But these stringent antimilitary restrictions were quietly watered down by the special parliamentary subcommittee on the constitution chaired by the Conservative Party leader Ashida Hitoshi, who added language that qualified Article 9. Nonetheless, the antimilitary tenor of the constitution was unmistakable and would have long-lasting consequences for the making of Japanese defense policy.

On the whole, the German Basic Law was more reserved in its expression of pacifist sentiments than Japan's postwar constitution. Nonetheless, it, too, included a clause, Article 87a, forbidding any future German government to conduct wars of aggression, and Article 66 established the right of an individual to refuse military service on the grounds of conscience (*Kriegsdienstverweigerung*). Other provisions of the Basic Law laid the groundwork for Germany's future multilateral approach to security, authorizing the government to enter into collective security arrangements. This provision was later to be interpreted as restricting German participation in military missions beyond its own borders to ones taken within a multinational framework.

These provisions in each constitution were designed to reassure both citizens and neighboring countries that there would be no reversion to militarism and aggressive expansionism. Nonetheless, two sets of factors made the Japanese commitment to antimilitarism much stronger than that of the Germans. The first had to do with the timing of the constitutional drafting process. In the Japanese case, the constitution was drafted in 1947, when U.S.-Soviet rivalry had still not crystallized and the Allies were more concerned with forestalling a revival of Japanese militarism than with guarding against a possible external security threat. The German Basic Law, in contrast, was formulated in 1948 and 1949, after East-West tensions had gained momentum. As a result, the drafters of the Basic Law were strongly conscious of the need to make Germany a part of the nascent Western alliance system and were less concerned with a possible reemergence of militarism.

The ways in which the two constitutions were drafted had further implications for the strength and character of antimilitarism in postwar Germany and Japan. The new Japanese constitution had been imposed on the government by the American military authorities. SCAP had originally believed that the constitution had best be drawn up by the Japanese themselves. It soon turned out, however, that even moderate conservatives such as Prime Minister Shidehara Kijuro essentially wanted a return to the limited Taisho democracy of the 1920s. Consequently, the draft proposal prepared by the Japanese government contained numerous provisions that were unacceptable to the Americans. SCAP Commander Douglas MacArthur had his staff hastily produce an alternative proposal—including Article 9—which was then forced upon the Japanese with the threat that if they did not accept the American version the emperor might be put on trial for war crimes. The German Basic Law, on the other hand, was written by a constitutional council consisting of the chief ministers of the German states, all of whom had been elected after the war. Unlike the Japanese proposal, it contained provisions that were by and large acceptable to the Western powers. As a result, the new German constitution enjoyed greater legitimacy than its Japanese counterpart.

Since their constitution had been forced upon them by a foreign power, one might have expected the Japanese to be more willing to reject, or at least modify, the document than the Germans. In fact, precisely the opposite occurred. Because the Basic Law was the product of their own labors, the Germans had greater confidence in their ability to change it when necessary, and in subsequent years they would do so fairly frequently. In contrast, in Japan there developed a deep-rooted fear not only among the Left but also among broad segments of the political center that democracy was a delicate, alien flower planted in inhospitable soil, and that constitutional revision could cause the fragile blossom of freedom to wither. For the next fifty years, despite ongoing debates, the Japanese would not revise their constitution.

Beyond the new constitutions, it should be emphasized that democratization in postwar Germany and Japan was closely linked to demilitarization. Most democracies, including Britain and the United States, have traditionally had an ambiguous relationship with their armed forces. On the one hand, they have been profoundly distrustful of such concentrations of power and antipathetic to the authoritarian values that military institutions typically embody. On the other hand, most major democracies are themselves products of a process of armed struggle against authoritarian forces and historically have relied on their armed forces to defend them from antidemocratic enemies. Consequently, democracies are suspicious of military establishments in general, while often being very supportive of their own armed forces in particular.

Postwar Germany and Japan represent a break with this pattern. For these two nations, democracy was the product not of military victory, but rather of military defeat. The Japanese Imperial Army and the German Wehrmacht not only failed to fulfill their traditional legitimating roles as defenders of the nation, but they had been in effect the tools of ruthless despotism. Thus, the link that in most nations ties together the political order, the nation, and the armed forces had been ruptured in Germany and Japan, complicating future efforts to justify rearmament and strongly reinforcing the innate distrust of the military that all democracies tend to harbor.

From Swords to Plowshares and Back

The Road to Rearmament

The Allied efforts to demilitarize Germany and Japan and banish the twin specters of Nazism and militarism proved successful beyond the expectations of all but the most optimistic of contemporary observers. Not only were the German and Japanese war machines successfully and peacefully dismantled, but during the occupation no evidence emerged to indicate that either nation harbored any thirst for revenge on its erstwhile opponents. With the gradual emergence of the Cold War in the late 1940s, however, issues of national security returned to the political agendas of both countries. West Germany's and Japan's economic potential and their strategic locations in Europe and Asia made their incorporation in the coalescing Western alliance against communism of paramount importance. It is one of the great ironies of recent history that, only a few short years after having forced its former adversaries to give up their weapons and renounce the use of force, the United States found itself trying to promote the remilitarization, or at least the rearming, of the now decidedly reluctant German and Japanese nations.

Given the widespread mood of war weariness permeating both countries and the antimilitary principles enshrined in their new constitutions, rearmament proved no easy task. Only the outbreak of the Korean War in 1950 made a public debate on self-defense possible. For the next decade West German and Japanese politics were racked by intense and emotional debates over defense and national security. The tensions and antagonisms that emerged were to decisively influence not only the policies that were adopted during this crucial formative period, but were to shape the terms of political discourse on national security for the rest of the Cold War era and beyond.

To be sure, the possibility of rearmament was contemplated in German and Japanese elite circles well before the Cold War began. On the day of Japan's surrender to the Allies, Rear Admiral Tomioka Sadatoshi told naval officers intent on continued resistance that "with the end of World War II there is sure to be a confrontation between the United States and the Soviet Union. In the rift Japan can find a chance to regain her feet."[2] Two weeks later, both the Imperial Army and the Imperial Navy produced proposals for a pared down military establishment, apparently using the post–World War I German Reichswehr as a model.[3] Similarly, prescient observers in Germany were quick to realize that tensions between the two superpowers eventually would generate pressures to create a new German military establishment.

Nor were such anticipations restricted to the losing side in World War II. A number of Allied leaders, including Winston Churchill, early on considered the possibility of using German military manpower for the defense of Western Europe against the Soviet Union.[4] Beginning in 1947, as tensions with the Soviet Union grew, American leaders as well began to quietly discuss the advisability of a limited German and Japanese rearmament.[5] After a fact-finding mission to Europe and Asia in 1948, George Kennan, the chief intellectual architect of the new policy of containment, wrote, "They [Japan and West Germany] should be reconstructed to the point where they can play their part in the Eurasian balance of power, but not so far advanced as to permit them again to threaten the interests of the maritime world of the West."[6]

Such considerations led the Allied intelligence services to assemble groups of former German and Japanese officers who, while officially engaged in research on the military history of World War II, could also serve as the nucleus of a general staff around which new armed forces could be mobilized if the need arose. Many of these officers would later become leading figures in the future German Bundeswehr and, to a lesser degree, in Japan's Self-Defense Forces.[7] Once a new civilian leadership began to emerge in the two occupied nations, unofficial discussions on the subject of rearmament occurred on various levels. In West Germany, the growing Soviet stranglehold over Eastern Europe prompted the newly installed German chancellor, Konrad Adenauer, to initiate a public debate on rearmament and to propose to the Allied High Commission the idea of recruiting German volunteers for an "international legion" to be created and trained in France.[8]

In Japan, resistance to broaching the topic of rearmament was greater than in Germany. Prime Minister Yoshida Shigeru was profoundly suspicious of members of the now-defunct Japanese imperial military forces, while MacArthur was adverse to reversing the pacifist policies in Japan for which he was in no small way responsible. Despite these obstacles, Yoshida's conservative rivals, such as Ashida Hitoshi and Hatoyama Ichirō, explored the possibility of Japanese rearmament and military alliance with the United States, making use of secret channels that circumvented both SCAP and Japanese public opinion.[9]

Although internally the U.S. government was increasingly receptive to the idea of rearming Germany and Japan, until the summer of 1950 no overt steps were taken in this direction. Domestically, it was feared that broad segments of the American public would be opposed to seeing the West's former adversaries rearmed so soon after the war while, internationally, strong resistance could be counted on, not only from the Soviets, but from many noncommunist Asian and European states as well, especially from France. In addition, German and Japanese public opinion polls and the fierce controversies sparked by limited preliminary discussions of rearmament suggested that it was far from certain that either country could form a consensus favoring rearmament even if the option were made available. This state of affairs changed abruptly on June 25, 1950, when communist forces crossed the 38th parallel and invaded South Korea.

In Japan, the security threat was felt more immediately, especially as large segments of the U.S. forces stationed there were drawn off to support the collapsing front in Korea. At the same time, the Japanese Communist Party, acting on instructions from Moscow, staged a series of violent incidents aimed at triggering a revolution in Japan. To counter the threat of insurrection, two weeks after the invasion MacArthur instructed the Japanese government to raise the lightly armed Police Reserve Forces (Keisatsu Yobitai) to replace some of the American troops being sent to Korea. Both MacArthur and Yoshida insisted, however, that this formation was merely a special branch of the police, and both SCAP and the Japanese government sought to avoid responsibility for the move by insisting that the decision to create the force had been made at the other side's behest.[10]

On the other side of the globe, it was widely feared that the invasion of South Korea was a diversionary maneuver designed to draw off American forces and open the way for an even larger communist offensive in Western Europe.[11] Fearing an outbreak of left-wing violence similar to the Communist Party's campaign in Japan, eighty thousand Germans in special services units were issued carbines and assigned to guard duty around Western military installations. The Allied High Commission authorized Adenauer to create a ten thousand–person gendarmerie, organized on a regional *(Länder)* level.[12]

Although no official decision to rearm Germany and Japan had been made, it was widely believed that it was only a matter of time until the two countries would be asked to do so. Almost immediately a storm of controversy was loosed as the topics of defense and national security moved to the center stage of West German and Japanese political debates. For the next decade the questions of rearmament and alignment with the West would remain at the heart of the ideological battles waged between the Left and the Right in each country.

On the one side of the debate stood conservatives and centrists like Konrad Adenauer in West Germany and Ashida Hitoshi in Japan. Backed by the business communities and more conservative segments of their respective societies (the Catholic Church and refugee organizations in Germany; farmers and ex-military men in Japan), they favored at least limited rearmament and alignment with the West. On the other side stood the leaders of the Communist and So-cialist parties. Supported by the labor unions, the media, and much of the in-telligentsia, they favored a posture of unarmed or minimally armed neutrality that would keep their nations out of the East-West conflict. This position seemed more in keeping with the pacifist sentiments of the general public and the antimilitary principles that had only recently been enshrined in the new German and Japanese constitutions. Underlying these divisions over defense policy were deeper differences over the nature of the domestic political order and national identity. Alliance with the United States implicitly meant accept-ing capitalism and a national identity anchored in the West, while neutralism left the door open for the creation of a socialist system and preserved Germany's and Japan's traditional ties with Central Europe and Asia respectively.

In both cases, public opinion was strongly divided between the two camps. In Japan a solid majority (53.8 percent) of those surveyed supported rearma-ment, but the public exhibited ambivalent feelings about the prospect of the continued stationing of U.S. troops in Japan, with 29.9 percent in favor and 37.5 percent opposed.[13] In Germany a substantial plurality opposed rearmament and a powerful, grass roots peace movement, the *ohne mich Bewegung,* protested the policies of the Adenauer government.[14]

The German peace movement's appeal was strengthened by a powerful na-tionalist element, for many West Germans feared that rearmament and an alli-ance with the West would cut off all hope of reunification with the eastern por-tion of the country. On a deeper level, raising the question of defense provoked a national identity crisis. If Germany was to be defended the question imme-diately arose: *Which* Germany should be defended, the historical German na-tion or only its much diminished successor state in the West? The Western Al-lies were interested only in the latter, but how could Germany protect itself if doing so meant abandoning nearly 30 percent of its territory and twenty mil-lion of its citizens? Many Germans refused to perform the act of psychic am-putation that Adenauer's policies in effect demanded. For them the territorial division of the nation effectively meant that the defeat in World War II had be-come frozen in time and that all efforts at national defense were a priori futile and self-destructive.

Despite the superficial similarities between the German and Japanese cases, there were many important differences between them. Two points in particular deserve attention. First, both before and after the Korean War, rearmament had been openly debated in West Germany. Neither Adenauer nor his opponents made a secret of their belief that alignment with the West and some degree of rearmament were necessary. In contrast, although Yoshida had in fact approved of the creation of the Police Reserve Forces, his government avoided responsibility for the move and insisted that military rearmament was not on the political agenda. At the time many conservative rivals of Yoshida were openly calling for rearmament and thereby undermining the credibility of the government's position. This made the Japanese government vulnerable to charges of duplicity and reinforced popular suspicions about the conservatives' true intentions.

Second, despite the fierce and often polemical battles over national security between Christian Democrats and Social Democrats in West Germany, there was greater room for cooperation and compromise between the right- and left-wing parties than was the case in Japan. The West German Social Democratic Party harbored harshly negative views of the Soviet Union, a historically grounded hostility that was greatly reinforced by the forcible partition of the nation. Many SPD leaders, like Otto Wehner, had firsthand knowledge of the brutalities of life under Stalin, and only recently the East German wing of the Social Democratic Party had been absorbed by the Soviet-backed Ulbricht regime. The Left in Japan, in contrast, often appeared almost hopelessly naïve about the nature of the communist system and prone to accept Soviet propaganda at face value. Over the course of the next ten years, as the basic German and Japanese policies toward their alliances and their new armed forces gradually took shape, the ideological differences between the Left and the Right were to sharpen and have a profound impact on the formation of the two countries' political-military cultures.

The Establishment of the Alliance Systems

Despite the many polemical battles waged during the 1950s over the advisability of joining the Western alliance system, in retrospect it would seem that Japan and Germany had little choice other than to do as they did. To maintain a neutral posture between East and West—as the Left in both countries advocated—would probably have been impossible. There was simply too great a risk that the Soviet Union would be tempted to use its political-military power to force both into its sphere of influence, and there was good reason to doubt that the United States would be willing to run such a risk, even supposing that German and Japanese leaders were.[15]

Once the basic decision to align with the West had been reached, however, there emerged a broad range of other questions whose resolutions were by no means self-evident. Chief among these matters were: what kind of alliance structure the two nations would participate in; the degree to which they were willing to integrate themselves into Western political strategy; and, finally, the way in which these decisions would be legitimated to the German and Japanese publics.

Both Yoshida and Adenauer saw in the outbreak of the Korean War an opportunity to bring the occupation of their nations to a speedy end. They perceived that this would give them a chance to win reacceptance and influence in the international community. The two men, however, had fundamentally different views of their respective countries' national interests. These dissimilarities were rooted in Germany's and Japan's different geostrategic positions and in their distinctive domestic political environments.

Although a quintessential realist in private, Yoshida believed that for the time being Japan should concentrate its energies on economic growth and reconstruction. He was concerned that rearmament would divert valuable resources from this goal and that Japan might alienate its Asian neighbors, with whom it would have to trade in order to become economically prosperous.[16] He also feared that rearmament might allow potentially subversive ex-military men to stage a political comeback.[17] Yoshida's preferred strategy was for Japan to continue to rely for its security on the United States. At the same time, he wanted to minimize involvement in American regional strategy, fearing that the United States would pressure Japan into committing forces abroad—possibly bogging it down in a land war in Asia—or force the country to build its military to the point where either a popular backlash or a right-wing coup would result.[18]

In pursuing this strategy, Yoshida faced a number of formidable challenges. On the one hand, he had to overcome fierce domestic political opposition, both from a Left violently opposed to capitalism and alignment with the West, and from his conservative rivals who favored a massive military arms buildup. On the other hand, the United States was pressuring Yoshida to raise 350,000 troops and join a NATO-like defense pact including Australia, New Zealand, the Philippines, and perhaps Indonesia.[19] Torn between these contradictory pressures, Yoshida was forced into compromises with the Americans and his domestic opposition in ways that made him appear duplicitous to both.

In contrast, Adenauer had few qualms about openly pressing for rearmament or joining a regional security alliance. Given the threat of a land invasion from the east, Germany was understandably more eager than Japan to build a substantial military establishment. As a front-line state in the Cold War that had only recently fought a war with the Soviet Union and had been brutally partitioned, Germany's fear that it might be abandoned by its new allies outweighed its fear of becoming entangled in conflicts not of its own making.

This did not mean, however, that West Germany was willing to become a totally pliant subject of the Western powers. The government was extremely sensitive to charges that the Western allies wanted to use Germans as cannon fodder for their own strategic purposes. In negotiations with the Western nations Adenauer insisted that West Germany be accorded equal treatment *(Gleichberechtigung)* in any future alliance, and that West Germans be allowed to participate in the military planning and operational command of allied forces. In addition, Adenauer extracted a guarantee that the newly formed North Atlantic Treaty Organization (NATO) would commit itself to meeting a Soviet assault at Germany's eastern border, abandoning a previous plans to conduct a mobile defense in depth, which would have implied surrendering much of the territory of the German Federal Republic to the enemy.

Given the overwhelming popular attachment to the ideal of national unity, Adenauer could not afford to abandon the goal of reunification. To reconcile the apparently irreconcilable objectives of seeking alliance with the West and reunification of Germany, Adenauer was forced to argue that by joining NATO, West Germany would increase its bargaining power vis-à-vis East Germany and thereby achieve reunification on better terms than it could by acting alone. To make this argument credible Adenauer had to induce the West to commit itself to pursuing the goal of eventual German reunification. In other words, while seeking to Europeanize West German security through a regional military alliance, Adenauer simultaneously tried to Europeanize the problem of German national partition.

Adenauer's and Yoshida's different conceptions of how their respective nations' alliances with the West should be structured, as well as the different types of pressures with which they had to contend, were in evidence in the early stages of formation of the two nations' alliance systems. In the Japanese case the first formal step was taken on September 10, 1951, when Japan signed the San Francisco Peace Treaty with forty-eight allied nations, excluding the Soviet Union and China, bringing the American occupation of Japan to an end. That same day, two additional agreements were signed, the Mutual Security Treaty (Sōgō Anzenhoshō Jōyaku, commonly referred to as Ampo), which defined Japan's security relationship with the United States, and an administrative agreement under which Japan granted the United States the right to continued use of its military bases in Japan. Shortly before the ceremony in San Francisco, John Foster Dulles, the American secretary of state, forced Yoshida to recognize the Chiang Kai-shek government in Taipei and thereby break relations with mainland China.[20]

For Germany, the defining moment came in May 1952, when the Federal Republic signed the General Treaty (Staatsvertrag), which returned to it a real, if limited, measure of sovereignty. At the same time it also signed the European Defense Community (EDC) Treaty, which committed it to joining the proposed multinational European army. In addition, the Federal Republic signed protocols concerning the stationing of Western forces on its territory, though now these forces were there to defend the West, rather than as occupiers. In a verbal promise to Dulles, Adenauer also agreed to forgo the development, production, and acquisition of so-called ABC (atomic, bacteriological, and chemical) weapons of mass destruction.[21]

The parallels between the two nascent alliances were many and obvious. Although all the implications of the agreements were not fully evident at the time, by forswearing weapons of mass destruction Germany and Japan effectively had agreed to place themselves under the aegis of the United States and rely upon its willingness to defend them in the all-important area of nuclear security. In this way, the two alliances served as a form of dual reassurance: They reassured the Germans and Japanese that they would not be abandoned in the event of a Soviet attack or attempt at nuclear blackmail; just as importantly, they reassured neighboring countries that feared the two former Axis powers might someday reemerge as security threats.[22]

In return for the American security guarantee, Germany and Japan both agreed to raise substantial military forces and to provide the United States with military bases on their territory. These bases were of vital importance, both for the defense of Germany and Japan and for the maintenance of America's military presence in the European and Eastern Asian theaters. Unless American forces were stationed in the two countries, it was feared the security guarantee would prove hollow, and the United States would have been hard-pressed to offer a credible defense of Western Europe or to pursue a strategy of containment in Eastern Asia. These two sets of interests, while overlapping, were by no means identical. At times they even contradicted one another, for there always existed the danger that American efforts to contain communism could spark a military confrontation whose main costs would have to be borne by countries in the region.[23] Consequently, both Adenauer and Yoshida sought ways to preserve some measure of control over the use of their forces and territories. The most important of these safeguards were the limitations placed by the legislatures of both nations on the overseas dispatch of their armed forces; in the German case they could only be used in the defense of alliance territory, while in Japan the armed forces could not be sent abroad at all.

Finally, both Germany and Japan were forced to pay a significant price in terms of their relations with their neighbors. For the Germans the cost of alliance was significantly higher, entailing as it did not only the severing of their traditional ties with most of Central Europe, but virtually guaranteeing the perpetuation of national partition. The cost to Japan of breaking off relations with mainland China should not be underestimated either, as many Japanese political and business leaders believed that Japan's long-term economic prosperity depended on maintaining its commercial relations with mainland Asia. On a deeper level, this policy was to have important implications for Japan's postwar identity. It enhanced Japan's isolation from the rest of Asia and compelled it to seek its destiny in the West, thereby breaking the pan-Asianist tradition of the 1930s and 1940s.[24]

Notwithstanding these broad similarities, the two alliances developed in significantly different directions. The first and most obvious point is that, whereas the Germans sought to enter into a close network of multilateral relations that included the United States and its Western neighbors, the Japanese alliance was a strictly bilateral affair. Germany's geographical location in the heart of Europe, facing the threat of a massive Soviet invasion, compelled it to build as strong a defensive coalition as possible. The fact that West Germany was not only under American, but also under British and French, control forced the Germans to negotiate with all three nations on matters pertaining to national sovereignty, including defense. Adenauer was compelled to reconcile the interests of all three Western powers, a task greatly complicated by French fears of a renewed German military threat.

Adenauer's solution to this dilemma was to seek security in a multinational alliance embracing all the Western powers. This policy was an integral part of the larger strategy of seeking European economic integration, and it led Adenauer to legitimate the new alliance on the basis of transnational ideals, such as the defense of democracy and Western civilization. This transnational idealism was reinforced by, and in turn served to reinforce, the general mood of antinationalism that had emerged in West Germany after the war.

In contrast, as an island nation Japan was less directly threatened than West

Germany, and the United States was its sole negotiating partner. Although there were other U.S. clients in the region, differences in their history, culture, and levels of economic and political development made for a far weaker push toward regional integration than that in Western Europe. To be sure, Yoshida and other Japanese conservatives felt that the containment of communism in Asia was a vital national interest. But he preferred that the costs of containment be borne by the United States and dreaded the domestic political consequences of allowing Japanese forces to become directly engaged in military operations overseas. Consequently, Japan sought a far more limited bilateral security pact with the United States, one that maximized American commitment to the defense of Japan while minimizing Japan's broader security obligations.

To legitimate this strategy to the Japanese people, Yoshida proposed a new national identity, that of Japan as a "merchant nation" *(chōnin kokka)*. Yoshida's definition of the national identity, like the Left's vision of Japan as a "peace nation," appealed to the powerful pacifist mood of the times and was in keeping with the demilitarizing impulse the American occupation had sought to impart. The image of Japan as a merchant nation was also intrinsically procapitalist, and left open the door for alignment with the United States. Yoshida's new conceptualization of the national identity was well designed to appeal to a broad spectrum of centrist opinion in Japan, which was profoundly weary of war and suspicious of the military, though at the same time, skeptical of the Left's socialist programs and neutralist pacifism.[25]

By 1952 the full contours of Germany's and Japan's alliance systems had not yet been fully defined, and a number of issues remained open. The resolution of these issues arrived sooner in Germany than in Japan. Initially the Federal Republic had been prepared to join the proposed EDC, which would have integrated German forces into a larger, multinational European military. However, in August 1954, the French National Assembly refused to consider the European Defense Community Treaty, thereby effectively killing the project.[26] The only practicable alternative was for Germany to join the existing NATO alliance. Having anticipated that the EDC proposal might run into difficulty in France, the Federal Republic applied for entry into NATO and its European sister organization, the Western European Union (WEU).[27]

Subsequently, the details of German entry into NATO were worked out at a series of conferences held in London and Paris. Under the London and Paris accords, the size of the West German force was set at half a million troops, organized into twelve divisions and placed under the command of the Supreme Allied Commander Europe (SACEUR). To further alleviate European anxieties over German rearmament, Adenauer reaffirmed his earlier pledge that Germany would not produce certain categories of weapons, including weapons of mass destruction, long-range missiles, heavy battleships, and strategic bombers.[28] In addition, in vowing that West Germany would never resort to force of arms in its search for reunification, Adenauer reassured West Germany's allies that it would not drag them into a conflict with the Soviet Union over the national issue. In return, the Western powers agreed that the Bonn government would be recognized as the sole legitimate representative of the German nation and that the question of Germany's eastern borders could only be settled after reunification.[29]

In addition to these new security treaties, the General Treaty of 1952 was renegotiated, returning full sovereignty to the West German government. In separate protocols, the Western allies retained special powers with regard to West Berlin, and the agreement to station troops in West Germany was renewed.[30] Adenauer even won concessions from the French on the disputed province of the Saar, one of the primary sources of tension between Germany and France that had greatly complicated his efforts to sell his policies to his more conservative political allies and the German public.[31]

In one masterful stroke, Adenauer thus succeeded in having West Germany join the ranks of the Western powers, complete with its own armed forces, and gaining near-equal status with other allied powers such as France and Britain. The great German goal of reunification, however, appeared more distant than ever. The Social Democrats criticized the government's foreign policy, and the Social Democratic leadership for the first time threw its full weight behind the peace movement. SPD leader Erich Ollenhauer called for a full year of political struggle, and the party began to explore the possibility of extraparliamentary opposition.[32] In January of 1955, close to two thousand SPD leaders joined peace activists at the Paulskirche in Frankfurt, one of the historical birthplaces of the nineteenth-century drive toward national unity. Together they issued the German Manifesto, rejecting the Paris treaties and demanding that the four occupying powers arrange a meeting on German reunification.[33]

Despite the aggressive response of the Socialist leadership, the Adenauer government had relatively little trouble pushing its program through the Bundestag, winning ratification of the Paris treaties by a margin of 324 to 151. Outside of the legislature as well, the opposition was largely ineffectual. Although there were protests and signature campaigns throughout West Germany, the average citizen appeared little moved by the polemics in Bonn.[34] The largest mass demonstration registered a turnout of little more than twenty-five thousand, mostly trade union members, and the public seemed more tranquil overall than in 1952.[35] It would require a new focus—that of nuclear weapons—and renewed hopes for reunification following a thaw in East-West relations to reinvigorate the peace movement in the late 1950s. Nonetheless, when West Germany's alliance system was formed, the basic patterns of the oppositional culture had been established as well. The *ohne mich Bewegung* and the Paulskirche protests became the models for the various cycles of protest that represent a central element in Germany's new culture of antimilitarism.

On the other side of the globe, the resolution of questions surrounding Japan's alliance with the United States moved more slowly, hindered by the increasing polarization of the Japanese domestic political environment after Yoshida's ouster from the prime ministership in 1954. Spurred on by the vigorous support of the business world and a general anxiety in conservative circles over the growing strength of the socialists, the conservative parties joined together to form the Liberal Democratic Party (LDP), which would dominate Japanese politics for nearly four decades.[36] The professed goal of the strongly anticommunist LDP was to revise the constitution, in particular Article 9, to create a large military establishment, and to pursue an independent foreign policy within the framework of the alliance with the United States. After opposition parties won more than one-third of the seats in the lower house in 1953, thus blocking any hope of constitutional revision, the government focused its attentions on revising the Mutual Security Treaty. In addition to rectifying various inadequacies in the treaty—such as clarification of America's commitment to defend Japan in the event of an invasion—the conservatives in the LDP government hoped to use the revision of the treaty to trigger a greater military buildup and pave the way for Japanese participation in a regional collective security system similar to NATO. Inevitably, it was believed, such an expanded military role would force the issue of constitutional revision back to the top of the political agenda.[37]

The domestic implications of this foreign policy agenda mobilized not only the political Left in opposition to the government's plans, but alarmed many in the center as well. Efforts by the government to prepare the way for revising the Mutual Security Treaty merely reinforced these fears. In particular, proposed legislation that would have greatly strengthened the powers of the police forces was widely believed to have been designed to suppress anticipated popular protests.[38] Suspicions that an authoritarian coup was in the offing were further reinforced in 1958 when Kishi Nobosuke, Tōjō's wartime munitions minister, became prime minister.

Consequently, in the summer of 1958, when the government announced its intention to revise the treaty, political unrest began to escalate to unprecedented levels. For the next two years protests and demonstrations spread across Japan, reaching their climax in the spring and summer of 1960. Confrontations between the police and protestors grew more and more violent, with groups of radical students repeatedly invading the Diet compound and clashing with police forces.[39] Meanwhile, inside the building, the Japanese public was treated to the unseemly spectacle of their elected representatives engaging in a form of parliamentary rugby as rival LDP and Japanese Socialist Party members of the Diet and their aides brawled with one another for control of the floor. When a desperate Kishi sought to use the Self-Defense Forces to reestablish order, the threat of civil war seemed eminent.

With increasing violence and political tension, there came growing criticism of the Kishi government in the mainstream media, the business community, and even within the LDP. The director general of the Self-Defense Forces, Akagi Munenori, refused to act on Kishi's request, and increasing numbers of Kishi's own government defected to the opposition. Ultimately, the LDP was able to ratify a revised treaty, but only at the price of Kishi's resignation on June 23, 1960. He was replaced by the more moderate Yoshida protégé, Ikeda Hayato. The changes in the treaty were for the most part incremental and hardly represented the quantum leap in defense policy that Kishi and other conservatives had hoped for.

On a deeper level, however, the battle over the revision of the Mutual Security Treaty was a defining moment in the development of Japan's new political-military culture. Kishi's defeat and removal led to a consolidation of the low-key, minimalist approach to defense and national security begun by Yoshida. Centrist political forces in the government, business, and the media, while not averse to Japan's taking a more active role in the alliance with the United States, were uneasy about Kishi's suspected hidden domestic political agenda and preferred gradual reform to violent confrontation with the Left over defense issues. Their concern with domestic stability was further reinforced by a rash of right-wing terrorist incidents in the wake of the treaty battle, including the assassination of the JSP secretary general, Asanuma Inejirō, the attempted assassination of Kishi, and the discovery in 1961 of a right-wing conspiracy to stage a coup d'état.[40] When push had come to shove, the political center chose to abandon Kishi, and it was this group, as much as or even more than the leftist protestors, who were responsible for his defeat.

The events of 1960 traumatized Japan's conservative political leadership, and Kishi's fall from power served subsequent generations of conservative politicians as a salutary lesson on the perils of pursuing the defense issue. For the next eight years, the LDP preferred to ignore the question of national security, and even after the original trauma had faded most LDP leaders dealt with defense only insofar as international pressures compelled them to do so. Although right-wing political leaders like Nakasone Yasuhiro would periodically rekindle the debate on defense, whenever they did so they were confronted by a political mainstream that, if not actively hostile, was deeply skeptical about their initiatives.

Far more so than in West Germany, the new political-military culture in Japan linked defense to the larger problem of democracy. The primary issue on which Kishi stumbled was not so much the Mutual Security Treaty itself (public opinion polls during the year-long crisis revealed decidedly mixed views on the issue),[41] but rather popular suspicion that his long-term political agenda and the hard-line measures used to ratify the treaty were inherently antidemocratic.

Of course, in West Germany as well there had been criticism of the substance of Adenauer's defense policies and the manner in which they were implemented. As in Japan, a close linkage existed between the German conservatives' domestic political goals and the often-controversial choices they made in the area of national defense (opting for capitalism versus socialism, integration with the West over pursuit of national unity, etc.). Unlike the situation in Japan, however, there was little popular anxiety that Adenauer and the Christian Democrats were seeking to undermine postwar democracy. The fact that Adenauer's government was a coalition government worked in his favor by reducing fears that the Christian Democrats Union might become too powerful. More importantly, however, Adenauer's credentials as a democrat were never seriously put into question. His leftist opponents on occasion questioned the strength of his prewar anti-Nazi record, but not even his archrival, SPD Chairman Kurt Schumacher, in his most venomous outbursts ever accused Adenauer of being a supporter of Hitler. Kishi, in contrast, with his dubious past and his close ties to various ultranationalist leaders, appeared to the Japanese public a far more sinister figure.[42]

Japanese anxiety over the strength of the democracy, coupled with popular fear that right-wing forces might undermine the democratic political order using national security as a pretext, turned the defense issue into a political taboo. Awareness of Kishi's and other LDP leaders' connections to the militarist regime strengthened these suspicions and further deepened the ideological polarization between the Left and the Right. Cooperation between the two camps was almost impossible, especially on defense and national security issues. Whereas consecutive West German governments were able to push through defense legislation despite violent opposition, whenever Japan's government sought to introduce new, important defense measures it was compelled to look for allies from other parties to lend its policies a cloak of democratic legitimacy.

Back in Uniform—The New Military Establishments

Parallel to the domestic political debates over the question of alliance with the United States, furious debates also took place over the size and structure of the armed forces and the ways in which they should be integrated into the new German and Japanese democratic systems. In Japan, the debates were triggered in 1951 when the Police Reserve Forces were established by American fiat. In Germany, the ongoing debate over the EDC and the character of West Germany's new alliance structures postponed serious discussion of rearmament until 1955.[43]

The new German and Japanese armed forces that emerged during this period were remarkably similar with respect to their pronounced defensive character. At the same time they differed drastically in other respects, especially in the ways in which the nations sought to establish civilian control over the armed forces, and in the ways in which they made defense policy.

The differences between the types of armed forces that the Germans and the Japanese created were in part a function of their very different geostrategic positions. Faced with the prospect of a massive Soviet ground offensive, West Germany initially sought to create heavily armored forces capable of mounting a mobile defense and attacking wherever possible to keep invading forces off balance. Japan, having rejected the option of joining a collective security arrangement and insulated from the threat of invasion by the overwhelming might of the U.S. Pacific fleet, viewed defending the nation from domestic subversion as the primary mission of its armed forces. The only part of Japan regarded as seriously threatened by conventional foreign attack was the northern island of Hokkaido, where the bulk of the Japanese heavy forces were eventually deployed.

International political factors played a decisive role in determining other aspects of German and Japanese defense policy. The anxiety of neighboring countries that rearmament might resurrect German and Japanese militarism led both countries to adopt basically defensive strategic doctrines and to forgo the acquisition of weapons systems, such as aircraft carriers or long-range bombers, that could be interpreted as offensive in nature.[44] Opposition from within the Western alliance, as well as from the communist countries, strongly discouraged German or Japanese acquisition of nuclear weapons, despite concerns of professional military men, especially in West Germany, that without nuclear weapons the conventional superiority of the Eastern bloc could not be countered.[45]

While international factors created some incentive for adopting a purely defensive military strategy, this inclination was greatly reinforced by domestic political factors. In neither country did the creation of armed forces generate any noticeable popular enthusiasm. German public opinion data from January 1955, when recruiting for the new army began, showed that only 19 percent of those surveyed said they would advise someone they knew to join the new Bundeswehr, while 47 percent said they would advise against it.[46] In the depressed Japanese economy of the 1950s it was somewhat easier to find recruits, and initially 382,000 people applied for 75,000 positions in the Police Reserve Forces.[47] Nonetheless, as in Germany, Japanese public opinion was extremely negative toward the new armed forces.

Antimilitary sentiments tended to become even stronger whenever the actual use of military power was contemplated. In Japan, even the suspicion that the armed forces might be used abroad met with violent resistance, and the fear that a closer security partnership with the United States might drag Japan into external conflicts helped to fuel opposition to the revision of the Mutual Security Treaty. Consequently, the U.S.-Japanese military alliance was largely passive for the first twenty-five years of its existence, and only very limited efforts were made to coordinate military planning and cooperation.

In West Germany, popular opposition to the use of force was greatly reinforced by the fear of nuclear weapons, whose presence on German soil was needed to compensate for superior Soviet conventional power, but whose actual use would have devastating consequences for the territory they were supposed to defend.[48] In 1955, when the influential West German journal *Der Spiegel* revealed that recent NATO exercises projected that 1.7 million Germans would die and 3.5 million would be wounded as the result of a *successful* defense of German territory, anxieties concerning rearmament switched focus from the alliance to nuclear weapons.[49] The same coalition of political forces that had opposed Adenauer in 1952—the SPD, the unions, and a powerful, grass roots peace movement led by intellectuals and the left wing of the Protestant Church—reignited the defense debate under the slogan "fight atomic death" (*Kampf dem Atomtod*). The strength of the antinuclear weapons movement, especially with the approach of federal elections in the fall of 1957, forced the government to abandon its original inclination to equip the Bundeswehr with tactical nuclear weapons, and instead made the introduction of nuclear weapons contingent on progress in arms talks between the superpowers. Thereafter, Bonn, with strong encouragement from the Americans, contented itself with a formula whereby it controlled short- and middle-range delivery systems while the United States retained control over the nuclear warheads themselves.[50]

While there were perfectly good strategic and international political reasons for Japan to limit its military integration with the United States, and for West Germany to forgo pressing for more control over nuclear weapons, good arguments to the contrary could also be made. The strategic stability of the East Asian region was of vital importance to the security of Japan. Not only was the United States eager for Japan to play a more active role in East Asian security, but many Japanese defense and foreign policy experts, as well as conservative politicians, felt that Japan should become more directly involved in the containment of communism in the region.[51]

In the case of West Germany, there was a general consensus that the development of an independent national nuclear force would needlessly provoke the Soviet Union and alienate Germany's Western allies, especially France. Nonetheless, strong arguments could be made that Germany should seek to acquire a greater degree of control over the nuclear weapons supplied by its allies in order to make the threat of nuclear escalation in the event of a Soviet invasion more credible and to enhance West German influence within the alliance.[52] Indeed, it was precisely the expectation that the Federal Republic eventually would push for "a German finger on the nuclear trigger" that encouraged the United States during the 1960s to undertake a number of initiatives designed to forestall such a development.

Domestic political pressures were clearly not the only reasons why Japan chose not to become involved in regional security affairs and why West Germany did not seek to acquire greater control over the nuclear weapons stationed in its territory. Nonetheless, the presence of large, virulently antimilitary coalitions of social and political forces, supported by widespread public antipathy toward the new military establishments in both countries, arguably tipped the balance.

Cultures of Antimilitarism

Domestic factors exerted even more influence in the area of civil-military relations. Given the historical association between the military and the forces of conservative authoritarianism, it is not surprising that the question of how to prevent the new armed forces from becoming a threat to the newly established democratic order emerged as a central issue in postwar German and Japanese defense debates. The two nations resolved this structurally similar problem in fundamentally different ways. Whereas the Japanese chose to rely largely on bureaucratic and legal external controls of their new armed forces, the West Germans combined external control mechanisms with internal controls in the form of an ideological program designed to integrate the military into the larger society.[53]

In the Japanese case the problem of containing the armed forces was primarily debated under the rubric of "civilian control" *(shiberian kontorooru).* The concept was originally imported into Japan by the American military advisors who assisted in the rearmament process. At first the Japanese had some difficulty understanding the concept; until the occupation, there were no Japanese terms that distinguished between military men and civilians. After the first briefing on the topic, one senior officer reportedly came away with the vague impression that it had something to do with the kinds of hats the new forces should adopt.[54] Despite this initial confusion, the Japanese government soon grasped the importance of the primacy of civilian authority and to this end created a large, civilian bureaucracy to oversee all aspects of the new armed forces.

A civilian director general, who was a member of the cabinet, was created to head the new apparatus of control. He was endowed with nearly complete executive authority, including the right to decide all personnel matters. Under the director general were created five internal bureaus *(naikyoku)* in charge of such key areas as military planning, procurement, training, and finances, and staffed by civilian bureaucrats. In addition, a National Defense Council (Kokubokaigi) was established, composed of members of the Diet and charged with the review of major defense decisions before they were sent to the cabinet for final approval. The military was denied any autonomy as an independent body, and the political activities of military personnel were tightly restricted. An active military officer was not allowed to publicly comment on defense issues without first obtaining approval by civilian bureaucrats. Disobeying this injunction was viewed as a severe violation of the principle of civilian control and could serve as grounds for dismissal.[55]

Moreover, whereas the Imperial Army and Navy of the prewar period had been semiautonomous agencies that could defy with impunity the policies made by the rest of the government, in the postwar era other bureaucracies exercised control over many aspects of defense policy making. For example, the Ministry of Finance (MOF) enjoyed ultimate authority with regard to budgetary issues, and the Ministry of International Trade and Industry (MITI) on procurement matters. Certain bureaus within the new armed forces were almost entirely staffed by bureaucrats on loan from other ministries. For example, the Finance and Accounting Bureau fell under the control of MOF, while the Procurement Bureau was colonized by the MITI, further reducing the new military's room for independent action.[56]

Yet, because of the vivid memories of the military takeover of government in the 1930s and continuing doubts about the strength of Japanese democracy, even these strict bureaucratic controls were regarded as insufficient to dispel popular fears that the armed forces might run amok. The surreptitious manner in which the new military establishment was created served to reinforce these fears and to greatly complicate the defense policy–making process. In 1950, when the Police Reserve Forces were established, the government denied that this represented a first step toward creating a military.[57] Pressures from the United States, however, compelled Yoshida to do more in terms of burden sharing, and the new institution gradually expanded. In 1952 the Police Reserve Forces evolved into the National Security Forces before turning into the Self-Defense Forces in 1954, acquiring increased military capabilities and external defense-oriented missions in the process. Under attack from opposition parties and unable to revise the constitution, the government was forced to reinterpret Article 9 and argue that the new forces, while more than a police force, were less than a true military. But as the armed forces continued to grow and develop, this position appeared increasingly disingenuous and entangled the government in a growing web of contradictions.

The steady buildup of military strength, together with the government's fluctuating interpretation of the constitution and of the armed forces' mission, created the impression of an inexorable march toward remilitarization. The Japanese public quite accurately perceived defense policy as being made by government fiat and supported by ad hoc legitimations. This process, labeled by critics an "accumulation of faits accomplis" *(kiseijijitsu no tsumiage)*, reinforced the opposition's doubts about the government's motives. In a vicious cycle, ideological cleavages over defense were deepened by the appearance of government duplicity, and, in turn, encouraged the government to avoid public debate of national security issues.

To alleviate public anxiety, the government was compelled to impose new limitations on the armed forces with each new defense initiative. For example, when the Self-Defense Forces were created in 1954, a National Defense Council was established to provide parliamentary oversight of the armed forces. In addition, the House of Councilors—the upper house of the Japanese legislature—passed a resolution forbidding the overseas dispatch of the new armed forces.[58] Such restrictions, referred to as *hadome*, or "brakes," became a fixed feature in the evolution of Japanese defense policy making and would seriously hamper the development of Japanese defense policy for decades to come.

In West Germany, a system of administrative controls was put into place whose purpose was to assure the subordination of the new armed forces to civilian authority and prevent them from becoming a "state within the state." The new Ministry of Defense was headed by a defense minister and two secretaries, all civilians, and was divided into four main sections, only one of which was run by professional military personnel. Although military men in Germany were given greater freedom than in Japan, civilians were firmly in control of all aspects of defense policy making. They swore an oath of allegiance to the constitution and democratic principles, instead of to the head of the nation, as had been the traditional practice.[59]

Beyond this program of external controls, the Bundeswehr adopted a far-reaching, almost radical program of indoctrination and reeducation known as internal leadership (Innere Führung) designed to democratize the new military from within and prevent it from becoming an instrument of authoritarianism. The concept of Innere Führung had emerged during the planning for rearmament and was originally proposed by Adenauer's military advisors, who were convinced that any new military institution was obliged to cleanse itself of the Nazi past and needed to be integrated into democratic society. The "new soldier" was no longer to fight on the basis of zombie-like obedience *(Kadavergehorsamkeit)*, but out of an inner conviction and belief in the values of freedom and democracy. While the principles of military hierarchy and discipline would be retained, the soldier was to be granted as many civil liberties as possible. No longer would he be elevated above his fellow countrymen, nor would he be reduced to a creature bound to slavishly follow his superiors' every command.[60]

From the perspective of its originators, the doctrine of Innere Führung was intended to prevent the abuse of the armed forces for criminal purposes as much as to protect civilian society from the pernicious influence of the military. At the same time, many ex-officers who joined the Bundeswehr were intensely suspicious of the new concept. They saw, not altogether incorrectly, that it represented a direct criticism of both themselves and the performance of the military during the World War II.[61] Adenauer himself felt that democratization of the army was thoroughly unnecessary to assure civilian control, and would have been content to rely on a system of purely external controls.[62]

Innere Führung, however, received strong popular support. Two groups in particular campaigned for the concept: the Social Democrats and various youth groups. Young German men were generally unwilling to subject themselves to the brutal regimen of traditional German army life and insisted on a far-reaching liberalization of conditions inside the new military. In order to raise the manpower German military planners believed necessary to counter the threat of a Soviet invasion, the new Bundeswehr was based on a system of universal conscription. The cooperation of youth organizations hence was seen as vital if the already politically unpopular program of rearmament was to succeed.[63] The Social Democrats, unlike their Socialist counterparts in Japan, decided that despite their general opposition to rearmament, they could not afford to remain uninvolved in the creation of the new armed forces.[64] Instead of blockading the deliberative process, as did the JSP, the SPD decided to help shape the new forces, making Innere Führung one of the preconditions for their support.

With strong support from all sides, Innere Führung became one of the cornerstones of the new Bundeswehr. The principles of Innere Führung were taught as an essential part of military training and profoundly influenced the formulation of military law, restricting the disciplinary power of officers and giving soldiers the right of appeal. In addition, an independent Office of the Parliamentary Commissioner for the Bundeswehr (Wehrbeauftragte) was created and charged with monitoring conditions within the military. The commissioner had broad investigatory powers and reported his findings directly to the Parliament.[65]

Inevitably, the ideal of reconciling principles of a democracy with the hierarchy and discipline of the armed forces proved difficult to achieve. By their very nature, armed forces require a certain degree of centralization of authority that is incompatible with grass roots democratic decision making. The soldier's duty to kill and to sacrifice his own life is almost by definition incompatible with a liberal view of human rights.[66]

Regardless of these difficulties, Innere Führung and the bipartisan manner in which it was created played a major role in legitimating the new armed forces in Germany. Just as importantly, the introduction of conscription made the Bundeswehr far more open to society than were the Japanese Self-Defense Forces. In subsequent decades millions of ordinary Germans were able to observe firsthand the inner workings of the new armed forces. While most them found military life rather unedifying, they nonetheless were reassured that it did not pose a threat to democracy.[67] In contrast, the isolated nature of the Self-Defense Forces made its internal mechanics far more opaque to outsiders and contributed to its sinister image in the public eye. Innere Führung and conscription were the two main pillars of opening the military up to society, instead of closing it off. Together they contributed greatly to the establishment of a relatively healthy climate of civil-military relations in West Germany, as compared to Japan.

3

The Anatomy of Two
New Political-Military Cultures

THE WAYS in which the various political actors in Germany and Japan interpreted the postwar approaches to defense and national security served to shape the new political-military cultures of both nations. Each country was influenced by several political-military subcultures, each of which held strong views about the military as an institution, the utility of force in international affairs, and national security interests. The ways in which these different subcultures were distributed within the postoccupation German and Japanese political systems on the levels of public opinion, among elite groups (e.g., the intelligentsia, the media, the business community, and so on), and among the political parties is worth analyzing. Such an analysis will permit an examination of the patterns of interaction that emerged among the subcultures in the political arena.

Using this type of analysis, this chapter produces a detailed "anatomy" of a given political-military culture at a particular point in time. Using this anatomy as a baseline, later chapters will compare changes in that culture, exploring whether changes in behavior are matched by corresponding changes in the two nations' political-military cultures and whether domestic political frictions emerged in those cases where policy initiatives ran against established patterns of behavior. Such an analytical procedure makes it possible to gauge of the strength of the political-military cultures of Japan and Germany and to judge whether they have had a significant impact on state behavior.

The Contents of the New Political-Military Cultures

In postwar Japan and Germany there emerged broad constellations of political forces that can be labelled as belonging to the Left, the Right, and the Center. These groups represented ideological subcultures within the larger West German and Japanese political cultures, each with distinctive views not only on the problems of national security, but also on a wide range of domestic and foreign-policy issues. The beliefs and values of these different subcultures were shaped by each country's unique historical circumstances as well as by the peculiar experiences and interests of the groups comprising them. What it meant to be on the Right, or the Left, differed greatly between the two countries. In order to differentiate between the Left, Right, and Center in each country, I will label them *Right-idealist, Left-idealist,* and *Centrist* in the case of Japan, and *West Europeanist, Central Europeanist,* and *Atlanticist* in the West German case.[1]

In each country, the Left and the Right were divided fundamentally by sharply diverging views of national identity. In Japan, the key questions of identity revolved around two major issues: the relationship between the new Japan and the old—whether to preserve the traditional values as much as possible or to abandon them as hopelessly outmoded—and the future social and economic systems that should be adopted—whether to follow the capitalist or the socialist model of development.[2] In West Germany, the central identity problem was a new version of the *deutsche Frage* (the German question) that had troubled German intellectuals and statesmen since the nineteenth century. The key question here was where to locate the geographical center of German cultural and national identity: whether it firmly belonged in Western Europe, whether it was a bridge between the East and the West, or whether it was part of a larger collectivity based on adherence to common political and economic principles. The division of Germany into two parts compounded this dilemma and introduced the additional question of how national unity could be restored.[3]

Japan: The Right-Idealists

The Right-idealists in Japan, as represented by Prime Ministers Kishi and Hatoyama, were distinguished from the Centrists and the Left-idealists by their reverence for Japan's historical and cultural traditions. It is possible to trace the Right-idealists' views back to the Meiji debate over the problem of how to preserve the essence of Japanese culture while meeting the technological and political challenges posed by the West. Like their Meiji predecessors, the postwar Right-idealists were preoccupied with strengthening Japan while controlling the modernization process and preventing it from eroding the core values of Japanese society. Without defining precisely what those core values were, the rightists in general agreed that they included a sense of pride and independence as a nation, the maintenance of a spirit of self-sacrifice, and the fostering of respect for the established social order—above all, for the institution of the emperor.

It would be a mistake to classify all the Right-idealists as reactionaries. Even the most fervent right-wingers were well aware of the enormity of Japan's defeat and recognized that the old system was in need of reform. Although they did not regard Japan's imperial expansion or the war against the United States as immoral, they were profoundly distrustful of the old military establishment, which they viewed as a potential hotbed of revolution and which they blamed for foolishly having dragged the nation into a futile and enormously destructive war.[4]

At the same time that they recognized a need for change, the Right-idealists strongly opposed the more liberal reforms of the occupation period, which they suspected were designed to permanently weaken the Japanese state. While their primary target was the elimination of the new constitution and its antiwar Article 9, they also were inclined to do away with a wide array of other American-initiated policies, such as unfettered trade unionism, a decentralized police force, and a liberalized educational system. On a more general level, the Right-idealists were sharply critical of the new, often crass materialist spirit of the times, with its disregard for old patterns of hierarchy and discipline and its adulation of individual rights over duty to the nation.

In the area of defense, the Right-idealists were inclined toward a traditional, realistic approach to foreign policy. Paradoxically, they were the strongest supporters of alliance with the United States because they saw communism as a greater threat to Japan than Western liberalism. In addition, they hoped to use American pressure on Japan to overcome domestic resistance to a military buildup. While they urged greater military cooperation with the United States, Right-idealists like Kishi and Hatoyama also favored the pursuit of a more independent foreign policy, including improved relations with communist nations so as to maximize Japan's room for diplomatic maneuvering.

In the minds of the Right-idealists a strong military was one of the necessary attributes of a truly sovereign nation. Consequently, they strongly advocated the abolition of Article 9 and revision of the constitution to rid it of its pacifist overtones. They also supported the removal of other legal and policy restrictions (*hadome*, or brakes) on the military, such as the prohibition on overseas dispatch and the bans on participating in collective defense, on arms exports, and on the acquisition of nuclear weapon. However, most Right-idealists, including ultrahawkish members of the Diet who otherwise advocated a massive military buildup and a more active military role abroad, felt that stringent civilian controls should be preserved in order to prevent the armed forces from once again becoming a threat to democracy.

Beyond their advocacy of constitutional revision, the Right-idealists tended to link a wide range of other nonmilitary polices with national defense. From their point of view, national defense required strengthening of the spiritual foundations of the military both within the armed forces and in the broader society. To this end, they advocated the development of a patriotic school curriculum, the free use of national symbols (including the emperor and the national flag), and cracking down on so-called subversive groups such as the teachers' union.

West Germany: The West Europeanists

The Right in West Germany was distinguished by its commitment to the ideals of defending the Christian civilization of West Europe *(christliches Abendland)* from the threat of bolshevism from the East. While reunification with the eastern part of the country was one of their chief objectives, West Europeanists like Konrad Adenauer and Defense Minister Franz Josef Strauss believed that national unity could not be soon reachieved. They hoped, however, that if West Germany, together with its Western allies, were sufficiently strong militarily and could demonstrate political will and solidarity, in the long run they could compel the Soviet Union to negotiate with them on terms of the West's choosing. In the meantime, however, any compromise with the forces of totalitarianism would be a serious mistake that would only encourage further Soviet intransigence and strengthen left-wing West German nationalism (i.e., the SPD).

On a deeper, historical and philosophical level, the West Europeanists were convinced that the primary cause of the tragedies of World Wars I and II could be found in Germany's geographical and spiritual position between East and West, which left it surrounded by potential adversaries and psychically torn between East European communitarianism and authoritarianism, on the one hand, and the pragmatic, individualist democratic traditions of Western Europe, on the other. They hoped that integration with the West would finally put Germany on the side of progress and enlightenment, and, at the same time, would help subdue the demons of nationalism, not only in Germany, but also in other Western nations. The renationalization of European defense and foreign policies was one of Adenauer's greatest fears, and it imparted an almost desperate quality to his determination to anchor the nation in the West.[5]

Unlike the Japanese Right-idealists, the German West Europeanists displayed a deep sense of remorse over the crimes of the Nazi era. At the same time, German conservatives tended to relativize Germany's crimes under Nazism by attributing them to the broader, not uniquely German, phenomenon of totalitarianism. By making a particular political system the culprit, as opposed to the German nation or people, this view absolved West Germany of at least some of the guilt it bore for the Holocaust and the war.

During the 1950s the West Europeanists were strong supporters of alliance with the West and rearmament. Profoundly suspicious of the various proposals for overarching collective security arrangements floated by some Western diplomats and German critics of the government, they argued that the ultimate effect of such agreements would be to undermine the unity of the alliance. West Europeanists like Adenauer were beset by the fear that the United States, given its geographical distance from Europe and its isolationist traditions, might one day strike a bargain with the Soviet Union—a second Potsdam agreement— allowing American disengagement in return for German neutralization.[6] As a way of hedging against a possible American withdrawal, the West Europeanists were eager to explore alternative security arrangements centering on France and the rest of Europe, especially after the United States took the first, tentative steps toward détente in the second half of the 1950s.[7]

In principle, the West Europeanists were in favor of a strong West German military. After 1950 they tended to discount any direct military threat from a Soviet invasion and viewed the armed forces first and foremost as an instrument of alliance politics and only secondarily as an instrument of defense. Building an overly large military, the Federal Republic's military planners feared, would impose unacceptable economic costs and increase the chance of a limited conventional war in Europe with devastating consequences for the two Germanys.[8]

Since the West Europeanists held Nazism to be the product of a now-defunct political system, they were far less concerned with Innere Führung as a means of strengthening civilian control over the military. Instead, conservatives tended to value the doctrine primarily for its public relations uses and as a form of anticommunist indoctrination. West Europeanists like Adenauer would have been perfectly willing to rely on external bureaucratic controls alone to ensure civilian primacy.

Japan: The Left-Idealists

At the opposite end of the political spectrum from the Right-idealists and the West Europeanists were the Left-idealists in Japan and the Central Europeanists in West Germany. The Japanese Left-idealists were determined to achieve a complete break with the old political, social, and economic order, which they saw as feudal and exploitative and whose pernicious influence they believed had survived into the postwar period, stifling the creation of a new, truly democratic, and more egalitarian Japan. While the Left-idealists wholeheartedly embraced modernization, unlike the Centrists, they favored a socialist model of development. There was also a strong strain of pan-Asian idealism in Left-idealist thinking, a feeling that Japan had a special contribution to make to the development of Asia. They believed that the security relationship with the United States prevented Japan from playing the kind of progressive role in Asia that they would like. This sense of mission was reinforced by feelings of recrimination on the part of many Japanese intellectuals over the atrocities committed by Japanese forces during the war, especially on mainland China.

It is important to emphasize that not all Left-idealists were pro-Soviet marxist ideologues. As with the other political subcultures, there existed a diversity of views within the leftist camp. The Left drew its mass appeal from the large segments of Japanese society who were profoundly dissatisfied with the status quo after having suffered through rapid industrialization, urbanization, and the havoc of war. This part of the population could just as easily have been organized under an entirely different ideological banner, as was demonstrated by the rise of the Buddhist Sokka Gakkai and its political arm, Komeitō, in the 1960s.

Central to the Left-idealists' agenda was their total rejection of alliance with the United States. The Left advocated adopting in its place a neutral stance between East and West while building closer relations with other Asian and developing nations.[9] Ironically, the Left-idealists' chief source of inspiration was of American origin, and they drew upon the pacifist ideals first formulated by MacArthur and Shidehara, which had been enshrined in the new constitution. They advocated a new national identity of Japan as a "peace nation," the harbinger of a new international morality offering a war-weary world an alternative to the endless cycle of violence that has characterized human history.

The Left-idealists viewed the Soviet Union and the People's Republic of China as essentially peace-loving nations forced to guard their ideals against the blandishments of the capitalist nations.[10] The pro-U.S. stance of their domestic political opponents, whom the Left-idealists viewed as dangerous reactionaries, reinforced this image. They feared that rearmament and integration into U.S. strategy would be the first steps toward the remilitarization of Japanese society and would drag the country into armed conflict on the Asian mainland. The Left-idealists insisted on nothing less than the immediate abolition of the Mutual Security Treaty and the dismantling of the Self-Defense Forces. Consistent with their vision of Japan as a "peace nation," they urged that Japan adopt a policy of unarmed neutrality *(hibusō chūritsu)* and pursue "peace diplomacy" *(heiwa gaikō)* in order to avert military threats. The Left-idealists believed the probability that Japan would be invaded was very low but, in the unlikely event of an attack, they advocated reliance on the force of world opinion, as expressed through the United Nations, and on passive resistance. In a country that had just experienced one of the most peaceful occupations in recorded history after waging a merciless war against an enemy it had demonized for more than a decade, these views were more persuasive than they might have been in many other countries.

West Germany: The Central Europeanists

The Central Europeanists in the Federal Republic, on the other hand, had a far harsher view of both war and the realities of life under communism than did their Japanese left-wing counterparts. Central to their core values was a deep commitment to the goal of speedy reunification of the German nation and a preference for some sort of socialist economic and social system. Central Europeanists like Kurt Schumacher felt that capitalism had been proven a failure. In their view, the excessive accumulation of wealth in private hands was antithetical to democracy and egalitarianism, and had been in no small measure responsible for the rise of National Socialism. The kind of socialism the German Left wanted to create, however, was very different from the totalitarian system that dominated Eastern Europe. True socialism, they believed, would represent a "third way" of solving the dilemmas of modernization and industrialization, striking a balance between the egocentric capitalism of the West and the authoritarianism of the East.

Far more so than other groups in Germany, the Central Europeanists were haunted by the Holocaust and the terrible burden of guilt they felt it placed upon the German nation. The Central Europeanists generally attributed Nazism to particular features inherent in German society. Consequently, they believed far-reaching reforms of German politics and society were needed to weed out the root causes of German authoritarianism and aggressiveness. This sense of guilt added a powerful moral dimension to the Left's opposition to rearmament and NATO nuclear strategy.

On issues of defense the Central Europeanists advocated the creation of a united, neutral Germany under the umbrella of some type of collective security arrangement involving all the major European powers, including the United

States and the Soviet Union. Throughout the late 1950s the Central Europeanists presented a series of plans that combined German unification with the creation of a collective security system.[11] They strongly opposed both military integration with the West through NATO and economic integration through the European Economic Community.

The Central Europeanists further opposed the creation of the Bundeswehr, not so much because they saw it as a potential tool of oppression (as the Left in Japan regarded military buildup), but rather because they feared it would provoke the Soviet Union and further dim prospects for an eventual, peaceful solution to German partition. Instead of a heavily armed Bundeswehr, the Central Europeanists, drawing on ideas of the iconoclastic government defense planner Bogislav von Bonin, favored the creation of a territorial militia armed mostly with antitank weapons. In the event of a Soviet attack, such a lightly armed force would rely on defensive tactics that would delay the invaders until outside help could arrive.[12] They categorically rejected the acquisition or even the stationing of nuclear weapons in Germany, condemning them as immoral, and warned that their use in the narrow confines of Germany would destroy precisely that which the weapons were intended to defend.

Despite the Central Europeanists' opposition to the Bundeswehr, the mainstream leadership of the SPD decided to accept the new military institution and participate in its creation so as to be able to influence its development and ensure that it would not become a threat to democracy. As the strongest advocates of the concept of Innere Führung, the Central Europeanists were extremely critical of subsequent failures to fully implement the concept in its original idealistic form.

Japan: The Centrists

The Japanese Centrists, like the Left-idealists, were strongly committed to modernizing and reforming Japan. Unlike the leftists, they sought their models in the capitalist West, particularly in the victorious United States. Although they were as critical of prewar Japan as were the Left-idealists, their confidence in the nation and its institutions had been severely shaken by the defeat and by the evident overwhelming superiority of the conquering Americans. The Centrists' idealization of the United States was comparable to the Left-idealists' idealization of the communist nations or the Right-idealists' glorification of Japan under the emperor system. The chief representatives of the Centrist camp were

Yoshida (though on domestic political issues Yoshida displayed strong Right-idealist tendencies) and the many ex-bureaucrats he brought into party politics, such as future Prime Ministers Ikeda Hayato, Satō Eisaku, and Miyazawa Kiichi.

Three core beliefs defined the Centrist position on defense. The first was that Japan was too vulnerable, both geographically and economically, to defend itself. The second tenet of the Centrist creed was the conviction that Japan, at least for the time being, should devote itself to the enterprise of economic reconstruction and modernization, with the emphasis placed on economic over social and political development.[13] Finally, Yoshida, like many other Centrists, feared that the creation of a powerful new military might pose a threat to Japanese democracy.

The Centrists hence were prepared to rely almost completely on an alliance with the United States for external security. At the same time they wanted to limit the alliance's scope and Japan's commitment to playing a military role in the Far East. Unlike the views of the Left-idealists, their concerns were largely pragmatic rather than ideological in character. The danger of being entangled in a conflict by the United States could not be discounted, and the economic costs of full-scale rearmament would have been considerable. On the other hand, if faced with the stark choice of alliance with the West or joining with the communist nations, there was never any doubt which side the Centrists preferred. The American economic and political systems were far more attractive to the Centrists. Measured in terms of either economic or military power, they believed the United States was far stronger than the Soviet Union.[14]

While largely discounting the threat of a military invasion, the Centrists believed that the Soviet Union presented at least a residual source of threat. Japan alone could not possibly cope with the threat posed by the Soviet Union; acquiring nuclear weapons was certain to provoke political chaos at home and hostility abroad. The obvious solution was to rely upon the United States to provide for Japan's external security, despite the not inconsiderable political costs of such a strategy. Under the U.S. alliance, Japan's room for diplomatic maneuvering was greatly reduced (especially with respect to its relations with China). It was obliged to provide the United States with military bases (which were the source of considerable domestic criticism). Finally, it was obliged to maintain some military force in order to satisfy U.S. demands on burden sharing. This high degree of dependence on America rankled national pride on both ends of the political spectrum. In the absence of the kind of clear security threat faced by West Germany, and without the German quest for moral redemption through integration, alliance with the United States created an impression of capitulation to superior force rather than one of joining a noble league dedicated to the defense of democracy.

The political center in Japan was thus less successful in articulating a clear ideological definition of what it stood for than were the centrist forces in West Germany. Whereas the Atlanticists were able to adopt a strong stance in favor of individual freedom and community in a transnational community of common ideals and institutions, the Japanese Centrists could only offer pragmatism and restraint. Caught in the ideological cross fire between old-style Right-idealist nationalism and Left-idealist pacifism, and led by people who for the most part had been professional bureaucrats rather than politicians, the Japanese Centrists were less able to articulate a philosophy legitimating their actions than were their counterparts in the Federal Republic.

West Germany: The Atlanticists

The center of the West German political spectrum was occupied by the Atlanticists, such as Ludwig Erhard and Gerhard Schröder of the CDU and Fritz Erler and Helmut Schmidt of the SPD. Like the Japanese Centrists, the Atlanticists were characterized by a strong emphasis on economic reconstruction and a generally pragmatic approach to politics. And like the West Europeanists, the Atlanticists were strongly committed to Western political values and were fond of speaking of a "community of values" *(Wertegemeinschaft)* that tied together the nations of the West. In contrast to the West Europeanists, the Atlanticists placed greater stress on common institutions and values than on geography and a putative common Western civilization. The Atlanticists' commitment to integration with the West was reinforced by their commitment to the capitalist market. Consequently, they were less insecure about America's long-term commitment to European defense than the West Europeanists were.

In the area of defense, the Atlanticists supported the West Europeanist program of joining NATO, economic integration with Western Europe, and rearmament. They would prove more ready to follow the American lead on foreign policy, including in the direction of détente, and they were less concerned with presenting a strong, anticommunist front than were the West Europeanists.

The following lists briefly summarize the views on selected key issues relevant to defense and security held by the Left, Right, and Center postwar forces in Japan and West Germany.

I. Japan

Issue	Right-idealist	Centrist	Left-idealist
Vision of national identity	A sovereign Japan	Merchant nation	Peace nation
Tradition vs. modernity	Protradition	Weakly antitradition	Antitradition
Capitalist vs. socialist model	Capitalist	Capitalist	Socialist
War guilt	None	Little or none	Some (toward Asia)
View of occupation reforms	Largely negative	Positive	Positive
Constitutional revision	Favor	Oppose	Oppose
Patriotism in education	Foster	Oppose somewhat	Oppose
Security treaty	Japan should support tactically	Support	Abolish
Self-Defense Forces	Expand	Support in current minimal form	Abolish
Overseas dispatch of SDF	Support	Oppose	Oppose
Nuclear weapons option	Support	Oppose	Oppose
Conscription	Support	Oppose	Oppose
Arms exports	Support	Mixed support	Support
Civilian control of the SDF	Mixed support	Support	Support

II. West Germany

Issues	West Europeanist	Atlanticist	Central Europeanist
Germany's cultural center	W. European civilization	Community of values	Bridge between East and West
Economic system	Latent mercantilism	Free market	Socialism
European integration	Support	Support	Oppose
View of United States	Ambivalent	Positive	Negative
Bundeswehr	Strong support	Mixed support	Support with reform
Collective security	EDC/WEU	NATO	Collective (CSCE)
Détente	Negative	Follow U.S. lead	Positive
Nuclear deterrence	European	NATO	Reject
Innere Führung	Token support	Support	Strong support
War guilt	Yes, with tendency to relativize	Strong	Very strong

Distribution of the Political-Military Cultures

As pointed out earlier, the overall constellation of political forces in Japan and West Germany closely resembled one another during the postoccupation period. In both nations, center-right coalitions had taken control of the government and were challenged on defense and security issues by left-wing oppositions backed by grass roots peace movements. At the same time, there were important dissimilarities in the way the right-wing, left-wing, and centrist political-military subcultures were distributed among the population as a whole and among the political elites in the two countries.

Public Opinion

German and Japanese survey data from this period reveal a profound ambivalence in public opinion with regard to foreign and defense policies. While Tables 3.1 and 3.2 show that there was little popular support for alignment with the communist bloc (no more than 1 percent in Japan and 4 percent in West Germany)[15], large minorities, even pluralities, favored some form of neutrality over alliance with the West. In Japan, support for alliance with the West fell in a straight line from a high of 55 percent in 1950 to a mere 26 percent in 1959, before recovering to 44 percent in 1960. Support for neutrality increased steadily over the same period, from 10 percent in 1950 to 50 percent in 1959, before returning to 32 percent in 1960.[16] Opinion surveys in the Federal Republic of Germany from the same period reveal that support for some form of neutralism was even greater there than in Japan, with the percentage of those surveyed favoring neutralism as high as 62 percent, against 32 percent supporting alignment with the United States in November 1956.[17]

The sources of the support for neutralism, however, differed in the two cases. In Japan, the primary fear was that an alliance with the United States would draw Japan into a war. There was also a general opposition to the presence of American bases in Japan.[18] In West Germany, support for neutralism was fed

Table 3.1
Japanese Attitudes toward Alignment

Year	Communist Nations (%)	Neutral (%)	Free World (%)
1950	0	10	55
1953	1	38	35
1959	1	50	26
1960	1	32	44

Note: Respondents were asked: Should Japan side with the communist nations, side with the Free World, or remain neutral?
Source: Adapted from Etō Shinkichi and Yamamoto Yoshinobu, *Sōgōampo to Mirai no Sentaku* (Tokyo: Kodansha, 1991), 223.12.

Table 3.2
FRG Attitudes toward Alignment

Year	Russians (%)	Neutral (%)	Americans (%)
1951	1	48	39
1952	1	44	41
1953	1	42	46
1954	2	48	48
1955	3	45	48
June 1956	4	64	38
November 1956	2	62	31
1957	2	55	39
1958	3	58	36
1959	2	54	41
1960	2	48	45

Note: Respondents were asked: What do you think is most important: that we as Germans have good ties with the Americans, have good ties with the Russians, or try to be neutral between the two?
Source: Adapted from Berthold Meyer, *Der Bürger und seine Sicherheit: Zum Verhältnis von Sicherheitsstreben und Sicherheitspolitik* (Frankfurt/Main: Campus, Verlag, 1983), 216, table 3.2.1.

above all by the popular longing for reunification. Reunification was consistently rated as the single most important issue by German voters during the 1950s, ahead of both the economy and peace.[19] West Germans on the whole, however, were far more favorably disposed toward the continued presence of U.S. forces on their territory than the Japanese were.[20]

On the other hand, in both countries support for a limited degree of rearmament was greater than that for alignment and alliance with the United States. In Japan, minorities favored either strengthening the Self-Defense Forces or eliminating them altogether (around 20 percent in both cases), but clear majorities agreed that the force was necessary (see Table 3.3). In Germany, data from 1955 and 1956 reveal that slim pluralities supported the new forces once they came into existence (Table 3.4). At the same time, however, large majorities opposed equipping German forces with atomic weapons.[21]

Table 3.3
Japanese Attitudes toward the Self-Defense Forces

Year	Should Be Strengthened (%)	Should Be Decreased/Eliminated (%)	Are Necessary (%)
1954	23	20	—
1955	22	23	—
1956a	17	17	58
1956b	29	19	—
1957a	27	19	—
1957b	30	19	—
1958	29	11	—
1959a	39	10	65
1959b	20	15	—
1960	19	15	—

Note: Respondents were asked: What do you think of the Self-Defense Forces: they should be strengthened; they should be decreased or eliminated; or they are necessary?
Source: Adapted from Etō Shinkichi and Yamamoto Yoshinobu, *Sōgōampo to Mirai no Sentaku* (Tokyo: Kodansha, 1991), 89.

Table 3.4
German Attitudes toward the Bundeswehr

Month and Year	For (%)	Against (%)	Undecided (%)
February 1955	39	42	19
May 1955	37	42	21
June 1955	42	38	20
September 1956	45	39	16
January 1956	44	40	16

Note: Respondents were asked: Are you for or against West Germany's creating a new army?
Source: Adapted from Berthold Meyer, *Der Bürger und seine Sicherheit: Zum Verhältnis von Sicherheitsstreben und Sicherheitspolitik* (Frankfurt/Main: Campus, Verlag, 1983), 261, table 9.1.2.

Cultures of Antimilitarism

Attitudes toward a number of other key issues worked in favor of the centrist position in both countries. Although only a minority of West Germans, around 20 percent, believed that reunification could be achieved through strengthening NATO's military capabilities, as Adenauer claimed, the Germans were equally unconvinced by the SPD's and the Left's argument that Germany's chances for reunification would be improved by not joining NATO.[22] In addition, many West Germans believed that the Federal Republic would become militarily more insecure if American forces were withdrawn.[23] In Japan, the Centrists' position was strengthened by growing opposition to constitutional revision, with a substantial plurality opposing revision after 1957.[24]

Perhaps most importantly, neither the Central Europeanists nor the Left-idealists were able to capitalize electorally on neutralist, antimilitary sentiments, although public opinion seemed to favor the left-wing point of view on defense more than either the centrist or right-wing positions.[25] In the Japanese case, the Socialists' political fortunes climbed steadily during the early 1950s, peaking in the 1958 general elections when they received 32.8 percent of the vote and 166 seats in the lower house (see Table 3.6). The Socialists were unable to win more than one-third of the electorate, leaving the conservatives firmly in control of the government. In this respect, the elections of 1960 should have served as a warning to the JSP. Encouraged by their success in toppling the Kishi government over the issue of revision of the Mutual Security Treaty, the Socialists tried to use the security issue to bludgeon the LDP. The LDP's electoral support under Ikeda Hayato, however, declined only marginally, from 57.8 to 57.6 percent.

In the West German case, the voters sent the SPD equally strong signals that the defense issue did not pay at the ballot box, as shown in Table 3.5. In the early 1950s the Socialists expected to become the dominant party in the new German landscape, reclaiming the position they had enjoyed during the Weimar Republic. The disintegration of the traditional nationalist right, the Socialists' strong anti-Nazi credentials, the popularity of pacifism, and the strong desire for reunification, all appeared to favor an eventual victory of the Left. Yet the CDU/CSU, campaigning on an agenda of stability and warning against SPD "experiments," garnered 45 percent of the vote in 1953 before peaking at 50 percent in 1957, while the SPD could not rise above one-third of the vote.

The electoral record of the early postwar period suggests that the antimilitary, antialliance themes of the West German and Japanese Left were incapable of taking the opposition above one-third of the electorate. Given the fractious history of the Right in Japan, the leftists had reason to hope that the LDP would disintegrate, allowing them to form a coalition government with the moderates

Table 3.5
Party Vote in FRG Elections, 1949–1957

Year	CDU/CSU (%)	FDP (%)	SPD (%)	Other (%)
1949	31	12	29	28
1953	45	9	32	14
1957	50	8	36	6

Note: On the second ballot
Source: Adapted from Russell J. Dalton, Politics in Germany, 2d. ed. (New York: Harper Collins, 1993), 286.

Table 3.6
Party Vote in Japanese House or Representative Elections, 1946–1960

	Year							
	1946 (%)	1947 (%)	1949 (%)	1952 (%)	1953 (%)	1955 (%)	1958 (%)	1960 (%)
LDP*	—	—	—	—	—	—	57.8	57.6
Liberal Party*	24.4	26.9	43.9	47.9	47.8	26.6	—	—
Democratic Party*	18.7	25.0	15.7	18.2	17.9	36.6	—	—
Independents**	20.4	5.8	6.6	6.7	4.4	3.3	6.0	2.8
JSP***	17.8	26.2	13.5	—	—	—	32.9	27.6
RS***	—	—	—	11.6	13.5	13.9	—	—
LS***	—	—	—	9.6	13.1	15.3	—	—
Labor-Farmer	—	—	2.0	0.7	1.0	1.0	—	—
DSP****	—	—	—	—	—	—	—	8.8
Communist	3.8	3.7	9.7	2.6	1.9	2.0	2.6	2.9
Other	14.9	12.4	8.6	2.7	0.4	1.3	0.7	0.4

*The conservative Liberal Democratic Party was formed out of the old Liberal and Democratic parties in 1955.
**Most of these independents can be viewed as quite close to the conservative parties.
***The Japanese Socialist Party split into separate Right and Left Socialist wings between 1950 and 1955.
****The Democratic Socialist Party split off from the JSP in 1960.
Source: Adapted from Bradley M. Richardson and Scott C. Flanagan, Politics in Japan (Boston: Little Brown, 1984), 76.

(as they had briefly in 1947). The Japanese Socialists, however, overlooked the fact that their stance on the alliance had created deep rifts within their own ranks, leading the right wing of the party to split off in 1952, and again in 1960. To understand why the Japanese Socialists—in contrast to the West German Social Democrats—chose to ignore these danger signs, one needs to look at how the different political-military subcultures were distributed among elite groups as well as within the political parties.

Elite Opinion and Interest Groups

Elite opinion and interest group politics played an important role in the debates over defense and national security of the 1950s, helping formulate many of the central ideas of the different political military subcultures and shaping the preferences of political actors. Among the elites, four groups were especially active during this period: the intelligentsia, the media, the labor unions, and the business world.

THE INTELLIGENTSIA

In both in the Federal Republic and in Japan, intellectuals were instrumental in defining the ideas of the Left and the peace movements. In West Germany, the Central Europeanist ideology was strongly influenced by contributors to the prominent intellectual journal, *Der Ruf,* and members of the informal literary circle, Gruppe 47, led by the novelist Hans Werner Richter. Richter and his group argued that the Soviet Union and the United States represented equally repugnant social systems. Taking advantage of the clean slate offered by its defeat in World War II, Germany should seek a "third way," and develop a new political and economic system based on humanistic socialism.[26] Other writers, such as Hermann Rausching, author of the 1950 best-seller, *Deutschland zwischen Ost und West (Germany between East and West),* added a strong nationalist element to this viewpoint by warning that entry into NATO would mean that Germany would abandon its Central European heritage.[27]

With the Adenauer government edging toward military alliance with the West and rearmament, left-wing German intellectuals organized a vast network of pacifist groups which protested against these policies through large-scale demonstrations and signature campaigns. Among the most prominent of these was the Nauheim circle, a group of left-wing intellectuals who met in the town of Bad Nauheim, which advocated strict, unarmed neutrality and argued that both East and West would accept a united Germany only if they were sure it

would not join the other side.[28] The peace movement received additional support from the churches, especially the German Evangelical Church; prominent
Protestant theologians like Martin Niemöller; and leading scientists like Carl
Friedrich von Weizäcker, who were concerned about the implications of the new
nuclear weapons.[29]

In Japan, the intellectual community was even more wholeheartedly engaged
on behalf of the Left-idealist cause. Prominent scholars such as the Socialist
Party leader Mori Nobutatsuo and president of Tokyo University Nambara
Shigeru proposed a new national identity: the concept of Japan as a peace nation. They argued that Japan should not be satisfied with its status as a disarmed
nation, but that it should become a true peace nation, one that cleansed itself of
all aggressive impulses. To achieve this end, the deeper roots of militarism in
Japanese society, the remnants of its feudal past and its capitalist system, had
to be rooted out. In its place a new democratic, socialist political and economic
order should be established. Supported by a cultural revolution, a society based
on these new ideals would wipe out inequality and the old authoritarian patterns of behavior.[30]

Inspired by this pacifist vision, during the 1950s leftist reform intellectuals
(*kakushin interii*) set up a myriad of organizations to protest the government's
defense policies. The most prominent of these groups was the Heiwa Mondai
Kenkyūkai (Peace Problems Study Group) formed in July 1949 by Abe Yoshige,
president of Gakushuin University; Ōuchi Hyo, a noted economist at Tokyo
University; Nishina Yoshino, a widely respected physicist; and other intellectual
luminaries such as Maruyama Masao and Shimizu Ikutaro. Over the next decade
the Heiwa Mondai Kenkyūkai published a series of highly influential statements
in the monthly *Sekai*, affirming their belief in human progress and severely criticizing the government's foreign and defense policies. Many of these prominent
figures lent their considerable prestige in support of the 1960 protests against
revision of the Mutual Security Treaty.[31]

Some Japanese intellectuals, including Fukuda Tsuneari, Etō Jun, and Inoki
Masamichi, defended the government and criticized the Left.[32] They were, however, an isolated minority within the Japanese intelligentsia. In the emotion-
ally charged atmosphere of Japanese academia in the 1940s and 1950s, they
risked condemnation and even physical assault from their students and colleagues for expressing views critical of the Soviet Union and China.[33] Moderate
leftists who had a more balanced view of the world were wary of the emotion-
alism exhibited by the communist firebrands in extremist student organizations

like Zengakuren. However, they were even more alarmed by the waxing influence of the Right-idealists in Japanese politics. Given Japan's recent history and the continued presence of seemingly unreconstructed Right-idealists like Kishi and Shigemitsu Mamoru in positions of power, many, such as Maruyama Masao, argued that the dangers associated with left-wing nationalism were preferable to those of nationalism on the right.[34]

In West Germany, in contrast, progressive figures comparable to Maruyama Masao, such as the philosopher Karl Jaspers and the sociologist Alfred Weber, who basically favored Social Democratic positions on social reform and other domestic issues, were harshly critical of communism. They shared the view held by Carl J. Friedrich and Hannah Arendt that the greatest threat of the age was totalitarianism, and they believed that the Soviet Union under Stalin was a totalitarian system qualitatively different from the liberal democracy, however imperfect, of the United States.[35] Although hope for reunification helped the Central Europeanists, their appeal to German nationalism was fundamentally flawed by the brutal Soviet occupation of the eastern half of Germany. Consequently, moderate German intellectuals were far more hostile toward communism than were their Japanese counterparts.[36] The Catholic Church tended to support the government's anticommunist position, and while the Protestant Church as a whole leaned toward the Left, many Protestants resisted siding with the peace movement. In October 1952, Bishop Otto Dibelius of the Evangelical Church of Germany (EKD) declared that the church would not interfere with matters that lay within the sphere of politics and that whether one chose to support the government or not was a matter of individual conscience.[37]

The German intelligentsia in general were less suspicious of the Christian Democrats than the Japanese intellectuals were of the Liberal Democrats. This combination of anticommunism and faith in the Christian Democrats' commitment to democracy allowed German academics to cooperate with the government. Many German intellectuals had no difficulty acting as advisors to the nascent German defense ministry during the rearmament period.[38] In Japan, on the other hand, more than a decade would pass before academics would play a similarly cooperative role.

THE MEDIA

Strikingly similar differences characterized the positions of the media elites in the two countries. As in the West German intellectual community, the German media were more balanced between the Left and the Center than the Japanese press. All three of Japan's major newspapers, the *Asahi*, the *Mainichi*, and the *Yomiuri*, each with a readership of several million, were in varying degrees critical of the government's defense policies and the alliance with the United States. This tendency increased during the 1950s and reached its peak early in the struggle over the Mutual Security Treaty. While the *Nikkei* and the *Sankei* were more Centrist in their views (there were no major newspapers that one could call Right-idealist in outlook), their readerships were smaller and were restricted largely to the business communities.[39] Yet all the major Japanese newspapers stopped short of supporting the Communist Party. They were united in their condemnation of both the Kishi government and the opposition's violent tactics at the height of the battle over the security treaty.[40]

In West Germany as well, segments of the media were highly critical of the government's positions on defense, none more so than postwar Germany's most influential news journal, *Der Spiegel*.[41] At the same time, many mainstream newspapers such as the prestigious *Frankfurter Allgemeine Zeitung*, the Catholic *Rheinischer Merkur*, and the more openly right-wing *Die Welt*, put out by the conservative publishing magnate Axel Springer, strongly defended the government's defense policies.[42] Although some correspondents, such as Paul Sethe and Adelbert Weinstein of the *Frankfurter Allgemeine*, were at times quite critical of Adenauer's policies, on the whole, there was remarkable consistency among these newspapers' editorial positions.[43]

LABOR UNIONS

Whereas the West German media and intellectual communities were marked by greater overall diversity than their Japanese counterparts, the opposite was true with regard to labor unions. The West German trade union movement was one of the largest in the world, with a total membership of over five million, and was organized under the German Trade Union Federation (Deutsche Gewerkschaftsbund—DGB). Except during the early 1950s when Adenauer reportedly bought off DGB chief Hans Böckler with compromises in labor-relations laws in order to gain union support on defense and foreign policy issues, the DGB was solidly behind the SPD and provided considerable logistical and organizational support to the peace movement.[44]

In Japan, in contrast, the labor movement was divided into two irreconcilable wings: the politically moderate private enterprise unions under the leadership of Nishio Suehiro and the more radical public service unions. While Nishio and other union moderates quietly supported rearmament and alliance with the United States, the public service unions were filled with ardent Left-idealists and helped spearhead the peace movement. In 1954 the Japanese labor movement split into two separate organizations, with Nishio leading the All-Japan Trade Union Congress (Zenrō, which later became the Japan Confederation of Labor, Dōmei) and the staunchly Left-idealist leadership of the public service unions' General Council of Japanese Trade Unions (Sōhyō).[45]

The divisions within the labor unions contributed to the fragmentation of the Japanese socialist movement. Together with the more leftist inclination of the Japanese intellectual and media worlds, the unions served to reinforce the Left-idealist cast of the Japanese Socialist Party. In West Germany, on the other hand, the unity of the labor movement and the moderation of its leaders helped push the SPD toward the political center.

BUSINESS

Finally, the Japanese and West German business communities were key supporters of the center-right coalitions that ruled the two nations during the 1950s. For the most part, business leaders were naturally inclined to support the Adenauer and Yoshida governments' policies of alliance with the West, believing that alliance would bring with it the trade and foreign assistance desperately needed to revive the economies of their countries.[46] The business communities were deeply suspicious of the Left's neutralist proposals, which they believed would lead to political instability and were linked to programs of social and economic reforms that ran counter to business interests.[47]

Although business supported alignment with the West, there were considerable divisions of opinion on the subject of rearmament, especially in Japan. In Japan, rearmament began earlier than in West Germany, in 1950 before the Japanese economy had recovered from the devastating aftermath of World War II. The new arms contracts from the U.S. military for its war in Korea was a veritable godsend for Japanese industries strapped for hard currency, and played no small role in getting Japan's economy back on its feet.[48] Consequently, many Japanese business leaders, especially those in heavy industry, hoped to profit from their considerable expertise in arms production and lobbied strongly for the creation of a large-scale military establishment and the passage of special legislation that would given arms manufacturers special subsidies and tax benefits. They were supported in these efforts by Japan's newly created Ministry of International Trade and Industry (MITI) and by the United States, which sought to tie its provision of foreign aid to an expansion of the Japanese armed forces.[49]

In 1953, the Defense Production Committee of Keidanren, the umbrella organization representing the interests of the major industrial groups, proposed the creation of a 300,000-person army, a 290,000-ton navy, and a 2,750-plane air force—over twice the numbers that the Japanese Defense Agency was requesting, but very close to what U.S. military planners at the time thought Japan needed.[50] If these plans and initiatives had been realized, Japan would have become a formidable military power. A military force of this size also would have created a natural constituency for the Right-idealists in the Japanese business world. Three groups of political actors, however, united to strangle this nascent military-industrial complex while it was still in the cradle: mainstream Japanese business leaders, especially those in the financial sector but also others in the top ranks of Keidanren, who felt it was dangerous for the economy to become overdependent on the weapons industry;[51] the Ministry of Finance (MOF), which automatically opposed any increase in government expenditures and argued that, given the unstable nature of the arms market, the defense industry and its allies would inevitably try to influence politics;[52] and, finally, Yoshida Shigeru and other Centrists in the LDP.

Together, the MOF and the banking industry sharply cut the flow of credit to firms engaged in weapons production, forcing the large conglomerates to shy away from defense contracting.[53] The MOF also blocked many of the MITI's proposals for treating defense as an infant industry.[54] Yoshida, together with his allies in the finance and foreign affairs ministries, managed to sufficiently delay the influx of U.S. military assistance funds and deemphasize its military character so as to frustrate any remaining hopes of nurturing a large-scale defense industry with American funds. Thereafter, Japanese industry, with the exception of the aeronautics sector, would retain only a residual interest in arms manufacturing. For the most part, business leaders supported a Centrist position on defense. Certain segments of the business community, however, continued to hope for an eventual expansion of military production and represented a latent constituency that Right-idealists could draw upon.

Rearmament in the Federal Republic started in the mid-1950s, after the German economic recovery had already taken off and further stimulation of the economy was no longer needed. Virtually all of the country's industrial and human resources were being used to the hilt, and German business leaders had considerable fears that resuming military production could develop into a major drag on economic growth. Consequently, those in German business circles were even less enthusiastic about a major military buildup than were their Japanese counterparts. To be sure, some firms were interested in defense production, especially in the aeronautics sector, but they represented a relatively small part of the huge West German manufacturing sector.[55] Although Germany's chief industrial organizations, BDI (Federation of German Industry) and DIHT (the German Chamber of Trade and Commerce), strongly supported Adenauer's policies of alliance with the United States, political and economic integration with the West, and rearmament, they also insisted that arms production should not come at the expense of production for the civilian economy.[56]

Defense Minister Franz Josef Strauss of the Christian Socialist Union (CSU) managed to allay these fears by reducing the length of military service and greatly slowing the pace of conventional rearmament. At the same time, Strauss sought to build a prodefense business lobby by promising to use defense as an instrument of industrial policy to increase Germany's competitiveness against other nations, including the United States. As in Japan, business leaders were interested in the potential technological benefits of defense research and in the licensing of technology from the United States, especially in the aeronautics field.[57] Not accidentally, Strauss's home state of Bavaria became a major beneficiary of these policies.[58]

As was the case in Japan, the defense industry remained a relatively small, though lucrative, sector within the German economy. For the most part, hopes that defense could be used to bolster the nation's technology base proved largely misplaced.[59] In those areas in which the German defense industry was especially competitive, such as tank building, technology imported from the civilian sector (so-called spin-ons) proved more useful than the technological benefits brought by military research (spinoffs).[60] Unlike Japan, where popular pressure and the Centrist efforts to constrain the defense industry led to a ban on weapons exports, the Federal Republic became a major exporter of weapons, with perhaps 20 percent of the weapons manufactured there going abroad. While the defense industries in both Japan and Germany gradually replaced the United States as their armed forces' main suppliers of weaponry, there is little evidence that these industries played a major role in shaping either public opinion or defense doctrine beyond the narrow area of defense procurement.

In sum, the broad contours of the debates on defense among elite segments in Germany and Japan bore considerable similarities. In both nations, the business communities favored alliance with the United States but resisted becoming dependent on arms production; the labor movements, for the most part, opposed rearmament; and the intelligentsia and the media tended to be highly critical of the government. In Japan, however, the Left was far more dominant in the intelligentsia and, to a lesser extent, in the media than in Germany. Moreover, the Japanese labor movement split in two over defense and national security issues, whereas in Germany the trade unions remained unified. At the same time, large-scale rearmament had stronger support in the Japanese business community and the economic bureaucracy than in these segments of the Federal Republic, thus encouraging the Japanese Right-idealists to pursue expansive military policies. This distribution of the political-military subcultures among elite sectors of Japanese society further reinforced the ideological polarization of these subcultures and reduced their propensity to cooperate with one another.

Political Parties

The turmoil of German and Japanese politics in the early postwar years made for highly fractious party systems. The uncertainty of the times produced a kaleidoscope of political factions and parties locked together in an intricate and shifting pattern of relationships. Over the course of the decade following the end of the war, these patterns began to settle into a relatively stable system of parties organized along a left-right spectrum.

In Japan the right end of the spectrum was occupied by the LDP, whose formation in 1955 created a coalition of Right-idealist and Centrist forces based on a platform supporting the capitalist system and the alliance with the United States. Those left-of-center Centrists who were not absorbed into the LDP were aggregated in the Democratic Socialist Party (DSP), which split off from the Japanese Socialist Party during the political struggle surrounding the revision of the Mutual Security Treaty. The main champion of the Left-idealist position was the JSP, while the more radical Japanese Communist Party (JCP) slowly grew stronger on the fringes.[61]

In the Federal Republic, the CDU emerged as the champion of the Europeanists and the Atlanticists after Adenauer successfully outmaneuvered his more Central Europeanist rivals in the party, Jakob Kaiser and Gustav Heinemann. The CDU's Bavarian sister party, the CSU, stood to the right of the CDU on most issues, including defense. Led by Defense Minister Strauss, the CSU lobbied for a "rational defense policy," by which it meant the creation of a powerful and technologically sophisticated Bundeswehr equipped with the "most powerful weapons" (a usefully ambiguous phrase that could be interpreted as including nuclear weapons). As debates during the 1960s would show, the CSU was more strongly inclined toward a Europeanist stance than was the CDU.

The SPD became the bastion of the Central Europeanist position. However, its tough anticommunism, particularly under Schumacher, and the presence of potential Atlanticists like Fritz Erler, Helmut Schmidt, and the charismatic young mayor of Berlin, Willy Brandt, prevented it from siding fully with the peace movement. This latent Atlanticism would become much stronger after the relaxation of U.S.-Soviet tensions in the late 1950s made it easier to reconcile the Federal Republic's membership in the Western alliance with the need to maintain a dialogue with the East. Eventually, these changes were to allow party reformers like Schmidt and Brandt to bring the Social Democrats into the Atlanticist mainstream at the SPD party congress at Bad Godesberg in 1959.

The Free Democratic Party (FDP), on the other hand, was in many ways the most divided party during this period. While its so-called nationalist wing, including Erich Mende and former Wehrmacht general Hasso von Manteuffel, were outspoken in their support of a large military establishment, other figures like ex-diplomat Karl Georg Pfleiderer promoted Central Europeanist plans for the creation of a united, demilitarized Germany. An important factor was the role played by veterans organizations in the early development of the FDP, which pulled it generally in a more nationalistic and strongly anticommunist direction.[62] Similarly, the party's strong pro–free market and protrade constituency among small and medium firms put the FDP firmly on the side of alliance with the United States.[63]

Two important institutional features of the two countries' party systems led to the development of very different politics on the issue of defense in Germany and Japan. First, the Federal Republic, unlike Japan, decided to outlaw the Communist Party. In 1956, the German Constitutional Court found the German Communist Party (DKP) to be "an enemy of the constitution" (*Verfassungsfeindlich*), opposed to the fundamental rights and freedoms sacred to postwar democracy, and ordered it to disband. The same range of repressive measures originally developed to counter neo-Nazi groups were now turned against the Communists. The DKP ceased to function as an effective political force and had little or no influence electorally or in the organization of labor.[64] While there remained many political movements to the left of the SPD, none was able to organize into a viable party organization until the late 1970s.[65]

Although the Japanese Communists garnered only a small percentage of the vote and largely discredited themselves by their efforts at sabotage during the Korean War, they never were officially outlawed. They were allowed to continue to operate on the fringes of the political system and eventually to expand their influence. Communists were particularly successful at penetrating both the peace movement and the trade unions in Japan, and they enjoyed the loyal backing of many intellectuals and of public service unions such as the Teachers Union.[66]

The existence of a well-organized alternative to the Left reduced the JSP's room for maneuver, forcing it to compete with the Communists for votes and constantly tempting it to increase its influence by cooperating with the JCP. These pressures increased during the late 1950s and 1960s, as the Communist Party got an increasingly larger share of the vote. A powerful left-wing faction within the Socialist Party, the Shakaishugi kyōkai (the Socialist Society) under Sakisaka Itsurō, advocated revolution and the development of closer ties with the JCP.[67] At the same time, the JSP's other natural partner, the DSP, was violently anticommunist. Trapped between these bitterly opposed forces, and with only dim chances of making a serious a bid for power without the cooperation of both, the JSP leadership found itself in an ideological bind making it difficult to move to the right, as the West German Social Democrats would do at Bad Godesberg in 1959.

A second important difference between the German and Japanese party systems relates to the highly factional character of Japanese parties. While battles between the different wings of a German political party *(Flügelkämpfe)* is far from unknown, Japan's parties are factionalized to an almost unique degree in the advanced industrial world.[68] During the time leading up to the battle over the revision of the Mutual Security Treaty, the LDP had as many as eight major factions, each seeking to maximize its political power and seize control of the office of the prime minister. The JSP for its part had four to five factions during the mid- to late 1950s, although its factions were said to be more ideologically than politically oriented.[69]

Factional struggles in Japan are fierce, merciless, and relentless. Since no faction is able to gain control over the party by itself, faction leaders are forced to constantly seek alliances with other factions in order to realize their political agendas. Such alliances, however, are marriages of convenience, lasting for relatively short periods before the leaders' mutually exclusive desires for power lead them to seek new allies. The old saw that politics makes for strange bedfellows is a truism the world over, but in Japan there is a virtual orgy of political maneuvering, as factional leaders hop from one alliance to the next, frequently involving not one but multiple partners. Since their power base within the party is inherently unstable, Japanese party leaders have great difficulty effecting radical changes in their parties' platforms. While Yoshida was able to realize highly controversial defense and foreign policies, he could only do so under the rather extraordinary conditions created by the American occupation, which served to insulate him from internal party pressures. Kishi, on the other hand, one of the most powerful of Japan's postwar prime ministers with one-third of the LDP under his control, was ultimately toppled by defections from both the left and right wings of his own party.

In West Germany, political parties are much more centrally organized. When Adenauer was chancellor, in particular, the CDU was under the sway of the party head, leading later analysts to refer to the Adenauerian political era as the Chancellor Democracy *(Kanzlerdemokratie),* to distinguish it from a normal democracy.[70] The SPD as well was characterized by a strong centralized organization that allowed the party leadership to push through controversial platform changes with a minimum number of defections. While often bitter personal rivalries and the realities of coalition government imposed sharp limits on the leadership's freedom of action, these were relatively mild compared to the constraints under which Japanese political bosses had to labor.

These two institutional features of the Japanese party landscape—the presence of a left-wing alternative to the JSP and the factionalized nature of politics—contributed enormously to their general immobility on defense and national security and helped to petrify the ideological rivalries born in the immediate wake of World War II. The Left in particular was disadvantaged by these developments (although there is no evidence that this was the result of calculated government action). As a result, it remained locked in an ideological stance that in the long run crippled its ability to take power from the LDP.

Patterns of Interaction and Strategies

The ways in which the contents and distribution of the political-military subcultures in Germany and Japan intersected produced very different patterns of interaction in each country. Even in the absence of consensus on many fundamental issues, the politics of defense in West Germany were characterized by a relative willingness to compromise. In Japan, on the other hand, debates over national security were marked by disagreement and strife before giving way after 1960 to what Japanese commentators later characterized as a general moratorium on the discussion of defense in the public arena.[71] These tendencies helped produce, and in turn were reinforced by, the peculiarities of the two nations' parliamentary procedures, which strengthened the propensity toward compromise on the part of the major German parties, while increasing the leverage of the minorities in the Japanese Diet.[72]

These distinctive patterns of interaction informed and shaped the very different German and Japanese models of defense policy making and civil-military relations. In Japan, the lack of willingness to compromise forced defense policy to advance through an accumulating series of government faits accomplis and led to the creation of an isolated, only quasilegitimate military establishment. Instead of trying to integrate the armed forces into society and win greater popular approval, the Japanese government chose to ensure civilian control of the new armed forces through a system of tight, external, bureaucratic controls together with a growing catalogue of self-imposed policy restraints.

In West Germany, defense decision making followed a more conventional pattern of bargaining among the contending political forces, with occasional instances in which the majority simply overruled the minority. While on rare occasions the majority in Japan imposed its will unilaterally—as it did over the revision of the Mutual Security Treaty—such measures were highly unpopular and raised doubts about the democratic process. The West Germans solved the problem of civilian control by democratizing and integrating the armed forces into society, an accomplishment that may be taken as yet a further reflection of that nation's capacity to create a societal consensus on defense.

In spite of these differences in the patterns of decision making, no single political grouping in either country was able to impose its vision of the world and its preferred policies. The subcultures within both countries were obliged to negotiate with one another, both over the contents of the policies at issue and the ways in which those policies were legitimated.

In Japan, the relative weakness of the Centrist position made this tendency especially striking. There is little indication that Yoshida was a pacifist out of conviction, and considerable evidence exists that he believed that in the long run Japan should once again become a great military power.[73] Nonetheless, Yoshida cultivated an antimilitarist public image by claiming that rearmament had been forced upon his government by the Americans. He tried to portray himself as the defender of Japan's new pacifist ideals, valiantly staving off demands by John Foster Dulles and others that Japan play a larger military role. While he certainly believed that Japan should become a merchant nation, in all probability the image he had in mind was more along the lines of nineteenth-century Britain than an unarmed economic superpower.

Yoshida's Right-idealist successors as well were forced to accept the rhetoric of Japan as a peaceful merchant nation. For example, in order to win acceptance of the Basic Principles of National Defense promulgated in 1957—a key document in defining postwar Japanese defense policy—the Kishi government felt compelled to include clauses that emphasized the role of the United Nations and stressed that Japan's military buildup would be constrained by economic needs and domestic politics.[74] Whenever it appeared that conservative leaders might swerve away from the low-key approach to defense associated with Yoshida, they were severely punished by Centrist political forces, including LDP leaders who on occasion defected from the ruling coalition to make common cause with the Left-wing opposition.

In contrast, during the 1950s the ruling West German center-right coalition was considerably more stable than that of Japan. The question of whether to give greater priority to the Atlantic or the European side of the alliance—the major point of disagreement between the Atlanticists and the West Europeanists—was just beginning to emerge at the end of the decade. In order to placate anti-military and nationalist sentiment in West Germany, Adenauer, like Yoshida, was compelled to adopt positions he only half believed in. Most importantly, Adenauer had to maintain that a policy of strength toward the East and integration with the West would hasten, not hinder, German reunification. In reality, however, it was painfully obvious that Germany's Western allies were less than fully committed to the goal of German national unity.[75] In 1958 the West German government was compelled by popular pressure to commit itself to the pursuit of arms control in order to win acceptance of NATO's nuclear deterrence strategy, even though arms control talks at that time had reached an impasse.[76] Finally, the conservative government chose to adopt the ideology of Innere Führung, even though Adenauer was far from convinced of its necessity, and many German military leaders believed that the democratization of the armed forces was inherently irreconcilable with the military's basic mission of preparing to fight a war.

In short, neither Japanese nor West German defense policies, or the ways in which those policies were legitimated, were purely the products of a single set of elites seeking to maximize their own expected utility or set of values. Nor did these policies simply result from the personal preferences of the political leaders, although undoubtedly both Yoshida and Adenauer left their own personal marks on their countries' national security policies. Rather, Japanese and West German leaders were forced to make compromises with their domestic rivals on both principle and substance in order to win passage of their plans and to minimize the political costs of doing so. Innere Führung was the price that had to be paid for rearmament based on conscription, the ban on overseas dispatch for the creation of the Self-Defense Forces. These compromises became the foundations of Japan's and West Germany's new political-military cultures and provided the basic templates for the defense policies that the two nations would adopt for decades to come.

Above all, domestic political pressures generated by their new cultures of antimilitarism inclined the governments of West Germany and Japan toward low-key approaches to defense and national security. Especially in the Japanese case the government's room for maneuver in the international sphere was relatively great. Had Japan wished to do so, it could have taken a more active role in regional security, integrating its forces with those of the United States and other Western allies in the region and offering to provide at least logistical support in the event of a regional conflict. Many Japanese leaders, including such relative moderates as Ashida Hitoshi, believed it was in Japan's national interest to do more to contain communism in East Asia.[77] Nonetheless, apprehensions of a possible right-wing revival, combined with the political strength of the left wing, induced the Japanese government to minimize the defense buildup and to rely primarily on the United States for external security. This strategy became known as the "Yoshida Doctrine" and was legitimated by a new national identity of Japan as a merchant nation *(chōnin kokka)*.[78]

The Federal Republic's latitude for action in international affairs was considerably smaller. Nonetheless, it would not have been surprising if West Germany had chosen to initiate a more active *Ostpolitik*, a policy toward the East, of its own in the 1950s, as many foreign observers, such as George Kennan, anticipated.[79] Adenauer feared, however, that such initiatives would strengthen his Central Europeanist opponents in the SPD and the peace movement and dislodge West Germany from the integrative structures he was painstakingly patching together. Instead, the CDU-led government chose to gradually build a substantial conventional defense force while relying upon its NATO partners to provide it with additional military reinforcement and a nuclear deterrent.

Central to the Federal Republic's strategy of integration with the West was the notion of *Souveränitäts Verzicht*, the calculated relinquishment of West German sovereignty in return for Western commitments to German goals and interests. In a wide range of areas, such as control over West Berlin or coal and steel production in the Ruhr, Germany deliberately offered to share decision-making powers with its Western allies. Born of the country's weakness during the occupation period, this strategy ironically needed the threat of potential German strength to make it work. From the point of view of its neighbors, integrating Germany into the West through NATO and the European Economic Community was the most cost-effective way of containing its economic and military power while at the same time making use of it to defend against the threat of Soviet invasion. What made this policy of self-containment domestically palatable in the Federal Republic was Germany's disillusionment with dreams of national grandeur and its burning desire to find a new national identity that absolved it of the sins of its past and promised a more stable and prosperous future.

The Yoshida Doctrine and Adenauer's policy of integration with the West were political solutions to the exigencies of both the international system and domestic politics in the 1950s. They are prime examples of how politicians cope with the dilemmas posed by what Robert Putnam has termed "two level games."[80] Both leaders offered new national identities based on orientation toward the West, renunciation of the use of force, and commitment to the pursuit of economic prosperity. While other policies were conceivable within the constraints imposed by the new international system of the Cold War, for domestic political reasons alternative policies would have been difficult to implement. Yet the Yoshida Doctrine and German integration with the West were far from being fully accepted, and the norms and policies they represented continued to be contested long after they first won the domestic political battles of the 1950s. It would take another twenty years for various tensions to be resolved and for the beliefs and values on which these strategies were based to take root and become integral parts of the new West German and Japanese political-military cultures.

4

The New Cultures of Antimilitarism
and the Challenges of Détente

In the decades that followed the emergence of West Germany's and Japan's new approaches to defense and national security, political support for the new policies gradually grew and their contours became more clearly defined. During that time the international system moved away from tight bipolar competition between the two superpowers toward multipolarity and greater East-West cooperation. The economies of the two countries took off in spectacular ways and their newly forged democratic institutions took root. By the late 1970s, other nations began to view both Japan and West Germany as models worthy of emulation.[1] These changes in their international and domestic political contexts created new opportunities and new pressures for both Japan and Germany to alter their approaches to national security. Instead of allowing them to take advantage of the opportunities created by the changing international environment to become great political-military powers, however, West Germany's and Japan's increasingly embedded antimilitarism induced their leaders to seek solutions that were basically consistent with the patterns of behavior established in the 1950s.

The two nations' defense and security policies evolved in three key areas—alliance politics, military doctrine, and civil-military relations—in response to domestic and international pressures. While some of these changes were quite significant, every effort to substantively alter the existing patterns of behavior prompted intense domestic political debate and often involved high levels of risk for the political leaders who engaged in them. As a result, abrupt departures in policies were eschewed in favor of a gradualist approach, and the underlying ideas and practices of the German and Japanese approaches to defense and national security remained the same.

The Politics of Alliance

The Berlin and Cuban missile crises that brought the United States and the Soviet Union to the brink of war in the early 1960s propelled the two superpowers toward a more cooperative stance vis-à-vis each other. This new era of détente posed new, albeit different, challenges for the alliance policies of Germany and Japan.

Germany: Oscillating between East and West

The Federal Republic's geographic location between East and West left it exposed it to the vagaries of the U.S.-Soviet relationship far more so than was Japan. Two shifts in particular served as triggers for West Germany's reappraisal of its relations with the United States and the West in general: the shift in U.S. nuclear strategy that began in the late 1950s and the deepening and broadening of U.S.-Soviet ties during the age of détente.

The U.S.-German crisis over nuclear strategy was rooted in a fundamental contradiction between the interests of West Germany and those of its allies. Most members of NATO, given the choice, had a natural interest in fighting a conventional war on German soil rather than risking a nuclear escalation which might put their own civilian populations in danger. The possibility of such a conventional war between the NATO states and the Soviet Union on German soil, however, was unacceptable from a German point of view. As early as the late 1950s Defense Minister Franz Josef Strauss and other West German military experts sought to ward off this danger by countering Soviet superiority in conventional military forces with the threat of strategic nuclear escalation in Germany. However, neither option for making West Germany a credible nuclear power was politically feasible—either equipping the Bundeswehr with nuclear weapons or extracting an unequivocal U.S. guarantee of the use of nuclear weapons in the case of a Soviet attack. As an alternative strategy, the Federal Republic sought to keep the conditions under which NATO might use its nuclear arsenal as vague as possible. This strategy, the Germans further hoped, would complicate Soviet military planning by creating the constant possibility that its military actions might trigger a nuclear exchange.[2]

In 1961, the newly inaugurated Kennedy administration, which already had offended Adenauer by offering tacit support to the SPD, set out to implement a new doctrine of flexible response designed to maximize American control over its nuclear weapons through a system of detailed contingency planning. Such a plan ran directly counter to German strategic interests as defined by Strauss and provoked a crisis in U.S.-German relations. Outraged by the apparent reversal in U.S. policy, Strauss argued that this shift increased the probability of war and accused the United States of conspiring to turn Germany into a nuclear battlefield.[3] The Soviet Union, he thought, might be tempted to use its conventional superiority to undertake a series of attacks, each designed to slice off as much German territory as possible short of provoking a nuclear confrontation. Over time, Strauss feared, such "salami tactics" might allow the Soviet Union to gobble up the entire Federal Republic.[4]

The crisis in U.S.–West German relations triggered by differences over nuclear strategy was further exacerbated by the Kennedy administration's handling of the Soviet blockade of Berlin. By acquiescing to the construction of the Berlin Wall, which defused the crisis from an American point of view, the United States became party to the solidification of German partition, a move that in the eyes of German diplomats violated U.S. obligations under the 1954 Treaty of Paris.[5] The subsequent American pursuit of a policy of détente with the Soviet Union further reinforced the impression that the United States was ready to freeze in place a status quo in Europe that undermined the positions with which Adenauer had legitimated his policies of integration with the West and his unwavering opposition to the East. The hope that German reunification might be achieved through a united Western show of force toward the Soviet Union no longer appeared credible, and the contention that the interests of the West and those of Germany were identical was shattered. As Heinrich Krone, one of Adenauer's closest allies inside the CDU, bitterly put it, "Everyone pushes for coexistence, coexistence on the basis of a divided Germany."[6]

The net effect of the crises over nuclear doctrine and relations with the Soviet Union severely shook German confidence in the United States. Increasingly, West German foreign policy seemed out of step with that of its allies and the changing international climate, provoking two very different responses in the German political culture. On the right, Adenauer and his West Europeanist allies in the CDU/CSU began to explore the possibility of creating exclusively West European alternative security arrangements. On the left, Central Europeanist tendencies, which only recently appeared to have been rejected at the SPD party conference in Bad Godesberg, reemerged in the guise of Ostpolitik.

The immediate impetus for the emergence of the West Europeanist debate on alliance policy was provided by the new French government of General Charles de Gaulle, who promoted the creation of an independent West European confederation capable of holding its own economically and politically with the two superpowers. Initially, Adenauer responded cautiously to the French general's enticements, but he soon became increasingly enthused. The two leaders initiated a series of meetings designed to promote European integration and to create closer Franco-German ties across a wide spectrum of activities that included political-military cooperation. Alongside progress on substantive political and economic issues, Adenauer adopted a new political rhetoric that stressed the two nations' common cultural bonds as members of a greater European civilization and implicitly suggested that the United States was not part of the historical entity represented by Europe.

Adenauer's motives for supporting de Gaulle's Europeanist vision were complex. While the wish for an alternative to Germany's one-sided reliance on its fickle transatlantic partner clearly played an important role, Adenauer was well aware of the practical limitations to the European enterprise being championed by the French. De Gaulle's charge that the United States, in a pinch, would not be willing to risk the survival of New York for Hamburg struck home, but it seemed even less plausible that the French would be willing to risk Paris, or that France would be willing to pursue German reunification at the possible expense of its own political paramountcy in Europe.[7]

Although Adenauer and other West German Europeanists may have been tempted by the vision of a European superstate independent of the United States and the Soviet Union, their immediate goals were of a more limited, tactical nature. By keeping open the option of creating a European alternative to NATO, West Germany was able to place pressure on the United States to pay greater respect to its interests. By indulging de Gaulle's greater Europe ambitions, Adenauer felt he could forestall the threat that France might pursue an independent policy of rapprochement with the Soviet Union, a move which would have further undermined Adenauer's overall strategy of solidarity with the West and isolation of the East.[8]

Adenauer's new policies, however, provoked concern not only abroad, but within his own party as well. The CDU split into two warring camps. On the one side were the Gaullists, led by Adenauer and Strauss, who were bitterly opposed to giving in to the rising tide of détente and seeking closer relations with Eastern Europe. On the other side were the Atlanticists, led by such figures as Finance Minister Ludwig Erhard and Foreign Minister Gerhard Schröder, who favored greater acceptance of the American policy of détente in order to preserve the alliance.[9] These differences over policy were reinforced by religious differences (Adenauer and Strauss were Catholics, Erhard and Schröder were Protestants), as well as by a strong element of political rivalry when Erhard became the prime candidate to replace the aging but still vigorous Adenauer as chancellor.

The struggle between the two camps paralyzed the CDU/CSU and stymied any hope Adenauer may have harbored for altering the structure of the alliance. Though it is unlikely that Adenauer and Strauss would have sought to abandon NATO altogether, it is perfectly conceivable that West Germany and France together might have been able to forge a stronger European entity within NATO. Although efforts in this direction ultimately failed because of French unwillingness to create a military partnership that would have respected German interests, the attempt to forge a tighter military bond with France foundered first because of political opposition within the ruling German coalition.

Supported by the FDP and the Federation of German Industry (BDI), the Atlanticists put pressure on Adenauer to adopt a more open stance on relations with Eastern Europe.[10] At the same time they worked to undermine the chancellor's policy toward France. When the Bundestag ratified the Franco-German Friendship Treaty in 1963, which included clauses on military exchanges and the development of "common conceptions" as a first step toward a new strategic partnership, the Atlanticists attached a preamble which reaffirmed the Federal Republic's commitment to NATO and the transatlantic relationship. As one French observer later put it, "One could hardly find a more complete contradiction of the entire principle of the treaty itself. Preamble? No, a declaration that all that followed was null and void. It was as if Ronald Reagan had written the preface to the *Capital* of Karl Marx."[11]

In April 1963, the solid Atlanticist Ludwig Erhard replaced Adenauer, putting an end to West Germany's flirtation with the creation of a European alternative to the Atlantic alliance. A basic rift in West German political culture had been revealed, however, and the Atlanticist-Gaullist rivalry over defense and foreign policy issues would continue to divide the CDU/CSU for the rest of the decade, hindering development of a coherent conservative response to the challenge of détente and ultimately leading to the Christian Democrats' fall from power.

On the left end of the West German political spectrum, the new international environment provoked a similarly far-reaching rethinking on the question of how the Federal Republic should best maneuver itself between East and West. The new U.S. policy of détente was eagerly embraced by the SPD. Although the Atlanticist wing had succeeded at Bad Godesberg in winning the party's acceptance of NATO, still harbored powerful yearnings for reunification and the forging of closer ties with Eastern Europe. Thus, during the dawning of détente in the early 1960s, Central Europeanism began to redefine itself by playing down the nationalist overtones it had displayed during the 1950s and placing greater emphasis on achieving peace through improved international cooperation.

The chief architect of the new Central Europeanist ideology was Egon Bahr, a close advisor to Willy Brandt, then mayor of Berlin. In an important 1963 speech at the Evangelical Academy at Tutzing, Bahr coined the concept of "change through rapprochement" *(Wandel durch Annäherung)*. Bahr argued that, instead of obstinately insisting on reunification and free elections in East Germany, the Federal Republic would better serve German interests by setting more modest goals and encouraging a gradual improvement in political conditions and human rights in the East through increased economic and political relations with the communist nations of Eastern Europe. Although in the short run such a policy of rapprochement implied acceptance of the de facto partitioning of Germany, in the long run, he argued, it might eventually open the door for reunification.

The ideas outlined by Bahr at Tutzing became the intellectual basis for the new *Ostpolitik* (policy toward the East). Though public opinion at the time still favored Adenauer's strategy of isolating East Germany, support for a more flexible stance toward the East began to snowball on the elite level.[12] Growing numbers of influential Christian Democratic and Free Democratic politicians, including the Atlanticist wing of the CDU under Gerhard Schröder, came out in favor of abandoning Adenauer's policy of confrontation vis-à-vis the German Democratic Republic (GDR) of East Germany.[13] Leading liberal newspapers and journals, supported by prominent intellectuals, launched an energetic media campaign in favor of improving relations with Eastern Europe.[14] Many business leaders expressed keen interest in gaining access to Eastern markets.[15] And in 1965 both the Protestant and the Catholic churches issued statements that supported establishing diplomatic relations with the governments of Eastern Europe.[16]

As the West German political environment shifted toward the Left during the late 1960s, the problem of improving relations with Eastern Europe became increasingly linked to a host of domestic political issues. The CDU government's continued inability to forge an internal party consensus in favor of recognizing the East German government or abandoning the Federal Republic's claim to being the sole legitimate representative of the German people became the symbol of what was perceived as a broader malaise of West German democracy and society. To its liberal critics, the CDU's hard-line anticommunist foreign policy reflected a conservative ideology that discouraged the further development of democracy at home and prevented the creation of a more peaceful environment abroad.[17] To a generation of West German students seeking to come to terms with the darker side of their nation's history, their government's refusal to recognize the governments of Eastern Europe, where the Nazis had perpetrated their greatest atrocities, was viewed both as an expression of unconscionable callousness toward the victims of German aggression and as the external symptom of a societal conspiracy to ignore the horrors of the Nazi era *(Vergangensheitsbewältigung)*. This combination in the general populace of an almost instinctive desire for democratic renewal and a need to come to grips with German national guilt lent a powerful moral dimension to the campaign to open ties to the East. Together with the incipient nationalist longing for reunification, these sentiments would propel the new *Ostpolitik* long after the original impetus from the international environment was spent.

In this way, domestic political developments, when joined with the external pressures toward détente, worked in favor of the SPD. The spirit of the age, or zeitgeist, seemed to smile upon the Social Democrats, and their share of the vote increased steadily, rising from 36 percent in 1961 to 43 percent in 1969. In 1966, the CDU/CSU invited the SPD form a grand coalition, giving Social Democrats the opportunity to participate directly in government policy making for the first time since the early 1930s. Finally, in 1969, the grand coalition came to an end. The SPD then became the dominant ruling party when it formed a new coalition with the Free Democrats.

The new government under the charismatic Willy Brandt made *Ostpolitik* its top priority. In his famous inaugural address, Brandt called on the nation to "risk greater democracy" *(mehr Demokratie wagen)*, and linked this project both to Germany's recognition of its responsibility for the crimes of World War II and to the normalization of relations with Eastern Europe—the new policy of *Ostpolitik*.

> This government acts on the assumption, that the questions which confront the German people as the result of World War II and the national betrayal of the Hitler regime, can be answered only in the new European peace order *(Europäische Friedensordnung)*. . . . The Germans are not bound together merely by their common language and, with all its glory and its misery, common history; we all dwell together in Germany. We have in addition also a

common mission and a common responsibility for peace among ourselves and in Europe. Twenty years after the foundation of the Federal Republic and the GDR we must prevent a further drifting apart of the German nation. . . . Even if *two German states* exist together in Germany, they cannot be as foreign lands to one another; their relationship can only be of a special nature.[18]

By tacitly acknowledging that there were indeed two German states, Brandt's speech marked a watershed in the history of postwar West German foreign policy. At the same time, Brandt's new foreign policy turned the Federal Republic from one of the principle obstacles to détente into one of its chief motors.

During the next two years Brandt and his chief foreign policy aide, Egon Bahr, undertook a complex and arduous series of negotiations with the governments of Eastern Europe. Using massive economic incentives in the form of trade and aid as negotiating levers, and assisted by the Soviet desire to encourage détente, Brandt and Bahr ultimately succeeded in normalizing relations between the Federal Republic and its Eastern neighbors. They obtained a number of important concessions from the Soviet and East German governments, such as Soviet acceptance of West Berlin as a separate entity from the GDR and improved access to West Berlin from West Germany.[19]

A fundamental objective of Brandt's and Bahr's diplomatic vision was the establishment of a new security order in Europe. This goal was partly realized through the creation of the ongoing Conference on Security and Cooperation in Europe (CSCE) in 1973 and the signing of the Helsinki Final Act in the summer of 1975. The thirty-five East and West European signatories of the Helsinki treaty agreed to accept the principle of the inviolability of borders, to respect each other's sovereignty, to enhance economic and political cooperation, and to respect human rights and civil liberties. The treaty also instituted a system of formal prior notification of military maneuvers and deployments known as CSBMs (military confidence and security-building measures).[20]

In many ways the CSCE and the Helsinki Final Act represented the culmination of the twenty-year-old Soviet diplomatic campaign aimed at winning the West's de facto recognition of the political and territorial status quo established in Central Europe at the end of World War II. Although the Final Act fell far short of the ultimate goal of luring Germany out of NATO or winning official Western approval of the division of Europe, it still represented the greatest Soviet diplomatic achievement of the Cold War. Although the SPD government was careful to emphasize the compatibility of the CSCE with NATO and took steps to reaffirm the Federal Republic's commitment to West European integration, clearly an important step had been taken toward realizing the Central Europeanist dream of eventually replacing NATO with some broader collective security arrangement.[21]

A combination of international and domestic factors, however, prevented *Ostpolitik* from evolving into a challenge to the NATO alliance. On the international level, many of the Federal Republic's allies, especially the United States, became apprehensive that the domestic political dynamics unleashed by *Ostpolitik* might tempt Germany to accept neutrality in return for the promise of reunification.[22] Domestically, Brandt found himself confronted with a potent Christian Democratic opposition that vociferously criticized him for making too many ill-considered concessions to the communists. During the Bundestag deliberations on the ratification of the Eastern treaties, the Christian Democrats fell only two votes short of passing a no-confidence motion, which would have toppled the government.[23] Although public opinion showed overwhelming support for the progress made in improving relations with the East, after 1972 popular interest in the issue decreased rapidly while, within the SPD, dissatisfaction with Brandt's leadership steadily grew. When it was revealed that Brandt's private secretary was an agent of the East German regime, the chancellor's party quickly moved to drop him, replacing him with the more reliable Atlanticist, Helmut Schmidt.[24]

Japan: Rejecting Gaullism

Because of Japan's very different geostrategic location and the peculiarities of its domestic political environment, its response to the challenges posed by détente differed considerably from that of Germany. Whereas the most significant political consequence of East-West rapprochement in Germany was that it revived the Left's hopes for the establishment of a collective security arrangement including the Soviet Union, in Japan it encouraged the Right to campaign for the adoption of a more autonomous defense posture. In the end, however, proposals for a dramatic departure from existing patterns were wrecked upon the shoals of strong domestic opposition, and only incremental changes were implemented, ones that, as in Germany, underlined the antimilitary character of the new political-military culture.

The initial impetus for the debate came from territorial issues, in this case the continued American occupation of Okinawa. In 1967, Prime Minister Satō Eisaku made the reversion of Okinawa the primary objective of his administration in order to strengthen his position within the LDP and to forestall left-wing exploitation of the nationalist issue during the struggles expected to erupt around the renewal of the Mutual Security Treaty in 1970.[25] Satō anticipated, however, that the negotiations with the United States over Okinawa would prove arduous, above all because of the American determination to retain control of its strategically important bases on the island. The issue was further complicated by the continued presence of nuclear weapons in Okinawa which, Foreign Ministry officials warned, the United States would not be willing to forgo. In order to get the United States to return control of the island, Satō concluded that Japan would have to more strongly support U.S. foreign policy in Eastern and Southeast Asia and show that it was ready to assume a larger regional security role.[26]

To strengthen domestic support for this change in policy, the LDP launched a comprehensive campaign to raise the public's "defense consciousness" and to rid the nation of its "nuclear allergy."[27] In the context of Japan's political-military culture, such efforts to rally support for the new defense policies soon took on strong Right-idealist overtones as the LDP stressed increased national pride, social order, and traditional values.

In January 1968, the party presented a new "Action Policy" program that placed heavy emphasis on the decline of public order and the deterioration of the unique features of the Japanese nation, a decline that it attributed to the pernicious influence of the postwar education system and left-wing propaganda. While stressing the party's continued support for the democratic order, the program called for a rejuvenation of the national spirit based on the five pillars of "human love," "public spirit," "love of homeland," "national spirit," and "defense consciousness" *(bōeiishiki)*.[28] At the same, Education Minister Nadao Hirokichi proposed reforming the educational curriculum in order to incorporate lessons on national defense in primary-school syllabi, revise textbooks to emphasize the positive aspects of the nation's past, and generally instill a sense of national pride and self-confidence in Japan's children.[29]

Satō's personal commitment to the Right-idealist agenda, however, was relatively tenuous. Political opinion against American military policy in Asia mounted in the wake of the 1968 Tet offensive in Vietnam and a series of incidents involving U.S. forces stationed in Japan.[30] A coalition was formed between LDP conservatives wishing to topple Satō or blackmail him for political favors, and the left wing of the party. Together they forced Satō to abandon his readiness to compromise with the United States, in particular on the sensitive issues of nuclear weapons and the American right to use the Okinawan bases for purposes other than the territorial defense of Japan.[31]

After long and tortuous negotiations in which the nuclear issue was basically papered over, the United States and Japan reached an agreement in November 1969, stating that administrative control of Okinawa would be formally returned to the Japanese government in 1972.[32] The ideological campaign favoring a more active Japanese defense role, however, had taken on a dynamic of its own and continued under the slogan of "Independent Defense" *(Jishubōei)*, even after it had fulfilled its original purpose of solidifying domestic support for Satō's policies. At the forefront of this movement was the conservative faction leader, Nakasone Yasuhiro, who became director general of the Japanese Defense Agency (JDA) in January 1970. Nakasone was supported by other conservative members of the LDP, such as fellow faction leader Funada Naka, and by large segments of the business community, which favored increasing domestic defense production and the maintenance of domestic security forces in the face of growing left-wing political agitation.[33] The concluding report of the Nikkeiren (the Japanese Federation of Employers) summer seminar of 1969 included passages calling for a reappraisal of the Mutual Security Treaty, increasing defense spending to 1.5 percent of GNP (gross national product), and development of a civilian nuclear power program in order to keep open the option of developing nuclear weapons.[34]

Nakasone was eager to use his new position to revitalize the defense debate, hoping in the process to spark a larger debate on Japanese nationalism. In interviews, he expressed the view that the main factors inhibiting the articulation of Japanese defense and national consciousness were obstacles from the elites, including politicians, intellectuals, and members of the educational establishment.[35] Nakasone felt that, in order to stimulate greater defense consciousness, Japan must accept greater responsibility for its own defense. To this end he called for a revision of the Basic Principles of National Defense that had defined the mission of the Self-Defense Forces (SDF) since 1957, to provide that Japan's armed forces would assume primary responsibility for national security, as opposed to relying on the United States.[36]

Like the West German Gaullists, however, Nakasone did not advocate abandoning the alliance with the United States. To moderate his hawkish image, he called for closer cooperation with the American armed forces and expressed support for Article 9 and the three non-nuclear principles (though he made that support conditional). At the same time, he argued that Japan would have to act as a non-nuclear mid-ranking nation *(hikaku chūkyū kokka)* in an increasingly multipolar world.[37]

Most of the changes Nakasone advocated as director general were on the level of rhetoric and served to define the SDF's mission. In terms of concrete procurement and force-planning goals, Nakasone's proposals differed little from those of his less controversial predecessors.[38] Symbolically, however, Nakasone's proposals represented a dramatic departure from Japan's postwar culture of antimilitarism. As a result, they provoked a powerful political reaction.

Bolstered by foreign apprehensions over Nakasone's rhetoric, Japan's opposition parties and left-wing intellectuals sounded the alarm that the government was preparing to lead Japan down the path to militarism and expansionism.[39] Centrists within the Japanese government, including segments of the LDP, the Foreign Ministry, and even the JDA, were disturbed by the foreign response to Nakasone's proposals and feared that, if the SDF were given the primary responsibility for Japan's defense, there would be no limit to the amount of money that eventually would be needed to achieve the requisite military capabilities.[40]

Consequently, once the treaty renewal crisis had passed and the Okinawa issue had been settled, Satō moved to reign in Nakasone and the Right-idealists. On July 15, 1970, the LDP leadership decided to reject Nakasone's proposed revision of the 1957 Basic Principles of National Defense, and in November of the same year the LDP Security Research Council published a "new vision" for national defense that underlined reliance on the military might of the United States. The Mutual Security Treaty would remain the main pillar of Japanese defense, while the SDF would continue to serve in secondary role.[41] In sum, Japan's conservative leadership had rejected the option of adopting a more independent posture on defense, despite the country's growing economic and technological prowess. The continued dominance of the Centrist antimilitarism had been reconfirmed.

Military Doctrine and Force Structure

The development of military doctrine and force structure in both Japan and West Germany was decisively influenced by each country's commitment to continue to rely primarily on its alliance with the United States for military security. Although the United States was unable to dictate military behavior to either nation, it wielded tremendous influence over their force postures, and shifts in American strategy compelled the Germans and the Japanese to make adjustments in their own military doctrines and the structures of their military forces. Such shifts in American policies frequently forced Germany and Japan to adjust and reexamine not only their military policies, but also some of their central strategic beliefs and the public justifications for their policies, generating considerable domestic political friction and, as a result, some intra-alliance conflict. Despite the costs, West German and Japanese leaders made the sometimes difficult, but necessary adjustments in the belief that failure to do so might jeopardize their nations' security and ultimately compel them to choose between even less palatable policy alternatives. At the same time, wherever possible, they sought to remain loyal to the broad core values of their postwar political-military cultures, often emphasizing their antimilitaristic features even more strongly in order to compensate for the wrenching changes caused by their alliances during this period of détente.

Germany

As was true with alliance policy, the winds of change brought by détente blew more strongly in Europe than they did in East Asia. The all-important political function of the German armed forces remained unchanged. By providing substantial military forces for the defense of Western Europe, the Federal Republic gained the status of equal, or near-equal, partner in NATO and was able to influence its allies' strategic decisions. The military mission of the armed forces, however, had to be redefined at least three times between 1951 and 1968, each time at considerable political cost.

West German military planners originally envisioned the creation of a powerful Bundeswehr, with twelve armored divisions and more than five hundred thousand troops, which would serve as the central component of a larger Western conventional force capable of containing a Soviet assault in Central Europe until an allied counteroffensive (including the use of nuclear weapons against military targets in Warsaw Pact territory) could be mounted.[42] This strategy, however, required the mobilization of German resources far beyond what other Western nations preoccupied with the task of economic reconstruction were willing to bear.[43] Beginning with the introduction of the Eisenhower administration's "new look" strategy in 1954, the United States moved toward a more economical approach that relied heavily on nuclear weapons to compensate for the Soviet superiority in conventional armaments.

Adenauer ignored these shifts in American military thinking for nearly two years. When U.S. plans to reduce the number of American ground forces stationed in Europe were leaked to the press, however, he was forced to acknowledge the new prominence of nuclear arms in NATO strategy and to adjust West German military planning accordingly. The pace of expansion of the Bundeswehr was reduced considerably and its function was redefined as one capable of localizing smaller-scale conflicts short of an all-out war. To counter a Soviet invasion, the German force could compel the Soviets to mass their forces to achieve a breakthrough, thereby making it more vulnerable to attack by Soviet tactical nuclear weapons.[44]

The subsequent deployment of NATO nuclear weapons systems in the Federal Republic triggered fierce domestic controversy and the mobilization of a massive peace movement. A complex mixture of moral abhorrence of nuclear weapons and widespread fears that Germany could be turned into a nuclear battlefield fueled the popular revolt against government policy. To mollify public criticism Adenauer was compelled to restrict the Bundeswehr to the control of delivery systems only, as opposed to that of nuclear warheads (a step which also reassured Germany's neighbors). Moreover, his government was coerced to pledge the pursuit of arms control as well as deterrence, even though at the time (1957) the arms control process had reached an impasse and considerable skepticism existed within the Adenauer administration about its overall political utility.[45]

No sooner had the Federal Republic come to terms with the major shifts in American strategy under Eisenhower than it felt pressure to readjust itself once more. The adoption of the Kennedy administration's doctrine of "flexible response" in 1961 represented an even more jarring blow to the West German government, raising suspicions that the United States was determined to confine any future conflict to the European theater.

For the next six years, the leaders of the NATO countries were preoccupied with finding ways to reassure the Federal Republic that American nuclear guarantees remained credible and with winning acceptance for the doctrine of flexible response, while at the same time trying to discourage Germany from seeking to create a purely European nuclear deterrent strategy in collaboration with the French. Ultimately, NATO efforts to create a multilateral nuclear force (MLF) proved unsuccessful, and the United States felt compelled to appease Germany by allowing it to participate in alliance nuclear planning through the Nuclear Planning Group (NPG) created in December 1966 and by drawing up new defense guidelines for the alliance.

As public opinion in West Germany had begun to shift in favor of détente, the Federal Republic in December 1967 at long last accepted the doctrine of flexible response with the adoption of the Harmel report by the North Atlantic Council of NATO. This report (named after its author, Pierre Charles Harmel, the Belgian foreign minister) became the centerpiece of NATO strategy for the next decade. It reaffirmed the West's resolution to maintain the military forces needed to provide an adequate deterrent to the threat of a Soviet military invasion. Beyond that it stressed the West's desire to achieve a peaceful resolution of the East-West conflict through arms control and closer political and economic relations with Eastern Europe. The Harmel report was thus a reflection of the trend toward détente, and it complemented the general shift in West Germany's political atmosphere in favor of an active *Ostpolitik*.[46]

The Harmel report also picked up on a strand of West German defense policy that was already discernible in 1957 when the Adenauer government had pledged the simultaneous pursuit of arms control and the introduction of nuclear weapons on West German soil.[47] Whereas the 1957 pledge was conceived largely as a symbolic concession to the opposition, in 1967 it was supported even by hard-line critics of arms control within the German government, who viewed it as a means of reconciling the alliance with the wave of détente that was rushing across the country.[48] In other words, the Harmel report did not indicate a triumph of pacifism over deterrence—rather to the contrary, it strongly reaffirmed the need for NATO and the maintenance of a strong military as prerequisites for a successful reduction of tensions. Yet the report served to elevate the pronounced antimilitary impulse in Germany's new political-military culture and raised it to a status equal to that of the military component. Henceforth, détente and arms control became the second pillar of the Federal Republic's approach to national security, along with the first pillar of defense and deterrence. The tensions between these two pillars, however, were not fully worked out, either in policy or in the West German political culture, leading to renewed controversy when the international climate shifted again in the late 1970s.

Japan

In Japan, the debate over military doctrine and force structure during this period focused far less on the dilemmas of extended deterrence than it did in Germany. Instead it centered on issues of how to define the mission of the Self-Defense Forces and, to a lesser extent, on questions of defense spending.

Any extensive debate over nuclear strategy was effectively precluded in Japan context in 1967 when, under pressure from popular antinuclear sentiment, Prime Minister Satō formulated the so-called three non-nuclear principles: Japan would not possess, manufacture, or permit the introduction of nuclear weapons on its territory.[49] Satō linked the non-nuclear principles to a broader policy that included the promotion of worldwide disarmament, reliance on the United States for nuclear deterrence, and the peaceful use of atomic energy.[50] Thereafter, the Japanese debate focused primarily on the largely symbolic question of whether the three non-nuclear principles were actually being respected, as opposed to serious consideration of the question of how Japan could best be defended from attack.[51]

During the first half of the 1970s, Japanese defense policy in the non-nuclear realm also became subordinated to a general approach that increasingly deemphasized the role of military instruments. At the forefront of this new movement stood Kubo Takuya, a prominent member of the Japanese Defense Agency, who in 1971 wrote a seminal internal memorandum that provided the intellectual foundations for a new Centrist defense philosophy. The memorandum argued that it was highly unlikely that Japan would become embroiled in a large-scale conflict in the near future and hence it was unnecessary to plan for meeting the maximum force that potential adversaries might bring to bear on Japan. Instead, the memorandum proposed the creation of a "standard defense force" (kibantekibōeiryoku), consisting of a relatively small, modern, well-equipped and highly professional military force. The basic mission of such a force would be to withstand a limited invasion on its own or, in the event of a larger assault, to hold the enemy until reinforcements from the United States arrived. Creation of such a force, Kubo argued, was more practicable than vainly seeking to maintain the forces needed for a full-scale conflict. It would also allay foreign and domestic fears about Japanese intentions. Above all, it would have a greater appeal for the Japanese people, whose support for any successful program of national defense was indispensable.[52]

Kubo's ideas won the support of moderate LDP leaders, including Prime Minister Miki Takeo and the new director general of the JDA, Sakata Michio. A further refined concept was presented to the public in 1975 by a blue-ribbon civilian advisory committee, the Research Group on Defense, under the directorship of Kyoto University Professor Kosaka Masataka, and by a government white paper. References in a previous white paper (put together while Nakasone was director general) to internal security missions were eliminated, and new emphasis was placed instead on the SDF's role in providing disaster relief, a function that opinion polls showed enjoyed widespread public support.[53]

Military leaders within the SDF as well as Right-idealists inside the LDP strongly resisted the new initiative. The opposition parties were also at first suspicious of the motives behind the proposed changes, fearing a government attempt to lure them into a recognition of the SDF that would open the way for a constitutional revision and a revitalization of the old-style, militaristic nationalism.[54] Despite these barriers, strong Centrist support for the project, coupled with changes in the international environment that reduced perceived threats of Japan's entanglement in foreign conflicts, allowed the Diet to approve the new plan, the Basic National Defense Policy Outline (or *Taikō*), which defined and laid out SDF procurement goals for the next decade.[55]

The Taikō, which had turned Kubo's concept of a standard defense force into the official basis for defense planning, justified the government's new policy stance by making reference to the global trend toward détente. Renewed emphasis was placed on the Mutual Security Treaty's role in contributing to the overall stability of the East Asian region, and more than ever military cooperation with the United States became central to Japanese defense planning.

In keeping with the established practice of creating new safeguards *(hadome)* every time a fresh defense initiative was taken, the government sought to reassure public opinion by offering a pledge that defense spending would not exceed 1 percent of GNP. The JDA managed to relativize the pledge somewhat by adding words implying that the 1 percent barrier was only a temporary measure and should be interpreted as a target, not an absolute limit.[56] Nonetheless, the pledge, together with the overall moderate tone of the Taikō and the Centrist character of the Miki government, succeeded in winning considerable support in the Diet, where both the Democratic Socialist Party and the Buddhist Clean Government Party helped pass the plan. Much to the dismay of liberal observers in the media, even the right wing of the Socialist Party appeared to approve of the Taikō.[57]

In certain respects, passage of the Taikō appeared to signal a revolution in the politics of Japanese defense. With the cooperation of at least some of the opposition forces that for the last twenty-five years had strenuously opposed government national security policy at every turn, for the first time a coherent rationale for Japanese defense efforts and weapons procurement had been submitted to and approved by the Diet. The Taikō also laid the groundwork for intensified military cooperation between the United States and Japan, apparently laying to rest the taboo against such cooperation for fear of becoming entangled in the United States's East Asia strategy.

Upon closer examination, however, it is apparent that the Taikō clearly was not so much a major departure from the existing approach to defense as in fact an elaboration on and reaffirmation of the old Centrist Yoshida Doctrine. When all was said and done, the Taikō represented a codification of the SDF's limited defense role. It even imposed new restrictions on the defense establishment in the form of the 1 percent limit on defense spending. The new emphasis on cooperation with the United States was also a continuation of the Yoshida strategy, which preferred relying on American military support to the economically costly and politically destabilizing alternative of developing a more autonomous defense capability. In addition, the intensification and formalization of Japanese defense cooperation with the United States further strengthened civilian control of military policy by allowing other arms of the government to monitor an area previously informally regulated by U.S. and Japanese military personnel.[58]

The apparent transformation of the political-military culture marked by the relatively tranquil passage of the Taikō also proved to be deceptive. The Right-Left divide in Japan's political-military culture did not vanish as the result of the development of détente. The Right-idealists in the LDP soon made their presence felt as they and other nonideological proponents of a larger defense establishment began to criticize the Taikō and the 1 percent limit as unrealistic and a grave danger to national security.[59] Likewise, the Left-idealist view continued to exert a powerful influence both on public opinion and the opposition parties.

What the passage of the Taikō represented was an important shift in the overall constellation of forces in Japan's political-military culture in favor of the Centrist position. Whereas in the 1950s the Centrists had been in the minority, by the mid-1970s support for their minimalist approach to national security had spread among the populace and the political parties. Having rejected the independent military option in 1970, the LDP leadership had now chosen to revitalize the existing Centrist approach to defense and adapt it to the exigencies of a more multipolar world. As one Japanese commentator put it, deterrence of the Soviet military threat could no longer be achieved through the mere *existence* of the Mutual Security Treaty system; it had to be made to *function*.[60] On the surface the new policy created the impression of a major shift to the right. In fact, however, it reflected a steady consolidation around the center.

Civil-Military Relations

The area of civil-military relations saw the fewest changes during the 1960s and the early 1970s. Whereas significant shifts had occurred in the formulation of alliance policies and military doctrine, civil-military relations experienced an impressive degree of inertia. This lack of change, however, does not indicate that questions of the relationships among the armed forces, the state, and society had been resolved. On the contrary, in both countries, the lack of any measurable change in civil-military relations was the result of a policy paralysis induced by widespread fears that the armed forces and a democratic government are fundamentally incompatible.

Japan

Because of the military's role in the destruction of democracy in the prewar period, civil-military relations continued to be a highly sensitive topic in Japan. Undiminished apprehensions about the intentions of the Right-idealist elements of the LDP further served to keep fear of the military alive. These fears resurfaced in 1965 when members of the Socialist Party surprised Prime Minister Satō during Diet interpellation with questions concerning secret contingency plans of the Defense Agency, known as the Three Arrows Plan, in the event of a new war on the Korean peninsula. Particularly provocative were proposed emergency laws that would allow the SDF to act without Diet approval, as were provisions for the wartime mobilization of national resources, including the introduction of the draft, and laws for suppressing internal subversive elements. In many other nations, including the United States and the Federal Republic of Germany, such contingency plans are regarded as an indispensable component of national defense, and similar legislation had been put in place with relatively little comment or dissent. Prime Minister Satō's evident ignorance of these plans strongly reinforced apprehensions that the military was acting independently of civilian authority.[61]

Satō himself was alarmed by the revelations and appointed a nonpartisan committee to investigate the incident.[62] Eventually Satō and the committee concluded that there was nothing wrong with the contents of the Three Arrows Plan, but they severely criticized the JDA for the secretive manner in which it had been drafted. The committee proposed various measures, not all of them successfully implemented, for increasing civilian control of the armed forces, and Satō insisted that henceforth all such plans had to be made public and authorized by the proper civilian authorities.[63]

Since such planning was bound to provoke a strong domestic response, the decision effectively acted as a moratorium on all such research. Rather than suffer the political costs of open discussion on the use the armed forces in an emergency, and fearing the possible consequences of conducting related research in secret, Japan's leaders preferred to ignore the issue altogether.[64]

Other incidents, such as the novelist Yukio Mishima's attempt to spark a military uprising before his spectacular suicide in 1970, served to reinforce public distrust of the military. The reactionary character of the writings and public statements of some former members of the Self-Defense Forces (including those of former Chief of Staff Sugita Ichiji) suggested that extreme right-wing views were far more prevalent in the armed forces than the JDA liked to admit.[65] As a result, a strict regime of civilian control over the armed forces was maintained and in certain respects even tightened. The JDA remained a junior player in the bureaucratic hierarchy, commanding a decreasing share of the government budget and subject to extensive colonization by other ministries.[66] Within the military establishment, civilian bureaucrats continued to dominate the decision-making process. Finally, new legislative safeguards were placed on the armed forces, such as the virtual ban on contingency planning, the three non-nuclear principles, the 1 percent barrier, and a further tightening of the ban on the export of weapons-related technology.

These self-imposed limits, however, frequently contained loopholes that allowed their circumvention at a later date or in case of emergency. For example, the government argued that although the acquisition of nuclear weapons would be *illegal* under the three non-nuclear principles, as long as the weapons were for the purpose of defense, their acquisition would not be *unconstitutional*. This suggested that at a later date such weapons could be acquired following a simple change in the law, rather than requiring a revision of the constitution.[67]

Despite this hedging, however, the policy limitations greatly restricted the scope of actions the government could legitimately undertake. For example, the limitations on overseas dispatch became one of the primary reasons why Japanese forces were not dispatched to the Persian Gulf during the crisis in the 1980s and 1990s, and the restrictions placed on weapons exports demonstrably delayed U.S.-Japanese cooperation in the defense technology field until the mid-1980s.

Germany

In the Federal Republic of Germany, the debate over civil-military relations centered on an entirely different set of issues. Rather than focusing on how to create formal instruments of control that could prevent the military from running amok, as was the primary issue in Japan, the West German debate revolved around the question of how to integrate the armed forces into a democratic society. Failure to do so, it was feared, would create a "state within the state" *(Staat im Staat)*, similar to the Reichswehr of the 1920s, which could have a corrosive effect on German democracy.

On one side of this debate stood the "reformers," who espoused a liberal interpretation of the doctrine of Innere Führung and insisted on a far-reaching democratization of the armed forces, strict protection of the civil rights of military recruits, and a highly selective approach to German military tradition. On the other side were the "traditionalists," who argued that certain aspects of all military organizations were inherently undemocratic and who called for the preservation of traditional German military values and practices in the interest of morale.[68] In the broader context of West German politics, supporters of Innere Führung tended to be more liberal, and their criticisms of the armed forces were often embraced by those eager to pillory the government's defense policies as a whole. The traditionalists were instinctively more conservative in outlook and generally found sympathy among those who favored a strong military defense.

The area of military education provided these two groups with their main battleground. The chief issue was what lessons and role models the members of the new Bundeswehr should draw from German military history. While this struggle appeared symbolic, it had very practical ramifications for vital military issues such as how to prepare recruits for combat or how to determine the limits of military obedience. While both camps agreed that the brutality of the World War II Wehrmacht must be condemned, other issues were less easy to resolve.

The evaluation of the military officers who, on July 20, 1944, attempted to assassinate Hitler and seize control of the German government presented a particularly thorny dilemma. On the one hand, the July 20 conspirators obviously had been tragic heroes who gave their lives opposing an evil and monstrous regime. On the other hand, they also were officers who had broken their pledge of obedience to duly constituted civilian authorities. German military history provides many examples in which considerably less serious acts of disobedience had grave consequences.[69]

Throughout the 1960s and 1970s the Bundeswehr was plagued by a string of scandals that raised doubts about the degree to which it had been successfully integrated into society. These incidents tended to belong to either of two general types. The first type of scandal involved the mistreatment of recruits, such as the so-called Nagold affair in 1963 in which a recruit in a paratrooper company died as a result of overly brutal training methods.[70] The second type revealed the existence of extreme right-wing views in the armed forces, exemplified by a 1976 incident in which a notorious neo-Nazi politician was invited to attend a veterans association meeting at a Bundeswehr base.[71]

The controversies between traditionalists and reformers intensified during the latter part of the 1960s when broader changes in German society, including the student movement, increased public interest in critically confronting the country's Nazi past. At the same time, the political sea change associated with the growing strength of the Social Democrats was spilling over into the Bundeswehr. Professional military men felt increasingly frustrated by the strict regime of civilian control as well as by the general public mistrust of the military institution, which they saw manifested in the doctrine of Innere Führung.[72] Their frustration was compounded by the difficulties they encountered in dealing with a new generation of Bundeswehr recruits, many of whom were long-haired, antidisciplinarian radicals opposed to the ideology of the Cold War on which the self-legitimation of the Bundeswehr rested.[73]

In 1969, these frustrations led to the development of what could be described as a traditionalist counterreformation within the Bundeswehr, as senior officers sought ways to restore order in the ranks and improve the Federal Republic's capacity to respond to a military crisis. These efforts culminated in an internal study commissioned by the Army Chief of Staff, General Albert Schnez, titled "Thoughts on Improving the Internal Order of the Army." The study advocated revision of the doctrine of Innere Führung so that it would not interfere with military effectiveness, placing a greater emphasis on military tradition, rewriting the Basic Law so as to give the military greater authority in case of a crisis, and restricting the right to conscientious objection. The study went so far as to suggest that, to increase the army's fighting power, German society would have to be reformed, echoing the reactionary philosophy of "total war" formulated by General Ludendorf during World War I.

The Schnez study triggered an avalanche of criticism. The sentiments it expressed met with considerable sympathy within the armed forces. The mainstream leadership in the Bundeswehr and the Defense Ministry, however, was less pleased with the tone of the report and moved quickly to reassert control. Although they decided not to take disciplinary action against the authors of the Schnez study, they insisted that it had been designed as a "think piece," and none of its proposals were adopted. Instead, new regulations were issued that forcefully reaffirmed Innere Führung and the goal of integrating the armed forces into society as the central legitimating principles of the Bundeswehr.[74]

After 1972, when the student movement subsided and the political controversy associated with Ostpolitik calmed down, the debate over civil-military relations lost much of its edge. Generational factors also played a role, as Bundeswehr officers socialized into the organizational culture of the Reichswehr and the Wehrmacht retired and were replaced by younger officers more open to the doctrines and ideals of the new armed forces.[75]

During the 1960s and early 1970s in both Japan and the Federal Republic, groups inside the new military establishments sought to challenge the system of civil-military control that had been instituted during the rearmament period. These groups were led by senior officers who had been trained in the much more militaristic and authoritarian cultures of the old Wehrmacht and the Imperial Army, and were critical of the directions in which society and the armed forces were developing.

In both cases these challenges appeared to culminate around 1970, when the domestic turmoil associated with the worldwide student antiwar and countercultural movement and the political spillover from détente reached their peaks. In both countries, the "rebels" enjoyed only partial support within the armed forces and were quickly suppressed. Although at the time, foreign and domestic observers pointed to the Schnez study and the Mishima incident as evidence that a reactionary takeover was imminent, the end result was an intensification rather than a weakening of civilian authority over the military.[76]

The ways in which civilian control was reasserted, however, differed greatly in Germany and Japan, and were consistent with their contrasting approaches to civil-military relations in general. In West Germany, emphasis continued to be placed on internal mechanisms of control and the further integration of the

armed forces into society. The doctrine of Innere Führung that súpplied direc-
tives for this purpose became even more clearly defined and codified with the
issuance of new regulations. In Japan, the response to the challenge relied more
heavily on external mechanisms of control, as civilian influence over defense decision making was reinforced and new restrictions *(hadome)* on the armed
forces were created, such as the 1 percent barrier (limiting military spending to
1 percent of GNP). In neither case can a deviation from the earlier established
pattern of civil-military relations be observed.

The Political-Military Cultures of West Germany and Japan, circa 1976

The 1960s and 1970s witnessed a general consolidation of the political-military cultures created during the rearmament period. The general contours and
contents of the two countries' political-military subcultures in 1976 differed relatively little from those that existed in 1960. In Japan, the defense debate continued to be highly polarized and dominated by prodefense, nationalistic Right-
idealists; pacifist-neutralist Left-idealists; and Centrists, who favored alliance
with the United States and concentrated on strengthening the national economy. In the Federal Republic, there was less polarization than in Japan, yet there
remained deep cleavages between West Europeanists, Atlanticists, and Central
Europeanists, who favored the forging of more cooperative relations with Eastern Europe.

New developments such as the Nuclear Nonproliferation Treaty and the Vietnam War placed new issues on the political agenda. Each political-military subculture's reactions to these events, however, were by and large consistent with
its earlier positions. For example, the stubborn opposition of German West Europeanists and Japanese Right-idealists to the ratification of the Nuclear Nonproliferation Treaty was unsurprising given the two groups' earlier emphasis on
developing strong, more independent defense and foreign policy postures. Some
issues, on the other hand, revealed splits between subcultures that had previously been hidden. For example, de Gaulle's offer of a Franco-German alliance
as an alternative to NATO brought to the fore differences between West Europeanists and Atlanticists within the CDU/CSU. Such cleavages, however, were
already in place, beneath the surface, prior to 1960.

What changed during the 1960s and 1970s period, however, was the *distribution* of the political-military subcultures within their respective political sys-

tems. In both nations a general trend of rising support for the minimalist, centrist approach to defense could be observed. This trend manifested itself at all three levels of the West German and Japanese political systems: public opinion, influential sectors of society (elite opinion), and political parties.

Public Opinion

Public opinion surveys from the 1960s and 1970s reveal a marked consolidation of West German and Japanese public support for the institutional pillars of their countries' security policy: their international alliances, political and economic integration with the West, and their new armed forces. Whereas in 1960 a substantial minority of Japanese (32 percent) supported neutrality over alignment with the United States (44 percent), by 1977 support for the West had increased to 48 percent while support for neutrality had declined to 26 percent. Undoubtedly external factors such as the end of the Vietnam War and President Richard Nixon's new China policy were at least partly responsible for this shift in Japanese attitudes.

In West Germany as well, a rise in popular support for the military alliance with the United States could be observed, albeit the rise was not as dramatic as that in Japan. In 1961, 42 percent were for neutrality, compared to 40 percent for the alliance with the United States. By 1975, pro-U.S. attitudes had risen to 48 percent versus 38 percent, and the percentage increased even more in the late 1970s.[77] Support for integration with Western Europe also increased during this period. While in 1965 the large majority (69 percent) of West Germans said that, if given a choice, they would prefer reunification of Germany over integration with Europe, by 1973 the balance had shifted dramatically, with 65 percent preferring European unity over German national reunification.[78]

As in Japan, external factors contributed strongly to this shift in German attitudes. Above all, détente and Ostpolitik reduced fears of war and offered a solution, albeit a far from perfect one, to the problems of national partition and a fractured national identity. Once West Germans had learned to tolerate, if not fully accept, the political status quo in Europe, other aspects of their external relationships, including those with NATO and the European Economic Community (EEC), became less problematic.

Tables 4.1, 4.2, and 4.3 present insight into the shifts in public opinion that occurred during the 1960s and 1970s.

The 1960s and 1970s also saw a growth in West German and Japanese popular support for their armed forces. The rise in support for the Bundeswehr and

Table 4.1
Japanese Attitudes toward Alignment

Year	Communist World (%)	Neutralism (%)	Free World (%)
1960	1	32	44
1963	1	28	45
1966	1	31	41
1969	2	30	44
1972	2	34	37
1975	2	29	41
1978	2	25	49
1980	2	25	55

Note: Respondents were asked: Should Japan join the Free World, join the communist camp, or be neutral?
Source: Adapted from Etō Shinkichi and Yamamoto Yoshinobu, *Sōgōampo to Mirai no Sentaku* (Tokyo: Kodansha, 1991), 223.

Table 4.2
What Is the Best Way of Defending Japan?

Year	Independent Defense* (%)	Alliance + SDF** (%)	Neutralist-Pacifist*** (%)
1969	14	41	10
1972	11	41	16
1975	9	54	9
1978	8	61	5

*The Right-idealist response (author's coding) includes: quit the Mutual Security Treaty, increase defense, and defend Japan by its own power alone.
**The Centrist response includes: remain in the alliance as now, defend Japan's security through the treaty system, and maintain the SDF.
***The Left-idealist response includes: quit the treaty and decrease or abolish the SDF.
Source: Asagumo Shimbunsha, *Bōei Handobukku* (Tokyo: Asagumo Shimbunsha, 1987), 498.

Table 4.3
West German Attitudes toward Alignment

Year	Neutral (%)	Ally with the United States (%)	Don't Know/Undecided (%)
1961	42	40	18
1965	37	46	17
1969	38	44	18
1973	42	41	17
1974	38	51	11
1975	36	48	16
1981	31	55	14

Note: Respondents were asked: What, in your opinion, would be the better foreign policy: Should we continue to ally ourselves militarily with the United States, or should we try to be neutral, like Switzerland for example?
Source: Adapted from Berthold Meyer, *Der Bürger und seine Sicherheit: Zum Verhältnis von Sicherheitsstreben und Sicherheitspolitik* (Frankfurt/Main: Campus, Verlag, 1983), 217, table 3.2.2.1.

the SDF did not mean, however, that popular sentiment now favored a significant increase in the size or mission of the armed forces. Public opinion in both countries indicated an overwhelming preference for the status quo.

In 1965, when the United States turned to its allies for support in the Vietnam War, public opinion in both Germany and Japan was overwhelmingly opposed to sending forces overseas, even in a merely logistic capacity. In West Germany, 88 percent of those surveyed opposed such a move, while a mere 3 percent were in favor.[79] In Japan as well, large majorities opposed the overseas dispatch of forces, even though another U.S. ally in the region, the Republic of South Korea, sent more than three hundred thousand combat troops.[80]

Neither the West German nor the Japanese public supported increases in defense spending, as shown in Tables 4.4, 4.5, and 4.6. Moreover, Japanese opposition to changing the constitution even increased, from 62 percent of all those surveyed in 1962 to 73 percent in 1978.[81]

At the same time, there was rising support for reliance on nonmilitary means of national security. After 1973, *Ostpolitik* and détente entered the repertoire of

Table 4.4
Japanese Attitudes toward the SDF

Year	Good to Have It (%)	Better Not to Have It (%)	Don't Know (%)
1959	65	11	24
1963	76	6	18
1965	82	5	13
1967	77	6	17
1969	75	10	15
1972	73	12	15
1975	79	8	13
1977	83	7	10
1978	86	5	9

Source: Asagumo Shimbunsha, *Bōei Handobukku* (Tokyo: Asagumo Shimbunsha, 1987), 496.

Table 4.5
West German Attitudes toward Defense Expenditures

Year	Too Much (%)	Just Enough (%)	Too Little (%)	No Answer (%)
1967	41	37	8	14
1969	31	36	16	17
1971	38	46	12	4
1973	35	39	10	17
1975	38	42	10	11
1977	27	50	12	11
1979	27	59	10	3

Note: Respondents were asked: In your opinion, does the Federal Republic spend too much, the right amount, or too little for defense?
Source: Adapted from Berthold Meyer, *Der Bürger und seine Sicherheit: Zum Verhältnis von Sicherheitsstreben und Sicherheitspolitik* (Frankfurt/Main: Campus, Verlag, 1983)', 270, table 11.2.1.

Table 4.6
Japanese Attitudes toward Defense Spending

Year	Increase (%)	Maintain at Present Level (%)	Could Be Decreased (%)	Don't Know (%)
1969	24	38	14	24
1972	10	42	23	25
1975	13	48	15	24
1978	20	48	10	22

Source: Asagumo Shimbunsha, *Bōei Handobukku* (Tokyo: Asagumo Shimbunsha, 1987), 499, table 7.

West German security policies, and public support for *Ostpolitik* continued to grow even after the mid-1970s, when popular distrust of the Soviet Union resurfaced. In 1973, 49 percent of those surveyed felt that *Ostpolitik* had been "worth it," and 29 percent did not. In January 1980, the level of support increased to 51 percent versus 28 percent, and the vast majority of West Germans supported the further promotion of détente—74 percent versus 17 percent.

In Japan, there was clear evidence of a strong popular preference for relying on nonmilitary instruments for national defense. A 1972 *Yomiuri* poll showed that only 6 percent of the respondents thought military power was a very effective way of defending the nation, and 32 percent said it was only somewhat effective, while 32 percent considered it not very effective and 14 percent thought it not effective at all. In contrast, the respondents rated diplomatic negotiations, improvement of the standard of living, and international economic and cultural exchange as more effective ways of ensuring national security.[82]

West German and Japanese survey data from the 1960s and 1970s reveal broadly similar trends toward greater societal consensus in favor of the existing, minimalist approaches to defense and national security. In both cases the immediate trigger for this difference in attitudes was the changed international environment associated with détente.

Beyond the reassuring impact of détente on public opinion, it appears likely that popular support for national institutions was growing on a deeper level in the two countries. The new political identities that West Germany's and Japan's moderate conservative leaderships had created proved overwhelmingly successful. After undergoing military defeats considered among the most devastating in history, both the German and the Japanese people had literally crawled out of the rubble and pulled off reconstructions among the most successful and rapid ever known.

Whereas in 1960 each country had a per capita GDP (gross domestic product) but a small fraction of that of the United States, by 1980 the Federal Republic's per capita GDP was virtually on par with the American figure, and Japan's was rapidly catching up. In absolute size, their economies were ranked behind only those of the United States and the Soviet Union. Their populations enjoyed a high standard of living and extensive protection of civil liberties. Their democratic systems had been proven stable and reasonably responsive to the wishes of their peoples.[83] While doubts remained about their defense policies, the basic mood in each country may be described as one of "don't upset the apple cart," or, as Adenauer had appealed in the 1957 election "no experiments!" This new centrist consensus would prove resilient even after the winds of change stirred again in the international arena and U.S.-Soviet tensions increased once more.

Elite Opinion

As general public opinion in Japan and West Germany during the 1960s and the first half of the 1970s tended toward a more centrist position on defense and security, elite views did the same. Overall, the basic predispositions of the elite sectors of society did not change fundamentally during this time; intellectuals, the media, and trade unions tended to be more inclined to Central Europeanist or Left-idealist views than the population as a whole, while the business community was more inclined toward prodefense and proalliance positions. Within these broad ideological parameters, however, relative shifts in favor of a moderate approach to national security occurred.

This was particularly true for Japan. In West Germany, elite opinion shifted toward the left as a powerful ground swell emerged in favor of détente. In Japan, however, the move was toward the right. For the most part the intellectual community and media remained committed to the ideology of Japan as a peace nation and were critical of the government's defense and security policies. Nonetheless, a growing number of intellectuals and media figures supported the Yoshida Doctrine, the Self-Defense Forces, and the Mutual Security Treaty.

At the forefront of this movement in Japan was a new generation of scholars, such as Kosaka Masataka and Nagai Yonosuke, who created the intellectual framework for legitimating Japan's postwar defense system by borrowing ideas from the American academic discourse on international relations.[84] Kosaka, Nagai, and others strongly supported alignment with the United States for classical balance-of-power reasons. At the same time they warned that Japan should not become overly entangled in U.S. strategy lest it be dragged into conflicts in which it had no interest.[85] Bolstered by the belief that the world was slowly moving from its focus on military competition to a greater concern with economic issues, these thinkers also expressed a fairly high degree of optimism that international institutions might develop the ability to mitigate the harshness of military competition between nations.[86] In short, despite great changes in the international system and Japan's position in it, they believed that the Yoshida Doctrine continued to be the most appropriate guide for Japanese foreign policy.

To be sure, Left-idealism remained a powerful, even dominant force in the Japanese intellectual scene, particularly as it was fed by the increased electoral strength of the Socialist and Communist parties and by popular opposition to the U.S. war in Vietnam. A new generation of Left-idealist scholars, such as Sakamoto Yoshikazu and Seki Hiroharu, continued to criticize the alliance with the United States and propagated the ideology of Japan as a peace nation.[87] Yet, whereas the 1950s and early 1960s defense discourse among intellectuals was dominated by Left-idealism, as of the mid-1960s the Centrist position was more clearly articulated and given a wider public hearing.

Two developments contributed to the emergence of this new Centrist cohort of scholars. The first was a shift to the center by the Japanese media, which began to publish the writings of Centrist scholars. This shift was most striking in the case of *Chūōkōron*, the nation's most prominent foreign policy affairs journal, which, along with *Sekai*, had been a platform for criticism of the Mutual Security Treaty system during the 1950s. In the 1960s *Chūōkōron* began to publish articles by Kosaka, Nagai, and others.[88]

The second development that encouraged the spread of Centrist thinking in the academic world was the Japanese government's efforts, beginning with Prime Minister Satō in the late 1960s, to court intellectuals and invite them to join government advisory groups and research councils. This strategy of incorporating intellectuals into government policy making continued and broadened after Satō's tenure and helped cultivate a more moderate climate in both academia and journalism.[89]

While in Japan the intellectual trend seemed on balance to be toward decreased opposition to government policies, in West Germany the intelligentsia ran toward greater criticism. Of course, before the 1960s, West German intellectuals and journalists had been relatively less strongly opposed to their government's defense policies than had their Japanese counterparts. In the mid- to late 1960s, however, détente and the general political shift to the left triggered a wave of support for a new approach to foreign policy as part of a broader renewal of West German society and politics.

This movement had at least two major components. The first was a liberal element represented by such influential intellectual figures as Karl Jaspers and Georg Picht, who was staunchly anticommunist but hoped for closer ties with East Germany and generally favored greater democratization of West German society.[90] While not always pro-American, these liberals were pro-Western and generally supportive of NATO and a measured Atlanticist position on foreign policy. The second component of this movement was drawn from the new generation of student protestors, who held more radical views. The young radicals, often coming out of the large West German countercultural scene, were generally less inclined than the liberals to draw a distinction between the liberal democracies of the West and the communist states of the East. Instead, they wished to create a new kind of egalitarian, participatory democracy. Their intellectual inspiration was derived from such respected scholars as Theodore Adorno, Max Horkheimer, and Herbert Marcuse (the founders of the so-called Frankfurt school of philosophy), as well as the rising star in the West German academic firmament, Jürgen Habermas.

While the West German student movement was part of a worldwide phenomenon, several specifically German factors gave the movement there a strength and staying power that it lacked in other countries.[91] First, the student radicals could build on the foundations of the old peace movement of the 1950s.[92] Second, the dark legacy of the past and the widely felt need in large sectors of German society to confront that legacy lent the student protestors an emotional edge it lacked elsewhere. Their spiritual patron within the SPD was Willy Brandt, who called on his party to take in the generation of unrest *(Die Generation der Unrast)* and who included many leading countercultural writers and journalists in his personal entourage.[93]

These two groups, the liberal reformers and the student radicals, were united during the late 1960s and early 1970s by the Brandt government and the common cause of opening relations with Eastern Europe. Their views on other issues, including defense, differed fundamentally. Whereas the liberals supported the Atlantic alliance and deterrence strategy, the 1968 generation, as the students were called, was instinctively hostile to the armed forces, nuclear weapons, and the alliance with the United States. With the successful implementation of *Ostpolitik* and Brandt's subsequent fall from power, they slowly drifted away from the Social Democratic Party and joined the ecological movement and the growing network of peace researchers. In short, while *Ostpolitik* enjoyed broad support among West German intellectuals and in the media, when international events in the late 1970s brought military issues back into the forefront of public attention, the coalition forged between liberals and radicals in support of *Ostpolitik* was destined to split apart.

Political Parties

During the 1960s and the first half of the 1970s there was considerable movement among the political party elites in both Germany and Japan toward centrist positions on defense and national security issues. This shift was most marked in West Germany, in part because various features of the party system there afforded German Social Democratic leaders greater room to maneuver than was true for their Japanese counterparts. Yet certain fundamental tensions that persisted even among the Social Democrats prevented the unhampered development of defense policy and made national security one of the most controversial and divisive issues in German and Japanese politics.

In West Germany, the single most important change was the SPD's conversion from staunch opposition to Adenauer's defense policies to ardent support of NATO and the Bundeswehr. The landmark event in this process was the famous Social Democratic Party congress in 1959 at Bad Godesberg, where the party accepted the principle of territorial defense *(Landesverteidigung).*[94] This shift on defense was no mere tactical adjustment for the purpose of winning more votes, but was part of a much larger transformation of the SPD's entire ideological self-definition. No longer did the SPD present itself as a classical Marxist party supporting the working class in the struggle against capitalism. Rather, it redefined itself as a people's party *(Volkspartei)* whose mission was to promote greater social justice and democracy for all classes. Marxism was replaced with an emphasis on humanism, classical philosophy, and Christian ethics.[95] In the economic sphere the SPD abandoned its traditional support for centralized economic planning and embraced instead the government's concept of the "social market" *(Soziale Marktwirtschaft),* or limited intervention in the economy to preserve social order.

Cultures of Antimilitarism

In short, the SPD underwent what in Kuhnian terms would be called a "paradigm shift." Not only did it modify its views on defense, it altered its entire world view in order to legitimate its changed stance on defense. Over the course of the next few months, the pragmatic party leadership under the direction of Herbert Wehner, Willy Brandt, and Fritz Erler managed to stifle all internal opposition to accepting the government's positions on defense, culminating in Wehner's watershed speech before the Bundestag in June 1960 announcing that henceforth the SPD would support NATO and the Paris treaties.[96]

Two key factors were behind the SPD's conversion. The first was the widespread perception that the party had failed to achieve any important objective through its opposition to Adenauer's policies. The Federal Republic was now in both NATO and the EEC with the apparent approval of most of the population. The second factor was the emergence of détente, which enabled the party to reconcile its antimilitary tendencies with support for American foreign policy. The shift in U.S. policy even allowed the SPD to turn the tables on the CDU/CSU. Whereas earlier the Christian Democrats could claim that they had the more pragmatic of the two parties, now they were hopelessly divided on détente, while the Social Democrats could claim to be more in step with the trend in world politics.

The Japanese Socialist Party, in contrast, did not see its electoral defeats as a sign that it was out of touch with the times. On the contrary, its success in unseating Kishi reinforced party members' belief that the party had made a major contribution to preventing the reemergence of reactionary forces. Through the 1960s and early 1970s the Left in Japan, including the Japanese Communist Party, enjoyed growing electoral success, culminating in its capture of the governorships of several major Japanese cities, including Kyoto and Tokyo, in the early 1970s. The LDP's electoral support, on the other hand, seemed to be slowly eroding, as shown in Table 4.7, apparently as a result of generational shifts and long-term demographic trends, and it seemed only a matter of time until the Liberal Democratic hegemony would be broken.[97] Moreover, the growing presence of the Communist Party to the left of the Socialists served to pin the party down on the left of center and weakened efforts to moderate its stands on defense and other issues.

These structural factors by themselves, however, cannot account for the persistence of the JSP's Left-idealist pacifism, for countervailing structural factors could have allowed for a quite different outcome. So-called middle-of-the-road parties emerged, including the Democratic Socialist Party (DSP) and the

Table 4.7
Japanese House of Representatives Election Results, 1960–1976

Date of Election	LDP	JSP	DSP	JCP	Komeitō	Other	Indepen-dent	Total
Nov 1960	296 (57.8)	145 (27.5)	17 (8.7)	3 (2.9)	— —	1 (0.3)	5 (2.8)	467
Nov 1963	283 (54.6)	144 (29.0)	23 (7.3)	5 (4.0)	— —	0 (0.1)	12 (4.7)	467
Jan 1967	277 (48.8)	140 (27.8)	30 (7.4)	5 (4.7)	25 (5.3)	0 (0.2)	9 (5.5)	486
Dec 1969	288 (47.6)	90 (21.4)	31 (7.7)	14 (6.8)	47 (10.9)	0 (0.1)	16 (5.3)	486
Dec 1972	271 (46.8)	118 (21.9)	19 (6.9)	38 (10.4)	29 (8.4)	2 (0.2)	14 (5.0)	491
Dec 1976	249/17[*] (41.7/4.1)	123 (20.6)	29 (6.2)	17 (10.3)	55 (10.9)	0 (0)	21 (5.7)	511

Note: Figures in parentheses represent percentage of votes.
[*]Figure after / represents the seats won by the New Liberal Club.
Source: Ronald J. Hrebenar, ed., *The Japanese Party System: From One-Party Rule to Coalition Government* (Boulder, Colo.: Westview Press, 1986), 301.

Buddhist-backed Komeitō Party, both of which were willing to accept with some reservations the Self-Defense Forces and the Mutual Security Treaty. A block of votes now existed to the right of the JSP that was at least as large as the number of voters it stood to lose to the Communists by moderating its politics on defense.[98] More important, forming a coalition with the moderate parties was the JSP's only realistic hope of taking power from the LDP. The JSP's continued refusal to accept the Self-Defense Forces and the Mutual Security Treaty, however, remained a major obstacle to the formation of a united opposition front.[99]

For these reasons, structural explanations for why there was no Japanese Bad Godesberg must be supplemented by ideological ones. The hold of Left-idealist thinking on JSP, fed by continued evidence of Right-idealism and the yawning chasm of mutual distrust and recrimination between the Left and the Right, cannot be underestimated. The JSP's inability to take power remained a source of great frustration. It was tempered, however, by the belief that its principled opposition to the government's policies was the chief barrier to a reactionary takeover.[100] More than a party seeking power, the JSP resembled a single-issue movement aimed at blocking military expansion. That it was so successful for so long is a testimony to the force of Japan's postwar culture of antimilitarism.

It is important to recognize that, while the JSP remained captive to Left-idealist ideology, significant shifts to the center occurred elsewhere in Japan during this period. Right-idealists, while still present, were clearly in the minority within the LDP, as the debate over a more independent stance on defense once again demonstrated. Among the opposition parties, the Komeitō and the DSP were both considerably more flexible on defense than the JSP. Especially during times of LDP weakness, the two middle-of-the-road parties displayed a marked readiness to compromise on defense in the hope that if the LDP lost its majority in the Diet it would turn to one of them to form a coalition.[101]

In the West German case, it would be a mistake to overestimate the strength of the Social Democratic consensus in favor of the Atlanticist position on defense. Even after 1960, there remained strong support for Central Europeanist positions on the grass roots level, and at party congresses through the 1960s and 1970s there were innumerable draft resolutions in favor of unilateral disarmament, dismantling the Bundeswehr, and creating a European peace order (*Friedensordnung*) that would replace NATO. A relatively small group of party reformers, however, were able to fend off these initiatives and prevent them from becoming part of the official Social Democratic platform by virtue of their positions of power within the disciplined, centrally organized structure of the SPD.[102] The more highly factionalized nature of Japanese party politics would have made it more difficult for Socialist leaders to implement such a strategy even if they had been inclined to do so.

The FDP, which during the 1950s had been in many ways to the right of the Christian Democrats on defense, shifted increasingly to the left, especially after they had been ousted from government by the Grand Coalition in 1966. Led by

Walter Scheel, Wolfgang Mischnick, and the young Hans Dieter Genscher (who were called the "Saxon guard" because of their origin in the East German region of Saxony), the party moved toward a national security policy designed to appeal to the SPD. At the 1969 Nürnberg party conference, the FDP adopted the idea of a European peace order based on the mutual renunciation of force, West German entry into the nuclear nonproliferation regime, and the adoption of a clearly defensive strategy for the Bundeswehr.[103] At the same time, the FDP reined in those within the party who were tempted to shift too far to the left.[104] Thereafter the FDP acted as a corrective to extremist tendencies in every party it formed a coalition with, leaning to the left on defense when allied with the CDU/CSU, and leaning to the right when together with the SPD.

Finally, whereas in Japan it was the JSP and the Left that were immobile on national security issues, in West Germany it was the conservatives and the CDU/CSU. Divided internally by the contending Atlanticist and Gaullist factions, the CDU was unable to achieve the kind of shift on national issues required for an adjustment to détente and the growing popular mood in favor of *Ostpolitik.* The price of that inflexibility was high as it relegated the Christian Democrats to the banks of the opposition for nearly fourteen years.

5

New Pressures, Old Responses—1976–1989

DURING THE SECOND HALF of the 1970s the trend toward détente and more relaxed East-West relations reversed itself. Growing Soviet military strength and continued efforts by the Soviet Union to expand its sphere of influence in the Third World, culminating in the 1979 invasion of Afghanistan, led to a hardening of American foreign policy. In the last years of President Jimmy Carter's administration, the United States returned to a strategy of containing Soviet power around the world politically, economically, and militarily. Increased aid was funnelled to anticommunist forces in the Third World; Western economic ties with the USSR and Eastern Europe were placed under tighter controls; and the United States embarked on one of the most massive rearmament programs of the Cold War.

During this period, West Germany and Japan continued to grow economically, solidifying their positions as the Western world's second and third strongest economies respectively, following the United States. Japan in particular emerged as an economic superpower, and its ballooning surpluses with its industrial trading partners became the source of considerable political friction. For the first time, economic tensions between Japan and the United States spilled over into their bilateral security relationship, threatening to erode the political basis of the alliance.

The United States, burdened by economic difficulties at home and less willing than ever to bear the main burden of Western defense, called on the Federal Republic and Japan to play a larger role in containing the Soviet Union. The West German and Japanese governments, already alarmed by their own analyses of the Soviet military buildup, came under tremendous diplomatic pressure to increase their defense efforts.

In response, both Japan and West Germany significantly increased their military capabilities. Their political leaderships, especially the conservative governments of CDU Chancellor Helmut Kohl and LDP Prime Minister Nakasone Yasuhiro, sought to rally domestic support for yet greater efforts. Alarmed by the nationalistic symbolism of Kohl's 1985 trip to Bitburg (where, among others, members of Hitler's Waffen SS were buried), and by Nakasone's almost simultaneous visit to the Yasukuni shrine (dedicated to the spirits of Japan's war dead), domestic and foreign observers feared that West Germany and Japan were shifting toward a more assertive approach to foreign affairs. Other analysts were alarmed by the size and virulence of the West German peace movement and the country's attachment to détente. Rather than increased military assertiveness, they contended, the Federal Republic was in danger of slipping toward a nationalism of a very different kind, a neutralist nationalism of the Left.

Despite these contradictory prophecies of doom, the policies West Germany and Japan chose to pursue remained broadly consistent with their behavior since the 1960s. Both nations continued to rely on their alliances with the United States for security, to restrict the scope and capacity of their armed forces, and to maintain a circumspect approach to civil-military relations that kept the military institutions under tight civilian control and eschewed linking nationalism with the armed forces. Despite mass protests in Germany and growing national self-confidence in Japan, a careful analysis of trends within the political systems of the two nations reveals the persistence of the core elements of their postwar political-military cultures and the continued dominance of antimilitary—but not pacifist—norms and values.

Alliance Politics

During the late 1970s and the 1980s the reintensification of the Cold War led the governments of the Federal Republic and Japan to rally behind their American ally and protector and adopt a more confrontational stance toward the Soviet Union. In both countries there was widespread criticism of the new American foreign policy, and the political costs of the governments' stances were considerable, cutting as they did against the grain of the two nations' minimalist approaches to national security. As in the 1960s, Germany, because of its exposed position, was hit harder politically by the shift in international politics than Japan was, and the domestic turmoil associated with the demise of détente was, if anything, even greater than that associated with its advent.

West Germany

The new debate over the alliance focused on NATO's "dual-track" decision to deploy medium-range missiles—the Pershing IIs—on West German soil, while pursuing arms control talks with the Soviet Union. In Germany, this shift toward a harder line vis-à-vis the Soviet Union triggered the fiercest political struggle since the founding of the Federal Republic. Many observers have argued that the force and intensity of these debates marked the end of the West German consensus on defense and national security.[1] Other commentators have maintained that the West German government's decision to deploy the Pershings despite mass demonstrations against doing so was a triumph of realism over left-wing hysteria.[2] Placing the events of 1979–1983 in the larger historical context of the 1980s, however, reveals that neither of these position is entirely accurate.

The decision to deploy the "Euromissiles" did indeed represent a crucial victory for Atlanticist and Europeanist forces who favored solidarity with the West in the face of growing Soviet power. As such the crisis reaffirmed the West German consensus in favor of the alliance. At the same time, the liberal-conservative government that pushed through the Pershing II missile deployment did not abandon the *Ostpolitik* policies of its predecessors. Despite considerable Western skepticism it continued to pursue détente with the Soviet Union and the GDR, even at the height of renewed East-West confrontation. The same voices in America who praised the Kohl government's decision to deploy the new intermediate-range nuclear forces in 1983 later bemoaned the détentist tendencies of Genscherism and the wild-eyed "Gorbymania" of the West German people.

Rather than representing a shift to the left or the right—toward Central Europeanism or toward hard-line West Europeanism/ Atlanticism—the German approach to the alliance during the 1980s remained consistent with the patterns that were already discernible in the 1957 Bundestag decision to deploy nuclear weapons on German soil and were reaffirmed in the 1967 Harmel report as well as the 1972 treaties normalizing relations with the East. Whenever it sought to pursue relations with the East, the Federal Republic was constrained to emphasize deterrence. Conversely, whenever it sought to strengthen deterrence it was compelled to underline its interest in East-West dialogue on arms control. Only this strategy made it possible for West German leaders from Adenauer to Kohl to resolve the tension between the values of deterrence and those of appeasement that had become part of the core of the Federal Republic's political-military culture.

The initial trigger for the new debate came in 1977 with the Carter administration's decision to seek funding for a new generation of tactical nuclear warheads (enhanced radiation weapons, commonly referred to as the neutron bomb).[3] To members of the SPD's left wing the issue seemed tailor-made to appeal to the radical members of the younger generation who had begun to drift away from the party since the early 1970s.

The neutron bomb, designed to produce more radiation while reducing blast and fire effects, could kill enemy soldiers without destroying physical structures and was thought to be especially useful as an antitank weapon. Although the neutron bomb made eminent sense from a military point of view—its development was supported by European military experts as well as the Pentagon—the weapon's emphasis on preserving property while taking lives made it a ready symbol of the apparent perversity of the strategy of nuclear deterrence.[4]

Faced with growing criticism within the SPD, Atlanticist Chancellor Helmut Schmidt encountered great difficulty securing Bundestag approval for the deployment of the neutron weapons, and the entire episode served to undermine his authority in the party. The neutron bomb controversy set the stage for the much bigger battle that broke out over the December 1979 NATO decision to deploy a new generation of intermediate-range nuclear forces (INF), including the highly accurate Pershing II missiles, to counter the ongoing Soviet deployment of SS-20s. Only two weeks after the INF decision the Soviet Union invaded Afghanistan, causing President Carter to postpone indefinitely the ratification of SALT and to begin a major U.S. military buildup. The era of détente came conclusively to an end and a new period of rising East-West tensions began.

The end of détente triggered a powerful reaction within the German political-military culture. The same coalition of forces that had opposed the neutron bomb now mobilized to stop deployment of the Pershing II missiles, which were made into a symbol of the new American foreign policy of confrontation with the Soviet Union. The new peace movement attracted considerable popular support for its antimissile crusade, for while the sense of threat increased significantly after 1979, attachment to détente remained high (74 percent overall; 59 percent even among CDU voters), and there was considerable popular ambivalence about the use of military force in general, and nuclear weapons in particular, for the defense of the nation.[5]

The end of détente also heralded the end of the fragile Social Democratic consensus in support of NATO. An open rift developed within the SPD. On the one side stood the proalliance Atlanticist wing of the party, led by Chancellor

Schmidt and his secretary of defense, Hans Apel. On the other side were the new Central Europeanists, represented by such figures as Brandt confidante Egon Bahr; the minister president of the Saar, Oskar Lafontaine; and the former Protestant minister and impassioned crusader for left-wing causes, Erhard Eppler. The Central Europeanists believed that the current escalation in East-West tensions was primarily the fault of American belligerence and that it was West Germany's duty to keep the peace by seeking to create a new security partnership that would unite the two halves of Europe.[6]

As left-wing criticism of U.S. policy escalated in Germany and the peace movement staged massive demonstrations to protest the planned deployment, Schmidt and his government were increasingly thrown on the defensive.[7] The formation of the radical Green Party in 1980 intensified the pressure on the chancellor. For the first time in the history of the Federal Republic, a significant political force to the left of the SPD existed, reinforcing pressures within the party to move further to the left on defense in order to win back left-wing voters and open the way for a coalition with the Greens. By 1982 Schmidt found himself increasingly isolated within his own party.[8]

As the SPD drifted back to its earlier Central Europeanist position on defense and the peace movement gathered momentum, the conservative CDU/CSU as well as the more moderate FDP began to voice alarm. In August 1982, FDP leader Hans Dieter Genscher openly sided with the CDU on the defense issue, warning that the SPD was beginning to blur the distinction between dictatorship and democracy, and insisting that West Germany had to comply with the dual-track decision for the sake of the alliance. The following month Genscher resigned his post as foreign minister and the FDP formed a new government with Helmut Kohl's Christian Democrats.[9] In the subsequent general elections the new CDU-FDP alliance won handily, with the CDU/CSU garnering 45.8 percent of the vote, the FDP 6.9 percent, and the SPD 38.2 percent (down 4 percent from the previous election). The Greens, however, came into the Bundestag for the first time, with 5.6 percent of the vote. Though large-scale protests and demonstrations continued, the Left was unable to prevent the deployment of the Pershing IIs. As in the 1950s, the Central Europeanist challenge to the alliance and to the West German approach to defense and security had failed, turned back by the Atlanticist consensus in the center and right wing of the political establishment and by the electorate's lack of enthusiasm for experiments in the area of security policy.[10]

The CDU/CSU–FDP victory did not imply, however, that the Federal Republic now wholeheartedly embraced the hard-line policies of the Reagan administration in the United States. In the late 1970s and early 1980s, the CDU underwent a transformation with regard to *Ostpolitik* comparable to the SPD's conversion at Bad Godesberg. Behind the CDU's conversion stood a variety of factors, above all the recognition that *Ostpolitik* enjoyed strong public support and had brought concrete benefits.[11] While stressing its solidarity with NATO and the need to increase defense spending, the CDU also embraced the CSCE and the Helsinki process as a means of eventually creating a lasting peace in Europe.[12]

Consequently, after 1982 the CDU/CSU–dominated government pursued *Ostpolitik* even as it pushed through the deployment of the Pershing II missiles. Despite the tense atmosphere between the superpowers, the CDU established its own minidétente with East Germany, signing a number of agreements pertaining to travel, cultural exchange, and economic and technological cooperation.[13] The high point of this minidétente came in 1987 with the long-delayed visit of the East German leader Erich Honecker to the Federal Republic.[14]

This diplomatic minuet between the two Germanys in the dead winter of East-West tensions of the mid-1980s was viewed with considerable apprehension by the Federal Republic's allies, who feared that the desire for reunification might undermine the West German commitment to NATO.[15] The Kohl government, however, would not be dissuaded by foreign misgivings. Its representatives argued that Germany was contributing to peace and stability on the continent and privately warned that an active stance on *Ostpolitik* was needed to prevent the peace movement and the opposition from exploiting the national mood.[16] SPD efforts to pursue negotiations with the East German government even while out of power greatly reinforced such apprehensions.[17]

In contrast to the Social Democrats, the CDU's *Ostpolitik* placed a greater emphasis on improving human rights in Eastern Europe as well as on the concept of using East-West relations for the "preservation of the substance of the nation" *(Erhaltung der Substanz der Nation)*, an idea with strong nationalist implications.[18] But whatever the differences in emphasis, substantively the new government's policies toward the East closely resembled those of the SPD. Rather than deepening the gulf between Left and Right in West Germany, the crisis of the early 1980s ironically resulted in a significant broadening of the consensus in favor of détente and the belief that national security could be enhanced through nonmilitary instruments. By the mid-1980s even such inveterate CDU hawks as Alfred Dregger and Jürgen Todenhöfer argued strongly in favor of détente and peaceful coexistence with the Soviet Union.[19]

Japan

The end of détente heralded changes in East Asia almost as far-reaching as those it brought about in Europe. The most important consequence from the Japanese point of view was the dramatic increase, especially after the Soviet invasion of Afghanistan, in U.S. pressures on Japan to increase its defense efforts and check growing Soviet naval power in the Far East.

Fortunately for the Japanese government, the domestic foundations for responding to these pressures had already been laid with the passage of Taikō during the mid-1970s. Consequently, the LDP and its allies in the bureaucracy were able to implement a rapid intensification of U.S.-Japanese military cooperation without much serious public controversy. Many observers, especially in the press, viewed these developments as a silent revolution that threatened to remilitarize Japan's foreign policy and undermine Japanese democracy.[20]

Yet, while the intensification of the military ties between the United States and Japan would represent the most important substantive change in postwar Japanese defense policy up to that time, it was more an adaptation of the Yoshida Doctrine to the shifting international political environment than a radical departure. In the first half of the 1970s, Japan's pragmatic Centrist mainstream had realized that "things must change to remain the same." Growing Soviet strength and the threat of U.S. disengagement impelled Japan either to adopt a far more independent defense posture, which would have increased international tensions and triggered a domestic political crisis, or to reinvigorate the alliance with the United States. Japan chose the latter option, even at the price of becoming more deeply entangled in U.S. strategy in East Asia.

The centerpiece of the new U.S.-Japanese military relationship was the 1978 "Guidelines on U.S.-Japanese Defense Cooperation," drawn up after three years of intensive negotiations.[21] The guidelines laid the groundwork for joint consultations on a wide range of security-related topics, including attack or the threat of attack on Japan, crises in the Far East with implications for Japanese security, and joint training and military maneuvers.[22] A special coordinating office was set up to facilitate cooperation between U.S. and Japanese forces in the event of an emergency. The Japanese government was also invited to participate in detailed discussions of U.S. strategic planning in the Far East.[23] Finally, for the first time the Japanese government openly acknowledged that one of the functions of the security relationship was to give Japan extended nuclear deterrence.[24]

Despite their enormous policy implications, the 1978 guidelines were ratified without Diet approval on the grounds that they represented merely the framework for further consultations and had no legally binding power, though they were approved by the National Defense Council and the Cabinet. To forestall any possible criticism, the government deliberately excluded from the discussions with the United States any questions relating to constitutional restrictions on defense and the three non-nuclear principles. Further, consistent with the goals established under Taikō, the SDF's mission was defined as being to repel only limited and small-scale invasions and to rely on the United States to cope with larger threats.[25]

These limitations notwithstanding, the guidelines set the stage for greatly intensified U.S.-Japanese defense cooperation. The most visible manifestation of the new collaboration was SDF participation in a broad range of joint military exercises with allied forces in the Pacific. Because these exercises occurred under the aegis of the United States, domestic fears of revived militarism remained largely muted.[26]

Over the course of the following decade, the U.S.-Japanese relationship continued to evolve and deepen. Beginning in 1979, Japanese defense officials and prodefense parliamentarians began to meet regularly with their American counterparts to discuss strategies for overcoming domestic resistance to increased defense efforts.[27] In 1981, Prime Minister Suzuki Zengo promised that Japan would take on responsibility for the defense of its sea-lanes for a range of one thousand nautical miles from the main islands.

Under Prime Minister Nakasone (formerly a proponent of independent defense), U.S.-Japanese defense cooperation intensified even further. Japan undertook responsibility for defending American ships in its territorial waters against possible Soviet aggression and pushed forward joint planning. In 1984, Nakasone signed an agreement permitting the export of military technology to the United States and promoting the joint development of weapons systems.[28] In 1978, Japan began to help pay for the maintenance of U.S. forces there; by the end of the decade, it was cheaper for the United States to maintain these forces in Japan than to have them stationed in the United States.[29]

Despite these developments, however, it is important to note what had *not* changed in the U.S.-Japanese military relationship. Although Japan now cooperated fully with the United States in preparing for the defense of the home islands, it continued to be uninvolved in regional security affairs. It remained an open question whether it would support the United States in a confrontation with the Soviet Union in which its own security was not directly threatened. For example, it was unclear whether the Japanese would close their straits to Soviet warships moving to challenge the United States in a showdown in the Middle East, even though Japan's own oil supplies would have been manifestly at risk in such a confrontation.[30] Nor did Japan integrate itself into a NATO-like defense structure, and it continued to define its relationship as being something other than a form of collective defense.

In short, despite considerable resistance from the media and the opposing parties, the LDP and its bureaucratic allies succeeded in achieving important changes in Japanese security policy. They did so through a process of low-key, graduated steps and the reinterpretation of policy, rather than through a dramatic redefinition that might have provoked a major political confrontation and triggered a defection of LDP Centrists to the opposition. The evolution of Japanese alliance policy in the late 1970s fit the familiar postwar pattern of establishing new defense policy by means of the accumulation of fait accomplis *(kiseijijtsu tsumoriage)*. Whenever government actions threatened to veer from the Yoshida Doctrine, as they did in the area of civil-military relations, Centrist pressures quickly forced a correction of course.

Military Doctrine and Force Structures

The West German and Japanese decisions to support the United States in its growing confrontation with the Soviet Union required that they agree to the adoption of new, more aggressive military missions and force postures. To many West German critics the deployment of a new generation of intermediate-range nuclear weapons and the Kohl government's willingness to join President Ronald Reagan's Strategic Defense Initiative (SDI) seemed to imply German acceptance of far more belligerent nuclear doctrines than ever before, which were paralleled in the area of conventional defense by the new American doctrine of Follow on Forward Attack (FOFA). Similarly, in Japan, Prime Minister Suzuki's pledge to defend his country's sea-lanes (or sea lines) of communication appeared to mark a drastic expansion of the SDF's traditional territorial defense role, while the overturning of the 1 percent of GNP limit on defense spending was taken by many as a sign that Japan was moving beyond its minimalist approach to force structure and preparing to become a great power. Yet once again, upon closer analysis, each of these apparent departures from exist-ing policy proves to be less dramatic than critics claimed.

West Germany

To be sure, the deployment of new INF in West Germany could be interpreted as a major shift in NATO military doctrine. The highly accurate Pershing II mis-sile could reach a strategic target in the Soviet Union within a matter of min-utes, theoretically making it the ideal weapon for the kind of surgical first strike aimed against the Soviet command and control structure advocated by some American strategic analysts.[31] Members of the peace movement argued that the deployment on German territory of INF capable of striking at targets in the Soviet Union risked creating a situation in which the United States might be tempted to wage a limited nuclear war in Western Europe.[32]

The military implications of the missile deployments, however, were at best ambiguous. It was unclear whether deployment of the new nuclear forces would decouple the U.S. strategic deterrent from Europe, as critics claimed, or whether— on the contrary—it prevented a decoupling by compensating for growing So-viet superiority in INF weapons. Supporters of the INF deployment warned that a new generation of Soviet weapon systems, in particular the highly accurate SS-20s, made it possible for the Soviet Union to destroy the existing NATO nuclear forces in Europe through a first strike, leaving the United States with the unpalatable choice of either accepting a Soviet victory or responding with nu-clear forces stationed outside of the European theater. The stationing of Persh-ing II and Tomahawk cruise missiles was intended to preserve the option of re-sponding to an attempted Soviet first strike on Western Europe with theater nuclear weapons.[33]

More important for this analysis, neither the West German government of Helmut Schmidt nor that of Helmut Kohl saw deployment of the INF missiles as a means of changing NATO strategic doctrine. Schmidt was primarily con-cerned with the political implications of the Soviet SS-20 deployment and feared that the United States was neglecting European interests in its eagerness to pur-sue arms control talks with the Soviets.[34] In addition, the Schmidt government attached a variety of conditions to the deployment of the new INF, including continued progress in arms control talks, that underlined West Germany's con-tinued adherence to a basically nonconfrontational stance on security issues.[35]

Although the CDU/CSU–led coalition that succeeded the Schmidt government in 1983 placed greater emphasis on the strategic military rationale for the missile deployment, it, too, stressed the importance of solidarity with the Western alliance over that of maintaining the balance of power against the Soviet Union. Similarly, the Kohl government's endorsement of SDI was primarily motivated by alliance and economic considerations rather than by a sea change in German strategic thought.[36] When, later in the decade, new U.S. arms control initiatives began to undermine the strategic rationale for INF deployment, Kohl and Genscher did not hesitate to overrule hard-liners who warned that German strategic interests were being sacrificed. In contrast to the 1960s, when the CDU split into warring camps of Europeanists and Atlanticists, the spread of norms of engagement and compromise in the German political system placed the hard-liners at a decisive disadvantage. Even the general inspector of the Bundeswehr, Wolfgang Altenberg, while admitting that the American proposals posed difficulties for NATO strategy, insisted that, "None of us will undermine a true zero solution, even I as a soldier will not, for the simple reason that no one can deny humanity's desire for denuclearization".[37] It is hard to imagine many American, British, or French generals at the time making such a bold statement.

German acceptance of aggressive new American conventional strategic doctrines that sought to use advanced technology to attack deep inside enemy territory was similarly motivated by alliance considerations. The practical consequences for West German force structure and military training was limited, and Germany's military leaders remained profoundly skeptical about the prospects for a conventional defense of Europe. As Bundeswehr General Inspector Klaus Naumann put it in an article written shortly before the end of the Cold War:

> Conventional war never succeeded in preventing war, the destructive power of nuclear weapons apparently does. Therefore German defense planners do not believe in strategists who advocate conventional deterrence. . . . Germany obviously wants to strengthen conventional capabilities in such a way that the risk of unacceptable damage for an aggressor is increased even in a conventional war and that the tight linkage between nuclear and conventional capabilities is maintained.[38]

In sum, the Bundeswehr was prepared to modernize its forces in order to take advantage of new technological developments. But German military planners and the federal government remained highly reluctant to pursue strategies that were sure to require an increase in the defense burden beyond what the public was willing to tolerate and that ultimately might encourage the waging of a conventional war.[39]

Japan

Japan also saw an intense debate over military doctrine and force structure during the 1980s, although the controversies were not as fierce as those in West Germany and the focus was rather different. Although the visits to Japanese harbors of U.S. warships believed to carry nuclear arms continued to be the target of opposition criticism, the nuclear issue remained relatively muted. The domestic political debate instead concentrated primarily on the issues of defense spending and what kinds of conventional missions the SDF should be allowed to engage in.

The most important apparent change in the definition of the armed forces' mission came during Prime Minister Suzuki Zengo's 1981 visit to the United States. After meeting with President Reagan, Suzuki announced that Japan would strengthen its alliance with the United States (*dōmeikankei*, a term that Japanese leaders previously had avoided when referring to the relationship with the United States because of its military implications) and was prepared to defend not only its own territory, but also its sea lines of communication up to one thousand nautical miles from the Japanese mainland. To this end, Suzuki continued, Japan would increase its "defense power" *(Bōeiryoku)* within the boundaries of what was permitted by its constitution.[40]

Suzuki's comments were widely interpreted as meaning that Japan was prepared to exercise control over a wide swath of the Western Pacific in the event of a military confrontation with the Soviet Union, enabling the U.S. Navy to concentrate its resources on other possible threats.[41] Coming only two months after Foreign Minister Itō Masayoshi had stressed that Japan was not willing to make such a commitment, Suzuki's announcement was a surprise to many, even in his own government, and it appeared to signal a major departure from the highly parochial definition of defense characteristic of postwar Japan's political-military culture.[42]

Yet it is doubtful that Suzuki's announcement marked quite the abrupt change in Japanese thinking that it at first appeared to. There remained a considerable gap between the American and the Japanese interpretations of what Suzuki had said. Whereas the Japanese government maintained it had committed itself only to the protection of shipping in its territorial waters and nearby shipping routes, the United States insisted that Japan was also responsible for clearing the area of all enemy vessels, including submarines.[43] Adding to the confusion was the fact that Suzuki himself had evidently been deceived by his Foreign Ministry handlers on how his statements would be interpreted. Once the prime minister's prestige had been committed, however, it became impossible for Suzuki or subsequent governments to back down on his promises, and the United States happily used Suzuki's pledge to pressure the Japanese for more burden sharing.[44] Suzuki's successor, the far more hawkish Nakasone Yasuhiro, went even further by promising to defend U.S. warships that came to the defense of Japan and stressing that, in the event of a war, Japan could serve as an "unsinkable aircraft carrier" against the Soviet Union.[45]

Although the Self-Defense Forces significantly increased its antisubmarine weapons capabilities and developed the ability to blockade straits and prevent Soviet naval forces in the Sea of Japan from breaking out into the Pacific, Japan continued to refrain from acquiring greater force projection capabilities, such as carriers (including helicopter carriers) or midair refueling facilities.[46] Nor did Japan acquire the capacity to defend its sea-lanes in the aggressive manner desired by U.S. force planners. Moreover, there was no guarantee that the SDF would defend U.S. forces unless Japan itself were directly attacked or threatened with an attack.[47]

This ambivalence was underlined in 1987 during the first Persian Gulf crisis, when the United States asked Japan to dispatch minesweepers to help clear Iranian mines that posed a threat to shipping in the region. Although Nakasone and some of his closest foreign policy advisors strongly favored responding to the American request, strong resistance from inside the LDP forced Nakasone to abandon the project. Chief Cabinet Secretary Gotoda Masaharu led the opposition to overseas dispatch, publicly arguing that, if the minesweepers were fired upon, they would be faced with an untenable choice of either not defending themselves or violating the constitution by shooting back. Privately he warned that overseas dispatch could start the nation down the road toward militarism.[48] Although the Japanese animus against military integration with the United States had been weakened, it was far from dead, and the overseas dispatch of forces in particular continued to be linked in the minds of many Centrist as well as left-wing leaders with the risk of a reversion to power politics, militarism, and war.

As in Germany, a further obstacle to Japan's assumption of a greater regional military role was the expected cost of such an enterprise. Although Japanese defense spending increased at a rapid average rate of 6.48 percent per year between 1980 and 1989, the defense budget barely went beyond 1 percent of total GNP in 1987, and public opinion polls showed overwhelming opposition to any further increase. According to one estimate, to acquire the kind of forces that would be needed to ensure control of the seas would have required a near doubling of the defense budget, to near 1.5 percent to 2 percent of Japanese GNP.[49] Of course, if Japan had chosen to do so, it could have increased its expenditures to such a level, but the domestic political consensus requisite for such a move was clearly lacking.

During the first half of the 1980s, East-West tensions were at their highest levels since the early 1960s, and conservative, prodefense governments were in power in both West Germany and Japan. But because of political constraints, defense spending as a percentage of GNP increased only slightly in Japan and actually declined in West Germany, as shown in Table 5.1.

Table 5.1
Defense Spending as a Percentage of GNP, 1975–1986

Year	United States (%)	Germany (%)	Japan (%)
1975	6.0	3.7	0.9
1980	5.1	3.3	0.9
1986	6.7	3.1	1.0

Source: From Simon Duke, The Burdensharing Debate (New York: St. Martin's, 1993), 116.

Civil-Military Relations

Conservative efforts to rally support for an increased defense program reignited the debate on civil-military relations in both West Germany and Japan. Because Japan did not have the kind of political consensus supporting the armed forces that had been forged in West Germany, the Japanese debate over civil-military relations was, on the whole, more intense and had greater implications for military policy.

Japan

The initial impetus for the new debate came in 1978, when the Fukuda government sought to introduce a broad package of legislation—called the Emergency Laws *(Yūjihōsei)*—designed to enable the military to respond efficiently to a military crisis. They contained provisions authorizing the armed forces to clear civilian roads for military traffic and to initiate civil defense and evacuation procedures, including various measures for protecting military secrets and so forth. In effect, this legislation posed a challenge to the taboo on planning for military emergencies that had been in effect since the Three Arrows incident of thirteen years earlier. In the mid-1970s, as the prospect of military conflict with the Soviet Union became more real and defense policy was reoriented toward meeting an external invasion, the Japanese government quietly resumed work on new emergency legislation.[50]

To avoid provoking popular apprehensions about a military coup d'état, the Japanese Defense Agency separated contingency planning from emergency legislation; in the Three Arrows Plan the two had been lumped together. Instead, contingency planning was now undertaken in the context of the new joint research to be conducted with the United States. Moreover, the government limited the scope of the new research, specifying that the constitution and the principle of civilian control would not be open to question; that the especially sensitive subjects of dealing with domestic unrest and internal subversion would be excluded; and that all planning would be based on the assumption that civilians would spontaneously cooperate with the armed forces (i.e., there was no plan for mass conscription or the placement of controls on the media or freedom of speech).[51] Against a background of softening opposition views on defense, many officials within the government hoped that these safeguards would allow speedy passage of the bill.[52] The established patterns of interaction in Japan's political-military culture, however, soon intervened and a major backlash, from both the Right and the Center, emerged.

Two incidents served to fan fears that the conservative government of Prime Minister Fukuda Takeo was opening the door to a reactionary takeover. The first came in July 1978 when, in a series of highly provocative interviews, Air Force General and Chairman of the Joint Chiefs of Staff Kurisu Hiromi suggested that in the event of a Soviet attack SDF pilots would not wait for government approval to engage in combat—as required by law—but would take matters into their own hands.[53] The JDA insisted that Kurisu's remarks were unrelated to the pending Emergency Law legislation and that it would quickly remove the general from his post. Nonetheless, even many Centrists expressed concern that the incident reflected a dangerous fraying of civilian control over the military.[54]

At the same time, a series of largely symbolic gestures by Prime Minister Fukuda, most notably his visit on August 15 (the date of Japan's surrender in World War II) to the Yasukuni shrine in Tokyo, compounded public misgivings about the government's intentions. While on the surface unrelated to defense and the Emergency Laws, these symbolic acts, taken together with Kurisu's comments and the inclusion of secrecy laws in the proposed emergency legislation, created the impression that the government was seeking to use the defense issue as a pretext to curtail civil liberties and effect a return to a more authoritarian political system.[55]

In the same month, the Japanese Socialist Party and Sōhyō, the federation of public-sector labor unions, held a rally in Tokyo to inaugurate the creation of a National Conference to Crush the Emergency Laws, reminiscent of the organizations formed in 1960 to oppose Kishi's revision of the Mutual Security Treaty. Socialist leaders expressed confidence that they could mobilize overwhelming mass support on the issue.[56] The middle-of-the-road parties as well expressed reservations regarding the new legislation. Democratic Socialist Party Chairman Sasaki Ryosaku announced that, while his party supported better rules of engagement, it opposed broader legislation that threatened the liberties of the individual.[57] Likewise, Kōmeitō charged the LDP with trying to mobilize support for changing the constitution and instituting a system of mass conscription.[58]

Faced with a united opposition, Centrist support within the government began to evaporate.[59] As a compromise solution the Fukuda government decided that research on the Emergency Laws would be allowed to proceed but that legislation would only be submitted to the Diet in the event of actual hostilities. To further defuse popular and opposition apprehensions, the JDA narrowed the scope of the hypothetical law, separating it from issues of counterespionage and rules of engagement.[60] While, by these modifications, the government succeeded in setting clear guidelines for the behavior of the armed forces in an actual crisis, continued tensions between Right-idealist, Left-idealists, and Centrists remained, hampering the rational development of defense policy and leaving unanswered vital questions about counterespionage and rules of engagement in the event of a surprise attack.

Similar dynamics were seen in 1985 when Prime Minister Nakasone chose to break the 1 percent of GNP limit on defense expenditures.[61] At its inception in 1976, the 1 percent barrier had been intended only as a temporary quid pro quo for the opposition's acceptance of Taikō.[62] Thereafter, however, the 1 percent barrier was enshrined by the media and the opposition as a symbol of civilian control of the armed forces. By the mid-1980s, rising costs and growing international pressures to increase defense spending made it seem that it was only a matter of time till the barrier would be broken.[63]

Nakasone took up the 1 percent barrier issue for both political and ideological motives. It is believed that he hoped to use the issue to dissolve the Diet and call for new elections, giving him a chance to solidify his power base within the LDP.[64] Like Hatoyama, Kishi, and other Right-idealist leaders before him, Nakasone wished to use the 1 percent barrier issue to stimulate a new debate on national defense, patriotism, and, ultimately, national identity. Unlike the JDA and many prodefense Diet members, Nakasone was intent on breaking the barrier in a highly visible fashion, marking a new consensus on defense and a radical departure from the established postwar pattern of advancing defense policy through the quiet accumulation of faits accomplis.

In July 1985, at the annual LDP summer seminar at the resort town of Karuizawa, Nakasone sounded the call to arms and expanded on one of his favorite themes, the "final resolution of postwar politics" (Sengoseiji no Sōkkessan). His comments revealed strong Right-idealist thinking:

> "After the defeat there emerged a view of history dominated by the Pacific war, in other words the historical perspective of the Tokyo War Crimes Tribunal. Under the laws of the Allied Nations Japan was accused and judged in the name of civilization, peace and humanity. With regard to [the validity of this verdict], history will eventually decide. Nonetheless, at that time, an intellectual current of self-flagellation that saw Japan as totally evil was born. This has remained with us to this day. . . . I am opposed to this tendency. Win or lose we are a nation. A nation casts aside past humiliations and marches forward in search of glory. From this perspective it is necessary to look at the accomplishments of the past and secure Japan's identity and independence. In this way . . . a national consensus will be formed and Japan will progress majestically toward the 21st century. This is the final resolution of postwar politics."[65]

In the speech, Nakasone also announced his intention to visit the Yasukuni shrine in Tokyo in his official capacity as prime minister. This shrine was dedicated to the spirits of Japan's war dead, including the seven Japanese wartime leaders executed as Class A war criminals. While these three issues—breaking the 1 percent barrier, the final resolution of postwar politics, and the visit to the Yasukuni shrine—were only loosely related, in the context of postwar Japanese political-military culture the connection was clear. Nakasone sought to use the 1 percent issue to call general elections, which would become a national referendum not only on defense but also on national identity. In the process, he planned to challenge the postwar taboo of linking defense to patriotism. His concept of the "final resolution of postwar Japanese politics" was a call to rid the nation of the debilitating burden of its past and to approach national defense in the presumably more rational manner of other countries. In other words, Nakasone wished to transform Japan's postwar political-military culture.

If this discussion had taken place in a country such as France or Britain, neither the removal of the 1 percent barrier nor Nakasone's other defense proposals would have appeared particularly ominous or unusual. The United States was actively pressuring Japan to increase its defense spending well beyond 1 percent of GNP, and there was nothing in Nakasone's proposals that need be construed as the beginning of a more bellicose foreign policy. Given the tense state of East-West relations and growing Soviet naval and air power in the Far East, Nakasone's actions could even be viewed as minimal responses to a worsening regional balance of power.[66]

Nonetheless, the domestic implications of Nakasone's plans sparked immediate resistance across the Japanese political spectrum. Within the LDP, former Prime Ministers Fukuda, Miki, and Suzuki stressed the importance of the 1 percent barrier as the basis of the people's trust in the government's defense policies and warned that removing the barrier might trigger out-of-control defense spending. Moreover, the party elders were concerned over the potential political costs of calling elections over the 1 percent issue and feared that the LDP might lose as many as thirty seats and be forced into coalition with the DSP.[67]

Other Centrist leaders soon turned against the plan, and many of Nakasone's allies opposed the idea of calling elections.[68] The leaders of the New Liberal Club, a splinter party with which the LDP had been forced into coalition, threatened to leave the government if the barrier was broken, while even the DSP, which originally had supported removing the 1 percent limit, now turned against the proposal. The JSP and Kōmeitō were even more outspoken in their criticism.[69]

Faced with overwhelming opposition, a bitterly disappointed Nakasone was forced to admit defeat and to postpone his plans indefinitely.[70] Yet only a few days later, the JDA and the Ministry of Finance negotiated a new five-year defense buildup program that virtually guaranteed that the barrier would be broken by 1987 at the latest. The very same leaders who earlier had opposed Nakasone now approved the plan in separate meetings of the National Defense Council and the Cabinet. Although the opposition swarmed to attack the new plan, the government largely ignored the criticisms, promising only to "respect the spirit of the 1 percent barrier" and to adhere to the barrier until at least 1986.[71]

A year later, in the fall of 1986, after the LDP had overwhelmingly won the June elections for the upper and lower houses following a campaign focused mainly on nondefense issues, the 1 percent barrier was broken with a minimum of commotion. To reassure the public that defense spending would not escalate out of control, the government replaced the barrier with a new policy brake in the form of a rolling budget system that fixed total spending for a five-year period and increased control over the defense budget by the Diet and other ministries.[72] Without Nakasone's provocative Right-idealist rhetoric to stimulate opposition, supporters of the 1 percent barrier were unable to mobilize the Centrist support needed to defeat the new policy. Had Nakasone chosen to adhere to a low-key approach to the issue in 1985, many in the JDA were convinced that the barrier could have been broken a year earlier.[73] As Foreign Minister Abe Shintarō commented, "One can pass the gate blowing a trumpet or bowing one's head, the result is the same. This is the problem with Nakasone's methods."[74]

Once again, Japanese defense policy had advanced by means of a fait accompli without any serious public debate of the strategic rationale for breaking the barrier. Although Nakasone had sought to challenge this surreptitious way of setting policy and the peculiar postwar Japanese mentality that made military security a quasilegitimate function of government, the continued weight of postwar Japanese attitudes toward defense forced him to pass through the gate with his head bowed in humble silence.

West Germany

In West German civil-military relations, the focus remained exclusively on symbolic issues rather than concrete military ones. The topic of how to structure and control the armed forces reemerged once more against the backdrop of renewed East-West tensions and a growing domestic peace movement, and raised questions about the purpose of the armed forces and about postwar German national identity. As in the 1950s and 1960s, the question of whether the Bundeswehr had been successfully integrated into German society became a primary point of contention.

During the 1970s, a series of incidents, such as the extension to a prominent neo-Nazi an invitation to a traditional Bundeswehr squadron's reunion, sparked criticism that the Bundeswehr had not been sufficiently purged of its prewar, antidemocratic ways of thought. Critics called for far-reaching reforms, including the expulsion of all references to the military's prewar past and the creation of a new, more democratic set of traditions drawing exclusively on postwar history.[75]

On the other side of the dispute stood more conservative forces, both in the CDU/CSU and within the armed forces, who felt that the Bundeswehr had been sufficiently integrated into democratic society and wanted to concentrate on increasing its military efficiency. While senior military officers sought to retain Innere Führung, the principles of democratization and civilian control of the military, they also criticized the bureaucratization of the armed forces that many officers associated with the doctrine and argued that the time had come to find other ways to improve morale and leadership.[76]

During the late 1970s left-wing criticism of the Bundeswehr intensified, culminating in 1980 in a series of riots triggered by the military ceremonies marking the twenty-fifth anniversary of the Bundeswehr.[77] Under pressure from the left wing of the SPD, in 1981 Defense Minister Apel issued a new set of instructions regarding the maintenance of tradition. The new guidelines stressed that soldierly virtues in the Bundeswehr must be subordinated to the values of a free, pluralistic democracy and that the armed forces' primary mission was not to prepare for war but to keep the peace. Former members of the Wehrmacht and the Waffen SS were to be excluded from the Bundeswehr list of role models, and new restrictions were placed on the kinds of rituals performed in the armed forces.[78]

After the SPD lost control of the government in 1982 the tide turned once more, and one of new CDU Minister of Defense Manfred Wörner's first acts was to promise to reverse the Apel decree.[79] In 1984, the Center for Innere Führung produced a new set of principles regarding the maintenance of tradition in the armed forces, resulting in 1985 in yet another decree on the subject. Now the primary mission of the Bundeswehr was the strengthening of deterrence by preparing to wage war. To increase the Bundeswehr's combat effectiveness, the cultivation of such traditional soldierly virtues as obedience, courage, stoicism, and camaraderie was to be encouraged. Figures from the Wehrmacht could be included in the Bundeswehr traditions but, as a gesture of compromise with the Left, so were the leaders of the July 20 revolt against Hitler.[80]

That same spring the issue of the relationship between Germany's military past and its new national identity drew international attention when Chancellor Kohl and President Reagan visited the German military cemetery at Bitburg, where, among others, members of Hitler's Waffen SS were buried.[81] While the motives and events leading to the visit were complex, the key factor was Chancellor Kohl's desire to underline German solidarity with the West. Viewed in a larger political context, the visit could be seen as part of Kohl's strategy of fostering a healthy sense of German patriotism centered on the country's relationship to the West and reconciled with the darker side of its past. In this respect, Kohl's trip to Bitburg was quite similar to Nakasone's visit to Yasukuni a few weeks later.

Unlike the event in Japan, however, Kohl's trip did not awaken fears of a renewed militarism. Kohl did not link the visit to an implicit rejection of German responsibility for the war. Although the Bitburg trip provoked considerable domestic controversy and international criticism, German public opinion data showed widespread support for the visit, and it may even have had a positive impact on the public's evaluation of the NATO alliance.[82]

In neither West Germany nor Japan did the essential features of the postwar approach to civil-military relations change significantly during the 1976–1989 period. To the extent that Kohl and Nakasone departed from established practices, their policies met with considerable resistance, though it is reflective of the quasilegitimate status of defense in Japan that only Nakasone's efforts met with near-complete failure.

In neither country did the armed forces gain in political influence or social stature, and neither departed from the basic strategies it used to keep the armed forces under control. The Japanese Self-Defense Forces continued to labor under a tight regime of bureaucratic and legal controls and, when military men challenged those controls, as General Kurisu did in 1978, they were summarily dismissed. While some safeguards, such as the 1 percent spending limit, were removed, they were replaced by new ones designed to reassure the public and the elites that the armed forces continued to be held in check. In the Federal Republic, the Bundeswehr continued to adhere to the doctrine of Innere Führung and the strategy of integrating the armed forces into society, though there remained sharp limits on the degree to which such integration could be accomplished.

The Political-Military Cultures of Japan and Germany, circa 1989

During the 1960s and early 1970s, the *content* (as opposed to the *distribution*) of the left, right, and center political-military subcultures in Japan and West Germany had changed relatively little from the 1950s. In contrast, by the late 1970s and 1980s more significant changes in content became discernible, as the Centrist and Atlanticist views on defense enjoyed increasing ascendancy across ideological boundaries, and issues such as capitalism versus socialism virtually disappeared. Slowly but surely, both countries' political-military subcultures moved toward positions of cultural hegemony.

West Germany

These shifts were more apparent in the West German context, where both the political Right and the Left continued to converge on certain key issues. In the 1950s and 1960s, the left wing of the SPD (but not its more centrist leadership) had bitterly resisted European integration because it feared integration would lock Germany into an exploitative capitalist system of production. By the late 1970s, however, Central Europeanists began to embrace the integration process. Similarly, in the 1980s conservative Europeanists accepted *Ostpolitik* and the CSCE process, which they had castigated earlier as a betrayal of German national interests and a threat to the Western alliance.

In both instances, the West Europeanists and the Central Europeanists reinterpreted the previously disputed policies and linked them to rather different goals. The Central Europeanists came to see the European integration process as a means of weakening the Atlantic alliance in the hope that a stronger united Western Europe could resist American pressures to adopt a confrontational stance vis-à-vis the Soviet Union.[83] Similarly, conservative Europeanists emphasized the usefulness of *Ostpolitik* as an instrument for preserving the substance of the German nation while helping the cause of human rights in Eastern Europe. This new acceptance of *Ostpolitik* led the Christian Democrats to formally redefine German security interests in 1980 under the rubric of "comprehensive policy" *(Gesamtpolitik)*, encompassing not only military defense, but also East-West cooperation, European integration, and ties with the United States.[84]

Japan

In Japan the change was less dramatic. Left- and Right-idealists remained almost as far apart in the 1980s as they had been in the 1950s and 1960s. Nonetheless, in Japan as well, subtle shifts in the way the different subcultures viewed defense and national identity were no less significant than the more noticeable changes in West Germany.

The most important change was the Right-idealists' increasing emphasis on economic over military power. Until the early 1980s, Right-idealist writers such as Shimizu Ikutarō still stressed the importance of military power and political stature for securing national independence and pride. As the 1980s progressed, however, and tensions between the United States and Japan over trade and other economic issues grew, nationalist Right-idealist commentators such as Etō Jun and Ishihara Shintarō increasingly focused on Japan's economic and technological prowess while downplaying the military security issue.[85] This shift in emphasis was accompanied by a new wave of anti-Americanism among Right-idealists. After forty years of professing to be staunch allies of the United States, Right-idealists began to vigorously criticize their Cold War ally, using the American political-economic challenge to stir up nationalist passions in much the same they way they had tried earlier to use the Soviet political-military threat.

Directly related to this shift in emphasis was a new focus on the economy as source of nationalist pride, a view that came to be widely shared among Japanese elites regardless of their political persuasion. Before 1945 Japan had defined itself as a warrior nation, the land of the samurai, whose martial values distinguished it from the spiritually weak and corrupt West. In the 1980s Japan came to view itself as a nation of merchants and manufacturers, endowed with a unique propensity for producing high-quality goods that other people, including Americans, simply could not match.[86]

Many Japanese elites, including army generals, prodefense members of the Diet, and hawkish members of the Ministry of Foreign Affairs, went further than Yoshida and argued that, not only was contemporary Japan no longer a warrior nation, but that in fact, it never had been one, at least not in the Western sense. Drawing on the vast popular and academic literature on Japanese national character, known as *Nihonjinron,* they maintained that because Japan was an island nation that supposedly had been insulated from the bitter interethnic conflicts common to Europe and the Asian mainland, the Japanese people were peculiarly inept at power politics as practiced by other nations. Consequently, Japanese society was unusually consensual and supportive of harmony compared to other nations.[87]

While this view of Japanese culture was widely shared by Japanese of all political stripes, various groups drew profoundly different conclusions from it. Right-idealists and prodefense Centrists argued that Japan had to work hard to overcome the "handicap" of its peaceful nature, whereas the Left-idealists maintained that this cultural predisposition made it all the more imperative for Japan to seek the status of complete and unarmed neutrality.[88] Centrists like former MITI Vice Minister Amaya Naohiro stressed that Japan should concentrate on being a merchant nation and leave the task of military defense to the new samurai nation, the United States.[89]

Despite these differences, the fact that all major ideological groupings now viewed economic rather than martial prowess as a constitutive feature of Japanese national identity signified that change had taken place on a very basic level in the overall political-military culture. One reflection of this shift in national identity can be found in the government's 1980 adoption of the concept of "comprehensive security" (Sōgōanzenhoshō), a holistic redefinition of national security somewhat akin to the CDU's concept of Gesamtpolitik, which embraced not only military security, but also energy security, foreign aid, closer relations with Eastern and Southeast Asian nations, and even secure food supplies.[90]

The contents of the major Left, Right, and Center political-military subcultures in Japan and West Germany began to converge during the 1980s, a fact often overlooked by commentators in both countries because of the continued raucous character of their defense debates. Behind this trend was the readjustment of political elites to domestic and international realities. In order to regain power, the Christian Democrats were compelled to reconsider their principled opposition toward closer relations to the East and promise to carry forth the politics of their predecessors. Likewise, Japanese Right-idealists, after forty years of vainly trying to use the political-military threat of communism to stir a debate on nationalism, discovered they could achieve far better results by focusing on the political-economic threat posed by the United States.

To this extent, the steps leading to changes in Japan's and Germany's political-military cultures could be interpreted as a rational learning process. These adjustments, however, came slowly and were accompanied by considerable domestic controversy. The CDU spent nearly ten years in the opposition before it could bring itself to change its platform, while the Japanese Socialist Party had to endure more than four decades in the political wilderness.

Moreover, these shifts in policy were also accompanied by shifts in the ways the policies were legitimated and ultimately in the political actors' fundamental beliefs about reality. It was not enough for the Christian Democrats to accept *Ostpolitik* in order to enter into coalition with the Free Democrats; they also had to redefine the policy to show how it realized some of their basic values—namely, the preservation of the substance of the German nation and fostering human rights in East Germany. Similar arguments had been made by Kurt Kiesinger and others in 1966, but it took another fifteen years before the party was ready to accept such views. Likewise in Japan, the Right-idealists and Centrists embraced not only a new vision of the national mission, but they altered their view of Japanese history and the defining characteristics of the Japanese people in order to give their positions greater legitimacy.

There was one important exception to this trend toward the forging of a consensus—namely, the emergence of a more radical leftist subculture associated with the new social movements and the Green Party in the West Germany of the late 1970s. The Greens espoused a brand of Universal Pacifism that had its intellectual and organizational roots in the Central Europeanist subculture, yet they differed dramatically in their highly ambivalent, even hostile, relationship to the concept of a German, or any other kind of, nation-state. Whereas Central Europeanists like Willy Brandt and Egon Bahr continued to hope for the eventual reunification of the two Germanys, a loose coalition of political activists that we can label "Universal Pacifists" resisted this concept, feeling that the proper locus of political loyalty is either to the individual or small group, or to humankind as a whole. Thus, the classical German question, "What is the geographical locus of the nation?," is for the Universal Pacifists an irrelevant, even pernicious, issue. This crucial difference between the Universal Pacifists and the Central Europeanists was starkly revealed in 1989–1991, as the two groups came to starkly different evaluations of German reunification.[91]

On balance, however, the core norms and values of the different subgroups since 1960 have displayed significant continuity. Continuities outweighed the changes by a good margin, despite at least two major shifts in the international environment, and despite important changes in the domestic political systems of both countries. In general the Right continued to rally for a strong defense, the Left for a neutralist position between East and West, and the Center supported a continuation of present policies. These positions on defense were reinforced by a broad range of preferences on other, primarily domestic political issues, such as education, the economy, and definitions of national identity.

The Distribution of the Political-Military Cultures

Public Opinion

During the 1980s Western leaders and analysts became increasingly concerned with the state of public opinion in Germany and Japan.[92] In West Germany, mass demonstrations and the ferocious political and media campaigns against the INF deployments raised anxiety that the Federal Republic was in danger of succumbing to pacifist neutralism. Pointing to public opinion data showing a growing perception of Soviet military superiority and American recklessness, and a concomitant rise in the fear of war and threat from the East (as illustrated in Tables 5.2 and 5.3), many German and foreign observers concluded that the Federal Republic's defense and national security policies had entered into a legitimation crisis that would undermine the Western alliance.[93]

After 1985, the fear of war subsided to its pre-1980 level. As public opinion data showed, precisely the opposite fear emerged: that Soviet leader Mikhail S. Gorbachev was more popular among West Germans than either Reagan or Kohl, and that the Soviet Union was perceived as being as committed, or even more committed, to peace as the United States (see Table 5.4). Many American analysts expressed concern that it was not the threat of war, but rather the threat of peace, that could prove the greatest danger to the Western alliance.[94]

Table 5.2
Fear of War in West Germany: German Perceptions of the Danger
of War in Europe

	High Danger (%)	Low Danger (%)	Don't Know/No Answer (%)
1977	11	74	15
1979	9	73	18
1980	14	72	14
1984	26	58	17
1986	15	65	20

Source: Hans Rattinger, "The Bundeswehr and Public Opinion," in Stephen F. Szabo, ed., The Bundeswehr and Western Security (London: Macmillan Press, 1990), 98.

Table 5.3
German Perception of the Balance of Power: Who Is Stronger Militarily?

Year	NATO (%)	Warsaw Pact (%)	Equal (%)	Don't Know (%)
1977	19	28	40	14
1981	20	42	24	14
1982	25	32	27	16
1983	13	36	37	13
1986	20	25	13	13

Sources: Adapted from Berthold Meyer, *Der Bürger und seine Sicherheit: Zum Verhältnis von Sicherheitsstreben und Sicherheitspolitik* (Frankfurt/Main: Campus, Verlag, 1983), 228, table 4.1.2, for 1977 data; Friedrich-Ebert-Stiftung, *The Germans and America: Current Attitudes* (Bonn: Friedrich-Ebert-Stiftung, 1987), 30, for later data points.

Table 5.4
German Views of the Superpowers: Which Superpower Wants Peace for the World?

Year	Only U.S.A. (%)	Only U.S.S.R. (%)	Both (%)	Neither (%)	Don't Know (%)
1980	52	3	29	7	9
1981	33	4	31	14	17
1982	25	3	45	16	11
1983	20	2	47	14	17
1986	22	3	56	12	8

Source: Friedrich-Ebert-Stiftung, *The Germans and America: Current Attitudes* (Bonn: Friedrich-Ebert-Stiftung, 1987), 45

In Japan as well, there was growing fear that the country could be dragged into a war. During the early to mid-1980s though, the shifting public perceptions did not coalesce into the kind of mass protest movement that emerged in West Germany. This may be partly attributed to political factors—the lack of a rallying issue comparable in its symbolic impact to the INF deployments or the absence of an institutional base comparable to the peace research centers created in West Germany—and partly to sociopolitical ones, such as the absence of a new class milieu that had given birth to the social-activist movements in Western Europe. As in the Federal Republic there was a decline in popular confidence in the United States, but the United States continued to be the foreign nation for which the Japanese expressed the greatest affinity.[95] According to one widely cited 1987 poll taken of Japanese junior high school students, only 38 percent thought that Japan might be involved in a war in the future. But more students thought that in the event of war the opponent would be the United States (49 percent) than thought it would be the Soviet Union (41 percent).[96] Results of other opinion polls on the danger of war are reported in Table 5.5. In addition, while Germans remained confident that the United States would come to West Germany's aid in the event of a Soviet attack, Japanese confidence in the American commitment appeared much lower.[97]

Table 5.5
Is There a Danger That Japan Will Be Dragged into a War?

Year	There Is a Danger (%)	Some Danger (%)	No Danger (%)	Don't Know/Other (%)
1975	14.9	28.7	34.3	22.1
1978	20.6	23.2	36.4	19.8
1981	28.0	32.2	21.3	18.5
1984	30.0	30.9	23.8	15.3
1988	21.5	32.1	31.3	15.1

Source: Adapted from Etō Shinkichi and Yamamoto Yoshinobu, *Sōgōampo to Mirai no Sentaku* (Tokyo: Kodansha, 1991), 441.

Despite growing fear of war and increased distrust of the United States, there was remarkably little observable change in West German and Japanese attitudes toward their central defense institutions. In both countries public opinion showed continued support for the alliance and defense structures. Tables 5.6, 5.7, 5.8, and 5.9 are examples of these findings. While in West Germany there was some support for a somewhat more independent European-led approach to de-

Table 5.6
German Attitudes toward NATO: Is NATO Essential to European Security?

Year	Essential (%)	Not Essential (%)	Don't Know (%)
1977	79	7	14
1978	84	5	11
1980	88	8	4
1981	62	20	20
1982	66	18	16
1983	86	12	2
1984	87	10	3
1987	70	15	15

Source: Richard Eichenberg, *Public Opinion and National Security in Western Europe* (Ithaca, N.Y.: Cornell University Press, 1989), 124.

Table 5.7
German Views of How to Provide for National Security

Date	NATO as It Now Stands	Eur. Command Allied to USA	Indep. Eur. Command	Independent Defense Effort	Accommodate Soviets	Don't Know
April 1979	55	—	11	8	—	17
March 1980	50	27	5	3	2	14
April 1980	47	19	9	4	4	17
Oct. 1980	57	18	3	10	2	11
Dec. 1982	60	22	8	2	4	4
Jan. 1987	54	—	—	25	—	2
Nov. 1987	45	28	6	11	—	10

Note: Interviewees were handed a card with a list of possible responses. The question reads: Which one of the following courses listed on the card seems to you the best way to provide for the security of our country?

*The full response for the "independent national defense" category read "rely on our own nation's defense forces without belonging in any military alliance." In 1979, this was changed to "do not participate in any alliance—take a completely neutral position." In 1980, this response was combined with an additional response, "withdraw our military forces from NATO, but otherwise remain in NATO for things such as policy consultation."

Source: Richard Eichenberg, *Public Opinion and National Security in Western Europe* (Ithaca, N.Y.: Cornell University Press, 1989), 128–129.

Table 5.8
Japanese Views of How to Provide for National Security

Year	Continue to Rely on the MST/SDF (%)	Quit MST and Reduce the SDF (%)	Defend by Japan's Power Alone (%)	Don't Know (%)
1978	61.1	8.2	5.0	24.9
1981	64.6	6.1	7.6	20.8
1984	69.2	5.0	6.8	17.9
1988	67.4	5.9	7.2	18.3

Source: Adapted from Etō Shinkichi and Yamamoto Yoshinobu, *Sōgōampo to Mirai no Sentaku* (Tokyo: Kodansha, 1991), 446.

Table 5.9
Japanese Views of the Alliance

Year	Useful (%)	On Balance Useful (%)	On Balance Not Useful (%)	Not Useful (%)	Don't Know (%)
1977	63	13	24		
1978	66	12	22		
1981	29.7 (65.8)	36.1	8.3 (12.7)	4.4	21.5
1984	33.9 (71.4)	37.5	6.5 (10.4)	3.9	18.2
1988	29.7 (68.8)	39.1	8.8 (12.5)	3.7	18.7

Note: Respondents were asked: Presently, Japan and the United States are tied together by the Mutual Security Treaty. Do you think that this treaty is useful or not useful?
Source: Asagumo Shimbunsha, *Bōei Handobukku* (Tokyo: Asagumo Shimbunsha, 1993), 519, and (1987), 498.

fense, overwhelming majorities expressed a preference for some sort of multi-lateral approach to security that included the United States (one of the core elements of the Atlanticist political-military culture) over any kind of more independent strategy, be it of the conservative Europeanist variety or the sort advocated by the left-wing Central Europeanists. Likewise, a large majority of Japanese supported the Mutual Security Treaty system and the Self-Defense Forces. Support for either the Right-idealist option of independent defense or the Left-idealist option of unarmed neutrality remained minimal.

The continued support for the security alliances, however, did not translate into popular favor for increased defense expenditures. As was true in most allied nations, German and Japanese support for increased defense expenditures was minimal, and large pluralities, if not even majorities, preferred keeping expenditures at current levels, as shown in Tables 5.10 and 5.11. Particularly in Japan, large majorities supported the various brakes *(hadome)* on defense, including the 1 percent of GNP barrier on defense spending (54 percent even after the barrier had been broken), the three non-nuclear principles (78 percent), and the restrictions on weapons exports (70 percent).[98] Moreover, popular support for the constitution remained high, well over 80 percent, and there was some indication that the public no longer thought constitutional revision a serious issue.[99] In West Germany, the question of the Bundeswehr's playing a role outside the NATO area received little support, and there was serious criticism of even allowing the United States to use bases in West Germany to launch a punitive strike against Libya in 1987.

In the second half of the 1980s, when asked to specify why they thought their existing military structures were useful, surprisingly large percentages of West Germans and Japanese gave responses that had little to do with military security. According to a 1988 study, the most frequently cited reason the Mutual Security Treaty was thought to be important was for stabilization of U.S.-Japanese relations (20 percent), followed by economic prosperity (9 percent) and the stability of East Asia (9 percent). The view that it was useful for the defense of Japan came only fourth (8 percent).[100] Likewise in the Federal Republic, evidence suggests that most West Germans supported the alliance for its political function of integrating West Germany into the West rather than solely for its military task of deterring aggression.[101]

As the polls cited have shown, public opinion data up to the end of the Cold War revealed a picture of increasing German and Japanese discomfort with U.S. policies and a decreasing belief in its military efficacy (early 1980s) or usefulness

Table 5.10
Japanese Views of Defense Spending

Year	Increase (%)	Maintain at Present Level (%)	Decrease (%)	Don't Know (%)
1978	20	48	10	22
1981	20.1	43.7	15	17.6
1984	14.2	54.1	17.7	14
1988	11.2	58	19.2	11.7

Note: Respondents were presented with a card showing Japanese defense expenditures compared to those of other countries. They were then asked: To defend Japan's peace and security, should defense expenditures be increased, maintained at the same level, or decreased?
Source: Asagumo Shimbunsha, *Bōei Handobukku* (Tokyo: Asagumo Shimbunsha, 1993), 517, and (1987), 490.

Table 5.11
German Views of Defense Spending

Year	Increase (%)	Keep the Same (%)	Decrease (%)	Don't Know (%)
1978	11	58	27	4
1981	14	52	34	1
1984	9	54	38	1
1987	6	47	45	2

Note: Respondents were asked: Should defense spending be decreased, kept the same, or increased?
Source: Richard Eichenberg, *Public Opinion and National Security in Western Europe* (Ithaca, N.Y.: Cornell University Press, 1989), 161–162.

(late 1980s). At the same time, they also showed a relatively small decline in support for Japan's and Germany's basic security institutions, which relied overwhelmingly upon the United States. The explanation of this apparent paradox is that, in the public mind, the technical-military rationales for the existence of the German and Japanese defense institutions did not weigh as heavily as the symbolic political ones. In the by-then firmly established political-military cultures of Japan and West Germany, the international alliances and the limited roles of the armed forces had become linked with a new political identity—in the German case based upon the vision of Germany as part of a larger Western community, and in the Japanese case on the image of Japan as a merchant nation seeking to foster international harmony while refraining from the pursuit of military power. By the 1980s these identities had taken a strong hold on the public mind and refused to be budged by political and economic tensions, changes in the balance of power, or fluctuations in the perception of threat.

Elite Opinion

During the 1980s the earlier shift of elite opinion toward the center halted, even as the differences between the ideological groupings were blurred by the convergence in the contents of their belief systems. While on balance the distribution of subcultures continued to favor centrist positions, distinct shifts occurred in either nation—to the right in Japan, and to the left in Germany. These changes were most apparent in the media and among the intelligentsia which, as in the 1950s, became embroiled in fierce public debates over defense and national security.

JAPAN

In Japan there was a remarkable upsurge in public debate over defense and national security in both the elite and the popular press.[102] Whereas until the late 1970s the main battle lines had been drawn between Left-idealists and Centrists, around 1980 the central debate became one between Centrists and Right-idealists.[103] The opening shot in this new ideological struggle came with the publication of Shimizu Ikutarō's *Nihon yo, kokka o tare!: Kakku no Sentaku (Japan Be a Nation! The Nuclear Option),* a national best-seller that perfectly crystallized the classic themes of postwar Right-idealism in calling for the revision of Article 9, increased veneration of the emperor, dissolution of the Mutual Security Treaty, and the acquisition of nuclear weapons.[104] Following Shimizu's lead, a small cadre of Right-idealist writers—including such figures as Etō Jun, Tetsuya Kataoka, Nakagawa Yasuhiro, and Miyoshi Osamu—attracted national attention.[105]

Alarmed by the Right-idealists' new ability to find an audience, the same Centrist intellectuals who had spent the 1960s and 1970s criticizing the anti-American idealism of the Left found themselves in a bitter, often polemical struggle with the anti-Americanism of the Right. Centrist intellectuals such as Inoki

Masamichi, Kosaka Masataka, and Nagai Yonosuke led the counteroffensive against the Right-idealists, while figures such as Satō Seizaburō and Okazaki Hisahiko, though more sympathetic to the Right-idealists, were equally critical of their anti-Americanism and exaggerated nationalist rhetoric.[106] Left-idealist intellectuals such as Sakamoto Yoshikazu and Kobayashi Naoki remained active, but their contributions no longer defined the defense debate as they had earlier. Trends in the media helped reinforce this rightward shift as the formerly left-of-center *Yomiuri* became markedly prodefense and the influential opinion journal *Bungeishunjū* increasingly promoted the work of Right-idealist writers.[107]

It is difficult to ascertain which subculture emerged as the winner in these debates. Clearly the Right-idealists had gained new legitimacy and national prominence. At the same time, they did not replace Centrists like Inoki Masamichi and Kosaka Masataka as leading advisors to the government, nor did they create influential defense-policy think tanks comparable to the West German peace research centers or the new Japanese Centrist think tanks that were founded during the same period.[108] After the mid-1980s the Right-idealists' output of articles and opinion pieces on defense dropped precipitously, as this group focused on the economic and trade fronts. The Left-idealists were even less successful in making headway, and by the second half of the 1980s the Centrists occupied the high ground of popular opinion almost by default.

WEST GERMANY

In West Germany, the course of events was a mirror image of that in Japan. Whereas in Japan it had been the prodefense Right that sparked the new defense debate, in the Federal Republic the initial impetus came from the Left. Supported by a network of peace research institutes and academic centers established in the 1960 and 1970s, a new generation of left-wing intellectuals provided the ammunition for a reinvigorated peace movement that opposed the neutron bomb and the INF missile deployments. At the forefront of the movement were military experts such as Gerd Bastian, Hans Günter Brauch, André Guhas, Dieter Lutz, Alfred Mechtersheimer, and Dieter Senghaas, as well as such prominent literary figures as Günter Grass, Heinrich Böll, and Siegfried Lenz. Additional support came from many radical young (especially Protestant) Christian groups and major weekly journals, including *Die Zeit, Der Spiegel,* and *Stern.*[109]

The peace movement's challenge to German security policy triggered what may be described as an intellectual counter-reformation on the right. Some of

Kohl's chief advisors, in particular the noted historian Michael Stürmer, argued that the peace movement embodied destructive nationalistic forces which, if left unchecked, could undermine domestic support for West Germany's anchorage in the West. To counter this dangerous current, they believed, West Germans needed to develop a healthy sense of patriotism, one which had come to terms with Germany's grim past and was no longer paralyzed in the security sphere by an overpowering sense of guilt.[110]

This conservative revisionism provoked savage counterattacks from liberal German scholars such as the philosopher Jürgen Habermas and the historian Wolfgang J. Mommsen, who saw it as one manifestation of a larger campaign to renationalize West Germany and reverse liberal policies in a broad spectrum of areas, including national defense and *Ostpolitik*.[111] Between these two camps were many intellectuals who, like the historian Hans Peter Schwarz and the political scientist Arnulf Baring, while wary of the thesis that Germany needed a new patriotism, were also critical of the SPD and the peace movement's idealism.[112]

As in the case of Japan, it is difficult to identify any winners or losers in this ideological struggle. On the whole, the right-wing position associated with the revisionist historians appeared to be held by a minority within the larger intellectual community. At the same time, the Central Europeanism and Universal Pacifism associated with the peace movement failed to achieve intellectual hegemony over defense thinking in Germany. While it made inroads among intellectuals and academics during this period, it also alienated many former Social Democratic intellectuals who in the 1960s and 1970s had been supporters of *Ostpolitik* and arms control.

Less visible but nonetheless significant shifts on defense issues can be detected among German and Japanese labor and business leaders as well. During the 1970s, Japan's leading federation of private unions, Dōmei (many of whose members worked in firms engaged in defense production), strongly supported the government's increased defense efforts.[113] Further moderating pressures developed with the formation in 1987 of the Private-Sector Japanese Federation of Trade Unions (Rengō), which joined Dōmei with the public-sector federation, Sōhyō, to form a single giant organization with 7.7 million members. The new Rengō leadership adopted a generally moderate, nonideological stance on defense issues that differed sharply from the Left-idealism of the earlier generation of labor leaders, particularly in the public-sector unions.[114]

During the 1980s Japanese business leaders exhibited a growing interest in defense, even though weapons procurement continued to represent only an infinitesimal fraction of Japan's overall industrial production (0.36 percent in 1980; 0.54 percent in 1989). No major Japanese firm relied on military contracts for more than 20 percent of its total business.[115] This increased interest in defense was initially sparked by a desire among some business leaders to use weapons exports as a means of currying favor with oil-exporting countries.[116] Subsequently, the prospect of gaining access to advanced American technology through joint research and development projects—legalized by the 1983 Reagan-Nakasone agreement that liberalized the export of military technology—attracted considerable interest among such giant Japanese defense contractors as Mitsubishi Heavy Industries and Kawasaki.[117] Opposition from mainstream business leadership soon stifled the campaign to use weapons export as a tool of diplomacy on the grounds that such a policy would cause problems in Japan's relations with the United States and could ultimately draw Japan into foreign conflicts.[118]

Heightened U.S.-Japanese trade tensions soon spilled over into the defense area, disrupting joint development ventures like the FSX fighter aircraft and dampening business enthusiasm for such projects.[119] Although the FSX and other projects survived, by the second half of the 1980s Japanese interest in defense production had cooled considerably and the Japanese government and Keidanren took steps to increase Japan's indigenous defense R&D capacity.[120] Most Centrist business and government leaders had little interest in exploring increased Japanese defense production, especially as they believed that large-scale defense spending and the orientation of research toward defense was a major factor in the relative decline of American economic competitiveness.[121] To put it simply, having succeeded so magnificently in global markets by concentrating exclusively on civilian production, why should Japan's business leadership change a winning formula?

In West Germany, on the other hand, pressures from business and labor unions tended to run in the opposite direction. During the early 1980s in particular, the trade union movement was racked by much the same type of internal dissension that affected the SPD, as the Atlanticist mainstream and member unions in arms-producing industries resisted the efforts of more radical unions to openly side with the peace movement. Although the leadership was compelled to publicly oppose the stationing of INF missiles, it managed to resist pressures to declare a general strike.[122] Nonetheless, West German political leaders constantly had to reckon with the possibility that the unions might rally again to pacifist causes if given a new focal point.

Cultures of Antimilitarism

For West German industry, weapons remained a small, if highly profitable, segment of its overall business, with especially high concentrations in aeronautics and the declining shipbuilding sector.[123] Certain aspects of the defense business made it a target of intense criticism, in particular with respect to arms exports to the Third World and German participation in SDI.[124]

Overall, in an age of declining defense budgets and concomitant defense-industry consolidation, the German business community tried to stay out of the limelight and was not the source of any significant defense proposals.[125] Only on the issue of straight sanctions on Eastern Europe did business leaders play an active role in politics, and then they joined defenders of *Ostpolitik* in successfully resisting American pressures to block the construction of a gas pipeline from the Soviet Union.[126]

As has been shown, although both West Germany and Japan experienced elite-based challenges to the Atlanticist and Centrist consensuses that had developed during the 1960s and 1970s, the distribution of political-military subcultures failed to shift decisively. To be sure, the impact of Universal Pacifism on the West German intellectual and media scenes was notable, yet it provoked countermovements on the right and was unable to rally much support beyond the media and academia. A confluence of international trends (the reintensification of the Cold War) and domestic events (generational change and the leadership struggle within the SPD) created the impression that the strategy of accommodation, the vital twin to deterrence in the context of West German political-military culture, was in danger. Once the Kohl government demonstrated its continued commitment to accommodation, however, the peace movement was defanged even before Gorbachev and the new détente finished it off.[127]

In Japan, Right-idealism enjoyed something of a revival as the new Cold War and hard-line Japanese governments gave it a degree of intellectual credibility that had been denied to it until then. Nonetheless, Left-idealism remained the dominant paradigm on Japanese campuses, while Centrist scholars and pundits were able to dominate the debate outside of academe. Unable to rally popular support on a promilitary message, after the mid-1980s the Right-idealists were compelled to find other issues to fan the flames of nationalism. Other segments of the Japanese elite showed few signs of significantly shifting in favor of a more independent stance on defense and, if anything, showed increased willingness to support the Centrist position of relying on the United States to provide military security.

Political Parties

In late 1970s and 1980s the political party systems of the Federal Republic and Japan underwent shifts in the distribution of subcultures, similar to the changes that had occurred in other elite sectors. In both nations challenges to the Atlanticist and Centrist consensuses of the 1960s and 1970s emerged. In the West German case the challenge came from the Left. In Japan the challenge was posed by the Right. These challenges were successfully resisted, although only after much controversy and, in the West German case at least, serious political upheaval.

JAPAN

In Japan, an apparent upsurge in Right-idealist ideology in the LDP was spurred by the growing Soviet threat, competition for the support of the party's right wing by rival conservative politicians, and growing media interest in the defense issue.[128] Increased defense spending also attracted interest among politicians, prompting two senior LDP leaders, Kanemaru Shin and Mihara Asao, to organize a so-called policy tribe *(zoku)* dedicated to promotion of the interests of the armed forces and the defense industry in return for political favors.[129] Defense thus took on the aura of an emerging area in which an ambitious politician could make a mark for himself and gain access to increased funding and influence.

These factors produced a dramatic increase in the number of openly prodefense LDP members.[130] The strongly conservative Fukuda and Nakasone prime ministerships of 1976–1978 and 1982–1987 contributed to this phenomenon. Both administrations sought to expand Japan's defense role and to foster a heightened "defense consciousness" through such measures as the expanded usage of the Japanese flag, trips to the Yasukuni shrine, and the increased use of nationalist-martial imagery in textbooks.

Much of this increase in Right-idealism, however, was more apparent than real. It was not so much the case that the number of Right-idealists increased during this period, but rather that the changed political and media environments encouraged them to be more open about their views. By the same token, while the perception of a growing Soviet threat and American pressures for greater burden sharing led to an increase in the number of LDP members in favor of greater defense expenditures and closer security cooperation with the

United States, the majority of these were Centrists interested in doing the minimum necessary to maintain their security relations with the United States rather than Right-idealists who saw a greater Japanese security role as a matter of national pride.

Likewise, while there were perhaps as many as one hundred nominal members on the LDP's defense committees, the number of those active in defense policy making was far smaller, perhaps only seventeen to eighteen.[131] Defense never accounted for more than 6.53 percent of total government expenditures during the decade, and it remained the conventional wisdom among politicians of all stripes that there was little electoral advantage to be gained from taking a strong stance on defense *(Bōei wa Hyō ni tsugaranai*—There are no votes in defense). Consequently, the defense issue was unable to generate the kind of lasting interest that other issues such as agriculture or construction did.[132]

Perhaps the most important evidence of the continued dominance of the Centrist viewpoint within the LDP is the resistance that invariably developed within the party whenever policies were proposed that were identified with a Right-idealist agenda. In 1978, support for the Emergency Laws legislation evaporated after Kurisu raised the issue of increased independence for the armed forces and Fukuda was perceived as seeking to revive nationalism. In 1985, Nakasone was stymied for similar reasons on his first attempt to break the 1 percent barrier. Likewise, in 1987, the dispatch of minesweepers to support U.S. naval operations in the Persian Gulf was blocked for fear that such a move could put Japan back on the slippery slope to entanglement in foreign military adventures. In sum, the LDP had become more active on defense during the 1980s, but it remained a very Centrist sort of defense activism, one which deepened the Japanese security partnership with the United States instead of seeking to develop a more independent Japanese military posture.

In the meantime the Japanese opposition parties continued to slowly drift toward greater acceptance of the Centrist approach to defense. Leading the way was the Democratic Socialist Party, which during the 1980s supported virtually every one of the government's defense initiatives, including increased military spending, defense of the sea-lanes, and breaking the 1 percent barrier.[133] Close behind the DSP was Kōmeitō, although it was more selective in its support of government policies.[134]

Behind the two middle-of-the road parties' steady shift to the right were the same factors that had inclined them toward moderation in the 1970s: increased popular acceptance for Centrist defense policies; the prospect of forming a coalition with the LDP; and the payments they reportedly received for cooperating with the government.[135] At the same time, countervailing pressures were exerted by the two parties' need to distinguish themselves from the LDP and by the continued prospect of forming a coalition government with the JSP. In addition, Kōmeitō was hampered by strong pacifist sentiments within some of its chief support groups, especially the Housewives Association.[136]

The Socialist Party, spurred on by its right wing, continued its glacial progress toward increased acceptance of Japan's current defense and security policies. The strongly ideological left wing of the JSP, however, while willing to abandon the party's marxist rhetoric and adopt more mainstream positions on domestic issues, resisted all efforts to moderate the platform on defense, threatening on at least one occasion to split the party over proposals that deviated too sharply from their Left-idealist principles. Although as many as two-thirds of the Socialist Diet members might have supported more moderation on defense, the farthest the JSP would go was to suggest that a Socialist-led government would not insist on an immediate abolition of the SDF and the Mutual Security Treaty, but would phase them out slowly.[137]

The JSP continued to oppose the government on virtually every piece of national security legislation, the only variation being in the degree to which that opposition manifested itself. The party paid a high price for its intransigence, however. Increasingly the public began to view the JSP as mired in anachronistic thinking, and the defense issue became a major stumbling block in negotiations with the other opposition parties and social groups in attempts to form an alternative coalition to the LDP.[138]

As a result of the opposition parties' inability to provide a viable alternative to continued LDP rule, and because of the LDP's ability to transform itself into a highly successful catchall party whose appeal reached beyond its traditional social bases of support, the LDP managed to reverse its long electoral decline of the 1960s and 1970s and hold firmly onto power in the 1980s. By the end of the decade the Left-idealist challenge to Centrism appeared increasingly impotent.

WEST GERMANY

In West Germany the most significant political event of this period was the emergence of the Green Party, which in 1983 broke into the Bundestag with 5.6 percent of the vote. Fiercely opposed to NATO and nuclear deterrence strategy, the Greens were the politically organized expression of Universal Pacifism.[139] Although the Greens were divided by contending factions, the pragmatic *Realos* and the idealistic *Fundis,* throughout the decade the party opposed government policy at every turn. Even the dramatic arms control proposal offered by Reagan at his 1987 meeting with Gorbachev at Reykjavik appeared inadequate in their eyes because the fundamental logic of deterrence had not been rejected.[140]

The emergence of the Greens had a devastating impact on the SPD's frail consensus in favor of an Atlanticist approach to defense and national security. For the first time in the history of the Federal Republic, there was a serious electoral alternative to the left of the SPD, leading Central Europeanists such as Willy Brandt and Egon Bahr to argue that the SPD should move to the left on security issues in order to win back the youthful support that the party had lost to the Greens.[141]

At the same time a new generation of SPD leaders came to the fore, such as Oskar Lafontaine, Erhard Eppler, and Karsten Voigt, who came out of the same social milieu as the Greens and who were highly sympathetic to the Universal Pacifist point of view.[142] The influx of new middle-class party members with university degrees reinforced this shift in leadership and took the party further away from its blue-collar, trade union roots.[143] Soon the Atlanticists Helmut Schmidt and Defense Minister Hans Apel found themselves completely isolated within the party, a situation that undermined the government's foreign policy and contributed greatly to the demise of the coalition with the Free Democrats.

Once the SPD was forced out of power, the trend toward a merger of Central Europeanism and Universal Pacifism quickly accelerated. Bahr and others developed new security concepts calling for a denuclearization of West German defense and the creation of purely defensive forces equipped with antitank weapons. Although the party urged both superpowers to disarm, it identified nuclear weapons and U.S. Reagan-era paranoia as greater threats to German security than the presence of massive Soviet forces in Eastern Europe.[144] The SPD did not convert completely to Universal Pacifism, however, and it continued to reject calls from more left-wing Social Democrats for exiting NATO and unilateral disarmament.[145] Nor did the SPD share the Greens' distrust of European integration, but instead argued that a united Europe would be less susceptible to U.S. pressures and could independently pursue a policy of peaceful diplomacy vis-à-vis the Soviet Union.[146]

This shift in SPD thinking signaled a resurrection of the old notion of Germany as a bridge between East and West that had enjoyed wide currency in the 1950s, only this time the Central Europeanists recognized that Germany by itself was too small to play such a role and needed to pool its strength with other European nations. Thus, even as the SPD abandoned its Atlanticist approach to defense, it reformulated its traditional Central Europeanism in a way that brought the party closer to the new West German political-military culture's core value of multilateralism.

The Free Democratic Party for its part continued to play the balancing role in German politics, leaning to the right during the early 1980s when its Social Democratic partners shifted too far to the left and after 1983 leaning to the left when the Christian Democrats moved to the right. While there continued to be some diversity of opinion within the party, the FDP leadership was compelled by the party's fragile electoral fortunes to pay close attention to public opinion and opt for positions that were likely to meet with broad public approval. Lacking a large electoral base like the two Volksparteien, or a highly committed core constituency like the Greens, the Free Democrats constantly faced political oblivion because of a peculiarity of the German electoral law, which stipulates that a party must get at least 5 percent of the popular vote if it is to be granted representation in the Bundestag.

As a result, FDP leaders, regardless of their own personal beliefs, were compelled to find ways of distinguishing themselves from their large Social Democratic or Christian Democratic coalition partners. When the CDU was in power the FDP regularly adopted more liberal positions on social and foreign policy. When in partnership with the SPD, the FDP would emphasize more conservative economic and defense policies. Consequently, at different times the FDP appeared to pursue quite different ideological agendas.

In 1983, after suppressing those within the party sympathetic to the peace movement, the FDP underlined its Atlanticist convictions when it abandoned the coalition with the Social Democrats.[147] Conversely, in the mid-1980s Genscher's staunch support of continued *Ostpolitik* and détente made him appear Central Europeanist and won him the opprobrium of many, especially in the American foreign policy establishment, who favored a harder line vis-à-vis the Soviet Union. Domestically, however, this stance paid off handsomely, contributing to the FDP's recovery from its 1983 electoral setbacks, especially among younger voters.[148] At times, Genscher and his colleagues even appeared Europeanist, advocating a stronger European pillar in NATO, perhaps by revitalizing the moribund WEU, and calling for the promotion of European patriotism.[149]

This ideological flexibility made the Free Democrats appear opportunistic. At the same time, it allowed the party to occupy the political center and exercise an influence over West German foreign policy totally out of proportion to its modest size. In the 1980s the FDP became the purest expression of West Germany's new culture of antimilitarism and, as the holder of the balance of power in the party system, its strongest guarantor.

The CDU/CSU continued to be dominated by its Atlanticist wing, led by Chancellor Helmut Kohl, Volker Rühe, and Manfred Wörner. The party also contained a powerful Europeanist contingent under Alfred Dregger, Jürgen Todenhöfer, and the CSU.[150] These two groups cooperated reasonably well during the first few years of the coalition, but tensions appeared over the question of how to respond to Gorbachev. In particular, the concessions offered in 1987 by Reagan at the Reykjavik summit outraged Dregger, who demanded that greater respect be paid to German strategic and national interests. At Dregger's behest, CDU Deputy Wilhelm Friedman even produced a proposal warning that the Federal Republic might renationalize its defense policies if the Western allies refused to link disarmament with German reunification.[151]

Such stirrings were quickly squelched by Kohl and Rühe, but nationalist pressures were reinforced by developments external to the party—especially by a new wave of small, far right-wing parties—and had an important impact on the leadership's thinking.[152] Mindful of the disastrous consequences of the Atlanticist-Gaullist struggle of the 1960s, and having just witnessed how the splintering of the Left had destroyed the Schmidt government, Kohl sought to contain the forces of nationalism in a variety of ways: through the pursuit of *Ostpolitik;* through symbolic gestures such as his visit to Bitburg—designed to foster a healthy West German nationalism; and through a new emphasis on the creation of a united Europe. The Atlanticists, however, were painfully aware that the French and the British were as little prepared to form a genuine European defense union in the 1980s as they had been in the 1950s and 1960s.[153] Consequently, Kohl and his allies in the party sought to ride two horses at the same time, supporting increased European integration and cooperation in defense and national security, while at the same time preserving the vital link to the United States.

Thus, whereas Japan's political parties had shifted to the right during the 1980s, in West Germany the trend was toward increased polarization, with the Left split between Universal Pacifism and Central Europeanism and the Right faced with a potential split between Europeanism and Atlanticism. As in Japan, however, the international environment and the distribution of ideological groupings favored the continued dominance of the moderate, centrist positions on defense and national security that had guided West German foreign policy for the past four decades, and the pro-Atlanticist parties maintained a modest, but decisive electoral advantage (over 53 percent).

6

Opting for Continuity: Germany and Japan after the Cold War

THE FALL OF THE BERLIN WALL in November 1989 ushered in a new era in international relations. The unexpectedly rapid collapse of communism, the reunification of Germany, and the end of U.S.-Soviet rivalry came as a shock to Germany and Japan and thrust both into a radically different international security environment. The two countries were not only presented with new opportunities for independent action but also came under pressure to assume new roles in world affairs. Each nation had to decide whether to support the emergent new international order spearheaded by the United States or, alternatively, to carve out their own spheres of influence and seek the status of a regional hegemony.

In the end they did neither. Almost by default, they fell back upon the same policies and patterns of behavior they had followed for the past forty years. While the end of the Cold War triggered major shifts in the domestic political environments of both countries—most notably the collapse of LDP rule in Japan and the political turmoil and anti-immigrant violence associated with reunification in Germany—their national security policies and the debates surrounding them did not change significantly. To be sure, events like the Persian Gulf War forced the Germans and the Japanese to modify some of their views and to adopt somewhat less parochial approaches to national security. Nonetheless, the changes that were made were largely incremental in character and served to confirm the antimilitaristic core values that had become part and parcel of the political-military cultures of post–World War II Germany and Japan.

The Immediate Reaction to the End of the Cold War

Germany

The impact of the end of the Cold War was particularly noticeable in Germany. The Soviet military threat that had hovered unremittingly for more than forty years faded, and by 1989 the end of the partition of the nation was in sight at long last.[1] The magnitude of these changes practically begged for an immediate and fundamental revision of postwar German policies on defense and national security. Many German leaders, including Hans Dieter Genscher and Egon Bahr, believed such a revision was both necessary and desirable if reunification was to be achieved. They argued that the end of the old superpower rivalry made the dissolution of the Cold War alliance system inevitable and advocated that it be replaced with a broader European security structure based on the Conference on Security and Cooperation in Europe (CSCE).[2]

Germany's neighbors feared that a reunited Germany might break loose from its Cold War moorings in NATO and the European Economic Community (EEC) and adopt a more independent, nationalistic approach to foreign policy. So great were these fears that the prime ministers of France and Great Britain, François Mitterand and Margaret Thatcher, initially sought to slow down the reunification process, even to stop it altogether. Moreover, there were numerous indications that France and Britain contemplated recreating the old pre–World War II balance-of-power system to contain the suddenly much stronger unified German state.[3]

Rather than exploiting the opportunity to create a more independent Germany—either as a classic great power or as a lightly armed neutral nation—the Kohl government embarked on a course of action which over the next year and a half would reconfirm virtually all of the main features of post–World War II West German national security policy in the areas of alliance politics, military doctrine, and civil-military relations. Mindful of his neighbors' misgivings about a reunified Germany, Kohl adopted exactly the opposite approach. Instead of going it alone, the Kohl government sought to strengthen and deepen the complex web of international institutions that had anchored West Germany in the Western alliance for the past forty years and took initiatives to extend it to cover the newly unified German state. Frequently quoting Thomas Mann's famous dictum that what was needed was to Europeanize Germany rather than to Germanize Europe, West German leaders insisted that unification made an acceleration of the European integration process necessary.[4]

Following the extraordinary EEC summit of April 1990, Kohl and Mitterand set in motion the diplomatic process leading to the signing of the December Treaty of Maastricht. Under the terms of the treaty, the EEC was given broad new powers and the member nations committed themselves, albeit in vague terms, to the "framing of a common foreign policy, which might in time lead to a common defense." At the same time, the European leaders agreed to revive the Western European Union (WEU) and turn it into the military arm of the EEC. Simultaneously they enjoined the WEU to collaborate more closely with NATO.

To reach this agreement, Germany was compelled to make concessions on a wide range of issues. The most important of these was its offer to sacrifice the German Mark—the most potent symbol of postwar West German economic prowess—in order to create a common European currency. In so doing Chancellor Kohl provoked powerful domestic political resistance—from the Bundesbank, from his coalition partners in the FDP, as well as from segments of the media. Despite the opposition, he forged ahead in the conviction that failure to strengthen the EEC might trigger a disintegration of the postwar order in Europe. He held that this would leave Germany once again isolated and vulnerable in the center of the European continent.[5]

Kohl also insisted that Germany remain in NATO, despite indications that the Soviet Union might refuse to allow unification to take place if Germany were to do so. Arguing against Foreign Minister Genscher and others, Kohl maintained that residual security threats in Europe required the ongoing presence of the Western alliance.[6] At the same time, in keeping with the well-established German dual-track approach of combining reassurance with deterrence, Kohl convinced Gorbachev to permit a united Germany to remain in NATO by offering various incentives and guarantees: He reaffirmed Adenauer's pledge that Germany would not acquire weapons of mass destruction; he agreed to reduce the size of the German armed forces to 370,000 by 1994; he agreed to accept the loss of Germany's Eastern territories beyond the Oder-Neisse line; he promised that no foreign (including non-German NATO) troops would be stationed on the territory of the former GDR; and he offered to take the lead in organizing the flow of aid to the Soviet Union, beginning with $8.4 billion to help pay for the relocation of the more than 300,000 Soviet troops stationed in East Germany.[7]

Germany also agreed to deepen its military integration into NATO. At the London NATO summit in July 1990 new emphasis was placed on the creation of multinational units, especially among combat-ready, rapid-reaction forces. While a number of factors motivated this policy, the desire to further contain German military power was a key element.[8] Germany also took a leading role in a redefinition of NATO's military doctrine designed to further reassure the Soviet Union by placing new emphasis on political cooperation with Eastern Europe and defining the alliance's primary mission as political rather than military in nature.[9]

Finally, the German government reaffirmed its commitment to Innere Führung and the universal male conscription system, even though many commentators suggested that the system was a Cold War anachronism and that Germany no longer needed a large standing conventional army with military reserves. Public opinion surveys at the time indicated that a majority of Germans would have welcomed the abolition of the highly unpopular military service, while the number of those who applied for conscientious objector status soared. Despite these pressures, the political elite preferred to continue some form of national service, including a strong military component, as a means of integrating the armed forces into civilian society and as a way of instilling an ethic of national service in the broader population.[10]

Japan

The end of the Cold War had less of an immediate impact on Japan than on Germany. Nonetheless, the Japanese, too, were faced with a dramatically changed international environment.

In certain respects Japan had a greater range of choice available to it than Germany, which was preoccupied with the reunification process and felt tightly constrained by intense pressures from its European neighbors in the East and the West. The threat of American military withdrawal loomed even larger in East Asia than in Europe, as reflected by the closing of American bases in the Philippines. Moreover, while the forces of liberalism and democracy appeared ascendant in Europe, authoritarian and potentially hostile regimes remained the norm in Asia. Japan was also considerably larger in population and more powerful economically than even a united Germany. If it so desired, Japan could have quickly created a formidable military establishment.[11] Given this environment, Japan arguably had a strong incentive to assume a more activist stance on national security either by increasing its independent defense ability or by reinforcing and perhaps expanding its security arrangement with the United States.

A domestic political consensus for a more activist defense policy, however, was entirely lacking. Instead, Centrist Japanese leaders such as Prime Minister Kaifu Toshiki envisioned that Japan would assume a more active global role as a nonmilitary, civilian power concentrating on economic and environmental issues.[12] In the area of military security very little changed as a result of the end of the East-West rivalry. While acknowledging that Soviet intentions had changed, the Japanese government pointed out that Soviet capabilities remained largely intact and that the kind of disarmament taking place in Europe had yet to occur in Asia.[13] Japanese defense spending and procurement policies changed little as well, although demographic pressures increased the difficulties experienced of the Self-Defense Forces in meeting personnel targets. As a result, the SDF was compelled to raise salaries and offer new, attractive benefits in order to make a career in the armed forces more appealing. In many respects, the life of a member of the Self-Defense Forces appeared considerably less regimented than that of the average Japanese white-collar office worker.[14]

A lively media debate over the meaning of the end of the Cold War ensued in Japan. Predictably, the Left insisted that the time had come to dissolve the alliance with the United States and dismantle the Self-Defense Forces, while the Right and the Center insisted on the undiminished usefulness of the Mutual Security Treaty.[15] The chief new element in the debate was a renewed interest on both ends of the political spectrum in forging foreign security ties with Asia. Bureaucratic inertia and continued American resistance to the formation of anything like an Asian version of the CSCE, however, prevented these sentiments from being translated into concrete policy.[16]

The Gulf War

Saddam Hussein's invasion of Kuwait in August 1990 and the subsequent military confrontation between the United States and Iraq came as a complete surprise to Germany and Japan, and placed both nations under immense pressure to take a more active role in global security affairs. Both countries are heavily dependent on oil from the region (Japan relies on the Persian Gulf for as much as 70 percent of its oil supplies), and both came under heavy pressure from the United States and other allies to become involved in what was widely viewed as the defining event of the new global order. Even France, a country traditionally ambivalent regarding U.S. strategic intentions, chose to follow the American-led effort for fear of being left out of world affairs.

Although a number of outside observers expected Japan and Germany to rise to the occasion and assume new leadership roles, it soon became apparent that no domestic political consensus existed in either country for such a dramatic expansion of their involvement in international security affairs. Both preferred to view the Persian Gulf crisis as a far-off event of relatively little concern to them. In any case, in the fall of 1990, the Kohl government was preoccupied with German reunification and did not want to do anything that might disquiet its neighbors or provoke negative public opinion on the eve of the first all-German elections, scheduled to be held in October through December of that year.[17]

In Japan, Prime Minister Kaifu enjoyed relatively greater room for maneuvering than Chancellor Kohl did. Ideologically, however, he was even less inclined to take an active role in the Persian Gulf crisis. Like Kohl, Kaifu preferred to believe that the crisis would soon blow over. The profound distrust of the military that had been so characteristic of Japanese postwar political-military culture fed this prevailing attitude in no small measure. So strong was the antimilitary animus that, for the first few months of the crisis, Kaifu excluded the Japanese Defense Agency from all cabinet deliberations in order to prevent civilian decision making from becoming contaminated by the presumably jaundiced views of professional military leaders.[18] It is probably safe to say that few governments in the world would deliberately deprive themselves of the advice of their own military experts in the midst of a major security crisis.

Public opinion in both countries was extremely critical of Saddam Hussein and the Iraqi invasion of Kuwait. The majority of Germans and Japanese, however, indicated that they would prefer greater reliance on diplomatic negotiations and economic sanctions to the use of arms. For instance, according to a survey conducted in November 1990, 70 percent of all Japanese opposed the use of force to resolve the confrontation.[19] Moreover, once the air war began, many Germans and Japanese, with their own memories of the devastating bombings of Dresden and Hiroshima still alive, found it easy to sympathize with the Iraqi people.[20] The citizens of both countries overwhelmingly rejected the view that their country should become directly involved in the fighting. In January 1991, 71 percent of all Germans supported allied actions, but only 20 percent would have supported Bundeswehr participation in the campaign.[21] Likewise in Japan, 48.5 percent of those surveyed indicated that they would oppose the dispatch of the Self-Defense Forces in any form, while 28.4 percent said they would support such a mission only if the forces were unarmed.[22]

At the same time, a fierce debate over the Gulf War was carried out in the German and Japanese media. In Japan the conservative *Sankei* and *Yomiuri* newspapers favored the dispatch of forces, while the traditionally liberal *Asahi* and *Mainichi* opposed such a move. The usually Centrist *Nikkei* waffled between the two positions and ultimately came out against the dispatch of the SDF to the Persian Gulf on the grounds that it might undermine the existing domestic political consensus on defense.[23] Similar views were echoed by other Centrist figures who argued that Japan should exercise power primarily through financial and diplomatic instruments.[24]

The German media debate was conducted along similarly predictable lines, with traditionally prodefense newspapers and pundits lobbying for greater activism and the Left advocating complete neutrality. For a brief period, when approximately two hundred thousand demonstrators gathered in Bonn to protest the government's support of U.S. policies in the gulf, it even appeared as if the Gulf War might revive the peace movement of the early 1980s.[25] The German debate over the Gulf War was complicated, however, by the comparisons between Saddam Hussein and Hitler drawn by American President George Bush, and by the threat posed by Iraq to Israel. Many left-wing commentators and opinion leaders such as Hans Magnus Enzensberger and, to a lesser extent, Willy Brandt argued that Germany had a moral duty to oppose Iraq precisely because its own history demonstrated the danger of allowing aggressive dictators to go unopposed.[26]

Left to their own devices, the two countries would probably have remained neutral during the Persian Gulf crisis. Intense American diplomatic pressure, however, soon compelled the governments of Germany and Japan to become more deeply involved in the conflict. Media critics in the United States and elsewhere lambasted the two countries for pursuing what some called a policy of "ostrich politik," accusing them of cowardice, "free riding," or both.[27] More ominously, many members of the U.S. Congress were outraged by what they perceived as blatant free riding on the part of the United States's two richest allies. In September 1990 the U.S. House of Representatives, angered by Japanese reluctance to provide financial support for the war effort, voted to reduce U.S. forces in Japan by five thousand troops a year unless the Japanese government took over the full cost of stationing those forces there.[28]

Rather than risk a serious rupture in their relationships with the United States, the German and Japanese governments felt compelled to provide vast amounts of financial and material assistance for the allied campaign in the Persian Gulf. Bonn provided a total of $10.6 billion, and Japan, after considerable foot dragging, over $11 billion. In both cases, however, the provision of aid provoked considerable domestic resistance. Both the Japanese Socialist Party and the left wing of the German SPD argued, in only slightly different terms, that the war was part of an American effort to maintain its global hegemony and that German or Japanese involvement might overturn their countries' post–World

War II pacifist traditions.[29] In order to secure the passage of the aid package in the Diet, the Japanese government had to make significant domestic political concessions to the Komeitō Party and was forced to attach the condition that Japanese aid could be used only for nonlethal purposes.[30] In comparison, the German government had relatively little difficulty supplying financial and material assistance for the Gulf War, including the provision of weapons and the use of NATO bases and facilities on German territory.

More controversial was the issue of sending troops and other personnel to support the allied war effort. Early in the crisis, Chancellor Kohl and Defense Minister Volker Rühe advocated sending some forces to the Middle East, albeit only in a logistic capacity, on the grounds that it was vital that Germany demonstrate solidarity with its allies.[31] The Kaifu government as well sought the passage of legislation that would permit Japanese forces to be dispatched to the gulf on noncombat support missions. Popular and parliamentary resistance to these proposals, however, proved overwhelming, and in both countries the projects had to be abandoned.[32] Subsequent efforts by the Kaifu government to send at least civilian volunteers to the gulf were similarly frustrated when it became apparent that volunteers were simply not available in sufficient numbers.[33]

On the whole, the barriers to the dispatch of forces in the German case were less pronounced than those in Japan, which may be attributed to Germany's integration into the NATO alliance. Early in the crisis German minesweepers were sent to the Western Mediterranean to relieve American forces deployed to the gulf. Later a squadron of eighteen Alpha jets was sent—over Genscher's strenuous objections—to Germany's NATO ally, Turkey, to help defend it in the unlikely event of an Iraqi aerial attack on its giant neighbor to the north. In all 3,100 German troops were mobilized in support of the allied campaign in the gulf.[34] Yet, though Kohl and his advisors were convinced that a more active role in the gulf was necessary, given the restraints imposed by the German political-military culture, these rather modest steps probably represented the maximum that could be done militarily at that time. Public opinion data showed that while many Germans (41 percent) thought that German forces could be permitted to participate in United Nations–led peacekeeping missions, only 17 percent supported allowing the Bundeswehr to engage in military missions under a UN command (similar to what British and French forces were doing in the gulf).[35] At the same time the number of conscientious objectors skyrocketed, including fifty of the soldiers scheduled to be sent to Turkey.[36]

The strength of the restraints imposed by the pronounced cultures of anti-militarism in Japan and Germany becomes all the more striking when compared to the responses to the Persian Gulf crisis of the United States's other allies. In their geostrategic situations, Britain and France closely resembled Germany and Japan, yet because of their very different political-military cultures their reactions were totally different. All four nations are what could be termed "middle powers" in the international system; all four, in varying degrees, are allies of the United States; all are similarly reliant on oil supplies from the Persian Gulf; and each supports the principles of sovereignty and the sanctity of national borders that were purportedly at stake in the conflict.

Admittedly, differences in their decision-making structures made it easier for British and French leaders to respond effectively to the crisis.[37] However, one should not overestimate the degree to which German and Japanese behavior was constrained by legal and other formal institutions. Many observers argued that had the leaders of either country wished to dispatch military forces—at least for noncombat missions—they could have done so without changing the laws governing their armed forces.[38] Similarly, Great Britain's and France's possession of nuclear arms cannot be argued to have played a significant role in their decisions to participate fully in the Gulf War. If anything, Germany and Japan should have been even more sensitive to U.S. pressures because their non-nuclear status made them more dependent on the United States for extended deterrence. Moreover, the fact that Germany and Japan were not members of the UN Security Council should have served as an additional incentive for them to participate in the conflict, for doing so would have underlined their eligibility for seats in this suddenly much more prominent international body.

Yet, in stark contrast to the near paralysis that characterized Germany's and Japan's responses to the crisis in the gulf, British and French leaders soon concluded that vital national interests were at stake, and they quickly came to realize that a military solution was quite possible, even probable. For Prime Minister Thatcher it was self-evident that the West would have to stand up to Saddam Hussein, and from the start of the crisis she urged President Bush to take strong action on the grounds that "aggressors must never be appeased."[39] Her successor, John Major, and his foreign minister, Roger Hurd, were no less resolute, and throughout the war Britain proved to be the United States's staunchest ally.

The French response was more complicated because of France's traditional ambivalence toward the United States and the alliance, and because of its ambition to play a mediating role between the West and the Arab world. Nonetheless, in the end Mitterand concluded that it was vital for France to participate in the war in order to preserve its status as a great power and not to forgo its chance to secure a central position for itself in the post–Cold War international arena.[40] Although there was some resistance from the Foreign Ministry and the left wing of the ruling Socialist Party (Defense Minister Chevènement resigned over the issue), in the end the French Parliament approved the dispatch of French forces by a margin of 523 to 43, and the popular opposition was largely muted.[41]

The two nations sent significant combat forces to the gulf—thirty-five thousand from Britain and twelve thousand from France—and made a substantial contribution to the execution of military operations against Iraq. Although other NATO allies—including Italy, Denmark, Holland, Spain, and Greece— did not play as large a role as these two countries, they did decide that some form of direct participation in the allied war effort was necessary. In order to demonstrate solidarity with the United States, all soon dispatched military forces to the region.[42] Germany and Japan, on the other hand, were conspicuous for their absence from the fighting, and they attracted harsh criticism from their allies, especially the United States. Both nations later sent minesweepers to help with cleanup operations, and after the hostilities had ended German forces helped to provide aid to the UN-protected Kurdish enclave in the north of Iraq. But the damage to the two nations' international standing had already been done.

In the aftermath of the conflict, mainstream leaderships in Germany and Japan concluded that they had had a close brush with disaster. American analysts frequently argue that German and Japanese behavior in the Persian Gulf must be understood as an extension of their traditional strategies of free riding on the international security order created by the United States during the Cold War. In actuality, however, the German and Japanese governments feared that their inactivity threatened to undermine the very free ride they had come to depend on. They worried that, if the United States had suffered the kind of massive casualties most American military experts and commentators predicted at the outset of the war, German and Japanese nonparticipation might very well have triggered a massive American backlash against U.S. military involvement overseas.[43] Despite the substantial financial support Germany and Japan provided, many in the United States would have been incensed if large numbers of American men and women had gone to fight and die in a war where, arguably, its allies had just as much at stake as the United States itself did. Anti-German and anti-Japanese resentment—already smoldering because of the widespread perception that it was the economically powerful Germans and Japanese, rather than the United States, who were the real victors of the Cold War—would have flared with white-hot intensity. Under such circumstances the United States might have easily reverted to its pre–World War II stance of isolationism, leaving Germany and Japan to fend for themselves in a chaotic and potentially unstable security environment, in which they were surrounded by deeply suspicious neighbors.[44]

The Gulf War made it amply evident that, even in the post–Cold War era, the threat of regional military conflict was far from over. Although no major German or Japanese leader directly advocated the assumption of a more independent military stance, in the foreign policy circles of both countries there was a growing sentiment that a revision of national security policies was imperative so that their nations would be better able to cope with such crises in the future.[45]

Soon after the Gulf War had ended, both the Kaifu and Kohl governments set out to build a domestic political consensus for a more active role in international security affairs. Kohl opened a debate on revising the German constitution to allow German forces to participate in military operations overseas.[46] Similarly, Kaifu, encouraged by public opinion data suggesting that support for nonmilitary SDF missions abroad had increased to 56 percent, once again tried to rally parliamentary support to secure the passage of a law permitting such operations.[47]

The Gulf War thus can be legitimately regarded as a watershed in the history of post-1945 German and Japanese debates on defense and national security. In its wake the mainstream elites of both nations came to realize that they had to face up to new realities calling for a departure from the decision-making patterns that had become established over a period of decades. Yet the sedimented beliefs and values surrounding defense and the use of force proved exceedingly tenacious. Both Kohl in Germany, and Kaifu and his successors in Japan, found that these beliefs could not be altered swiftly. The antimilitary animus that had informed German and Japanese national security behavior for four decades continued to pose potent barriers to increased activism in the area of national security.

The Post–Gulf War Debate

After the Persian Gulf War, the German and Japanese debates over defense and national security reached a degree of intensity that arguably had not been seen in either country since the 1950s. At the center of these debates stood the issue of whether, and in what form, the Bundeswehr and the Self-Defense Forces should be allowed to participate in military missions beyond the boundaries of their Cold War alliances. In the case of Japan, the question was whether the SDF should be allowed to operate beyond the limits of the nation's immediate territory and the one thousand–nautical mile corridors through which its sea lanes run. In the Federal Republic, the debate centered on whether the Bundeswehr should be deployed outside the NATO alliance. Despite the shock of the Gulf War and many newly emerging security threats, remarkably few changes were effected in the time-tested patterns by which issues pertaining to national security were handled in both nations. In the late 1990s, despite radical changes in the international environment, few significant differences in the political-military cultures of Japan and Germany are in evidence, nor can we identify any major modifications in the political processes by which national security policies are formulated.

Public Opinion

Public opinion in both countries appears today to favor the status quo. In Germany, reunification with the Eastern part of the country had little impact on West German attitudes toward NATO and integration with the EEC. In 1991, 49 percent of all Germans said European integration was more important than ever before, while 12 percent said it had become less important; 57 percent said NATO remained the best guarantor of peace, against 28 percent who favored neutrality. Although a majority of East Germans—51 percent—were for neutrality in 1991 (reflecting their very different historical and political socialization), 1995 data reveal that their attitudes on issues of defense are becoming rapidly similar to those of their West German cousins.[48] The same 1991 set of polls also shows that, while support for the stationing of foreign troops on German soil declined somewhat at the end of the Cold War, a solid majority of 55 percent remained in favor.[49]

Despite some signs of rising German nationalism—which in its most extreme form manifested itself in a wave of neo-Nazi attacks on foreigners—public opinion data, to date, reveal continued, strong anti–right wing sentiments in

Germany.[50] There is little indication that rising national sentiments are translated into more assertive attitudes vis-à-vis issues of foreign affairs. Soon after reunification the majority of Germans listed Switzerland (40 percent) and Sweden (29 percent) as models they wished their country would emulate, far ahead of great powers such as the United States (6 percent), France (8 percent), and Great Britain (2 percent).[51]

After the Gulf War the majority of Germans said their country needed to make a larger contribution to the international order, including German participation in United Nations peacekeeping missions (50 percent according to studies by the Allensbach Public Opinion Research Center). Yet resistance to participation in overseas combat missions remained high.[52] Some 62 percent of Germans said they opposed the participation of German forces in the defense of other European countries, while 53 percent rejected joining UN-mandated combat operations.[53] In 1992, by a margin of 58 percent to 37 percent, Germans said they would prefer to restrict the Bundeswehr to noncombat missions.[54] When violence began to escalate on one such mission—during the 1993 Bundeswehr humanitarian mission to Somalia—surveys showed that the majority of Germans (51 percent to 42 percent) were for an immediate withdrawal.[55]

In Japan, support for the institutional underpinnings of national security also decreased only slightly after the end of the Cold War, despite continued U.S.-Japanese tensions over trade and other economic issues.[56] Although 24 percent of the respondents to a 1991 *Yomiuri* poll identified the United States as Japan's greatest security threat (more than any other country), 56 percent rated the United States as the country Japan could most rely on.[57] By the same token, government studies revealed that the percentage of Japanese in favor of continued reliance on mutual security defense mechanisms and the Self-Defense Forces for purposes of national security decreased only marginally, from 67.4 percent in January 1988 to 62.4 percent in February 1991. Those favoring either an independent military policy or abolishing the Self-Defense Forces and the U.S.-Japanese Mutual Security Treaty remained in the minority at 7.3 percent and 10.5 percent respectively.[58]

After the Gulf War, Japan, like Germany, cautiously began to participate in UN-sponsored peacekeeping missions. In general, the public approved of Japan's dispatch of minesweepers to the Persian Gulf (once the war had ended), and considerable support was registered for Japanese participation in peacekeeping operations in Cambodia—despite the fact that the operation claimed two Japanese lives.[59] There remained, however, strong public reservations about whether such missions should be allowed in the future, with 49.3 percent in favor of either reducing or abandoning all such operations and only 6.8 percent for becoming more actively involved.[60]

Japanese respondents were equally negative in their assessment of UN Secretary-General Boutros Boutros-Ghali's proposals to strengthen UN forces so that they could not only keep the peace, but also enforce it. Some 40 percent of the Japanese surveyed supported Boutros-Ghali's suggestion, and 46 percent were opposed. This level of opposition was considerably higher than that in the United States and other Western powers, where support ranged from 53 percent to 68 percent. The German support for Boutros-Ghali's proposals—a strong 57 percent in favor, with 18 percent opposed—may be seen as a reflection of greater German faith in the capability of multilateral institutions to deal with security problems.[61] Most Japanese also remained highly ambivalent about the utility of force in foreign policy. According to a December 1991 survey conducted simultaneously in the United States and Japan, 72 percent of Americans indicated that the use of force in the maintenance of international justice and order was an appropriate measure whereas only 26 percent of the Japanese respondents considered it appropriate.[62]

Elite Opinion

Similarly, the distribution of prodefense and antidefense views among German and Japanese opinion elites has altered little since 1989. In Germany there remains a substantial community of peace researchers and activists in the churches and the academy who may be counted on to generate mass protests against increased government activism on defense, as they did during the Gulf War when they staged demonstrations mobilizing hundreds of thousands of protestors across the country.

The Bosnian conflict, and in particular reports of the systematic rapes of women and television footage of other atrocities in Serbian concentration camps, provoked an emotional debate inside the peace movement. A number of Greens and pacifists, including many members of the traditionally antimilitarist feminist movement, argued in favor of military intervention by the international community to counter Serb aggression and to stop the abuses of human rights in the Balkans.[63] According to observers inside the peace movement, however, these views were in the minority, and the Left's opposition to Bundeswehr involvement in military missions abroad, on the whole, remained undiminished.[64] More typical was the Left's response to government plans for the creation of a command and control infrastructure needed for out-of-area operations. Left-wing commentators invariably labeled such attempts as assaults on the civilian control of the armed forces and saw them as warning signs of an imminent renationalization of German foreign policy.[65]

In Japan, there has been an even greater degree of continuity in the intellectual debate over defense. Left-idealist positions, such as opposition to the overseas dispatch of the SDF and the further intensification of ties to the United States, have continued to be strongly represented in the editorial pages of *Asahi* and *Mainichi* as well as in the traditional flagship of the left-wing intelligentsia, *Sekai*. In contrast, right-leaning newspapers and journals such as *Yomiuri*, *Sankei*, and *Bungeishunjū* consistently take the opposite position, calling on the government to play a more active role in global security affairs. More Centrist journals such *Nikkei* tend to strike a balanced position, favoring continued reliance on the United States for security, but expressing reservations with regard to military missions overseas.

Japanese business groups, for their part, continue to advocate policies designed to foster Japanese independence in technology. The ban on the export of arms, however, has remained in effect, and there are few signs that the business community is interested in expanding domestic arms production.[66]

Japanese labor unions, on the whole, remain silent on national security issues. However, they continued to drift toward the center in 1993 and 1994 when the giant Private Sector Japanese Federation of Trade Unions, Rengō, indicated it would abandon its exclusive support for the Japanese Socialist Party and became active in the formation of a new left-of-center coalition.[67]

Political Parties

The greatest changes caused by the German and Japanese defense debates after the Gulf War took place within the political parties. In the German case the end of the Cold War initially appeared to strengthen the Atlanticist political consensus. Some in the Social Democratic Party, including most visibly that longtime champion of Central Europeanism, Egon Bahr, argued that NATO had become an anachronism and that it should be gradually dismantled and replaced with an expanded and strengthened CSCE. The party leadership, however, decided that such a platform was imprudent on the eve of the first all-German elections in 1990, and Bahr and other Central Europeanists soon found themselves isolated inside the party. The differences among the political parties thereafter were more in nuance than in substance, with the CDU and CSU adopting a more nationalistic tone while the SPD placed greater emphasis on disarmament. The Greens, as usual, were the exception. They continued their stubborn opposition to virtually every aspect of German defense policy, existing or contemplated.[68]

This apparent consensus soon evaporated, however, with the issue of the Gulf War and the subsequent debate over German military involvement in so-called out-of-area operations. The SPD in particular was deeply torn between the Left and the more pragmatic Atlanticist wings of the party. The former remained deeply ambivalent about the Atlantic alliance and opposed any military role for Germany beyond a minimal defense of its own territory, whereas the latter argued that Germany was obliged to participate in some, albeit limited, fashion in UN peacekeeping missions abroad.

After many bitter internal battles, at the party congress in Bremen in 1991 the pragmatists under the direction of Björn Engholm managed to win the party's approval for the dispatch of Bundeswehr forces in connection with so-called Blue Helmet UN peacekeeping missions. However, the key arguments Engholm and his successor, Rudolf Scharping, employed to win party approval were more tactical than ideological in nature. Rather than arguing that Germany had not only an interest in bolstering its security ties with its allies and partners, but also a moral obligation to do so, or that it was necessary for Germany to win increased international stature, the SPD's pragmatic leadership maintained that a Centrist policy stance on security issues was needed to win voters who might otherwise cast their ballots for the CDU or the FDP.[69]

Moreover, the Left remained a powerful presence inside the Social Democratic power structure. In order to maintain party unity going into the 1994 election year, Scharping, the new party chairman, appointed a large number of left-wing leaders to the committee charged with the drafting of a new party platform.[70] The person put in charge of writing the Social Democrats' new defense and security policy proposals was Heidemarie Wiezorek-Zeul, a member of the traditionally left-wing Frankfurter Kreis and keeper of the flame of many Central Europeanist views on defense.[71] Consequently, SPD members such as Karsten Voigt who expressed support for allowing the Bundeswehr to participate in armed missions remained isolated voices in party debates.[72]

In keeping with its traditional role as the balancing force in the German political system, the FDP sought to strike a balance between the CDU and the SPD. Its representatives undertook tortuous efforts to solve the controversy over out-of-area missions. In general, the Free Democrats under the direction of Klaus Kinkel, Genscher's successor as foreign minister, in principle favored allowing the Bundeswehr to participate in such operations, including combat missions, but insisted that a revision of the German constitution was needed first.

In the absence of such a constitutional revision, the FDP was compelled to question the constitutionality of the few highly restricted out-of-area operations Germany participated in after the Gulf War. As a result the FDP found itself in the highly embarrassing position of filing petitions with the federal Constitutional Court that requested a restraining order be placed against such missions—thereby challenging the policies of the government in which it was a member—and then being perversely relieved when its petitions were rejected.[73]

The CDU/CSU, for its part, adopted a more hawkish stance on defense and national security. On the one hand, it accepted the legitimacy of the other parties' position that a constitutional revision was needed, and it agreed to make Bundestag approval a prerequisite for the dispatch of German forces on combat missions. On the other hand, by requiring only a simple majority for approval, the Christian Democrats sought to set a lower threshold for the employment of German forces abroad. The CDU also wanted to avoid restricting the use of the Bundeswehr to missions sanctioned by the United Nations. In arguing that combat missions in other multilateral frameworks such NATO or the WEU should be permissible, the CDU favored a policy that would leave the door open for German participation in future Gulf War types of conflicts.[74] The Constitutional Court accepted the CDU proposals almost in their entirety when it ruled in July 1995 that German forces could participate in out-of-area operations provided the government obtained prior Bundestag approval and operated within a multilateral framework.[75]

In Japan, the defense debate among the political parties was complicated by the long-anticipated yet quite unexpected end of thirty-eight years of LDP rule, brought on by a combination of factors that made for a split within the ranks of the party and by long-term trends predating the end of the Cold War. The resultant reorganization of the Japanese political landscape blurred many of the traditional lines between the Left-idealist, Centrist, and Right-idealist positions and held out the promise of dispelling Japan's long-held fears vis-à-vis its armed forces.

The pivotal event in this process came in 1993 when three offshoots of the LDP—the Japan New Party (JNP) under Hosokawa Morihiro, the Renewal Party headed by Ōzawa Ichirō, and the New Harbinger Party under Takemura Masayoshi—succeeded in finally cobbling together a coalition of opposition parties, including the Japanese Socialist Party,[76] the Komeitō, the Democratic Socialist Party, and the Social Democratic League.[77] In order to build a coalition, however, this ideologically diverse group of former adversaries first had to achieve a minimum level of consensus. As in previous efforts to form a united front, this proved to be particularly difficult in the controversial area of defense. Whereas the left wing of the Socialist Party remained wedded to its demands for the abolition of the Mutual Security Treaty and for adopting a posture of unarmed neutrality, the most powerful LDP offshoot, the Japan Renewal Party, led by Ōzawa Ichirō, advocated the revision of Article 9 of the constitution as well as the assumption of a more assertive stance on international security issues, including the overseas dispatch of Self-Defense Forces on combat missions.[78]

After difficult and protracted negotiations, the various parties managed to paper over their differences and produce a joint platform that advocated keeping the treaty and the SDF while, at the same time, seeking to promote disarmament and improving Japan's relations with its Asian neighbors.[79] After winning the general elections, the new Hosokawa government assumed a basically left-centrist position on defense, taking pains to reassure the United States that Japan would remain a loyal ally and appointing former LDP members to sensitive positions in the Ministry of Foreign Affairs and the Defense Agency.[80] The Socialists received mainly domestic political posts and, prodded by their allies in the new Japanese Federation of Trade Unions (Rengō), they indicated that they were willing to go along with the government's new policies as long as Japan committed itself to fostering greater regional dialogue and the promotion of arms control and disarmament. These trends continued even after the JSP abandoned the Hosokawa coalition and formed a new government in partnership with its long-time nemesis, the LDP. In order to remain in power, the Socialists once again made major concessions by formally announcing their acceptance of both the Self-Defense Forces and the Mutual Security Treaty.[81] Yet beneath the surface, tensions remained and the two partners clearly held very different views on security issues.

For a brief while it seemed that the reorganization of politics (or *Seiji Sai-*

hensei) might do more to clear away Japan's inhibitions vis-à-vis defense and national security than Nakasone had done in five years of preaching Cold War nationalism. With the Cold War over and with a chance to join in governing the nation, the Socialists appeared ready to moderate their strong antimilitary attitudes. As occurred in Germany immediately after reunification, a remarkable degree of consensus on national security seemed to be emerging among Japan's political parties.

Beyond its impact on the Socialist Party, *Seiji Saihensei* had deeper implications for Japan's political-military culture as a whole. Japanese suspicions about the reliability of their armed forces had been a reflection of their fears that democracy in Japan was inherently unstable—a beautiful but fragile foreign blossom transplanted to alien soil that had to be protected from indigenous antidemocratic infections. The end of thirty-five years of single-party rule should have reassured the Japanese about the strength of their democracy and, by extension, should have reduced their fears that democracy might be used as an instrument for a takeover by reactionary forces.

The appearance of a growing moderation on defense proved short-lived, however, as deep differences over national security issues soon reemerged. One of the first manifestations of this reversal was the enormous controversy generated when Nakanishi Keisuke, the new director general of the Japanese Defense Agency and close confidante of Ōzawa, suggested at a meeting of an unofficial study group that the time had come to revise the Japanese constitution and allow the Self-Defense Forces to participate in combat missions under UN command. Although Nakanishi emphasized that Japan should continue to respect the spirit of the constitution by not seeking great-power status, the Socialist Party was outraged and demanded that Nakanishi be removed from the government. Rather than risking a crisis with his Socialist coalition partners, Hosokawa was compelled to accept Nakanishi's resignation.[82]

In an odd way, the same constellation of fears and suspicions that paralyzed the Japanese defense debate during the long decades of the Cold War now reappeared, even though the political landscape had been fundamentally transformed. Instead of the Liberal Democrats being the target of Left-idealist suspicions, it was Ōzawa and other conservatives, both inside and outside the government, who combined their calls for a more active Japanese global military role with proposals for the strengthening the state. Although the tone of the debate had become more muted than it was during the Cold War, the themes of Japan's political-military culture lived on, exciting similar passions and exerting similar constraining effects on the kinds of policies the government could pursue.

The Evolving German and Japanese Security Policies since the Gulf War

Given the domestic political constellations in both countries, it should come as no surprise that changes in German and Japanese defense policies since the Gulf War have been cautious and incremental in character. While some important new steps were taken—above all in the area of international peacekeeping—the degree of continuity remains greater than the degree of change in the central areas of alliance relations, civil-military relations, and military mission.

Alliance Relations

In its approach to international alliances, Germany continued to exhibit a strong preference for dealing with security issues within the context of multilateral security institutions and to promote the further development and expansion of virtually every major multilateral organization of which it was a member—NATO, the WEU, and the CSCE. The often frenetic German campaigns to strengthen international institutions soon triggered fierce consternation among Germany's alliance partners, many of whom were inclined to detect in these initiatives signs that Germany was leaning toward closer relations with one partner over the other—France, Russia, or the United States. The Germans, however, consistently tended to view institutional membership as a type of public good, one that benefitted all partners equally, and to ignore the possible implications its policies might have for the balance of power.[83]

German relations with France became one of the first foci of activity following reunification as Kohl sought to reassure the French that Germany would remain a reliable partner. In October 1991 Kohl and Mitterand agreed to upgrade the French-German brigade to corps level, and in June 1992 the two nations underlined the importance of the WEU as an instrument for the creation of a common European defense and foreign policy.[84] Comments by German political and military leaders at the time suggested that Germany was interested in Europeanizing NATO now that the Cold War was over.[85] While they may have provided some reassurance to the French, these measures immediately triggered fears in London and Washington that Germany was reverting to a new form of Gaullism. In response, the Bush administration sent an unusually harsh diplomatic cable to warn Bonn that Germany's new policies ran the risk of undermining the Atlantic alliance.[86] Bonn, for its part, promptly began to look for ways to reassure Washington, initiating various measures designed to demonstrate the compatibility of NATO and the WEU and privately arguing that, rather than weakening the Atlantic alliance, improved German ties to Paris would help coax France back in.[87]

To improve its relations with Eastern Europe, Germany turned to the mechanism of the CSCE, trying to strengthen it so that it could become an effective instrument for crisis prevention and promotion of democracy and human rights.[88] These principles were institutionalized in the Declaration of Prague in January 1992. Various German proposals for expansion of the CSCE's institutional apparatus—including the creation of a Council of Ministers, a High-Level Group, a Conflict Prevention Center, and an Election Observation Center—soon followed. Other European nations and the United States considered these measures to be major, even daring, innovations. Kohl and Genscher, however, viewed them as merely first steps toward the creation of a new network of multilateral ties that would bring peace and stability to Eastern Europe.[89]

NATO, on the other hand, remained the centerpiece of German security policy. Now redefined as a political alliance, NATO restated its mission to include crisis prevention, combat of the proliferation of weapons of mass destruction, and, through the newly created mechanism of the North Atlantic Council, the organization of aid to Eastern Europe.[90] Militarily NATO forces were reconfigured to adapt to the new security environment. The bulk of NATO forces were placed in a territorial defense mode, and only relatively small groups of newly created multinational rapid-reaction forces were maintained in a high state of readiness.[91] With the possible exception of the rapid-reaction forces, these steps fit well with Germany's traditional antimilitarist preferences. The integration of the German military into multilateral forces was in good measure designed to serve as an additional barrier against the renationalization of European defense policies and can be seen as an extension of the well-established German strategy of entangling its allies through self-entanglement.

The one apparent exception to German multilateralism was the strong position the country took on the issue of extending diplomatic recognition to the newly independent republics of Croatia and Slovenia. Against the wishes of almost all of its partners, Germany insisted in December 1992 that the EEC recognize the two republics, threatening to do so unilaterally if the other nations did not comply. This hard-line strategy was widely interpreted by its allies as a sign of renewed German assertiveness and sparked fears that Germany might begin to develop an independent foreign policy in Eastern Europe.[92]

On closer examination, however, it appears that Bonn's policy was primarily motivated by the fear that failure to face up to the nationalist Serb dictatorships threatening Croatia and Slovenia would encourage other nationalist leaders, including those in the former Soviet Union, to attempt similar acts of aggression. In addition, Christian Democratic leaders felt that Germany could not stand up for the principle of self-determination for the German people and deny its applicability elsewhere in the world.[93] Despite the threat of unilateral action, Germany did not believe it could cope with the Yugoslav crisis on its own, and hoped—correctly, as it turned out—that through the threat of unilateral action it could force the United States and European countries to support its position. While the Yugoslavian incident may have signalled greater German willingness to use multilateral institutions to achieve its own objectives, it hardly pointed toward a renationalization of German foreign policy.

Japan, like Germany, remained wedded to its close military relationship with the United States. While some Asian leaders, such as Prime Minister D.S. Mahathir bin Mohamed of Malaysia, proposed the creation of an East Asian economic bloc capable of standing up to NAFTA (the North American Free Trade Agreement) and the EEC, Japanese political and economic elites preferred to continue to work within the framework of the General Agreement on Tariffs and Trade (GATT). Japan was profoundly leery about the prospects of creating a new East Asian economic bloc. Instead, it was one of the chief supporters of the newly created of APEC (Asian Pacific Economic Cooperation), which includes the United States and Canada along with a number of Asian countries.[94]

In security matters Japan continued to see no alternative to the Mutual Security Treaty with the United States. Since the end of the Cold War, Japanese governments, including the Hosokawa coalition, have reaffirmed their undiminished commitment to the alliance and have sought to improve foreign policy coordination between the two countries. For instance, in 1991 when North Korea appeared to be on the verge of acquiring nuclear weapons, the Japanese Defense Agency investigated the possibility of acquiring antimissile defense technology from the United States, rather than creating its own deterrent capability.[95]

Yet Japan's traditional ambiguity concerning its commitment to regional military security remains. As a result, even though the prospect of a military crisis on the Korean peninsula grew in the mid-1990s, Japan adopted a hands-off attitude and emphasized that, in the event of an emergency, even the logistical support it might offer to U.S. forces would be provided only within Japanese territory.[96] Thus, should hostilities erupt on the peninsula, a political crisis of even greater dimensions than the Persian Gulf War seems almost inevitable.

At the same time, Japan also became interested in fostering a security dialogue with neighboring countries in East Asia. Beginning with Prime Minister Miyazawa Kiichi's speech in Bangkok in January 1993, Japan—with the tacit support of the new Clinton administration in the United States—sought to create a number of security institutions designed to increase stability by improving the flow of information in the region and improve the capacity of Asian governments to communicate with one another in the event of a security crisis.[97] Of equal importance was the increase in bilateral security discussions initiated by Japan, including most notably dialogues with the People's Republic of China, which growing numbers of Japanese conservatives perceive as a potential security threat.[98] On a number of occasions Japan sought to encourage China toward increased moderation on national security issues, prodding it toward a diplomatic resolution of the Spratley Island issue—a much disputed group of strategic islands in the South China Sea—and urging it to reduce its burgeoning defense budget.[99]

In terms of force structure, similar patterns can be observed in both Germany and Japan. After a brief hiatus, the end of the Cold War led to significant reductions in the size of the German and Japanese armed forces as well as in their defense budgets. This was particularly true of Germany, where the Bundeswehr was reduced from more than 600,000 (including the former East German army) to 370,000, with comparable reductions in the stocks of tanks, artillery, and armored vehicles.[100] Similarly in Japan, the steady increase in defense spending was greatly slowed. While some modernization of Japan's SDF was undertaken, most notably through the acquisition of advanced AWAC command and control aircraft, there were no overt moves toward the acquisition of increased power projection capabilities.

Civil-Military Relations

The basic patterns of civil-military relations have seen little change in Japan and Germany since 1989. The end of the Cold War had its greatest impact on civil-military relations in Germany, where the conscription system was sharply attacked by domestic critics. Yet, despite powerful demographic and political forces that made the abolishment of conscription plausible, both the SPD and the CDU favored the retention of universal conscription as a means of integrating the armed forces into society.[101] In Japan there was less debate on the issue, but social and political pressures to keep the armed forces on a tight leash persisted and must be seen to reflect the continuation of the long-established pattern to place *hadome* on the armed forces whenever new defense initiatives were proposed.

Military Missions

The most important new development in German and Japanese defense policies since the Gulf War is the expansion of the mission of both nations' armed forces to include participation in UN peacekeeping operations. The German government was able to send forces to Somalia and Cambodia in a noncombat role without the passage of a new law specifically authorizing such missions. In July 1995, after securing the approval of the federal Constitutional Court, the Kohl government dispatched a squadron of Bundeswehr Tornados for possible combat in Bosnia. For the first time since 1945, regular German military forces were placed in a position in which they might have to fire on an enemy.[102]

Despite the importance of this move, two important points must be kept it mind. First, the German decision to allow forces to participate in possible combat missions in Bosnia was not easily made and came at the end of nearly four years of fierce political fighting and debate. Prior to this decision, three cases had to be resolved by the judiciary on the basis of its reading of German law and not on the basis of traditional realist considerations of the balance of power. Had the court ruled differently, the Kohl government would have had to abide by its decision regardless of what action it believed was in Germany's national interest.

Second, the new policy is broadly consistent with the pronounced multilateralism that has become a prominent feature of the German approach to national security. German participation in such missions was largely justified as fulfilling Germany's international obligations and supporting the cause of peace. Nowhere in the mainstream of German political debate is there to be found the skepticism regarding collective security arrangements that is commonplace in other Western nations such as Britain, France, and, above all, the United States.

In Japan, after nearly two years of ferocious political infighting, the Miyazawa government finally managed to pass legislation allowing Japanese forces to participate in United Nations peacekeeping operations. Subsequently a fairly large contingent of Self-Defense Forces personnel was dispatched to Cambodia, where it remained until peaceful elections could be held there. The new law marked a watershed in post–World War II Japanese defense policy and was viewed with apprehension, not only by Left-idealist critics in Japan, but also by many of Japan's neighbors. Singaporean Prime Minister Lee Kuan Yew, for instance, remarked that having the Japanese participate in military missions was like giving liqueur chocolates to a former alcoholic.[103]

The new law, however, in keeping with the well-established Japanese pattern of instituting fresh legislative brakes with every new defense initiative, placed a large number of restrictions on such missions. Among other things the law requires that the dispatch of forces be approved and periodically reviewed by the Diet, that the number of forces be limited to two thousand lightly armed troops, and that their mission be carefully circumscribed so as to minimize the chance that they would be dragged into combat. For instance, Japanese forces are not allowed to assist in the removal and disposal of mines, nor are they permitted to help with the collection of weapons. Moreover, to minimize the chance of entanglement, dispatch of forces is permitted only if all the warring parties have agreed to a cease-fire. Japanese commanders are even forbidden to give their troops the order to fire—each soldier is expected to determine on his own recognizance if he is in a position that justifies the use of firearms in self-defense.[104]

Perhaps the most significant aspect of Japan's new involvement in peacekeeping missions is that the initial stimulus came from the Gulf War. Concerned with the isolation of their country in the international community, Japanese leaders concluded that they had to overcome the country's traditionally parochial approach to military issues. It is therefore ironic that today Japanese experts agree that their forces are still legally unable to participate in a Gulf War type of operation. Were a new test of the military solidarity of the major industrialized democracies to emerge, chances are that Japan would be nearly as poorly prepared to react as it was in 1990 and 1991.

There should be little doubt by now that the root cause of the two nations' delayed response to the changed international environment is the continued strength of the antimilitary animus that informs Germany's and Japan's political-military cultures. The persistence of fears in the two countries that military action could lead to the remilitarization and renationalization, not only of their foreign policies but also of their societies, remains to this day the lasting heritage of their dismal twentieth-century past and makes their continued preference for diplomacy and engagement over military power and confrontation understandable. While their new activism in international affairs and the gradual development of their domestic political debates indicate that these political-military cultures are slowly adapting to changes in their security environments, it is also evident that the external shock of the Gulf War by itself was of insufficient magnitude to overcome their deeply sedimented antimilitarist values.

7

Conclusions: Culture, Cultural Change, and the Future of German and Japanese Defense Policy

THIS BOOK SET OUT to chart the complex relationship between political culture and national security policy. Post–World War II Germany and Japan—the two cases explored here—clearly demonstrate that cultural forces have a profound influence on a nation's approach to the problems of defense and national security. More than half a century after the end of World War II, the memories of the disastrous events of the 1930s and 1940s still haunt the minds of contemporary Germans and Japanese. The lessons drawn in the immediate postwar period continue to shape German and Japanese state behavior, encouraging them in the direction of low-key, antimilitaristic approaches to defense and foreign policy. In short, new cultures of antimilitarism have emerged and become constitutive features of the larger political cultures of these two nations.

In examining the broader theoretical and foreign policy implications of this study, several questions arise. Is it possible to generalize from models of political culture? Can a political-cultural model allow us to advance projections for the future of Germany and Japan?

The Impact of Culture on German and Japanese Security Policy

In the five decades that have followed the end of World War II, Germany and Japan have consistently pursued unusually guarded, low-key approaches to defense and national security. Despite dramatic shifts in the international balance of power as well as in their own domestic political environments, they continue this approach. Regardless of their military potential—which, given their economic and technological prowess and the size of their populations, is formidable—the two countries have displayed a pronounced aversion to the use of force and military power in any form and have gone out of their way to reassure their neighbors of their peaceful intentions.

This antimilitarist policy stance is consistent with the post–World War II German and Japanese domestic political discourses on defense and national security. There are few countries in which pacifist sentiments find a deeper political resonance than in Germany and Japan. The same antimilitary themes and rhetoric that were prevalent in the 1950s continue to be voiced in the 1990s with scarcely diminished fervor. Hence, it may be plausibly argued that these attitudes have caused the patterns of behavior observed in defense and foreign policy. Still, it is possible to ask to what extent these attitudes and behaviors are the result of historically grounded beliefs and to what extent they are attributable to other factors, such as the desire to minimize the costs of paying for security, the constraining effects of international institutions, or the interests of business, labor, and other elites in minimizing the power of the military establishment. In other words, it has to be determined to what degree German and Japanese behavior can be explained through reference to cultural and ideological forces and to what degree it is better explained by noncultural forces such as the distribution of military power in the international system, the impact of growing economic interdependence and international institutions on state behavior, or domestic political actors pursuing their economic interests.

Our review of the evolution of German and Japanese defense policy making has identified a number of cases in which the impact of historically grounded cultural beliefs and values was clear and unambiguous. This is particularly true in the area of civil-military relations. In Japan the deep-rooted fear of the military has sharply constrained defense planning and, to a lesser extent, the development of force structures. The 1965 leak of the Defense Agency's Three Arrows Contingency Plan, designed to respond to a possible war on the Korean peninsula, triggered widespread fears that the military was planning a coup and resulted in what amounted to a thirteen-year ban on military contingency planning. Although the 1978 controversy surrounding the Emergency Laws partially reversed this ban, persistent fears that the armed forces could run amok prompted the extension of legal restrictions on the military's ability to act in times of war. More generally, Japan's distrust of its own armed forces has created a pattern of policy making in which every new defense initiative has been accompanied by a new set of institutional *hadome* on the military establishment.

In Germany, the main source of controversy has been of a quite different nature. The central focus of the German debate has been on the beliefs and values propagated within the armed forces rather than on the formal institutional structure within which the military is expected to operate. The underlying premise of this debate has been the belief that the armed forces are trustworthy only if they are integrated into civilian society. Consequently, efforts to develop independent military traditions have been met with suspicion, leading to a series of conflicts between the proponents of using tradition as a tool for fostering military cohesion and the guardians of the civilizing doctrine of Innere Führung.

In both Germany and Japan, leaders have made many efforts to alleviate these tensions in civil-military relations and to heal the historical rupture between the nation and its armed forces. Various instruments have been used to this end, including changes in the school curriculum and symbolic acts of state, such as Nakasone's visit to Yasukuni and Kohl's trip to Bitburg. Yet in both countries such efforts generated intense controversy, leading not only to criticism from domestic political opponents but, on occasion, rousing suspicions in neighboring countries as well.

These controversies over civil-military relations have had negative consequences for military efficiency. Japan's lack of a rational policy on rules of engagement and its self-imposed restrictions on contingency planning and military exercises have increased its vulnerability in the event of a military emergency. If there had been a renewal of hostilities in Korea or a serious military confrontation involving Soviet forces in the Far East, Japan would have been as poorly equipped to respond as it was during the Persian Gulf War, with far more immediate consequences for its national security. Likewise, many German military professionals felt that the doctrinaire application of Innere Führung prevented them from recreating the level of unit cohesion and discipline that historically made the German armed forces so effective in combat.[1] Similarly, there were vain efforts by Japanese conservatives to foster a patriotic "defense consciousness" *(Bōeiishki),* resulting in policies that often had a deleterious impact on Japan's relations with its neighbors and complicated the task of creating even a rudimentary security regime in East Asia.

In other areas the impact of cultural beliefs and values on German and Japanese defense policy making is less obvious, though still quite discernible. The power of cultural forces was particularly evident at critical junctures in postwar history when a variety of equally plausible options seemed available to policy makers. At such times, both nations invariably opted for those policies that were most consistent with the established antimilitary patterns of behavior. For instance, at the height of the Cold War in the 1950s and 1960s, Japan stubbornly refused to become involved in any form of regional security affairs, even though many Japanese conservatives and moderates felt that their country could and should do more to bolster the containment of communism in Asia. The sort of U.S.-Japanese cooperation in training and defense planning that began in 1978 could have been initiated at a much earlier date and would have brought substantial improvements in military readiness and in Japan's relations with the United States. Moreover, an improvement in defense cooperation could have been achieved without embroiling Japan in military confrontations or increasing the economic costs of defense. Likewise, Nakasone's 1970 proposals for a more independent defense posture within the framework of the Mutual Security Treaty and his efforts to adopt a hard-line posture vis-à-vis the Soviet Union in the 1980s were, from a realist point of view, perfectly rational responses to increasing regional instability and the perceived decline in U.S. power and commitment to East Asian security.

The failure of these initiatives was not the result of geostrategic factors. Nor can their failure simply be attributed to domestic political groups with a concrete interest in frustrating closer relations with the United States. Rather, they were blocked by ad hoc alliances between the political Left and Center who saw these proposals as the first steps toward the dismantling of postwar Japanese democracy. The widely shared suspicion that antidemocratic forces are afoot in Japan seeking to exploit the security issue to engineer a reactionary takeover has remained a deeply ingrained feature of that nation's political-military culture. It has endured despite the gradual moderation of the right-wing rhetoric and the reformation of the Japanese party system following the end of the Cold War.

West Germany's *Ostpolitik* of the 1970s and 1980s can be viewed as a logical effort to preserve national and humanitarian ties to East Germany after hopes for a speedy end to German partition faded. From a sophisticated realist point of view, *Ostpolitik* may even be seen as a clever strategy to subtly play the East against the West, and to leave open the possibility of eventual reunification and thus a considerable increase in German national power. Similarly, neoliberal institutionalists might hypothesize that the partition of Germany and the isolation of West Berlin created a demand for increased East-West cooperation that, after a series of negotiating games had been played out, led to the creation of a set of international institutions embodied in the Federal Republic's treaties with Eastern Europe.

The problem, however, is not to explain why West Germany chose to pursue *Ostpolitik*, but why it took so long for it to do so. The timing of this shift in German strategy required a dramatic change in the domestic political environment. The first overtures to the East became possible only after there had been two changes in government and German society had been shaken to the core by the outbreak of the student revolt of the 1960s. The opening to the East was viewed not solely as a diplomatic maneuver, but was defined by Willy Brandt as a part of a larger program of democratic renewal and of Germany's new determination to confront its Nazi past.

These ideological elements lent *Ostpolitik* a moral impetus that was missing in other countries in similar structural positions—for instance, South Korea in its relations with the North.[2] Despite serious misgivings by many of West Germany's allies, including the United States, *Ostpolitik* paved the way for a broader East-West dialogue, culminating in the 1975 Helsinki agreements. As a result, despite the reintensification of the Cold War during the first half of the 1980s, the Federal Republic continued to pursue closer ties to East Germany.

Of course, it is possible to devise ingenious, noncultural, rational actor explanatory models to make sense of these events. For instance, it could be plausibly argued that in any given case the German and Japanese governments were acting on the basis of rational calculations of their nations' or their own parochial political interests. Any set of leaders, a rationalist would contend, regardless of cultural background—be it French, Indian, or Eskimo—would have acted in much the same way. The situations cited above, however, were highly ambiguous and it was often unclear whether a single "Pareto-efficient" set of policy choices could be found. Rational actor theory offers little guidance on how states should behave in such ambiguous situations. Arguably, it is precisely at such critical junctures in history that ideas and cultural values play a particularly large role in determining outcomes.[3] The fact that time and again over the past fifty years German and Japanese foreign policymakers opted for nonconfrontational, nonmilitary solutions strongly bolsters such an interpretation.

On those occasions when international pressures did push German and Japanese decision makers to adopt policies running counter to their culturally determined preferences, they invariably encountered fierce domestic political resistance. For example, the reversion of Okinawan sovereignty to Japan led to widespread popular protests and fissures within the LDP over the question of whether to allow the continued presence of American bases and nuclear weapons on the island. Similarly, the Japanese government's decision to commit itself to the defense of its sea-lanes unleashed such strong domestic protests that Foreign Minister Itō Masayoshi was compelled to resign and Prime Minister Suzuki Zengo's administration was dealt a blow from which it never recovered. In much the same way, the German decision to deploy Pershing II and cruise missiles in response to the Soviet military buildup in Eastern Europe provoked the largest mass demonstrations in the history of the Federal Republic and helped topple the government of Helmut Schmidt.

Since the end of the Cold War the continued potency of cultural forces has been exceptionally evident in areas outside of civil-military relations. In particular, German and Japanese inactivity during the Gulf War is hard to explain without making reference to the peculiar political-military cultures of the two countries. Here was a crisis almost tailor-made for each country to assume a larger international role. Many other countries in structurally similar situations saw some degree of involvement in the allied war effort as vital to their national interests. Yet, although the governments of both countries strongly favored greater action, the antimilitary animus rampant in the two societies prevented them from mustering even a token show of military support in the Persian Gulf.

These and other examples demonstrate that the domestic political costs of violating cultural norms can be enormous. Therefore, it should come as no surprise, except perhaps to the most committed adherent of structural determinist theories of state behavior, that Germany's and Japan's deeply ingrained cultures of antimilitarism have imposed powerful restraints on the kinds of policies their leaders have chosen to pursue.

The Evolution of Germany's and Japan's Political-Military Cultures

The clearly identifiable antimilitary beliefs and values regarding national security that were institutionalized in West Germany and Japan during the 1950s have since become permanent features of their political cultures. Contrary to what more static notions of political culture might predict, there is little evidence in either country of a reversion to older, pre–World War II patterns of behavior even as the physical trauma of defeat has receded. The traditional links among the nation, the state, and the armed forces, which had been one of the most distinctive features of German and Japanese history before 1945, remained broken during the postwar period despite efforts by some, like Nakasone at Yasukuni and Kohl at Bitburg, to revive or repair it.

This remained true even in the 1980s and 1990s when national pride was clearly on the rise. As Germans and especially Japanese became increasingly confident of the virtues of their own economic and political systems, many observers feared a revival of their old patterns of assertive foreign policy behavior. Instead of rediscovering their martial pasts and traditions, however, Germans and Japanese took pride in doing precisely the opposite. They celebrated their countries' identities as civilian mercantile powers that had freed themselves of the destructive delusions of power politics and had found success in other areas, above all in the economic sphere. A wide range of indicators reflects the steady consolidation and remarkable robustness of this new national self-understanding in which a pronounced antimilitarism plays a pivotal role. In the 1980s this trend had gone so far that even traditionally prodefense conservatives came to see Japan's alleged cooperative, mercantile, and essentially nonmilitary culture as its most distinctive feature. By embracing Japan's identity as a "merchant nation" they stood the prewar cult of Bushido and the Japanese warrior spirit on its head.

The development of these distinctive new cultures of antimilitarism was far from a straightforward process. Immediately after the war the moderate, pro-Western German and Japanese political-military subcultures were in the minority in the larger political systems. Public opinion data show that in both countries large reservoirs of popular support for a more neutralist stance on defense and national security existed. Moreover, in Japan at least, there was also a readiness in certain elite sectors of society to adopt a more assertive stance on defense and national security; this view was closely linked to a vision of a strong Japanese state and a patriotic, conservative social order.

The antimilitary political cultures, offering different definitions of national identity and of their nations' mission in world affairs, ultimately lost out in the political struggles of the 1950s—in Germany to the pro-Western Atlanticists and in Japan to the moderate Centrists. In both countries the neutralist, leftist subcultures were placed at a disadvantage by the enormous benefits that were to be gained from alliance with the United States, beginning with the return of sovereignty and access to the newly emerging international trading order.

The right-wing political-military subcultures, on the other hand, were also handicapped by a variety of factors. In Germany conservative forces advocating the creation of a European-centered alternative to the Atlantic alliance were undercut by both international and domestic developments. Internationally they were damaged by the obvious impracticality of the Gaullist option. Domestically the conservatives were put on the defensive by the tidal wave supporting détente and a new opening to the East in the 1960s and 1970s. In Japan the prodefense Right was held in check by widely shared suspicions regarding its political agenda. In both countries the Right, with its emphasis on strengthening the armed forces, was crippled by a prevailing mood of disillusionment and war weariness.

Over time a deeper consensus emerged in favor of the moderate, middle-of-road approach to national security. At first this took the form of a shift in the distribution of political-military subcultures in the political system. Public opinion increasingly supported the basic institutions on which the German and Japanese approaches to national security were based—their alliances with the West, their new armed forces, the pacifist constitution in Japan, and a moderate form of *Ostpolitik* in Germany. This process reached its peak in the late 1970s and owed much to the tangible benefits the two countries enjoyed under the aegis of a U.S.-guaranteed peace. Countries that experience the kind of economic growth and relative political stability that Germany and Japan did during this period are understandably disinclined to rock the boat.

After the 1970s, and to a certain degree even before then, there were signs of a growing convergence in the contents of the different political-military cultures as well as in their distribution. Factions that operated at opposite ends of the political spectrum increasingly opened up to each other's ideas and normative and cognitive understandings of the world. In Germany the first manifestations of this process came in the late 1950s when the SPD at Bad Godesberg underwent a remarkable conversion to the principles of the Atlantic alliance. The CDU's conversion to *Ostpolitik* and arms control in the 1980s and the Japanese conservatives' gradual acceptance of a nonmilitary approach to national security policy—perhaps best symbolized by the promulgation of the concept of comprehensive security—provide yet further important examples of this phenomenon.

Certainly a considerable degree of tactical calculation was involved in each of these political developments. In Germany the SPD in 1959 and CDU in 1969 were interested in winning elections and building coalitions so that they could take power. In Japan Prime Minister Ōhira was interested in log-rolling the defense issue through the bureaucracy while at the same time redefining national security so as to reduce American pressure for greater burden sharing. Nonetheless, once these policy switches had been effected, German and Japanese leaders were compelled to legitimate their actions to the broader public. In so doing they often adopted the arguments and rhetoric of their opponents. In this sense reality, including strategic reality, was being negotiated in the domestic political arena of both countries. This negotiating process led to a deepening of the

German and Japanese antimilitarist bias and helps explain why by the end of the Cold War the two nations were so reluctant to assume larger international security roles.

The emergence of the Greens and the German peace movement of the late 1970s presented the major exception to the trend of convergence and consensus building. The Greens, however, remained a relatively small, if influential, portion of the German electorate and political elite. They must be seen as the political outgrowth of the social protest movement of the 1960s and represent a new culture of Universal Pacifism without the specifically nationalist component of the old German Left. The 1960s saw similar activity in Japan, but there the peace movement was unable to institutionalize itself as successfully as its counterparts in the West. Preliminary evidence suggests that the Greens are slowly being incorporated into the larger camp of the German Left as their leaders—especially so-called *Realos*—readjust their views on defense and other issues in order to build political coalitions.

As the Greens negotiate compromises with their mainstream rivals, they will come under pressure to moderate their more extreme ideological positions. As we can see in the debate over German participation in peacekeeping operations in Bosnia, Green leaders are already beginning to redefine the ideals of their party and temper the strict pacifism they once espoused. Such a move, however, does not imply that the Greens will suddenly become adherents of some form of realpolitik. A strong antimilitarist, antinationalist animus will certainly remain a core element of the movement's identity and have concrete implications for the kind of foreign policies the party will be willing to endorse. At the same time, through compromise the Greens will increase the cohesiveness, and thus the political influence, of the German Left. The net result is likely to strengthen, rather than diminish, the antimilitary bias of Germany's political-military culture as a whole.

Implications for Theory

The findings about postwar German and Japanese antimilitarism raise important questions for theories of international relations and comparative politics. First, they suggest that international systemic factors alone do not determine defense policy formation and indicate that greater attention should be paid to domestic political forces. Second, having made the case for the inclusion of domestic political factors in the analysis of defense policy making, this study suggests that a structural analysis focusing solely on the material interests of various groups in the political system is insufficient. Widely shared cultural norms and values also need to be factored into the policy equation. Finally, the examination of Japan and Germany has demonstrated the utility of an approach that combines the analysis of political institutions with an investigation of the broader ideational-cultural context within which such institutions are embedded.

In recent years it has become virtually axiomatic among international relations theorists that systemic models of state behavior need to be supplemented by approaches that take into account subsystemic, state-level factors.[4] Since the late 1970s domestic-level explanations of states' economic and trade policies have become popular in the field of international political economy. At the forefront of this movement stand such scholars as Peter Katzenstein and Peter Gourevitch.[5] In the field of international security, however, systemic explanations of national defense and security policies remain, with a few notable exceptions, the norm.[6]

As a consequence of this general preoccupation with structural explanations, international security analysts have had difficulty in accounting for deviations from their models. So for example, classical realists such as John Mearsheimer, Christopher Layne, and, in a more popular vein, George Friedman and Meredith Lebard argue that Germany and Japan are bound to seek a political-military role commensurate to their enormous economic and technological power.[7] Yet as we have seen, to date Germany and Japan have acted in precisely the opposite manner expected by these theorists. Nor does it appear likely that either nation will readily assume the role of great military power in the near future. While it is possible that at some time Germany and Japan may opt to play a greater military role, the relationship between potential military power and its realization is far weaker than adherents of classical realism assume.

Likewise, neoliberal scholars who argue that systemic changes in the international environment incline states toward decreased reliance on force as an instrument of foreign policy encounter problems explaining German and Japanese national security policy behavior.[8] Analysts like Richard Rosecrance, who maintain that increased economic interdependence and technological developments make states give greater weight to economic rather than military power, frequently cite Japan and Germany as providing evidence for their views.[9] Such arguments, however, overlook the fact that antimilitarism in Germany and Japan is far stronger than it is in comparable classical trading states such as Sweden, Switzerland, and Singapore. Other theorists, such as Jeffrey Anderson and John Goodman, stress the role of international security institutions like NATO, the EEC, and the CSCE in pacifying Germany. A comparison with the Japanese case, however, reveals that although Japan has but one single external security tie—its bilateral relationship with the United States—it is, if anything, even more antimilitaristic than Germany.[10]

To mitigate the shortcomings of purely structural approaches in the explanation of defense policy formation, the findings of this study indicate that it is useful to focus on how differences in the ideas that nations come to hold and the kinds of institutional arrangements that they possess explain much of the variation in their response to the international security environment, much as scholars working in the field of international political economy have done. Such an approach does not deny the powerful constraints that international forces, such as the balance of power, place on state behavior. Both Germany and Japan have responded to changes in their international environments, although the direction of their responses has remained consistent with their firmly ensconced antimilitarism. To make these observations does not imply a rejection of the claims made by either neorealist or neoliberal theorists concerning the nature of the international system as a whole.[11] Rather, an approach that combines investigations of domestic as well as international political factors enables analysts to construct more powerful explanatory models of foreign policy and allows them to arrive at better predictions of individual state behavior.

In exploring the impact of the domestic political system on defense policy, it is not enough to examine only the concrete interests of various domestic political actors. Although political scientists who study defense policies from a comparative perspective give at least token recognition to the impact of cultural forces, for the most part they prefer to focus on variables that better fit a rational actor account of human behavior, such as bureaucratic or interest group politics.[12] As with international structural explanations, such a focus on the interests of political actors cannot adequately account for many important features of actual policy making. The empirical evidence from the German and Japanese cases reveals a number of instances in which larger, culturally determined considerations shaped how domestic actors defined their own as well as the national interest, causing them to behave in a manner quite different from what a rational actor model might predict.

For instance, it is perfectly natural that Japanese defense manufacturers have lobbied for an increase in defense spending and a loosening of controls on arms exports. Yet one cannot understand why Japanese mainstream business leaders have consistently opposed such initiatives unless one takes into account their historically grounded fear that a large defense industry might strengthen the far Right and their extreme sensitivity to the antimilitarist sentiments rampant in Japanese society. In Germany, in contrast, there is a far weaker fear of a right-wing takeover. Hence, German business leaders have made no concerted effort to hinder the growth of the German defense industry even though their objective interests are not much different from those of their Japanese counterparts.

Finally, this study has demonstrated the utility of an approach to political culture that combines the study of formal political institutions with the investigation of their broader cultural-ideological context. In the field of comparative politics there has recently been an upsurge of interest in the way ideas, norms, and values interact with institutions to influence state policies. In this regard Peter Hall's work on the development of British and French economic policy has been particularly influential.[13] A growing number of international relations theorists, among them John Odell, Judith Goldstein, Emmanuel Adler, and Peter M. Haas, have made use of similar approaches to explore the impact of ideas on foreign policy making.[14] While acknowledging the power of public opinion, these theoretically sophisticated approaches generally focus on the formalized ideas and beliefs prevalent in elite sectors of society.[15] They tend to neglect, however, the role of less clearly articulated but widely shared societal beliefs and values that inform political behavior.

A clear illustration of the shortcomings of focusing on formal ideas and institutions alone is provided by the way in which Japanese defense policy has progressed through the imposition of a succession of legal restrictions *(hadome)* on the military establishment. An institutionalist approach would duly note the existence of policies such as Article 9 of the Constitution, the three non-nuclear principles, and the 1 percent limit on defense spending, and would correctly identify them as important barriers to the expansion of the Japanese military. What would be overlooked by such an analysis is the fact that these institutions originate in the broader, historically grounded Japanese conviction that the armed forces are a potential threat to democracy that must be isolated and carefully constrained by civilian authorities. Thus, even when one of these safeguards is dropped or altered, it is invariably replaced by a new policy whose underlying objective—to contain the military—is much the same. Try as one might, one can find no requirement anywhere in the Japanese constitution or in the laws governing the Self-Defense Forces that such an endless succession of brakes be imposed. Yet the existence of such practices is itself one of the primary handicaps under which Japanese defense planners have to labor. The safeguards are symptoms, not the cause, of Japan's culture of antimilitarism.

Independently of the institutionalists, researchers such as Ronald Inglehart, Robert J. Putnam, and Aaron Wildavsky have succeeded in breathing new life into the political-culture paradigm developed in the 1950s and 1960s. They have analyzed the impact of culture and ideology on a broad range of social and political phenomena, including the emergence of new social movements, the effectiveness of civic organizations, and the increased risk aversion in advanced industrial nations.[16] In a certain respect, however, this new wave of political-cultural research suffers from the reverse problem of the institutional approach. Scholars working in this paradigm have focused on culture as it is rooted in the microlevel institutions of society—the family, the church, and so forth. Consequently, all changes in political culture are seen as bubbling up from changes occurring at this level. Hence, these scholars tend to neglect the impact of forces flowing from the macroinstitutional level, which in turn can shape and give direction to widely held beliefs and behavior.

In short, the historical-cultural approach developed in this study bridges the institutional and the political-cultural literatures. To remedy the shortcomings of the structural approaches to ideas, it uses the insights provided by the concept of political culture to put ideas back into their larger domestic political context. On the other hand, in focusing on how cultural norms and beliefs are shaped and operate in the political arena, this approach remedies the bias of culturally inclined analyses to ignore the influence of elites and elite bargaining in the formation and maintenance of cultures. In other words, the present approach proposes a pluralist model of culture formation that puts politics back into political culture without necessarily resorting to Gramscian notions of intellectual hegemony.[17]

The Generalizability of the Cultural Model

By its very nature, the concept of culture inclines the analyst to focus on the unique aspects of states and societies. Hence, any analysis that stresses the importance of the cultural dimension raises the question of whether the model it proposes can be generalized to other cases, or whether the social sciences in dealing with cultural variables are condemned to return to purely idiographic studies of individual countries or political systems.

The answer to this question depends in part on whether it is possible to identify common processes in the development of all cultures. Although the political-military culture of any particular country is unique, the way in which it is formed and evolves may follow universal patterns.[18] The notion of process generalizability can, of course, be challenged, and this is precisely what many postmodernist theorists do when they argue that each culture develops according to its own rules and dynamics.[19]

The research findings presented here suggest that some such general processes were at work in the development of postwar German and Japanese political-military cultures. The differences between German and Japanese society are many and profound, beginning with the fact that Germany is a European nation that shares with other Western cultures the classical Greco-Roman and Judeo-Christian intellectual heritage. Japan, on the other hand, is an Asian society steeped in the Confucian tradition and its own syncretistic blend of Buddhism and Shintoism. Yet, despite these and many other differences, the historical development of postwar German and Japanese antimilitarism followed remarkably similar paths of development.

Against a backdrop of widespread war weariness and disillusionment in the wake of World War II, confusion reigned in both countries over how to deal with security issues. Ideological boundaries were fluid, and former militarists like Ishiwara Kanji became pacifists while antiwar liberals like Ishibashi Tanzan became proponents of rearmament. In both countries three subcultures gradually emerged, forming along a left-center-right spectrum according to their views of the economic, social, and political status quo. Each of these distinctive subcultures was supported by a coalition of political interests, and each sought to propagate its own distinctive vision of national identity and the nation's mission in world affairs based on its interpretation of recent history. Moreover, the composition of these ideological coalitions in the two countries were broadly similar with much of the intelligentsia and labor movement on the Left and business groups on the Right or Center.

In the ensuing political battles, a number of external factors were important. Above all, the Allied occupation after World War II and American foreign policy tipped the balance in favor of moderate, pro-Western forces. Thereafter a consensus on defense gradually emerged in both countries in remarkably similar ways. During the first twenty years of its existence this hard-won and, at first, somewhat fragile political consensus grew by making shifts toward the political center, as public opinion and a number of elite political groups came to accept the new policies and the arguments made to legitimate them. Eventually, as we have seen, this shift toward the center in the distribution of attitudes toward defense was followed by a deeper shift in the content of the views of the different political-military subcultures. Increasingly, the political Left, Right, and Center in both Germany and Japan came to share similar beliefs and values concerning defense, even though deep-rooted differences over many issues remained, and changes in the international system sparked new controversies. Driving the trend toward consensus was a process of negotiated reality, as political groups accepted each other's views as part of the coalition-building process.

It is possible to generalize the processes of cultural evolution identified in the analysis of German and Japanese national security policy to other countries and other issue areas. Among the central features of this process model are: first, a pattern of political fragmentation following a major shock; second, the emergence of a number of subcultures bound together by common ideological interpretations of history and definitions of reality; and third, the development of a consensus, first on the level of the distribution of the coherent subcultures, and subsequently reinforced through a negotiated transformation of the views of the different groups themselves.

To put it differently, a process that begins as debate over highly fluid ideas and notions about defense and national identity coalesces and becomes sedimented and institutionalized through a process of negotiation, ultimately culminating in a relatively stable new political-military culture. In the German and Japanese cases this new political-military culture happened to be profoundly antimilitaristic in character. This does not have to be so in other cases. The examination of a broader range of cases could help refine our understanding of the process of historical and cultural change and make these preliminary findings more robust.

Variations on the Political-Cultural Model

After study of a larger number of cases, it might be possible to create a typology of different of kinds of political-military cultures and the conditions under which they emerge. Postwar Germany and Japan may be seen as unusually pure examples of a larger category of antimilitarist cultures. Although it may be difficult to identify other examples of antimilitarism as pure as those of Germany and Japan, it is possible to locate other cases in which comparable conditions existed and to inquire whether similar patterns of political behavior emerged. In cases where this did not occur, the researcher would set out to isolate cultural and institutional features that led to the development of a different political-military culture. Italy is a prime candidate for such an investigation, as are the Netherlands, Belgium, and the United States. An examination of U.S. bouts with isolationism in the 1930s and 1970s suggests itself here.

Jack Snyder's study of the sources of overexpansion suggests the existence of another category of hyperaggressive states whose attitudes toward the military and the use of force are diametrically opposite those of antimilitarist cultures.[20] Further research may make it possible to identify yet more varieties of political-military cultures, to specify their features, and to analyze the structural and ideational forces that cause them to come into being.

Implications for Foreign Policy

In terms of their practical implications, the findings of this study offer a peculiar combination of "good news" and "bad news" for American foreign policy and world politics. The good news is that, contrary to the pessimistic expectations of many observers, it is highly unlikely that either Germany or Japan will aspire to the status of great military power for some time to come. Neighboring countries need not fear a resurgence of German or Japanese adventurism, nor should the United States worry about their emergence as rival hegemonic powers in their respective regions.

In this connection it is worth noting that the widely held view that Japan's antimilitarism is less genuine than Germany's, and hence more easily discarded, is entirely mistaken. Proponents of this point of view typically point to two factors. First, they cite Japan's failure to face up to the atrocities committed by its military during the 1930s and 1940s as evidence that the forces of aggressive nationalism are still smoldering and could be easily rekindled. Second, they maintain that the relatively unstable East Asian security environment creates powerful incentives for Japanese policy makers to take greater responsibility for their own security.

Yet paradoxically, both of these factors may in fact have the opposite effect: They make it more rather than less likely that Japan will be able to handle issues of military security in an effective manner. Japan's continued inability to face up to the demons of its recent past has fueled fears both there and abroad of the danger of an aggressive nationalism. As we have seen, such fears have acted as a powerful constraint on the Japanese government's ability to respond to security threats and historically have strengthened antimilitarist sentiments rather than weakened them. Similarly, Germany's memberships in NATO and the EEC have made it easier for German leaders to legitimate the Bundeswehr's participation in military operations as long as they are conducted in a multilateral framework. Japanese leaders, on the other hand, have no similar multilateral crutch to fall back on. Hence, the political threshold that needs to be crossed before the Self-Defense Forces can engage in combat is much higher than in Japan than in Germany. In sum, instead of weakening Japan's antimilitarism, the country's unwillingness to confront its past has strengthened its pacifist inclinations. And instead of increasing the likelihood of a military buildup, Japan's relatively unstable security environment has only served to heighten its desire to avoid conflict.

This latter point brings us to what can be described as the "bad news" of the findings of this study. Germany's and Japan's unwillingness or inability to respond to military security threats is much greater than is assumed by those who believe that their behavior is merely the consequence of the free ride on security they receive from the United States. This, of course, makes the problem of achieving an equitable sharing of the burden of international security far more intractable. If the United States were to reduce its commitment to European and East Asian security, it is far from certain that either country would be ready to take up the slack. Although American policy may have created the conditions that allowed Germany's and Japan's cultures of antimilitarism to take hold and flourish, they have since taken on a dynamic largely independent of American actions.

In the long run it is neither desirable nor possible for the United States alone to bear the primary responsibility for world order. A precipitous U.S. withdrawal is likely to trigger destructive regional conflicts that, like World Wars I and II, would eventually draw the United States in at a far higher cost in lives and treasure than it would have to pay to sustain its present commitments. Fortunately, as the findings of this study suggest, Germany's and Japan's political-military cultures are continuing to evolve and develop in response to changes in their external circumstances, albeit at a sometimes maddeningly sluggish pace. A rapid shift in attitudes is only likely if the German and Japanese political systems experience massive shocks that conclusively demonstrate that their present approaches to national security have failed. The most plausible scenarios for such a shock would involve the simultaneous disintegration of their current alliance structures combined with the emergence of a serious security threat, perhaps in the form of a resurgent, nationalist Russia or a militarily belligerent People's Republic of China. Alternatively, an incident of nuclear threat by terrorist groups or rogue states such as North Korea could shake German or Japanese security policy to its core.

Even were a shock of such magnitude to materialize, in all likelihood a severe domestic political crisis would ensue and neither nation would, on its own, be able to respond quickly or effectively. As occurred after World War II, new coalitions of political actors would emerge, each offering new interpretations of recent and past events designed to legitimate their preferred policies. It is difficult to predict what kind of new political-military cultures would emerge at the end of such a process. A hard-nosed realism might take hold. In the most extreme scenario, nationalist sentiments might be rekindled and combined with a mood of resentment directed at a real or imagined betrayal by the outside world.

If pragmatic realism were to win out, the international system that would emerge would be at once more complex and unstable than the one we see today. In the long run, such an outcome may be inevitable, even without a major external shock, if the United States allows the Cold War alliance structures to decay. Given their demographic weight, industrial strength, and political importance, Germany and Japan are eventually likely to regain a greater sense of national self-confidence and purpose. In the absence of a set of international institutions that can both harness and constrain their potential, the international system would move "back to the future," to the balancing and shifting alliances that characterized Europe before World War I.

To avoid such a scenario it is desirable for the United States, together with its other allies, to reinvigorate the current system of multilateral ties and reforge them into effective instruments for dealing with the security problems of the post–Cold War world. Such a strategy need not entail the acceptance of a Wilsonian vision of a global collective security order. The practical difficulties of achieving a true collective security system may well be insurmountable.[21] Nonetheless, multilateral security arrangements are useful devices, not so much as tools of international diplomacy per se, but rather as instruments for legitimating military action on the level of domestic politics. The aim of such arrangements would not be to maximize the inclusiveness of their memberships, as was the case with classical collective security initiatives, but rather to endow them with a maximum degree of flexibility. The United Nations in this respect may be the worst candidate for serving as a centerpiece for a new world order. At the same time, NATO, with its European origins, may be too limited in geographic scope. A new institutional structure could be created that would embrace the current members of NATO together with Japan and perhaps a few other advanced industrial democracies.

Whatever institutional form such a new alliance may take, it would be highly desirable to encourage Germany and Japan to become active not only in peace-keeping operations, but also in more offensive military missions under its auspices. While at first such missions would probably have to be restricted to logistical and support roles, eventually both nations should be expected to commit their forces to regular combat missions, sharing the same risks that are borne by the troops of other democratic nations. With the help of pragmatic leaders in both countries, the United States could thus help these two nations transcend their overly parochial approaches to military security issues while at the same time preserving the most laudable aspect of their new political-military cultures—their determination not to succumb to revived dreams of martial glory and the quest for power.

Notes

Chapter 1. The Cultural Context of Defense Policy Formation

1. Hans J. Morgenthau, *Power among Nations: The Struggle for Peace and Power*, 5th ed. (New York: Alfred A. Knopf, 1978), remains the classic statement of this point of view. For a more recent formulation see Christopher Layne, "The Unipolar Illusion: Why New Great Powers Will Rise," *International Security* 17, no. 4 (1993).

2. For an overview of the German response to the Gulf War see Karl Kaiser and Klaus Becher, "Deutschland und der Irak-Konflikt," *Arbeitspapiere zur Internationalen Politik* 68 (Bonn: Forschungsinstitut der Deutschen Gesellschaft für Auswärtige Politik, 1992); and Michael J. Inacker, *Unter Ausschluß der Öffentlichkeit: Die Deutschen in der Golfallianz* (Bonn-Berlin: Bouvier, 1992). On Japan see Courtney Purrington and K.A., "Tokyo's Policy Responses during the Gulf Crisis," *Asian Survey* 21, no. 4 (1991); and Asahi Shimbun Wangankiki Shuzaihan, *Wangan Sensō to Nihon* (Tokyo: Asahi Shimbunsha, 1991).

3. For examples of these criticisms, see Michael Lind, "Surrealpolitik," *New York Times*, March 28, 1991; "Germany's Ostrich Politik," *New York Times*, January 26, 1991; Alan Sked, "Cheap Excuses: Germany and the Gulf Crisis," *National Interest* no. 24 (1991); "Stand Up, Japan," *Economist*, September 1, 1991, 12. See also Jeffrey Garten, *A Cold Peace: America, Japan, Germany, and the Struggle for Supremacy* (New York: Times Books, 1992), 162–67.

4. See, for example, Okazaki Hisahiko, *Senryakuteki Shikō to wa Nani ka* (Tokyo: Chūōkōshinsho, 1983), ch. 1.

5. For a penetrating analysis of German and Japanese guilt about World War II, see Ian Buruma, *The Wages of Guilt* (New York: Farrar, Straus & Giroux, 1994).

6. See Jeffrey Anderson and John B. Goodman, "Mars or Minerva?: A United Germany in a Post–Cold War Europe," in Robert O. Keohane, Joseph S. Nye, and Stanley Hoffman, eds., *After the Cold War: International Institutions and State Strategies in Europe, 1989–1991* (Cambridge, Mass.: Harvard University Press, 1993).

7. Richard Rosecrance, *The Rise of the Trading State* (New York: Basic Books, 1986).

8. See Stephen Welch, *The Concept of Political Culture* (New York: St. Martin's Press, 1993), esp. 64–72, on the problems of retracing cause and effect.

9. See Carole Pateman, "Political Culture, Political Structure, and Political Change," *British Journal of Sociology* 1, no. 3 (1971), 291–306.

10. See Gabriel Almond and Sydney Verba, *The Civic Culture* (Boston: Little Brown, 1965), 11–14, for the now-classic formulation of the concept of political culture.

11. On the notion of cultural congruence see Harry Eckstein, *Regarding Politics: Essays on Political Theory, Stability, and Change* (Berkeley, Calif.: University of California Press, 1992), ch. 5.

12. It is undoubtedly possible to identify further levels of political culture and refer them to different levels of behavior, though the two levels identified here probably represent the ends of a continuum. It remains an open question, however, to what degree and in what manner historical and anthropological political culture influence one another.

13. Peter Hall, *Governing the Economy: The Politics of State Intervention in Britain and France* (New York: Oxford University Press, 1986), 19.

14. See Kathleen Thelen, Sven Steinmo, and Frank Longstreth, eds., *Structuring Politics* (Cambridge and New York: Cambridge University Press, 1988), 2, esp. n. 9.

15. Michael Thompson, Richard Ellis, and Aaron Wildavsky, *Cultural Theory* (Boulder, Colo.: Westview Press, 1990), 21.

16. See Talcott Parsons, *Social Systems* (Glencoe, Ill.: Free Press, 1951).

17. See Imre Lakatos, "Falsification and the Methodology of Scientific Research Programs," in Imre Lakatos and Alan Musgraves, eds., *Criticism and the Growth of Knowledge* (Cambridge and New York: Cambridge University Press, 1970).

18. Eckstein, *Regarding Politics,* 268.

19. For a more sophisticated version of this type of analysis, see Archie Brown, "Ideology and Political Culture," in Sewryn Bialer, ed., *Politics, Society, and Nationality inside Gorbachev's Russia* (Boulder, Colo.: Westview Press, 1989), esp. 19.

20. Thompson, Ellis, and Wildavsky, *Cultural Theory,* 69–70. Care should be taken, however, to define human needs broadly so as to include subjective cultural needs, such as those for meaning or solidarity, as well as objective needs such as human life or material prosperity.

21. Thomas Kuhn, *The Structure of Scientific Revolutions,* 2d ed. (Chicago: University of Chicago Press, 1970).

22. Jack Snyder, *The Soviet Strategic Culture: Implications for Nuclear Options,* R-2154-AF (Santa Monica, Calif.: Rand, 1977); Colin Gray, "National Styles in Strategy: The American Example," *International Security* 6, no. 2 (1981); Colin Gray, *Nuclear Strategy and National Style* (Lanham, Md.: University Press of America, 1986); Colin Gray, "American Strategic Culture," *Comparative Strategy* 5, no. 3 (1985); Yaacov Vertzberger, *The Worlds in Their Minds: Information Procession, Cognition, and Perception in Foreign Policy Decision-making* (Stanford, Calif.: Stanford University Press, 1990); Yitzak Klein, "A Theory of Strategic Culture," *Comparative Strategy* 10, no. 1 (1991).

23. For a related line of argument, see Friedrich Kratochwil, "On the Notion of 'Interest' in International Relations," *International Organization* 36, no. 2 (1982).

24. Similar arguments are made in Jack Snyder, *The Myths of Empire: Politics and International Ambition* (Ithaca, N.Y.: Cornell University Press, 1991), ch. 1. On the notion of multiple equilibria games, see Geoffrey Garret and Barry Weingast, "Ideas, Interest, and Institutions: Constructing the European Community's Internal Market," in Judith Goldstein and Robert O. Keohane, *Ideas and Foreign Policy: Beliefs, Institutions, and Political Change* (Ithaca, N.Y.: Cornell University Press, 1993).

25. See Brian Barry, *Sociologists, Economists, and Democracy* (London: Collier-Macmillan, 1970); and Carole Pateman, "Political Culture, Political Structures, and Political Change," *British Journal of Sociology* 1, no. 3 (1971), 291–306.

Chapter 2. From Swords into Plowshares and Back

1. Lutz Niethammer, *Die Mitläuferfabrik: Die Entnazifierurung Am Beispiel Bayerns* (Berlin: Dietz, 1982), 16–16n.

2. See Hata Ikuhiko, "The Post War Period in Retrospect," *Japan Echo* 11 (1984), 13–14.

3. See Hata Ikuhiko, *Shiroku Nihonsaigumbi* (Tokyo: Bungeishunjū, 1976), 43–46.

4. See Rolf Steininger, *Wiederbewaffnung: Die Entscheidung für einen westdeutschen Verteidigungsbeitrag: Adenauer und die Westmächte 1950* (Erlangen: Straube, 1989), 76–93.

5. See Meirion and Susie Harries, *Sheathing the Sword: The Demilitarization of Postwar Japan* (New York: Macmillan, 1987), 193, 231; Michael Schaller, *The American Occupation of Japan* (New York: Oxford University Press, 1985), 90.

6. Schaller, *The American Occupation of Japan*, 90. On the importance of Germany and Japan to U.S. strategy in this period, see John Lewis Gaddis, *Strategies of Containment: A Critical Appraisement of American Postwar National Security Policy* (London: Oxford University Press, 1982), 38–39, 114–15.

7. See Mary Ellen Reese, *General Reinhard Gehlen: The CIA Connection* (Fairfax, Va.: George Mason University Press, 1990), esp. 82–85. On the German side, these officers included Adolf Heusinger, future inspector general of the Bundeswehr, and Reinhard Gehlen, founder of the West German intelligence service. On Japan see Hata, *Shiroku Nihonsaigumbi*, 156–57; and Harries, *Sheathing the Sword*, 226–27.

8. See Gerhard Wettig, *Entmilitärisierung und Wiederbewaffnung* (Munich: Oldenbourg, 1967), 276–81; Norbert Wiggershaus and Roland G. Foerster, eds., *Die westliche Sicherheitsgemeinschaft 1948–1950* (Boppard: MGFA, Militärgeschichte seit 1945, 8, 1988, 37–41; Steininger, *Wiederbewaffnung*, 43–45; Hans-Peter Schwarz, *Adenauer der Aufstieg, 1876–1952* (Stuttgart: Deutsche Verlags-Anstalt, 1986), 740–45.

9. John Welfield, *An Empire in Eclipse: Japan in the Postwar American Alliance System* (London and Atlantic Highlands, N.J.: Athlone Press, 1988), 205; Martin E. Weinstein, *Japan's Postwar Defense Policy: 1947–1968* (New York: Columbia University Press, 1971), 20–22; Hata, *Shiroku Nihonsaigumbi*, 88–89.

10. See *Asahi*, August 10, 1950; and Hata, *Shiroku Nihonsaigumbi*, 143.

11. Ernst Nolte, *Deutschland und der Kalte Krieg*, 2d ed. (Stuttgart: Klett-Cotta, 1985), 242.

12. Wettig, *Entmilitärisierung und Wiederbewaffnung*, 91, 276; Schwarz, *Adenauer der Aufstieg*, 748–49.

13. *Asahi*, November 15, 1950.

14. For public attitudes toward rearmament at the time, see Berthold Meyer, *Der Bürger und seine Sicherheit: Zum Verhältnis von Sicherheitsstreben und Sicherheitspolitik* (Frankfurt: Campus Verlag, 1983), 261, table 9.1.1. For more about the German peace movement, see Mark Cioc, *Pax Atomica: The Nuclear Defense Debate in West Germany during the Adenauer Era* (New York: Columbia University Press, 1988); Hans Karl Rupp, *Außenparlamentarische Opposition in der Ära Adenauer—Der Kampf gegen die Atombewaffnung in den fünfziger Jahren* (Köln: Pakl-Rugenstein, 1970); and Nolte, *Deutschland und der Kalte Krieg*, esp. 41–85, 382–90.

15. Hata, *Shiroku Nihonsaigumbi*.

16. John Dower, *Empire and Aftermath: Yoshida Shigeru and the Japanese Experience* (Cambridge, Mass.: Harvard University Press, 1979), 16–17, 387, 425, 428.

17. Dower, *Empire and Aftermath*, 134–35, 235–40, 257–65.

18. Dower, *Empire and Aftermath*, 388–89; Frank Kowalski, *Nihon no Saigumbi* (Tokyo: Simul Press, 1969), 72–73.

19. See Hata, *Shiroku Nihonsaigumbi*, 131–35; Weinstein, *Japan's Postwar Defense Policy*, 49–50, 50–61, and Dower, *Empire and Aftermath*, 393.

20. Dower, *Empire and Aftermath*, 400–414; Welfield, *An Empire in Eclipse*, 52–54.

21. Catherine Kelleher, *Germany and the Politics of Nuclear Weapons* (New York: Columbia University Press, 1976), 11–28; Hans-Peter Schwarz, *Die Ära Adenauer, 1949–1957*, vol. 2 of *Geschicte der Bundesrepublik Deutschland* (Stuttgart: Deutsche Verlags-Anstalt; Wiesbaden: Brockhaus, 1981), 144–49. When Adenauer pledged not to produce ABC weapons, he made clear in response to questions from Dulles that he considered the pledge *rebus sic stantibus*, that is, valid only so long as the conditions under which it was concluded exist.

22. Conversely, the alliances could also be viewed as a form of dual containment: They were means of containing both the Soviet Union and the former Axis powers.

23. The clearest and most succinct description of the dilemmas of Cold War alliance politics remains A.W. DePorte, *Europe between the Superpowers: The Enduring Balance* (New Haven, Conn.: Yale University Press, 1979).

24. Dower, *Empire and Aftermath*, 400–414; Welfield, *An Empire in Eclipse*, 52–54.

25. Kosaka Masataka, *Saishō Yoshida Shigeru* (Tokyo: Chūōkōgyōsho, 1968), 64–71.

26. For more on the French decision, see Raymond Aron and Daniel Praeger, *France Defeats the EDC* (New York: Praeger, 1957); Alfred Grosser, *Deutschland im Westen* (Munich: Deutscher Taschenbuch-Verlag, 1985), 132–42; Schwarz, *Die Ära Adenauer*, 221–28.

27. The WEU was set up in 1948 in order to placate the French, who wished to ensure that control of German forces not rest exclusively with U.S.-dominated NATO, but was shared with a purely European organization as well.

28. The new pledge represented a significant watering down of the original 1952 promise insofar as West Germany agreed only to forgo the *production* of nuclear weapons, leaving open the option that it might acquire them through other means (presumably from its allies). See Matthias Küntzel, *Bonn und die Bombe: Deutsche Atomwaffenpolitik von Adenauer bis Brandt* (Frankfurt/Main: Campus Verlag, 1992), 19–21.

29. The text of the agreement can be found in Klaus von Schubert, *Sicherheitspolitik der Bundesrepublik Deutschland*, vol. 1 (Köln: Verlag Wissenschaft und Politik, 1978), 153–70. See also Dennis L. Bark and David R. Gress, *From Shadow to Substance* (Oxford: Basil Blackwill, 1989), 330–32.

30. See von Schubert, *Sicherheitspolitik der Bundesrepublik Deutschland*, vol. 1, 153–70. See also Bark and Gress, *From Shadow to Substance*, 330–32.

31. See Schwarz, *Die Ära Adenauer*, 254–57.

32. Udo F. Löwke, *Für den Fall, daß ... die Haltung der SPD zur Wehrfrage, 1945–1955* (Hanover: Verlag für Literatur und Zeitgeschehen, 1969), 207.

33. The text of the German Manifesto can be found in Christoph Butterwegge and Heinz-Gerd Hofschen, *Sozialdemokratie, Krieg und Frieden,* (Heilbronn: Distel, 1984), 289–91.

34. See Butterwegge and Hofschen, *Sozialdemokratie, Krieg und Frieden,* 289–91.

35. See Schwarz, *Die Ära Adenauer,* 259–62.

36. See Nobuo Tomita, Akira Nakamura, and Ronald J. Hrebenar, "The Liberal Democratic Party of Japan: The Ruling Party of Japan," in Ronald J. Hrebenar, ed., *The Japanese Party System: From One-Party Rule to Coalition Government* (Boulder, Colo.: Westview Press, 1986), 237–41.

37. Many in the Foreign Ministry were concerned that these inadequacies could spark a crisis. Hara Yoshihisa, *Sengo Nihon to Kokusai Seiji: Ampokaitei no Seijirikigaku* (Tokyo: Chūōkōronsha, 1988), 86; Weinstein, *Japan's Postwar Defense Policy,* 64. On the LDP's hidden agenda, see Welfield, *An Empire in Eclipse,* 120–22.

38. See Hatakeyama Hirobumi, "Keishokuhō kaisei to Seijiteki Riidaashippu," in Ōtake Hideo, ed., *Nihonseiji no Sōten* (Tokyo: Sanichi Shobo, 1984), esp. 85–87; Fuji Shoichi and Ōe Shinobu, *Sengo Nihon to Rekishi,* vol. 2 (Tokyo: Aoki Shoten, 1974), 37–55; George R. Packard, *Protest in Tokyo: The Security Treaty Crisis of 1960* (Princeton, N.J.: Princeton University Press, 1966), 101–3, 126.

39. See Packard, *Protest in Tokyo,* ch. 3, for a discussion of the genesis of the radical protest groups.

40. Welfield, *An Empire in Eclipse,* 140.

41. See ibid., 162–63.

42. See Karel van Wolferen, *The Enigma of Japanese Power* (New York: Alfred A. Knopf, 1989), 103.

43. See Bark and Gress, *From Shadow to Substance,* 280–81.

44. In the German case in particular this was to prove rather difficult, since the type of armored forces needed to implement a mobile defense of German territory could just as easily be used to engage in offensive activities.

45. See John E. Endicott, *Japan's Nuclear Option: Political, Technical, and Strategic Factors* (New York: Praeger, 1975); and Kelleher, *Germany and the Politics of Nuclear Weapons,* esp. 18.

46. Elisabeth Noelle-Neumann, *The German Public Opinion Polls 1947–1966* (Westport, Conn.: Greenwood Press, 1981), 436–37.

47. See Osamu Nishi, *The Constitution and National Defense Law System in Japan* (Tokyo: Seibundo, 1987), 40–41.

48. Initially Adenauer's military advisors planned a conventional defense, but it soon became apparent that neither the United States nor its allies were willing to shoulder the costs of creating and maintaining the necessary massive military force. Thereafter, NATO was compelled to rely on nuclear weapons to compensate for its weakness in conventional forces. Lawrence S. Kaplan, *NATO and the United States* (Boston: Twayne, 1988), 50–62.

49. See Cioc, *Pax Atomica,* 29–31.

50. Cioc, *Pax Atomica,* 36–37, 42–50; Küntzel, *Bonn und die Bombe,* 34–38; Schwarz, *Die Ära Adenauer,* 356–63.

51. See, for example, Welfield, *An Empire in Eclipse,* 201–5; Sugita Ichiji, *Wasurerarete iru Anzenhoshō* (Tokyo: Jiji Tsūshin, 1967), esp. 270–80. See ch. 6 with regard to the Three Arrows incident.

52. Küntzel, *Bonn und die Bombe,* 34–36.

53. For more on the concept of internal vs. external controls, see Samuel P. Huntington, *The Soldier and the State* (Boston: Little Brown, 1957).

54. Kowalski, *Nihon no Saigumbi*, 129–33.

55. See Nishi, *The Constitution and the National Defense Law System*, 119–30; Leonard A. Humphrey, "The Japanese Military Tradition," in James H. Buck, ed., *The Modern Japanese Military System* (Beverly Hills, Calif.: Sage Publications, 1975); Nishioka Akira, *Gendai no Shiberian Kontroru* (Tokyo: Chishikisha, 1988); and Hirose Katsuya, *Kanryō to Gunjin: Bunmintōsei no Genkai* (Tokyo: Iwanami Shoten, 1989), 60–77.

56. It appears likely that Yoshida and his advisors initially viewed the PRF as an extension of the police forces, and evidence suggests that until 1952 Yoshida hoped to create a separate, high-quality military force free of the influence of the old military. See Ōtake Hideo, *Saigumbi to Nashyonarizumu* (Tokyo: Chūōkōshinsho, 1989); Peter J. Katzenstein and Nobuo Okawara, *Japan's National Security: Structures, Norms, and Policy Responses in a Changing World* (Ithaca, N.Y.: Cornell University Press, East Asia Series, 1992), 21–56.

57. Ōtake, *Saigumbi to Nashyonarizumu*, 87–89; Masuhara Keiichi, "Keisatu Yobitai kara Jietai made," in Ando Yoshio, ed., *Shōwa Keizaishi e no Shōgen*, vol. 3 (Tokyo: Mainichi Shimbunsha, 1966), 390; Katō Yozo, *Shiroku Jietaishi* (Tokyo: Bōei Kōsaikai, 1979), 45.

58. Welfield, *An Empire in Eclipse*, 61–62; Joseph P. Keddell, Jr., *The Politics of Defense in Japan: Managing Internal and External Pressures* (Armonk, N.Y.: M.E. Sharpe, 1993), 32–35; *Asahi*, June 2, 1954.

59. Wolfgang R. Vogt, *Militär und Demokratie: Funktionen und Konflikte der Institution der Wehrbeauftragften* (Hamburg: R.V. Decker's Verlag G. Schenk, 1972), 12–25.

60. Wolf Graf Baudissin, *Soldat für den Frieden: Entwürfe für eine zeitgemässe Bundeswehr* (Munich: R. Piper and Co., 1969); Vogt, *Militär und Demokratie*, 24–88; Ulrich Simon, *Die Integration der Bundeswehr in die Gesellschaft: Das Ringen um die Innere Führung* (Heidelberg/Hamburg: R.V. Decker's Verlag G. Schenk, 1980), 24–88; Donald Abenheim, *Reforging the Iron Cross* (Princeton, N.J.: Princeton University Press, 1988), ch. 2. The original ideas were present in the Himmerdoder Denkschrift that laid the foundations of the new armed forces; see Hans-Jürgen Rautenberg und Norbert Wiggershaus, *Die Himmeroder Denkschrift vom Oktober 1950* (Karlsruhe: MGA, 1985), 37–38, 57.

61. Simon, *Die Integration der Bundeswehr in die Gesellschaft*, 96–197; Dietrich Genschel, *Innere Führung 1951–1956: Eine Fallstudie zur Vorbereitung einer Reform* (diss., Freiburg University, 1972) and (Hamburg: R.V. Decker's Verlag G. Schenk, 1972). Quotations here are from the Genschel dissertation and Norbert Wiggershaus, "Zur Debatte un die Tradition Künftiger Streitkräfte 1950–1955–6," in MGFA, *Tradition und Reform in den Aufbaujahren der Bundeswehr* (Herford: E.S. Mittler, 1985).

62. See Schwarz, *Die Ära Adenauer*, 291–92.

63. Author's interview with Willi Weiskirch in Bonn, June 1990. Weiskirch is a former member of the CDU and Wehrbeauftragften. During the 1950s he was a leading member of the Christian Democratic youth wing. CDU pamphlet by Willi Weiskirch, *Nie wieder Kommiß: Es muß alles anders werden*, c. 1955.

64. Abenheim, *Reforging the Iron Cross*, 123–25; Udo F. Löwke, *Für den Fall, daß . . . die Haltung der SPD zur Wehrfrage, 1949–1955;* Gordon D. Drummond, *The German Social Democrats in Opposition, 1949–1960: The Case against Rearmament* (Norman, Okla.: University of Oklahoma Press, 1982), 121–24.

65. Abenheim, *Reforging the Iron Cross*; Vogt, *Militär und Demokratie*; Genschel, *Innere Führung 1951–1956*, 200–204; *Innere Führung und Recht*, Texte und Studien Zentrum Innere Führung, Heft no. 1, (Koblenz 1983), esp. 33–34.

66. Simon, *Die Integration der Bundeswehr in die Gesellschaft*, 97–111; Genschel, *Innere Führung 1951–1956*, 216–22.

67. See Karl Hegner, Ekkehard Lippert, and Roland Wakenhut, *Selektion oder Sozialisation* (Opladen: Westdeutscher Verlag, 1983), 107–29, esp. 112–14.

Chapter 3. The Anatomy of Two New Political-Military Cultures

1. For other descriptive typologies of the ideological groupings in Japan, see Michael Mochizuki, "Japan's Search for Strategy," *International Security* 8, no. 3 (1983/1984); Umemoto Tetsuya, "Arms and Alliance in Japanese Public Opinion" (Ph.D. diss., Princeton University, 1985); Ito Kobun, *Japan's Defense: Its Present and Future* (Tokyo: National Institute for Defense Studies, 1985); Chuma Kiyofuku, *Saigumbi no Seijigaku* (Tokyo: Chishikisha, 1985), 177–80. For typologies for West Germany, see Thomas Risse-Kappen, *Die Krise der Sicherheitspolitik* (Mainz-München: Kaiser Grünwald, 1988); Anne-Marie Barley, "The Once and Future German Question," *Foreign Affairs* 68, no. 5 (1989–90); David P. Calleo, *The German Problem Reconsidered: Germany and the World Order, 1870 to the Present* (Cambridge and New York: Cambridge University Press, 1978), esp. 177; and Stephen F. Szabo, *The Changing Politics of German Security* (London: Pinter, 1990), ch. 1.

2. See Joji Watanuki, "Pattern of Politics in Present Day Japan," in S.M. Lipset and Steiner Rokkan, eds., *Party Systems and Voter Alignments* (New York: Free Press, 1967). For a recent reevaluation, see Miyake Ichirō, *Tōhyōkōdō* (Tokyo: Tokyodaigaku Shuppankai, 1989), 151–68.

3. See Calleo, *The German Problem Reconsidered*, 177; Barley, "The Once and Future German Question"; and Szabo, *The Changing Politics of German Security*, ch. 1.

4. John Dower, *Empire and Aftermath: Yoshida Shigeru and the Japanese Experience* (Cambridge, Mass.: Harvard University Press, 1979), ch. 7.

5. Hans-Peter Schwarz, *Die Ära Adenauer, 1949–1957*, vol. 2 of *Geschicte der Bundesrepublik Deutschland* (Stuttgart: Deutsche Verlags-Anstalt; Wiesbaden: Brockhaus, 1981). Similar feelings were exhibited by Adenauer's self-described "grandson," Helmut Kohl, following German reunification in 1989.

6. Schwarz, *Die Ära Adenauer*.

7. These tendencies of the West Europeanists came to the fore in the 1960s, leading to the famous Atlanticist versus Gaullist split in the CDU discussed in ch. 4.

8. See Szabo, *The Changing Politics of German Security*, ch. 1.

9. See J.A.A. Stockwin, *The Japanese Socialist Party and Neutralism* (Melbourne: Melbourne University Press, 1968), ch. 3.

10. Kojima Ryo, *Hangarii Jiken to Nihon* (Tokyo: Chūōkōshinsho, 1987).

11. See Eckhardt Contze, "Von Genf nach Ottawa: Zum Zusammenhang von deutscher Einheit, europäischer Sicherheit und Internationaler Abrüstung am Ende der Fünfziger Jahre und Heute" (Ebenhausen: Stiftung Wissenschaft und Politik Working Paper, 1990).

12. See Mark Cioc, *Pax Atomica: The Nuclear Defense Debate in West Germany during the*

Adenauer Era (New York: Columbia University Press, 1988), 25–28; Bogislav von Bonin, *Atomkrieg—Unser Ende* (Recklinghausen: J. Bauer, 1955).

13. See Kent E. Calder, *Crisis and Compensation: Public Policy and Political Stability in Japan* (Princeton, N.J.: Princeton University Press, 1988), esp. 349–52, 362.

14. On the economic benefits of the alliance, see Jitsuo Tsuchiyama, "The Origins of the U.S.-Japanese Alliance," *Aoyama Kokusai Seiji Review Ronshu* no. 5 (1986), 41, 58–59.

15. See Etō Shinkichi and Yamamoto Yoshinobu, *Sōgōampo to Mirai no Sentaku* (Tokyo: Kodansha, 1991), 223; and Berthold Meyer, *Der Bürger und seine Sicherheit: Zum Verhältnis von Sicherheitsstreben und Sicherheitspolitik* (Frankfurt: Campus Verlag, 1983), 216, table 3.2.1.

16. Etō and Yamamoto, *Sōgōampo*, 223.

17. Meyer, *Der Bürger und seine Sicherheit,* 216.

18. Nishihara Kazukichi, "Nichibei Ampotaisei," *Jiyū* (January 1981), 19–20.

19. In a 1956 survey, 38 percent rated reunification as the most important issue, followed by the economy (28 percent) and peace (16 percent). This trend increased during the decade. Elisabeth Noelle-Neumann, "Die Verklärung Adenauer und die öffentliche Meinung 1949–1976," in Dieter Blumenwitz et al., eds., *Konrad Adenauer und seine Zeit, Persönlichkeit und Politik des ersten Bundeskanzlers* (Stuttgart: Deutsche Verlags-Anstalt, 1976), 531; Meyer, *Der Bürger und seine Sicherheit,* 234–47; Hans-Adolf Jacobsen, "Zur Rolle der Öffentlichen Meinung bei der Debatte um die Wiederbewaffnung, 1950–1955," in Militär-Geschichtliches Forschungsamt, ed., *Aspekte der Wiederbewaffnung, bis 1955* (Boppard: Harald Boldt Verlag, 1985), 65–67.

20. In response to the question, "In light of the current world situation should American forces stay in Germany or leave?," even at the height of neutralist sentiment in 1956 a plurality of Germans preferred that they remain, 43 to 41 percent. For most of the period 1950–1957, majorities as high as 71 percent supported U.S. presence. See Meyer, *Der Bürger und seine Sicherheit,* 221, table 3.8.2.1. However, approximately two-thirds of those who supported U.S forces in Germany regarded them as an unavoidable necessity rather than as welcome protectors. See Meyer, *Der Bürger und seine Sicherheit,* 221, table 3.8.1.

21. See ibid., 271, table 11.3.1. See also tables 11.3.2.1 and 11.3.2.2.

22. See ibid., 240, table 5.1.6.1.1.

23. Ibid., 219, tables 3.3.6 and 3.3.7.

24. Nishihara Kazukichi, "Nihon Kempō," *Jiyū* (February 1981), 157. See also Etō and Yamamoto, *Sōgōampo*, 87.

25. On a number of issues, many Germans had right-wing ideas. For example, solid majorities rejected the acceptance of the loss of German territories absorbed by Poland, Czechoslovakia, and the U.S.S.R. Meyer, *Der Bürger und seine Sicherheit,* 243, table 5.1.9.3.1. On the far right in West Germany during this period, see Manfred Rowold, "Im Schatten der Macht: Die nicht-etablierte Kleinparteien," in Heinrich Oberreuter and Alf Mintzel, *Parteien in der Bundesrepublik Deutschland* (Munich: Olzog, 1990), 316–31; and Ekkart Zimmerman and Thomas Saalfeld, "The Three Waves of West German Right-Wing Extremism," in Peter H. Merkl and Leon Weinberg, eds., *Encounters with the Radical Right* (Boulder, Colo.: Westview Press, 1992).

26. See Bob Burns and Wilfred van der Will, *Protest and Democracy in West Germany* (New York: St. Martin's Press, 1988), 28.

27. Hermann Rausching, *Deutschland zwischen Ost und West* (Berlin: 1950).

28. Ernst Nolte, *Deutschland und der Kalte Krieg,* 2d ed. (Stuttgart: Klett-Cotta, 1985), 252–56.

29. See Nolte, *Deutschland und der Kalte Krieg,* 256, 280–91; Cioc, *Pax Atomica,* ch. 3 and 4.

30. Morito Tatsuo, "Heiwa Kokka no Kensetsu," *Kenso* (January 1946); Nambara Shigeru, *Heiwa no Sengen* (Tokyo: Tokyodaigaku Shuppanbu, 1951).

31. See George R. Packard, *Protest in Tokyo: The Security Treaty Crisis of 1960* (Princeton, N.J.: Princeton University Press, 1966).

32. Fukuda Tsuneari, *Jyōshiki ni Kaere* (Tokyo: Shidōsha, 1960); Etō Jun, *Hisuke ga aru Bunsho* (Tokyo: Chikuma Shobō, 1960); Inoki Masamichi, "Seijiteki no Kiki no Soko ni aru Mono," *Chūōkōron* (August 1960).

33. The author is grateful to Professors Inoki Masamichi, Satō Seizaburō, and Munakata Iwao for discussions of the intellectual climate of the period.

34. For a frank discussion of the nationalist character of the neutralist movement in Japan, see Maruyama Masao, "Nationalism in Post-War Japan," *Institute of Pacific Relations Bulletin* (October 1950); Ōtake Hideo, *Saigumbi to Nashyonarizumu* (Tokyo: Chuōkōshinsho, 1989), 177–78.

35. See Burns and van der Will, *Protest and Democracy,* 27–31.

36. See Kojima, *Hangarii Jiken to Nihon,* esp. ch. 2 and 52–57.

37. Jacobsen, "Zur Rolle der Öffentlichen Meinung," 76–81.

38. See Jacobsen, "Zur Rolle der Öffentlichen Meinung," 89–90. Many of the scholars, such as Theodor Adorno and Max Horkheimer, who acted as advisors to the Defense Ministry were far from conservative and had views quite close to those of the SPD.

39. See Jung Bok Lee, *The Political Character of the Japanese Press,* International Study Series, no. 6 (Seoul: Seoul National University, Institute of Social Studies, 1985), 62–73.

40. Lee, *The Political Character of the Japanese Press;* Packard, *Protest in Tokyo.*

41. See, for example, chief editor and founder Rudolf Augstein's editorials (written under the pen name Jens Daniel) in *Der Spiegel,* October 2, 1948, and March 27, 1951.

42. See Hans Dieter Fischer, *Handbuch der Politischen Presse in Deutschland, 1480–1980* (Düsseldorf: Droste Verlag, 1981), esp. 321–54, for an overview of the development and political orientation of the postwar West German press.

43. Paul Sethe, for example, argued strongly that government should not ignore Stalin's note of 1952 offering to open negotiations on German reunification on the eve of the ratification of the EDC treaty. This stance contributed to Sethe's removal from the newspaper in 1955. See *Frankfurter Allgemeine Zeitung,* April 15, 1952.

44. See Reiner Steinweg, "Die Bedeutung der Gewerkschaften für die Friedensbewegung," in Reiner Steinweg, ed., *Die Neue Friedensbewegung* (Frankfurt/Main: Suhrkamp, 1952); and Ernst-Dieter Köpper, *Gewerkschaften und Außenpolitik* (Frankfurt/Main: Campus Verlag, 1982).

45. See Ōtake, *Saigumbi to Nashyonarizumu,* ch. 4.

46. Important minorities in Japan's business community were interested in preserving their traditional business ties to the East. See Sadako Ogata, "The Business Community and Japanese Foreign Relations: The Normalization of Relations with the People's Republic of China," in Robert A. Scalapino, *The Foreign Policy of Modern Japan* (Berkeley, Calif.: University of California Press, 1977), 179–81.

47. See Chitoshi Yanaga, *Big Business in Japanese Politics* (New Haven, Conn.: Yale University Press, 1968); Arnulf Baring, *Im Anfang war Adenauer* (Stuttgart: Deutsche Verlags-Anstalt, 1971), 322. See also *Jahresbericht des Bundesverbandes der Deutschen Industries* (1952–1953), 9.

48. See Arizawa Hirotatsu and Ineba Yuzo, *Shiryō Sengo Nijyūnenshi*, vol. 2 (Tokyo: Nihon Hyōronsha, 1966), 160.

49. On MITI's interest during this period, see Ōtake Hideo, "Nihon ni okeru 'Gunsankan fukugōtai' keisei no Zasetsu," in Ōtake Hideo, ed., *Nihonseiji no Sōten* (Tokyo: Sanichi Shobo, 1984), 34–37. On U.S. efforts to tie aid to increased Japanese defense spending see ibid., 45–59; Sakanaka Tomohisa, "Jietai no Jitai," in *Nihon no Jieiryoku* no. 8 (Tokyo: Asahi Shimbun Shakan, 1968), 25–30; Daniel I. Okimoto, "The Economics of National Defense," in Daniel I. Okimoto, ed., *Japan's Economy: Coping with Change in the International Environment* (Boulder, Colo.: Westview Press, 1982), 239.

50. See *Sankei Shimbun*, February 28, 1953.

51. See Ōtake, "Nihon ni okeru 'Gunsankan fukugōtai' keisei no Zasetsu," 19–20; *Zaikai*, August 1953, 12–13; *Zaikai*, January 1954, 9–107; and *Ekonomisuto*, September 19, 1953.

52. Ōtake, "Nihon ni okeru 'Gunsankan fukugōtai' keisei no Zasetsu," 51–56.

53. Ibid., 23.

54. Ibid., 34–37.

55. In 1956, weapons production represented a mere 0.76 percent of total manufacturing in the Federal Republic, and in the following twenty-five years it never exceeded 2.18 percent. See Michael Brzoska, *Rüstungsexportpolitik* (Frankfurt/Main: Haag+Herschen, 1986), 159.

56. Regina S. Cowen, *Defense Procurement in the Federal Republic of Germany: Politics and Organization* (Boulder, Colo.: Westview Press, 1986), 6–7; Gerhard S. Brandt, *Rüstung und Wirtschaft in der Bundesrepublik Deutschland* (Witten and Berlin: Eckart Verlag, 1966), 163–64; *Jahresbericht des BDI* (1954/1955), 198–201.

57. Cowen, *Defense Procurement*, 25–26; Detlef Bischoff, *Franz Josef Strauß, die CSU, und die Außenpolitik: Konzpetionen und Realität am Beispiel der Großen Koalition* (Meisenheim am Glann: Anton Hain, 1973), 120–31; Gerd Schmückle, *Ohne Pauken und Trompeten* (Stuttgart: Deutsche Verlags-Anstalt, 1982), 175–76.

58. Before the war there had been little military production in Bavaria, but in the postwar period it became home to some of Germany's most important defense contractors. See *Rüstungsindustrie in Bayern* (Frankfurt/Main: Campus Verlag, 1990).

59. See Karl Hegner, Ekkehard Lippert, and Roland Wakenhut, *Selektion oder Sozialisation* (Opladen: Westdeutscher Verlag, 1983), 107–29, esp. 112–14.

60. Brzoska, *Rüstungsexportpolitik*, 161–62.

61. The JCP was not truly Left-idealist because, although it supported a policy of strict neutrality, it did not advocate complete disarmament. Instead, the party advocated the creation of a socialist people's army free of any residue of the militarist past.

62. Eckhard Opitz, "Die Sicherheits—und wehrpolitische Diskussion in den Politischen Parteien 1949–1955," in *Aus Politik und Zeitgeschichte*, special supplement to *Das Parlament* B35 (September 3, 1983), 35–36.

63. Dietrich Wagner, *Die FDP und Wiederbewaffnung* (Boppard am Rhein: Harald Boldt Verlag, 1978), 39 and 56.

64. See Rowold, "Im Schatten der Macht," 349.

65. Rowold, "Im Schatten der Macht," 348–62.

66. See Peter Berton, "The Japanese Communist Party: The 'Lovable' Party," in Ronald J. Hrebenar, ed., *The Japanese Party System: From One-Party Rule to Coalition Government* (Boulder, Colo.: Westview Press, 1986), esp. 129–38; and Robert A. Scalapino, *The Japanese Communist Movement, 1920–1966* (Berkeley, Calif.: University of California Press, 1967).

67. See Gerald L. Curtis, *The Japanese Way of Politics* (New York: Columbia University Press, 1988), 133–38.

68. Only Italy has comparably factionalized political parties. See Giovanni Sartori, *Parties and Party Systems: A Framework for Analysis* (Cambridge and New York: Cambridge University Press, 1976), 20.

69. See J.A.A. Stockwin, "The Japanese Socialist Party: The Politics of Permanent Opposition," in Ronald J. Hrebenar, *The Japanese Party System*, 101–6.

70. See Arnulf Baring, *Aussenpolitik in Adenauer's Kanzlerdemokratie: Bonn's Beitrag zur Europäischen Verteidigungs Gemeinschaft* (Munich: Oldenbourg, 1969).

71. Nagai Yonosuke, "Moratoriumuron," *Chūōkōron* (spring 1980).

72. On the functioning of the Japanese Diet and the tools available to the opposition to slow proceedings, see Michael Mochizuki, *Managing and Influencing the Japanese Legislative Process* (Ph.D. diss., Harvard University, 1982), esp. ch. 2. On how the German system functions to encourage cooperation and consensus building, see Uwe Thaysen, "Representation in the Federal Republic of Germany," in Uwe Thaysen, Roger H. Davidson, and Robert Gerald Livingston, *The U.S. Congress and the German Bundestag* (Boulder, Colo.: Westview Press, 1990).

73. During the original cabinet meetings regarding the American proposal for a new constitution Yoshida had opposed the proposed reforms, Dower, *Empire and Aftermath*, 318–20. Furthermore, there are signs that he hoped to create a professional military force separate from the Self-Defense Forces. Ōtake, *Saigumbi to Nashyonarizumu*, 59–69. During the 1960s Yoshida even made comments suggesting he supported the acquisition of nuclear weapons, although it should be pointed out that he was close to senile at the time.

74. See Joseph P. Keddell, Jr., *The Politics of Defense in Japan: Managing Internal and External Pressures* (Armonk, N.Y.: M.E. Sharpe, 1993), 35–39.

75. Wolfram F. Hanrieder, *Germany, America, and Europe* (New Haven, Conn.: Yale University Press, 1989), 150–66.

76. Cioc, *Pax Atomica*, 49–50.

77. It might be argued that such a stance would have embroiled Japan in regional conflicts and been prohibitively expensive. But Japan could have retained the right to refuse to dispatch forces to conflicts in which it had no interest, for example, Vietnam. Moreover, countries such as South Korea and Taiwan have achieved high economic growth rates despite spending a large percentage of GNP on defense.

78. Yoshida Shigeru, *Memoirs* (Westport, Conn: Greenwood Press, 1973), 6–12; Kosaka Masataka, *Saishō Yoshida Shigeru* (Tokyo: Chūōkōgyōsho, 1968), 128–38.

79. John Lewis Gaddis, *Strategies of Containment: A Critical Appraisement of American Postwar National Security Policy* (London: Oxford University Press, 1982), 74–76, 78–79.

80. See Robert J. Putnam, "Diplomacy and Domestic Politics: The Logic of Two-Level Games," *International Organization* 42 (summer 1988).

Chapter 4. The New Cultures of Antimilitarism and the Challenges of Détente

1. See Andrei S. Markovits, ed., *The Political Economy of West Germany: Modell Deutschland* (New York: Praeger, 1981); and Ezra Vogel, *Japan as Number One* (Cambridge, Mass.: Harvard University Press, 1979).

2. See Hans-Jürgen Grabbe, *Unionsparteien, Sozialdemokratie, und die Vereinigte Staaten von Amerika, 1945–1966* (Düsseldorf: Droste Verlag, 1983), 277–80.

3. See interview with Franz Josef Strauss in *Frankfurter Allgemeine Zeitung*, March 8, 1962.

4. Thomas Enders, *Franz Josef Strauss—Helmut Schmidt und die Doktrin der Abschreckung* (Koblenz: Bernard & Graefe, 1984), 139–41.

5. Wilhelm G. Grewe, *Rückblenden 1976–1951: Aufzeichnungen eines Augenzeugen deutscher Außenpolitk von Adenauer bis Schmidt* (Frankfurt/Main: Propyläen Verlag, 1979), 487–97.

6. Heinrich Krone, "Aufzeichnungen zur Deutschland—und Ostpolitik 1954–1969," in Rudolf Morsey und Konrad Repgen, eds., *Adenauer Studien Bd. III: Untersuchungen und Dokumente zur Ostpolitik* (Mainz: Matthias-Grünewald-Verlag, 1974), 136.

7. See Nicole Gnesotto, "Le dialogue franco-allemande depuis 1954: patience et langueur de temps," in Pierre Lellouche et Karl Kaiser, eds. *Le couple franco-allemand et la defense de Europe* (Paris: Institut Français des Relations Internationales, 1986), 18–19.

8. See Lothar Ruehl, "Adenauer's Politik und das Atlantische Bündnis—eine schwierige Balance zwischen Paris und Washington," in Dieter Blumenwitz et al., eds., *Konrad Adenauer und seine Zeit, Persönlichkeit, und Politik des ersten Bundeskanzlers* (Stuttgart: Deutsche Verlags-Anstalt, 1976), esp. 61–80.

9. See Dennis L. Bark and David R. Gress, *From Shadow to Substance* (Oxford: Basil Blackwell, 1989), 484–86.

10. Grabbe, *Unionsparteien, Sozialdemokratie, und die Vereinigte Staaten von Amerika*, 314–21; and Arnulf Baring, *Aussenpolitik in Adenauer's Kanzlerdemokratie: Bonn's Beitrag zur Europäischen Verteidigungs Gemeinschaft* (Munich: Oldenbourg, 1969), 45–55.

11. Jean Lacoutre, *Le Souverain 1959–1970*, vol. 3 of *De Gaulle* (Paris: Seuil 1986), 308.

12. As late as 1967 public opinion surveys showed that only 26 percent of West Germans supported recognition of the East German government, while 61 percent opposed such a step. See Berthold Meyer, *Der Bürger und seine Sicherheit: Zum Verhältnis von Sicherheitsstreben und Sicherheitspolitik* (Frankfurt: Campus Verlag, 1983), 247, table 5.7.4.

13. See Clay Clemens, *Reluctant Realists: The Christian Democrats and West German Ostpolitik* (Durham, N.C.: Duke University Press, 1989).

14. See Klaus Hildebrand, *Von Erhard zur Grossen Koalition* (Stuttgart: Deutsche Verlags-Anstalt, 1984), 325–26.

15. See Wolfgang von Amerongen, "Aspekte des deutschen Osthandels," *Aussenpolitik* (March 1970). For an overview see Michael Kreile, *Osthandel und Ostpolitik* (Baden-Baden: Nomos Verlag, 1978); and Angela Stent, *From Embargo to Ostpolitik: The Political Economy of West German–Soviet Relations 1955–1980* (Cambridge and New York: Cambridge University Press, 1981).

16. William E. Griffith, *The Ostpolitik of the Federal Republic of Germany* (Cambridge, Mass.: MIT Press, 1978), 126–27.

17. Karl Jaspers, *Wohin treibt die Bundesrepublik?* (Munich: R. Piper and Co., 1966).

18. Presse and Informationsamt der Bundesregierung, *Bundeskanzler Brandt: Reden und Interviews* (Bonn: Presse and Informationsamt der Bundesregierung, 1971), 14.

19. For more on the evolution of *Ostpolitik* see Griffith, *The Ostpolitik of the Federal Republic of Germany;* Wolfram F. Hanrieder, *Germany, America, and Europe* (New Haven, Conn.: Yale University Press, 1989), 195–205; and Günther Schmid, *Entscheidung in Bonn: Die Entstehung der Ost—und Deutschlandpolitik, 1969–1970* (Köln: Verlag Wissenschaft und Politik, 1979).

20. The text of the final act can be found in U.S. Department of State, *Department of State Bulletin*, no. 78 (September 1, 1975), 323–50. The German version can be found in Klaus von Schubert, *Sicherheitspolitik der Bundesrepublik Deutschland*, vol. 1 (Köln: Verlag Wissenschaft und Politik, 1978), 433–43. For more on the diplomatic process leading up to Helsinki, see Helga Haftendorn, *Sicherheit und Entspannung, Zur Aussenpolitik der Bundesrepublik Deutschland*, 2d ed. (Baden-Baden: Nomos Verlagsgesellschaft, 1986), 413–91; Jonathan Dean, *Watershed in Europe* (Lexington, Mass.: Lexington Books, 1987); Vojtech Mastny, *Helsinki, Human Rights, and European Security* (Durham, N.C.: Duke University Press, 1986).

21. See Christian Hacke, *Weltmacht wider Willen* (Stuttgart: Ernst Klett Verlag, 1988), 210–17. On Brandt's and Bahr's motivations, see also Walter S. Hahn, "West Germany's *Ostpolitik:* The Grand Design of Egon Bahr," *Orbis* 16 (winter 1973).

22. See, for example, Henry Kissinger, *The White House Years* (Boston: Little Brown, 1979), 380, 408, 422, 529, 964; on French apprehensions, see Willy Brandt, *Begegnungen und Einsichten: Die Jahre 1960–1975* (Hamburg: Hoffman und Campe, 1976), 380ff.

23. See Arnulf Baring, *Machtwechsel: Die Ära Brandt-Scheel* (Stuttgart: Deutsche Verlags-Anstalt, 1982), 422–23, 583.

24. Revelations concerning Brandt's personal life were also decisive in his downfall. See Baring, *Machtwechsel*, 739–55.

25. See Ōtake Hideo, *Nihon no Bōei to Kokunai Seiji, Detanto kara Gunkaku e* (Tokyo: Sanichi Shobo, 1984), 47.

26. *Asahi*, October 3, 1967, evening edition.

27. See John Welfield, *An Empire in Eclipse: Japan in the Postwar American Alliance System* (London and Atlantic Highlands, N.J.: Athlone Press, 1988), 232.

28. *Asahi*, January 17, 1968.

29. Ōtake, *Nihon no Bōei to Kokunaiseiji*, 30.

30. Thomas Havens, *The Fire across the Sea: The Vietnam War and Japan 1965–1975* (Princeton, N.J.: Princeton University Press, 1987), esp. 151–63.

31. *Mainichi*, February 4, 1969, evening edition. For more on the background of the agreement, see Welfield, *An Empire in Eclipse*, 227–30; and Senda Hisashi, *Satō Naikaku Kaisō* (Tokyo: Chūōkōronsha, 1987), 78–81.

32. *Asahi*, November 22, 1969.

33. See Ōtake, *Nihon no Bōei to Kokunaiseiji*, 32–33.

34. See Ōtake, *Nihon no Bōei to Kokunaiseiji*, ch. 3, esp. 32, 55–56. See also interviews with

Senga Tetsuya, long-time head of Keidanren's Defense Production Committee, in "Bōei-seisan no Kiseki 11: Tenkikaku shita Nakasone Kōzō," in *Ekonomisuto*, September 6, 1977. On the student protests of the time, see Havens, *The Fire across the Sea*, esp. ch. 6 and 7.

35. See interview with Nakasone Yasuhiro in *Ekonomisuto*, August 18, 1970.

36. Ōtake, *Nihon no Bōei to Kokunaiseiji*, 31. See also Nakasone's comment in *Asahi*, January 3, 1970; March 19, 1970, evening edition; and May 18, 1970; as well as the round table discussion including Nakasone, "Seijizadankai: Kokubō o Saikentō suru," *Kokubō* (October 1970).

37. Ōtake, *Nihon no Bōei to Kokunaiseiji*, 39–42.

38. Hirose Katsuya, *Kanryō to Gunjin: Bunmintōsei no Genkai* (Tokyo: Iwanami Shoten, 1989), 27; and Ōtake, *Nihon no Bōei to Kokunaiseiji*, 64, 69.

39. Hirose, *Kanryō to Gunjin*, 138–43. See also *Kokubō* (January 1971) for a sampling of foreign reactions.

40. Hirose, *Kanryō to Gunjin*, 142–43; See the round table discussion, "Hikakuchūkyūron to Kokubō no Hōkō," in *Kokubō* (January 1971); and Doba Hajime, "Nihon no 'Jishuōbei' wa Kanōka," in *Chūōkōron* (September 1970).

41. Ōtake, *Nihon no Bōei to Kokunaiseiji*, 35–37; *Nikkei*, November 7, 1970.

42. See Haftendorn, *Sicherheit und Entspannung*, 150–51, 155–56; Mark Cioc, *Pax Atomica: The Nuclear Defense Debate in West Germany during the Adenauer Era* (New York: Columbia University Press, 1988), 4–5, 14–15.

43. At the NATO meeting in Lisbon, it was decided that ninety-six divisions were needed to implement this strategy.

44. Catherine Kelleher, *Germany and the Politics of Nuclear Weapons* (New York: Columbia University Press, 1976), ch. 2 and 3; Hans Speier, *German Rearmament and Atomic War* (Evanston, Ill.: Row, Peterson, 1957).

45. See David Schwarz, *NATO's Nuclear Dilemmas* (Washington, D.C.: Brookings Institution, 1983), 70–72; Richardson, *Germany and the Atlantic Alliance: The Interaction of Strategy and Politics*, (Cambridge, Mass.: Harvard University Press, 1966), ch. 3; Hans Speier, *German Rearmament and Atomic War*, pt. 1; Haftendorn, *Sicherheit und Entspannung*, 162ff.

46. See Hanrieder, *Germany, America, Europe*, 50ff.

47. See Cioc, *Pax Atomica*, 46–63.

48. See Grewe, *Rückblenden*, 668–69.

49. *Asahi*, January 31, 1968, and November 25, 1971.

50. See Glenn D. Hook, "The Erosion of Antimilitaristic Principles in Contemporary Japan," *Journal of Peace Research* 25, no. 4 (1988), 387.

51. The evidence strongly suggests that the three non-nuclear principles are not strictly applied. As major U.S. naval bases in the Far East, Japanese ports are regularly visited by U.S. warships. Many of these ships probably carry nuclear weapons. Declassified U.S. documents and American newspaper accounts suggest there was a verbal agreement at the time of the Okinawa negotiations exempting U.S. ships visiting Japan from the non-nuclear principles. See Reinhard Drifte, *Japan's Rise to International Responsibility* (London and Atlantic Highlands, N.J.: Athlone Press, 1990), 225–26.

52. See Kubo Takuya, "Heiwaji no Bōeiryoku—hitotsu no apurochi," *Kokubō* (April 1973), and "Nichibei Ampōjyōyaku o Minaosu," *Kokubō* (June 1972), esp. 113, 136–37, and 142–44. See also Kubo's critique of the fourth defense buildup plan, written under the pen name

Tashima Ryosuke, "Daiyoshibōeiryoku Seibi Keikaku no Haikei to sone Mondaiten," in *Kokubō* (March 1971).

53. See the published version of the report, Bōei o Kangaerukai, *Wagakuni no Bōei o Kangaeru* (Tokyo: Asagumo Shimbunsha, 1975).

54. Ōtake, *Nihon no Bōei to Kokunaiseiji*, 89–96, 115–17. *Asahi,* September 10, 1972; November 13, 1972, evening edition; January 5, 1973; February 6, 1973, evening edition; and February 13, 1973. Author's interview with Itō Kobun, Tokyo, May 1988.

55. The fall of Saigon in 1975 brought an end to the conflict in Vietnam, while the U.S.-China alliance against the Soviet Union greatly reduced fears that by siding with the United States Japan might be drawn into conflict with mainland China.

56. Kaminishi Akio, *GNP 1% Waku* (Tokyo: Kadokawa Bunko, 1986), 176–78; Itō Keiichi, "Zenkokubōkaigi Jimukyokuchō to shite Bōeihi 1% waku o ronzuru," *Chūōkōron* (March 1985).

57. *Asahi,* November 15, 1976. See also Kaminishi Akio, *GNP 1% Waku.*

58. Hirose, *Kanryō to Gunjin,* 187–88.

59. Ōtake, *Nihon no Bōei to Kokunaiseiji,* 137–38; Chuma Kiyofuku, *Saigumbi no Seijigaku* (Tokyo: Chishikisha, 1985), 160.

60. Ōtake, *Nihon no Bōei to Kokunaiseiji,* 143.

61. See *Chūōkōron* (April 1965), which contains the entire Diet protocol. See also *Asahi,* February 10, 1965; Hirakawa Kuro, "Mitsuya kenkyū to sono ato no Shinso," *Ushio* (April 1965). For good overviews of the controversy, see Ishikuro Takeo, "Mitsuya Kenkyū to Shiberian Kontroruurongi," in *Rippō to Chosa* (June 1980); and Hans Georg Mammitzch, *Die Entwicklung der Selbsterveteidigungs-Streitkräfte und Aspekte der zivil-militärischen Beziehungen in Japan* (Ph.D. diss., Rheinische Friedrich-Wilhelms-Universität, Bonn, 1985), esp. 156–74.

62. *Asahi,* March 11, 1965.

63. The text of the committee's report can be found in Nishioka Akira, *Gendai no Shiberian Kontroru* (Tokyo: Chishikisha, 1988), 264–79. See also Fukushima Gengo, "Shiberian Kontroru wa ika ni arubeki ka," *Asahi Jyānaru* (February 1965).

64. Author's interview with General Goda Yutaka, Tokyo, June 24, 1988.

65. In his writing, Sugita Ichiji compared U.S. efforts to demilitarize Japan to the Soviet Union's massacre of Polish officers at Katyn. He supported alliance with the United States only because he felt marxism posed an even greater threat to Japan than Western liberalism. See Welfield, *An Empire in Eclipse,* 377–403, nn. 697 and 698.

66. The process of colonization increased when a former Ministry of Finance bureaucrat became the JDA vice minister in 1974. Thereafter, a long internal struggle was waged between the MOF and the "native" bureaucrats, backed by the Police Agency, for control of the top slot in the JDA.

67. See Asagumo Shimbunsha, *Bōei Handobukku* (Tokyo: Asagumo Shimbunsha, 1995), 410–13.

68. The best account of this debate in English can be found in Donald Abenheim, *Reforging the Iron Cross* (Princeton, N.J.: Princeton University Press, 1988). See also Ulrich Simon, *Die Integration der Bundeswehr in die Gesellschaft: Das Ringen um die Innere Führung* (Heidelberg/Hamburg: R.V. Decker's Verlag G. Schenk, 1980).

69. See Abenheim, *Reforging the Iron Cross,* 142–44, 1155–57, 206–7.

70. Ulrich Simon, *Die Integration der Bundeswehr in die Gesellschaft,* 61–62.

71. See Abenheim, *Reforging the Iron Cross,* 256–63.

72. A good portrayal of these views can be found in Hans-Georg von Studnitz, *Rettet die Bundeswehr!,* 3d ed. (Stuttgart: Deutsche Verlags-Anstalt, 1967).

73. Heinz Karst, "Die Bundeswehr—eine Armee die keine sein soll: Ketzereien eines Bundeswehroffiziers der ersten Stunde," in Gerd-Klaus Kaltenbrunner, ed., *Der Soldat: Dienst und Herrschaft der Streitkräfte* (Freiburg-Basel-Wien: Herder, 1981).

74. For a complete discussion of the Schnez affair and the controversy it triggered see Abenheim, *Reforging the Iron Cross,* 240–55; and Simon, *Die Integration der Bundeswehr in die Gesellschaft,* 64–68.

75. See Simon, *Die Integration der Bundeswehr in die Gesellschaft,* 110–20.

76. See Albert Axelbank, *Black Flag over Japan* (Tokyo: Tuttle, 1973).

77. Likewise, the view that NATO brought more benefits than disadvantages increased steadily. See Meyer, *Der Bürger und seine Sicherheit;* 217, table 3.2.2.1.

78. In 1976, 61 percent of Germans hoped for reunification while only 36 percent attached no importance to reunification. There was a clear generational gap on this issue, with a majority of West Germans between the ages of sixteen and twenty-nine viewing reunification as not so important (52 percent versus 44 percent). From Meyer, *Der Bürger und seine Sicherheit,* 243.

79. Grabbe, *Unionsparteien, Sozialdemokratie, und die Vereinigte Staaten von Amerika,* 455.

80. In a 1973 *Yomiuri* survey, 65.5 percent said the SDF should be restricted to a territorial defense role, 3 percent said that maritime escort operations would be permissible, and only 11 percent said there should be no limits on SDF activities. See Welfield, *An Empire in Eclipse,* 425. On Japanese views of the army in general, see Havens, *The Fire across the Sea,* esp. 89–91 on the popular outcry over the logistical role played by Japanese civilian sailors in supporting the U.S. war effort.

81. See Umemoto Tetsuya, "Arms and Alliance in Japanese Public Opinion," (Ph.D. diss., Princeton University, 1985), 87.

82. See Akio Watanabe, "Japanese Public Opinion and Foreign Affairs 1964–1973," in Robert A. Scalapino, *The Foreign Policy of Modern Japan* (Berkeley, Calif.: University of California Press, 1977), 115.

83. For a discussion of Japanese democracy, see Ellis Krauss and Takeshi Ishida, "Japanese Democracy in Perspective," in Ishida and Krauss, eds., *Democracy in Japan* (Pittsburgh, Pa.: University of Pittsburgh Press, 1989).

84. See Kosaka Masataka, *Kokusaiseiji* (Tokyo: Chūōkōronsha, 1966); and Nagai Yonosuke, *Heiwa no Daishō* (Tokyo: Chūōkōronsha, 1967).

85. See Kosaka Masataka's op-ed piece in *Yomiuri,* May 30, 1966, evening edition; and Nagai Yonosuke, *Heiwa no Daishō,* 64–66.

86. See Kosaka, *Kokusaiseiji,* 200–204; Kosaka, "Kaiyō Kokka Nihon no Kōzō," *Chūōkōron* (September 1964); and Kosaka, "Kokusaiseiji no Tagenka," *Chūōkōron* (December 1964).

87. Sakamoto Yoshikazu, *Kakujidai no Kokusaiseiji* (Tokyo: Iwanami Shoten, 1968); and Seki Hiroharu, *Kiki no Nishiki* (Tokyo: Kukumura Shuppan, 1969).

88. Terazawa Hitsohi et al., "Shinampojyōyaku," *Chūōkōron* (June 1960). A key factor

in this conversion was reportedly a sometimes violent right-wing campaign of intimidation against the Left-idealist media. In 1962, rightists attacked the home of a senior editor at *Chūōkōron*, killing his maid and wounding his wife. Author's interview with Yasue Ryosuke, August 1988.

89. Author's interviews with Yasue Ryosuke, Tokyo, August 1988, and Inoki Masamichi, Tokyo, April 1989. On the incorporation of intellectuals into the policy-making process, see Frank Schwartz, "Of Fairy Cloaks and Familiar Talk: The Politics of Consultation," in Gary D. Allinson and Yasunori Sone, eds., *Political Dynamics in Japan* (Ithaca, N.Y.: Cornell University Press, 1993).

90. See Georg Picht, *Die deutsche Bildungskatastrophe* (Olten and Freiburg: Walter Verlag, 1964); and Jaspers, *Wohin treibt die Bundesrepublik?*

91. On the origins of the Green Party and the new social movements, see Hans Georg Betz, *Postmodern Politics in Germany: The Politics of Resentment* (New York: St. Martin's Press, 1991); Andrei S. Markovits and Philip S. Gorski, *The German Left: Red, Green, and Beyond* (New York: Oxford University Press, 1993). See also R. Roth and D. Rucht, eds., *Neue Soziale Bewegungen in der Bundesrepublik Deutschland* (Bonn: Bundeszentrale für Politische Bildung, 1987).

92. See Bob Burns and Wilfred van der Will, *Protest and Democracy in West Germany* (New York: St. Martin's Press, 1988), 91–94.

93. Martin und Sylvia Greiffenhagen, *Ein Schwieriges Vaterland: Zur politischen Kultur Deutschlands* (Munich: List Verlag, 1978), 186–89.

94. See esp. Joachim Hütter, *SPD und Nationale Sicherheit: Internationale und innenpolitische Determinanted des Wandels der Sozialdemokratischen Sicherheitspolitik 1959–1961* (Meisenheim: Anton Hain, 1975); and Lothar Wilker, *Die Sicherheitspolitik der SPD 1956–1966: Zwischen Wiedervereinigungs—und Bündnisorientierung* (Bonn-Bad Godesberg: Verlag Neue Gesellschaft, 1977).

95. Bark and Gress, *From Shadow to Substance*, 445–46.

96. See *Verhandlungen des deutschen Bundestages*, June 30, 1960, 7052–61.

97. See Gerald L. Curtis, *The Japanese Way of Politics* (New York: Columbia University Press, 1988), 120–22.

98. See Horie Fukashi and Ikei Masaru, *Nihon no Seitō to Gaikō Seisaku* (Tokyo: Keio Tsūshin, 1980); Yoshihara Tsuneo and Nishi Osamu, *Nihon no Anzenhoshō to Kakutō no Bōeiseisaku* (Tokyo: Kyōikusha, 1979), and Ōtake, *Nihon no Bōei to Kokunaiseiji*, esp. 98–99 and 331–43.

99. *Asahi*, August 21, 1976; and *Yomiuri*, December 2, 1976. Similar problems hampered opposition efforts to form a united front in the 1980s, especially after the LDP was rocked by the recruit scandal.

100. See Yoshihara Tsuneo and Nishi Osamu, *Nihon no Anzenhoshō to Kakutō no Bōeiseisaku*, 20.

101. See Kaminishi Akio, *GNP 1% Waku*, 216–23; Umemoto, "Arms and Alliance in Japanese Public Opinion," 175–80.

102. See Thomas Enders, *Die SPD und die äußere Sicherheit* (Melle: Knoth, 1987), esp. 160–63, 205–23.

103. See Peter Juling, *Programatsiche Entwicklung der FDP 1946–1969: Einführung und*

Dokumentation (Meisenheim: Anton Hain, 1977); Baring, *Machtwechsel*, 209–11, 218–26; and Dennis L. Bark and David R. Gress, *Democracy and Its Discontents, 1963–1988* (Oxford: Basil Blackwill, 1989), 90–94.

104. See Thomas Risse-Kappen, *Die Krise der Sicherheitspolitik* (Mainz-München: Kaiser Grünwald, 1988), 146–48. Author's interview with Berthold Meyer, Frankfurt, June 1990.

Chapter 5. New Pressures, Old Responses—1976–1989

1. See, for example, Hans Günter Brauch, ed., *Sicherheitspolitik am Ende* (Gerlingen: Bleicher Verlag, 1984).

2. Jeffrey Herf, *War by Other Means: Soviet Power, West German Resistance and the Battle over the Euromissiles* (New York: Free Press, 1991).

3. The timing of the debates contradicts those who place blame for the conflict on the Reagan administration's Manichean view of East-West relations. For a different view see, for example, Wolfram F. Hanrieder, *Germany, America, and Europe* (New Haven, Conn.: Yale University Press, 1989), 113–15, 363–64.

4. Lothar Ruehl, "Die Nichtentscheidung über die 'Neutronwaffe'," *Europa Archiv* 34, no. 5 (1979); David S. Yost and Thomas C. Glad, "West German Party Politics and Theater Nuclear Modernization since 1977," *Armed Forces and Society* (summer 1982). Also see Shirley Wasserman, *The Neutron Bomb Controversy: A Study in Alliance Politics* (New York: Praeger, 1983); Volker Mathée, *Die Neutronwaffe: zwischen Bündnis und Innenpolitik* (Herford und Bonn: Verlag E.S. Mittler & Sohn, 1985); and Hubertus Hoffman, *Die Atompartner Washington—Bonn und die Modernisierung der Kernwaffen* (Koblenz: Bernard & Graefe, 1986).

5. In July 1979, 2 percent felt a new world war was likely, 17 percent thought one possible, and 80 percent held it unlikely. In January 1980, in contrast, 10 percent saw a war as likely, 48 percent as possible, and only 41 percent as unlikely. See Berthold Meyer, *Der Bürger und seine Sicherheit: Zum Verhältnis von Sicherheitsstreben und Sicherheitspolitik* (Frankfurt: Campus Verlag, 1983), 197.

6. For views of these leaders, see Erhard Eppler, *Wege der Gefahr* (Reinbeck bei Hamburg: Rowohlt, 1981); Oskar Lafontaine, *Angst vor den Freunden* (Reinbeck bei Hamburg: Rowohlt Verlag, 1983); and Egon Bahr, "Zehn Thesen über Frieden und Abrüstung," in Hans Apel et al., *Sicherheitspolitik contra Frieden? Ein Forum zur Friedensbewegung* (Berlin und Bonn: Verlag Dietz, 1981).

7. For examples of media criticism see the editorials by Rudolf Augstein in *Der Spiegel*, July 20, 1980; May 24, 1981; and February 22, 1982; Wilhelm Bittorf, "Euroshima, Mon Amour," *Der Spiegel*, February 9, 1981; and *Stern* editor Wolf Perdelwitz, *Wollen die Russen Krieg?* (Hamburg: Stern Bücher, 1980), esp. 274.

8. Herf, *War by Other Means*, 153–56; Thomas Enders, *Die SPD und die äußere Sicherheit* (Melle: Knoth, 1987), 218–19.

9. Herf, *War by Other Means*, 159–63. See also R.E.M. Irving and W.E. Paterson, "The Machtwechsel of 1982–1983: A Significant Landmark in the Political and Constitutional History of West Germany," *Parliamentary Affairs* (autumn 1983). Although the proximate cause of the coalition's dissolution was a disagreement over social policy, the SPD's drift toward the peace movement was a key factor in the FDP's decision to dissolve the coali-

tion. Author's interviews with Berthold Meyer, summer 1989, and FDP Bundestag member Uwe Ronneburger, spring 1989.

10. Robert Gerald Livingston, "The 1983 National Elections: Three Winners and a Loser," in Robert Gerald Livingston, ed., *The Federal Republic of Germany in the 1980s* (New York: German Information Center, 1983).

11. See Clay Clemens, *Reluctant Realists: The Christian Democrats and West German Ostpolitik* (Durham, N.C.: Duke University Press, 1989), 237–67; and Christian Hacke, *Weltmacht wider Willen* (Stuttgart: Ernst Klett Verlag, 1988), 365–67, 457.

12. Clemens, *Reluctant Realists*, 198–203, 218–25; Thomas Risse-Kappen, *Die Krise der Sicherheitspolitik* (Mainz-München: Kaiser Grünwald, 1988), 140–42.

13. See Clemens, *Reluctant Realists*, postscript; Ernst Martin, *Zwischenbilanz, Deutschlandpolitik der 80iger Jahre* (Stuttgart: Bonn Aktuell, 1986).

14. Karl Wilhelm Fricke, "Der Besuch Erich Honeckers in der Bundesrepublik Deutschland," *Europa Archiv* 23 (December 10, 1987).

15. See *International Herald Tribune*, September 7, 1987; and Christopher Layne, "Deutschland über Alles," *New Republic* (September 1987). See also Eberhard Schulz and Peter Danylow, eds., *Bewegung in der deutschen Frage? Die ausländischen Besorgnisse über die Entwicklung in den beiden Deutschen Staaten* (Bonn: DGAP, 1985).

16. See Horst Teltschik, "Aspekte der deutschen Außen—und Sicherheitspolitik im Rahmen der Ost-West Beziehungen," *Aus Politik und Zeitgeschichte* (February 16, 1985), 12–13; Volker Rühe, "Gemeinsame Sicherheit in der Allianz als Grundlage für gegenseitige Sicherheit zwischen Ost und West," in Daniel Proekter, Volker Rühe, and Karsten Voigt, *Mehr Vertrauen, Weniger Waffen: militärische Entspannung in Europa aus sowjetischer und deutscher Sicht* (Stuttgart: Bonn Aktuell, 1987).

17. *Die Zeit*, September 18, 1987; Dennis L. Bark and David R. Gress, *Democracy and Its Discontents, 1963–1988* (Oxford: Basil Blackwell, 1989), 462–63; Teltschik, "Aspekte der deutschen Außen—und Sicherheitspolitik," 4–6; Clemens, *Reluctant Realists*, 293–99. The author thanks Michael Stürmer, Uwe Nerlich, and Gebhard Schweigler for insights on these issues.

18. See Hacke, *Weltmacht wider Willen*, 395.

19. See Alfred Dregger, "Disarmament and Security: A German View of Current Alliance Developments," *Atlantic Community Quarterly* (winter 1987–1988), esp. 411–12; and Jürgen Todenhöfer, "Plädoyer für eine neue *Ostpolitik* des aktiven friedlichen Wettbewerbs," *Beiträge zur Konfliktforschung* (March 1986).

20. See, for example, Yasuhara Kazuo, "Kishihajimeta Sengo Bōei no Wakugumi: Shūdanjieiken, Hikaku 2.5 Genzoku e no Kennen," *Ekonomisuto* (July 10, 1980); and Masuda Koji, "Shindankai ni haitta Nichibei Kankei: 'Keizai' to 'Ampo' de Semegiai," *Ekonomisuto* (November 20, 1980).

21. The text of the guidelines is available in Oga Ryohei, Takeda Gorō, and Nagano Shigeto, *Nichibei Kyōdō Sakusen: Nichibei tai Soren Tatakai* (Tokyo: Asagumo, 1982), 281–87.

22. The basic range to be covered by the guidelines had been determined by 1976. See *Nikkei*, December 7, 1976.

23. *Asahi*, January 9, January 18, and January 19, 1978.

24. *Yomiuri*, November 20, 1978.

25. *Nikkei*, December 7, 1976.

26. See Sasaki Yoshitaka, "Rimupakku 80 Shuzai Nisshi," *Asahi Jyānaru,* April 11, 1980, esp. 31.

27. See Ōtake Hideo, "Bōeihizogaku o meguro Jiminto no Tonairikigaku," in Ōtake Hideo, ed., *Nihonseiji no Sōten* (Tokyo: Sanichishobo, 1984); Joseph P. Keddell, Jr., *The Politics of Defense in Japan: Managing Internal and External Pressures* (Armonk, N.Y.: M.E. Sharpe, 1993), ch. 3.

28. See Chuma Kiyofuku, *Saigumbi no Seijigaku* (Tokyo: Chishikisha, 1985), 141–46. For Nakasone's original comments and the controversy surrounding them see Yoshimura, *Soridaijin no Hatsugen, Shitsugen* (Tokyo: Bunjūbunko, 1988), 10–12. Author's interviews with Foreign Ministry and Defense Agency officials, 1989.

29. See *Asahi,* January 8, 1988, 1; Keddell, *The Politics of Defense in Japan,* 68.

30. Although partly in response to U.S. prompting, Japan did acquire the capability of closing off the straits. The author thanks Professor Satō Seizaburō and Professor Nishihara Masashi for discussions of this complex subject.

31. Colin S. Gray and Keith Payne, "Victory Is Possible," *Foreign Policy* 89 (summer 1980).

32. For West German criticisms of the new weapon systems, see Hans Günter Brauch, *Die Raketen Kommen!* (Köln: Bund Verlag, 1983), esp. 96–112, 136–49; Dieter S. Lutz, *Weltkrieg wider Willen* (Reinbeck bei Hamburg: Rowohlt, 1981); Alfred Mechtersheimer, *Rüstung und Frieden* (Munich: Langen-Müller und Herbig, 1982); and Gert Krell and Hans-Joachim Schmidt, *Der Rüstungswettlauf in Europa* (Frankfurt: Campus Verlag, 1982).

33. See Thomas Risse-Kappen, *Null-Lösung: Entscheidungsprozesse zu den Mittelstreckenwaffen 1970–1987* (Frankfurt/Main: Campus Verlag, 1988), 20–21, 24–25; and Hanrieder, *Germany, America, and Europe,* 110–11.

34. See Helga Haftendorn, *Sicherheit und Entspannung, Zur Aussenpolitik der Bundesrepublik Deutschland,* 2d ed. (Baden-Baden: Nomos Verlagsgesellschaft, 1986), 237–42; H. Hoffman, *Die Atompartner Washington;* Lothar Ruehl, *Mittlestreckenwaffen in Europa: Ihre Bedeutung in Strategie, Rüstungskontrolle, und Bündnispolitik* (Baden-Baden: Nomos Verlag, 1987); and Risse-Kappen, *Null-Lösung.*

35. The text of the decision can be found in Auswärtiges Amt, *Aussenpolitik der Bundesrepublic Deutschland, Vom Kalten Krieg zum Frieden in Europa* (Munich: Bonn Aktuell, 1990), 503–5. See also Haftendorn, *Sicherheit und Entspannung,* 250–51.

36. Hacke, *Weltmacht wider Willen,* 334–41; and Carl Otto Czempiel, "SDI and NATO: The Case of the Federal Republic of Germany," in Sanford Lakoff and Randy Willoughby, eds., *Strategic Defense and the Western Alliance* (Lexington, Mass.: D.C. Heath-Lexington Books, 1987).

37. Quoted in Risse-Kappen, *Null-Lösung,* 152.

38. See Klaus Naumann, "The Forces and the Future," in Stephen F. Szabo, *The Bundeswehr and Western Security* (London: Macmillan, 1990), 174.

39. For a skeptical view of conventional deterrence, see Robert W. Kommer, "A Credible Conventional Option: Can NATO Afford It?," *Strategic Review* (spring 1984).

40. *Asahi,* May 9, 1981; *Nikkei,* May 8, 1981, evening edition.

41. For a summary of the evolution of this issue, see Chuma, *Saigumbi no Seijigaku,* 110–14.

42. *Asahi,* March 29, 1981. See also Chuma, *Saigumbi no Seijigaku,* 115–16.

43. Chuma, *Saigumbi no Seijigaku,* 122–23.

44. Ibid.; author's interviews with Japanese government officials indicate that some inside the Foreign Ministry were not unhappy to see Suzuki make a fool of himself.

45. Ibid., 141–46; *Japan Times,* August 11, 1988.

46. Chuma, *Saigumbi no Sejigaku,* 123–24; *Japan Times,* November 26, 1988, p. 3; *Asahi,* November 14, 1988.

47. At the end of the Cold War these questions remained unsettled. See *Asahi,* December 11, 1988.

48. See *Asahi,* July 7, 1987, evening edition, 1; *Asahi,* September 5, 1987, 3; *Japan Times,* October 8, 1987, 1; Gotoda Masaharu, *Seiji to wa Nanika* (Tokyo: Kodansha, 1988). Author's discussions with Satō Seizaburō, September 1987.

49. See NHK Shuzaihan, *Bōei Shiireen no Umi* (Tokyo: Nihonhōsō Shuppankyokai, 1983), 269–86.

50. *Mainichi,* June 27, 1978; *Nikkei,* August 17, 1978.

51. *Asahi,* June 22 and August 26, 1978. This point was the subject of controversy within the Defense Agency. Many military men feared that Japan would need a system of mass mobilization in a major conventional struggle.

52. *Nikkei,* July 6, 1978.

53. *Asahi,* January 20 and July 20, 1978.

54. *Asahi,* July 27, 1978; Ōtake Hideo, *Nihon no Bōei to Kokunai Seiji Detanto kara Gunkaku e* (Tokyo: Sanichi Shobo, 1984), 186–87.

55. See Ōtake, *Nihon no Bōei to Kokunai Seiji,* ch. 18.

56. See Ishigawa Masanobu, "Zensenshiko to Sengokaiki ni," *Asahi Jyānaru,* September 22, 1978.

57. *Asahi,* September 2, 1978.

58. *Asahi,* August 31 and September 7, 1978. The party's youth wing was especially opposed to the Emergency Laws.

59. *Asahi,* September 13 and September 16, 1978. See also Prime Minister Ōhira Masayoshi's comments in *Nikkei,* October 16, 1978.

60. Ōtake, *Nihon no Bōei to Kokunai Seiji,* 236–39.

61. Keddell, *The Politics of Defense in Japan;* and Kaminishi Akio, *GNP 1% Waku* (Tokyo: Kadokawa Bunko, 1986). Other useful sources include Akasaka Tarō, "1% Waku de Tsumazuita Nakasone Shushō," *Bungeishunjū* (November 1985); Shioda Ushio, "Kane to Bōei," *Chūōkōron* (May 1986); Shioda Ushio, "1% Waku Kekkai no 500 hi," *Chūōkōron* (April 1987); Itō Keiichi, "1% Waku no Rekishi no Mondaiten," *Seiron* (March 1987); and Takeuchi Yasuo, "GNP 1% Waku Rongi o Warau," *Bungeishunjū* (January 1986).

62. Itō Keiichi, "1% Waku no Rekishi no Mondaiten," 58; Takeoka Katsumi, "1% Waku Kenji o Kitai suru," *Sekai* (1986), 67; author's interview with Itō Keiichi, Tokyo, winter 1988.

63. Takeoka, "1% Waku Kenji o Kitai suru," 143.

64. Kaminishi, *GNP 1% Waku,* 24–25.

65. Ibid., 21–22.

66. See Satō Seizaburō "Naze, soshite dono yō na Gunjiryoku ka," *Chūōkōron* (December 1985).

67. Kaminishi, *GNP 1% Waku,* 52–54, 66–68; Akasaka, "1% Waku de Tsumazuita Nakasone Shushō"; Fukuda Takeo, "Rekishi no Kyōkun ni manabu Heiwadaikoku e no Michi," *Asahi Jyānaru,* October 4, 1985.

68. Kaminishi, *GNP 1% Waku,* 62–64; Akasaka, "1% Waku de Tsumazuita Nakasone Shushō."

69. Akasaka, "1% Waku de Tsumazuita Nakasone Shushō."

70. At a meeting ten days after the 1 percent issue had been postponed, the despondent prime minister reportedly sang an antiwar song to astonished bureaucrats and remarked bitterly that he had "withdrawn all his savings," i.e., squandered his public approval ratings. Kaminishi, *GNP 1% Waku,* 73.

71. Kaminishi, *GNP 1% Waku,* 85–92; *Asahi* and *Mainichi,* October 18, 1985.

72. Takeoka, "1% Waku Kenji o Kitai suru," 142–51; Itō, "1% Waku no rekishi to Mondaiten," 57.

73. Author's interviews with JDA officials, fall 1987.

74. Akasaka, "1% Waku de Tsumazuita Nakasone Shushō."

75. See Manfred Messerschmidt, "Das Verhältnis von Wehrmacht und NS Staat und die Frage der Traditionsbildung," in *Aus Politik und Zeitgeschichte* 17 (April 25, 1981); Bernd Hesselein, ed., *Die Unbewältigte Vergangenheit der Bundeswehr* (Reinbeck bei Hamburg: Rowohlt, 1977); Donald Abenheim, *Reforging the Iron Cross* (Princeton, N.J.: Princeton University Press, 1988), 263–70.

76. *Führungsfähigkeit und Entscheidungs Verantwortung in den Streitkräften* (Bonn: Ministry of Defense, 1979), 24–27.

77. Lucian Kern, Herbert Krause, and Siegfried Petrelli, "Die Argumentationsmuster in den Auffassungen gesellschaftlich relevanter Gruppen zur Traditionspflege in der Bundeswehr," *SOWI Bericht* 23 (Munich: 1981), 20–26.

78. Helmut Froechling, "Identitätsprobleme moderner Streitkräfte: Die Traditionsdebatte in der Bundeswehr im Zeichen gesellschaftlichen Wandels," in Wolfgang R. Vogt, *Sicherheitspolitik und Streitkräfte in der Legitimitätskrise* (Baden-Baden: Nomos Verlagsgesellschaft, 1983), 215.

79. Bundesminister der Verteidigung, *Weißbuch 1985: Zur Sicherheit der Bundesrepublik Deutschland und zur Luge der Bundeswehr* (Bonn: 1985), 304–5.

80. Zentrum Innere Führung, rev. ed., *Eine Darstellung der Konzeption der Bundeswehr und des Auftrages des Zentrum Innere Führung* (Koblenz, 1984).

81. For an extensive documentary overview, see Ilya Lefkov, ed., *Bitburg and Beyond: Encounters in American, German, and Jewish History* (New York: Shapolsky Books, 1987).

82. See Elisabeth Noelle-Neumann, *Frankfurter Allgemeine Zeitung,* June 25, 1985. Some 70 percent of Germans were in favor of the trip to Bitburg, and only 17 percent were against it.

83. See Horst Ehmke, "Eine Politik zur Selbstbehauptung Europas," *Europa Archiv* (April 10, 1984); Karsten Voigt, "Die Vereinigung Europas—westeuropäische Integration und gesamteuropäische Kooperation," *Europa Archiv* (July 10, 1989); and Karsten Voigt, "Defense Alliances in the Future: West European Integration and All-European Cooperation," *Bulletin of Peace Proposals* (December 1989).

84. Clemens, *Reluctant Realists,* 198–203.

85. Compare Shimizu Ikutarō, *Nihon yo Kokka o tare!: Kaku no Sentaku* (Tokyo: Bungeishunjū, 1980), with Etō Jun, *Nichibei Sensō wa owatte inai: Shukkumei no Taiketsu—Sono Genzai, Kakko, Mirai* (Tokyo: Nesco Books, 1986); and Ishihara Shintarō and Morita Akira, *No to ieru Nihon e* (Tokyo: Kobunsha, 1989).

86. For discussions of the new Japanese ideology, see Kosaku Yoshino, *Cultural Nation-*

alism in Contemporary Japan: A Sociological Enquiry (London and New York: Routledge, 1992); and Peter N. Dale, The Myth of Japanese Uniqueness (New York: St. Martin's Press, 1986).

87. A sophisticated version of this argument can be found in Okazaki Hisahiko, Senryakuteki Shikō to wa Nani ka (Tokyo: Chūōkōshinsho, 1983), 9–13, 24–26.

88. See Okazaki, Senryakuteki Shikō to wa Nani ka.

89. See Amaya Naohiro, "Chōnin koku Nihon tedai no kurigoto," Bungei Shunjū (March 1980).

90. See the report of the Comprehensive Security Research Group, Sōgōanzenhoshō kenkyū gruupu hōkokusho, delivered to the prime minister on July 2, 1980.

91. See Hans-Georg Betz, Postmodern Politics in Germany: The Politics of Resentment (New York: St. Martin's Press, 1991), 11–18, 64–80.

92. See, for example, Washington Post, July 31, 1983.

93. See Vogt, Sicherheitspolitik und Streitkräfte in der Legitimitätskrise.

94. "CDU/CSU Wähler: Gorbatschow besser als Kohl," Der Spiegel, June 6, 1989; Friedrich-Ebert-Stiftung, The Germans and America: Current Attitudes (Bonn: Forschungsinstitut der Friedrich-Ebert-Stiftung, 1987), esp. charts on 45–47; and Stephen F. Szabo, The Changing Politics of German Security (London: Pinter, 1990), ch. 3.

95. Between 1978 and 1990, around 70 percent of Japanese said they felt close to the United States, with a low of 67.5 percent in 1986 and a high of 78 percent in 1979. Etō Shinkichi and Yamamoto Yoshinobu, Sōgōampo to Mirai no Sentaku (Tokyo: Kodansha, 1991), 450.

96. Asahi, June 18, 1984.

97. In a 1984 Asahi poll, only 29 percent of Japanese thought the United States would make a serious effort to defend their country if attacked and 56 percent said it would not. In 1981, 59 percent of Germans expressed confidence that the U.S. would come to their aid in a Soviet threat and 28 percent did not. See Richard Eichenberg, Public Opinion and National Security in Western Europe (Ithaca, N.Y.: Cornell University Press, 1989), 53–58; and Japan Times, September 1, 1987, 3.

98. Asahi, November 6, 1988; Umemoto Tetsuya, "Arms and Alliance in Japanese Public Opinion" (Ph.D. diss., Princeton University, 1985), 87.

99. Nishihara Atsuki, "Nihon Kempō no Hyōka to Kaisei," Jiyū (February 1981), 162.

100. Asahi, November 6, 1988.

101. See Clay Clemens, "Changing Public Perceptions of NATO," in Stephen F. Szabo, The Federal Republic and NATO (New York: St. Martin's Press, 1990).

102. See Michael Mochizuki, "Japan's Search for Strategy," International Security 8, no. 3 (1983/1984); Umemoto, "Arms and Alliance."

103. Umemoto, "Arms and Alliance," 120.

104. Shimizu, Nihon yo Kokka o tare!, 9–23, 27–32, 53–59, 90–94.

105. Etō Jun, Nichibei Sensō ga owatte inai; Tetsuya Kataoka, Waiting for Pearl Harbor (Stanford, Calif.: Hoover Institution Press, 1980); Nakagawa Yasuhiro, Chōsenshinkoku Nihon: Nihon Seiji no Shindansho (Tokyo: Kodansha, 1980); Nakagawa, Shin Nihon Kokukempō Sōan (Tokyo: Yamate Shobo, 1984); Miyoshi Osamu, "Shūdanteki Jieiken: Genyo Henko Ka, Kokusaiteki Koritsu Ka," in Nihon Senryaku Kenkyō Sentaa, ed., Tabu e no Chōsen: Hadaka no Bōeiron (Tokyo: Nihon Kōgyō Shimbunsha, 1984).

106. See, for example, Inoki Masamichi, Gunjitaikoku e no Gensō (Tokyo: Bungei-

shunjū, 1981); Nagai Yonosuke, "Rekishi no Owari ni mieru mono," a colloquy with Etō Jun, *Chūōkōron* (March 1990); Okazaki Hisahiko, *Senryakuteki Shikō to wa Nani ka;* Satō Seizaburō, "Jidai no Henka ga yori Kyōkō na Dōmei o motomeru," *Chūōkōron* (March 1990).

107. See *Yomiuri,* January 31, 1980; August 15, 1983; November 19, 1986; August 29, 1981.

108. The Research Institute for Peace Studies (RIPS) under the direction of first Inoki Masamichi and then Kosaka Masataka, and the more conservative International Institute for Global Peace Studies (IIGPS) founded by Nakasone and directed by Satō Seizaburō.

109. For more on the role of the churches in the peace movement, see Risse-Kappen, *Die Krise der Sicherheitspolitik,* 214–17; David R. Gress, *Peace and Survival: West Germany, The Peace Movement, and European Security* (Stanford, Calif.: Hoover Institution Press, 1985), 71–76, 143–50; Hans Josef Legrand, "Friedensbewegungen in der Geschichte der Bundesrepublik Deutschland: Ein Überblick zur Entwicklung bis Ende der siebziger Jahre," in Josef Janning et al., eds., *Friedensbewegungen: Entwicklung und Folgen in der Bundesrepublik Deutschland, Europa, und den USA* (Cologne: Verlag Wissenschaft und Politik, 1987); and Günther Schmidt, "Zur Soziologie der Friedensbewegung," in Dieter S. Lutz, *Sicherheitspolitik am Scheideweg* (Baden-Baden: Nomos Verlagsgesellschaft, 1982). Author's interviews with German journalists Josef Joffe, Thomas Kielinger, Joachim Maitré, and Uwe Simonetto.

110. Michael Stürmer, *Deutsche Fragen: Oder die Suche nach der Staatsräson* (Munich: Piper, 1988), 113–16, 122–24. The author is also indebted to conversations with Wolfgang Bergsdorf and Michael Stürmer on this subject.

111. Jürgen Habermas, "Eine Art Schadenabwicklung: Apologetische Tendenzen in der deutschen Zeitgeschichtenschreibung," *Die Zeit,* July 11, 1986; Wolfgang J. Mommsen, *Nation und Geschichte: Über die Deutschen und die deutsche Frage* (Munich: Piper, 1990); Hans Jürgen Wehler, *Entsorgung der deutschen Vergangenheit? Ein polemischer Essay zum 'Historikerstreit'* (Munich: C.H. Bech'sche Verlagsbuchverhandlung, 1988).

112. Hans-Peter Schwarz, *Die gezähmten Deutschen: Von Machtbesessenheit zur Machtvergessenheit* (Stuttgart: Deutsche Verlags-Anstalt, 1985); and Arnulf Baring, *Unser neuer Größenwahn: Deutschland zwischen Ost und West* (Stuttgart: Deutsche Verlags-Anstalt, 1988).

113. Horie Fukashi and Kobayashi Yoshiaki, "Minshatō no Anzenhoshōseisaku," in Horie Fukashi and Ikei Masaru, *Nihon no Seitō to Gaikō Seisaku* (Tokyo: Keio Tsūshin, 1980); and Umemoto, "Arms and Alliance," 135ff.

114. For more on Rengō, see Yutaka Tsujinaka, "Rengō and Its Osmotic Networks," in Gary D. Allinson and Yasunori Sone, eds., *Political Dynamics in Japan* (Ithaca, N.Y.: Cornell University Press, 1993). Rengō's pragmatic new leadership sought contacts with government defense and foreign policy experts. See *Aera,* December 6, 1988, 22.

115. Peter J. Katzenstein and Nobuo Okawara, *Japan's National Security: Structures, Norms, and Policy Responses in a Changing World* (Ithaca, N.Y.: Cornell University Press, East Asia Series, 1992), 66. Certain industrial sectors did rely heavily on military contracts, especially aeronautics—74.64 percent in 1989, down from 81.54 percent in 1984; followed distantly by shipbuilding—7.15 percent in 1989, up from 5.15 percent in 1984. See Asagumo Shimbunsha, *Bōei Handobukku* (Tokyo: Asagumo Shimbunsha, 1987), 244, and (1993), 252.

116. Oikawa Shoichi, *Jietai no Himitsu: Tōzai Gunji Baransu no Henka no Naka de*

(Tokyo: Ushiobunsha, 1981), 171–76; Funabashi Yōichi, "Fukken suru Bōei Sangyō," *Sekai* (June 1978); Maeda Tetsuo, *Heiki Daikoku Nihon* (Tokyo: Tokumashoten), 101–3; Ōtake, *Nihon no Bōei to Kokunai Seiji,* 319–28.

117. See Marie Söderberg, *Japan's Military Export Policy* (Stockholm: University of Stockholm, 1987); Greg A. Rubinstein, "Emerging Bonds of U.S.-Japanese Defense Technology Cooperation," *Strategic Review* 15, no. 1 (1987).

118. Oikawa, *Jietai no Himitsu,* 174–76; *Nikkei,* April 9, 1980; *Asahi,* January 15, 1981.

119. For more on the Toshiba controversy, see *Asahi,* July 18, 1987, 11; August 19, 1987, 4; and March 23, 1988, 5. On the FSX, see Richard Samuels, *Rich Nation, Strong Army* (Ithaca, N.Y.: Cornell University Press, 1994), 231–44; Clyde Prestowitz, *Trading Places: How America Allowed Japan to Take the Lead* (New York: Basic Books, 1990); and Teshima Ryuichi, *Nippon FSX o Ute* (Tokyo: Shinchosha, 1991). On the debate sparked by FSX in Japan, see *Asahi,* February 27, 1989, evening edition.

120. *Aera,* May 30, 1989, 17; and *Asahi,* March 18, 1989, Miritech series no. 22. Already in 1985 trade frictions had led to an increased emphasis on domestic military research. See Kurogawa Shuji, "Bōeiseisaniinkai no Seijikōdō," in Nakano Minoru, *Nihon Seisaku Kettei no Henyō* (Tokyo: Tōyō Keizai, 1988), 226, 230–31.

121. Author's interviews with Moroi Ken, president of Chichibu Cement, and Chiba Genya, director of the Research Development Corporation of Japan.

122. Risse-Kappen, *Die Krise der Sicherheitspolitik,* 210–14.

123. Regina S. Cowen, *Defense Procurement in the Federal Republic of Germany: Politics and Organization* (Boulder, Colo.: Westview, 1986), 194.

124. *Der Spiegel,* February 4, 1991.

125. Manfred Timmerman, "Weniger Waffen—Mehr Wettbewerb," *Die Zeit,* June 6, 1991; Christian Deubner, "Rüstungs Export und Arbeitsteilung in West Europa: Risiken einer Fusion," in *Neue Gesellschaft/Frankfurter Hefte* (November 11, 1989), 972.

126. See Angela Stent, *Soviet Energy and Western Europe,* Washington Paper no. 90 (New York: Praeger, 1982); and Jonathan Stein, "U.S. Controls and the Soviet Pipeline," *Washington Quarterly* (autumn 1982).

127. Josef Joffe, "Peace and Populism: Why the European Antinuclear Movement Failed," *International Security* 11 (spring 1987).

128. See Ōtake, *Nihon no Bōei to Kokunai Seiji,* ch. 7.

129. Habara Kiyomasa, "Kokubōzoku to wa Dare ka," *Sekai* (December 1986), 84–85; unpublished paper by Michael Green on the LDP's defense policy tribe.

130. There were 184 "hawks" in the LDP, 151 "doves," and 61 "neutrals." *Asahi,* September 20, 1981.

131. Green, unpublished manuscript. Inoguchi Takashi and Iwai Tomoaki, *Zoku Giin no Kenkyū* (Tokyo: Nihon Kezai Shimbunsha, 1987), 304. Both give figures of twenty-one to twenty-five.

132. This was the opinion of nearly all the LDP Diet members interviewed by the author, including Nakao Eiichi, Mori Kiyoshi, Kamei Shizuka, and Hiranuma Takeo.

133. See Horie and Ikei, *Nihon no Seitō to Gaikō Seisaku,* 51–59 nn. 1074, 1075.

134. Yamaguchi Sadamaru, "Komeitō no Mezasu 'Genjitsu' to wa nani ka," *Sekai* (January 1981), esp. 34–35.

135. Kamanishi, *GNP 1% Waku,* 184, 195–97, 236–37, 249–55.

136. Ōtake, *Nihon no Bōei to Kokunai Seiji*, ch. 26.

137. Author's interviews with Eda Satsuki, Maruyama Hiroyuki, and Takazawa Torao. By the end of the decade the JSP made the abrogation of the Mutual Security Treaty contingent on American consent, thus giving the United States a de facto veto.

138. For unsuccessful efforts of the opposition parties to form a coalition to take advantage of the scandal-ridden Takeshita government's weakness, see *Asahi*, February 4 and August 15, 1988; and April 9, April 13, April 18, and May 27, 1989. Defense also damaged the Socialists' credibility with the business community. Mainichi Shimbun Seijibu Keizaibu, *Zaikai to Seikai: Saihen e no Taidō* (Tokyo: IPEC Press, 1991), 286–89.

139. For more on the Green Party, see Werner Hülsberg, *The German Greens* (London: Verso, 1988); and Hans-Joachim Veen and Jürgen Hoffman, *Die Grünen zu Beginn der neunziger Jahre* (Bonn: Bouvier Verlag, 1992).

140. See comments by Angelika Beer, member of the Green Party's Subcommittee on Disarmament, "Deutsche Interessen contra Abrüstung," *Blätter für deutsche und internationale Politik* (June 1987), 722–25; and *Die Grünen Bundestagwahlprogram* (Bonn: 1987), 26–31. For the Greens' views on foreign and defense policy see William E. Griffith et al., *The Security Policies of the West German Left: The SPD and the Greens in Opposition* (Washington, D.C.: Bergamon-Brassey's, 1988).

141. See Egon Bahr, *Was wird aus den Deutschen* (Reinbeck bei Hamburg: Rowohlt, 1982), 229–30.

142. See, for example, Oskar Lafontaine, *Angst vor den Freunden: die Atomwaffenstrategie der Supermächte zerstört die Bündnisse* (Reinbeck bei Hamburg: Rowohlt, 1983).

143. See William E. Paterson, "The German Social Democratic Party," in William E. Paterson, ed., *The Future of Social Democracy: Problems and Prospects of Social Democratic Parties in Western Europe* (Oxford: Clarendon Press, 1986); Erwin Scheuch, *Wie Deutsch sind die Deutschen* (Bergisch Gladbach: Gustav Lüber Verlag, 1991), esp. 153.

144. See, for example, Egon Bahr, *Zum Europäischen Frieden: Eine Antwort an Gorbatschow* (Berlin: Siedler, 1988).

145. See Peter Glotz, "Die Linke und die Friedensbewegung," *Neue Gesellschaft/ Frankfurter Hefte* (January 1, 1984).

146. See Ehmke, "Eine Politik zur Selbstbehauptung Europas"; and Voigt, "Die Vereinigung Europas."

147. See Risse-Kappen, *Die Krise der Sicherheitspolitik*, 256–61, 318–20, on contending views on national security in the FDP; and Herf, *War by Other Means*, 158–60, on the FDP's decision to leave the coalition.

148. Karl Cerny, "Campaign and Election Outcome," in Karl Cerny, ed., *Germany at the Polls: The Bundestag Elections of the 1980s* (Durham, N.C.: Duke University Press), 245–46, 251–52.

149. See Berthold Meyer, *Die Parteien in der Bundesrepublic Deutschland und die Sicherheitspolitische Zusammenarbeit in Europa* (Frankfurt: Hessische Stiftung fur Friedens und Konflikt Forschung, Report 2, 1987), 42–45; Wolfgang Mischnick, "Die Einheit Deutschlands, der Frieden Europas—Perspektiven der Freiheit," *Liberal* (August 1989), 110; and Christian Stechow, "Sicherheitspolitische Perspektiven der neunziger Jahre," in W. Heisenberg and Dieter S. Lutz, eds., *Sicherheitspolitische Kontroverse: auf dem Wege in der neun-*

ziger Jahre vol. 247 (Bonn: Schriftenreihe der Bundeszentrale für politische Bildung, 1987), 835–38.

150. See Kurt Biedenkopf, "Wir können nicht einfach aussteigen, aber Friedenssicherung durch atomare Abschreckung ist kein Dauerzustand," in Heisenberg and Lutz, eds., *Sicherheitspolitische Kontroverse;* Kurt Biedenkopf, "Und christliche Demokraten für Schritte zur Abrüstung," in *Sicher auf neuen Wegen: Impulse für christlich-demokratische Friedenspolitik* (Warendorf: Diethelm Gohl und Heinrich Niesporek, 1986); and Clemens, *Reluctant Realists,* 289–97.

151. Risse-Kappen, *Null Lösung,* 150–70, esp. 158–60 and 169–70.

152. For more on the Republicans, see Class Leggewie, *Die Republikaner: Phantombild der Neuen Rechten* (Berlin: Rotbuch Verlag, 1991); and Betz, *Postmodern Politics,* esp. ch. 4 and 5. On the potential impact of the new Right, see Peter Glotz, *Die deutsche Rechte* (Stuttgart: Deutsche Verlags-Anstalt, 1989).

153. See David Yost, "Franco-German Defense Cooperation," in Robert Gerald Livingston, *The Bundeswehr and Western Security* (London: Macmillan, 1990), 238–42.

Chapter 6. Opting for Continuity: Germany and Japan after the Cold War

1. On the events leading up to reunification, see Philip Zelikow and Condoleezza Rice, *Germany Unified and Europe Transformed: A Study in Statecraft* (Cambridge, Mass.: Harvard University Press, 1995). On the immediate impact of unification, see Peter H. Merkl, *German Unification in the European Context* (University Park, Pa.: Pennsylvania State University Press, 1993).

2. Horst Teltschik, *329 Tage: Innen Ansichten der Einigung* (Berlin: Siedler, 1991), 149–52.

3. Margaret Thatcher, *The Downing Street Years* (New York: Harper Collins, 1993), 790–99, 813–15; Stanley Hoffman, "French Dilemmas and Strategies in the New Europe," in Robert O. Keohane, Joseph S. Nye, and Stanley Hoffman, eds., *After the Cold War: International Institutions and State Strategies in Europe, 1989–1991* (Cambridge, Mass.: Harvard University Press, 1993), 130; Anne-Marie Legloannec, "The Implications of German Unification for Western Europe," in Paul B. Stares, ed. *The New Germany and the New Europe* (Washington, D.C.: Brookings Institution, 1992), 252. See also Ingo Kolboom, *Die häßlichen Deutschen: Deutschland im Spiegel der westlichen und östlichen Nachbarn* (Darmstadt: Wissenschaftliche Buchgesellschaft, 1991). The Germans were well aware of their allies' misgivings. See Teltschik, *329 Tage,* 37–38, 59–61, 95–102.

4. Hans Dieter Genscher, *Die Zeit,* August 30, 1991, 5–6; and Horst Teltschik, "Was die anderen von den Deutschen erwarten," *Die Zeit,* May 3, 1991, 6; April 1990.

5. The Germans attached a number of stringent provisos regarding monetary union. As the German Finance Minister Theo Waigel put it, "(Germany) will bring the German currency order to Europe." See Peter Rudolf, "Doomed to Lead? German Foreign Policy in a New Europe," unpublished manuscript (Cambridge, Mass.: Center for International Affairs, Harvard University, February 1992), 2–3; Harald Müller, "German Foreign Policy after Unification," in Stares, *The New Germany and the New Europe,* 158–60; Waigel cited on 159. For the factors that led to Maastricht, see Alberta M. Sbragia, "Introduction," in Sbragia,

ed., *Europolitics: Institutions and Policy Making in the "New" European Community* (Washington, D.C.: Brookings Institution, 1992); and Wayne Sandholtz, "Monetary Policy and Maastricht," *International Organization* 47, no. 1 (1993), esp. 31–34.

6. Teltschik, *329 Tage*, 138–41, 163, 168–69, 185–87.

7. Teltschik, *329 Tage*, 313–45; Karl Kaiser, "Germany's Reunification," *Foreign Affairs* 70 (winter 1991); Jeffrey Anderson and John B. Goodman, "Mars or Minerva?: A United Germany in a Post–Cold War Europe," in Keohane et al., *After the Cold War;* Rudolf, "Doomed to Lead?"; Catherine Kelleher, "The New Germany," in Paul B. Stares, ed., *The New Germany and the New Europe,* 22.

8. Ottfried Nassauer, "Die NATO—Aufbruch zu neuen Ufern?," in Erich Schmidt-Eenboom and Jo Angerer, eds., *Siegermacht NATO* (Berg am See: Verlagsgessellschaft Berg, 1993), 75–84; Thomas-Durrell Young, *The New European Security Calculus: Implications for the U.S. Army* (Carlisle, Pa.: U.S. Army War College, Strategic Studies Institute, March 1, 1991).

9. Kelleher, "The New Germany," 24–25.

10. See the published version of a special parliamentary commission's report on the future of the Bundeswehr, Hans-Adolf Jacobsen and Hans-Jürgen Rautenberg, eds., *Bundeswehr und Europäische Sicherheitsordnung* (Bonn: Bouvier, 1991), 50–51, 55–59; Jürgen Kuhlmann and Ekkehard Lippert, "Wehrpflicht Ade? Argumente für und wider die Wehrpflicht in Friedenszeiten," in Geld Kladrack and Paul Klein, eds., *Die Zukunft der Streitkräfte Angesichts Weltweiter Abrüstungsbemühungen* (Baden-Baden: Nomos Verlagsgesellschaft, 1992). For criticisms of the draft system, see Gerd Schmückle, "Neue Lösungen müssen her," *Der Spiegel,* December 21, 1990; and Schmückle, "Wehrpflicht am Ende," *Der Spiegel,* February 8, 1993.

11. According to one estimate, if Japan were to spend approximately 5 percent of GNP per year on defense, within ten years it could have a navy with six to eight aircraft carriers, fifty to sixty nuclear-powered attack submarines, three hundred surface vessels, one thousand land-based fighters, fifteen aerial and assault divisions, and a total military force of over one million. Richard Halloran, "The Chrysanthemum and the Sword Revisited: Is Japanese Militarism Resurgent?" (address to Pacific and Asian Affairs Council, Honolulu, Hawaii, December 6, 1990), 9–10. With plentiful nuclear fuel and advanced technological resources, a number of nuclear weapons could be assembled within months if not weeks. In a couple of years Japan could develop a respectable force de frappe, with a second strike capability. See Selig E. Harrison, "Japan and Nuclear Weapons," in Harrison, ed., *Japan's Nuclear Future: The Plutonium Debate and East Asian Security* (Washington, D.C.: Carnegie Endowment for International Peace, 1996).

12. See Kaifu Toshiki, "Japan's Vision," *Foreign Policy* no. 80 (fall 1990). See also Yōichi Funabashi, "Japan and the New World Order," *Foreign Affairs* 70, no. 4 (1991). Some German commentators were making similar arguments. See Hans W. Maull, "Germany and Japan: The New Civilian Powers," *Foreign Affairs* 69, no. 1 (winter 1990–91).

13. The 1990 *Defense White Paper* dropped all reference to the Soviet Union as a threat. Tsuneo Akaha, "Japan's Comprehensive Security Policy: A New East Asian Environment," *Asian Survey* (1991), 328.

14. Fuji Sadao, "Maniawase no 'Nobiritsu' shōmetsu," *Ekonomisuto* (February 1, 1993).

For more on problems in the armed forces, see "Jietai futatsu no Kiki ga ou," *Aera* (November 26, 1991).

15. For the left-wing view, see Igarashi Taieshi, "Sekimatsu no Nihon no Anzenhoshō-seiasku," *Sekai* (July 1990), esp. 54–56.

16. Eugene Brown, "Contending Paradigms of Japan's International Role: Elite Views of the Persian Gulf Crisis," *Journal of Northeast Asian Studies* (spring 1992). Author's interviews with Douglas Pall, U.S. National Security Council, and Desai Anderson, U.S. State Department, Washington, D.C., spring 1992.

17. Thomas Kielinger, "The Gulf War and Consequences from the German Point of View," *Aussenpolitik* 42, no. 3 (March 1991), 244–45.

18. Sassa Atsuyuki, "Nihon wa Wangansenso e no Taio kara nani o manabubeki ka," *Shinbōeironshu* 19, no. 2 (September 1991). Interviews with mid-level Self-Defense Forces and Foreign Ministry officials, Cambridge, Mass., fall 1991 and spring 1992.

19. *Discord or Dialogue: The United States and Japan in 1991* (Washington, D.C.: The Edward O. Reischauer Center for East Asian Studies at the Paul H. Nitze School of Advanced International Studies, Johns Hopkins University, 1991), 20.

20. See *Asahi*, March 8, 1991; *New York Times*, November 2, 1990, and October 6, 1991; Steven R. Weisman, "Pearl Harbor in the Mind of Japan," *New York Times Magazine*, November 3, 1991, esp. 32; Colin Nickerson, "The Worrier Nation," *Boston Globe Magazine*, September 8, 1991. Japanese and other Asians often saw the Persian Gulf War as an extension of traditional Western gunboat diplomacy. *Far Eastern Economic Review* (January 24, 1991), 10–14; *Far Eastern Economic Review* (March 7, 1991), 8–12.

21. Karl Kaiser and Klaus Becher, "Deutschland und der Irak-Konflikt," *Arbeitspapiere zur Internationalen Politik* 68 (Bonn: Forschungsinstitut der Deutschen Gesellschaft für Auswärtige Politik, 1992). See also *Der Spiegel*, January 28 and March 11, 1991.

22. A mere 10 percent supported SDF dispatch with no limitations; even among LDP supporters opponents outnumbered proponents by 41 percent to 14.9 percent. *Nikkei*, October 15, 1990.

23. Itō Kenichi, "The Japanese State of Mind: Deliberations on the Gulf Crisis," *Journal of Japanese Studies* 17, no. 2 (1991), 281–86.

24. See, for example, the discussion between Kato Koichi, Yamazaki Taku, and Koyama Shigeki, "Ima koso Pax Nipponica no Kakuritsu o," *Ekonomisuto* (February 19, 1991).

25. *Der Spiegel*, January 28, 1991.

26. For examples of the Left's arguments see Peter Glotz, "Der ungerechte Krieg," *Der Spiegel*, February 25, 1991; and "Wider den Feuilleton-Nationalismus," *Die Zeit* 17 (April 26, 1991), 19; Rudolf Augstein, "Sterben für Kuweit?" *Der Spiegel*, November 12, 1990. Compare with Hans Magnus Enzensberger, "Hitler's Widergänger," *Der Spiegel*, February 4, 1991. Also see Cora Stephan, "An der deutschen Heimatfront," *Der Spiegel*, March 4, 1991.

27. For some of these criticisms, see Michael Lind, "Surrealpolitik," *New York Times*, March 28, 1991; "Germany's Ostrich Politik," editorial in *New York Times*, January 26, 1991; Alan Sked, "Cheap Excuses: Germany and the Gulf Crisis," *National Interest* no. 24 (summer 1991).

28. Jeffrey Garten, *A Cold Peace: America, Japan, Germany, and the Struggle for Supremacy* (New York: Times Books, 1992), 162–67.

29. See Ito, "The Japanese State of Mind," 279; and Courtney Purrington, "Tokyo's Policy Responses during the Gulf War and the Impact of the 'Iraqi Shock' on Japan," *Pacific Affairs* 65, no. 2 (1992), 168. For German Social Democratic views see *Der Spiegel*, February 4 and 11, 1991.

30. Purrington, "Tokyo's Policy Responses during the Gulf War," 164–65; Inoguchi Takashi, "Japan's Response to the Gulf Crisis: An Analytic Overview," *Journal of Japanese Studies* 17, no. 2 (Summer 1991), 259.

31. *New York Times*, September 10, 1990, A1.

32. A summary of the proposed legislation can be found in *Yomiuri*, October 16, 1990. See also Asahi Shimbun Wangankiki Shuzaihan, *Wangan Sensō to Nihon* (Tokyo: Asahi Shimbunsha, 1991); Inoguchi, "Japan's Response to the Gulf Crisis"; Courtney Purrington and K.A., "Tokyo's Policy Responses during the Gulf Crisis," *Asian Survey* 21, no. 4 (April 1991), esp. 314–19. On the German side, see Michael J. Inacker, *Unter Ausschluß der Öffentlichkeit: Die Deutschen in der Golfallianz* (Bonn-Berlin: Bouvier, 1992).

33. For example, only fourteen doctors out of a planned delegation of one hundred could be found who were willing to go to the gulf. *Asahi*, February 5, 1991. See also Purrington, "Tokyo's Policy Responses during the Gulf War," 165–67.

34. *Der Spiegel*, February 4, 1991; and interview with Genscher, 22. According to one survey, 58 percent of Germans said the government did the right thing in sending Bundeswehr jets to Turkey; 32 percent did not. The majority, however (51 percent versus 43 percent), thought that if Iraq attacked Turkey those jets should not be used in combat, indicating that many Germans supported the dispatch of jets as a purely symbolic act. *Der Spiegel*, January 28, 1991.

35. *Der Spiegel*, March 11, 1991.

36. *Der Spiegel*, February 4 and 11, 1991.

37. On the British and French defense policy-making processes, see Alan Ned Sabrosky, "France," esp. 229–36, and David Greenwood, "The United Kingdom," esp. 272–77, in Douglas J. Murray and Paul R. Viotti, *The Defense Policies of Nations* 2d ed. (Baltimore, Md.: Johns Hopkins University Press, 1989). See Purrington and K.A., "Tokyo's Policy Responses during the Gulf Crisis," esp. 314–19; and Sassa Atsuyuki, "Posuto Maruta ni okeru Nihon no Chii," *Chūōkōron* (March 1991), esp. 55–56, for overviews of weaknesses in the Japanese institutional mechanisms for crisis management.

38. See comments by Nishihara Masashi, *Japan Economic Journal* (March 16, 1991), 3.

39. Thatcher, *The Downing Street Years*, 816–28, quote on 817.

40. See Pia Christian Wood, "François Mitterrand and the Persian Gulf War: The Search for Influence," *French Politics and Society* 10, no. 3 (1992), 45–49.

41. See Hughes Portelli, "Union sacrée?," *Pouvoirs* 58 (1991). See also Paul-Marie Couteaux, "L'Opposition Française à la Guerre: Persistance d'un Indépendantisme Français," in Lucien Poirier, ed., *Strategique—La Guerre du Golfe* 3, no. 4 (1991); and Dominique Moïsi, "Le Quai d'Orsay et la Crise du Golfe," *Pouvoirs* 58 (1991), esp. 50.

42. *Economist*, September 22, 1990, 45–46.

43. For American estimates of expected casualties, see U.S. Congress. Senate. Committee on Armed Services. *Crisis in the Persian Gulf Region: U.S. Policy and Objectives, Hearings before the U.S. Senate*, 101st Cong., 2d sess., 2d hearing, 101–1071, November 30, 1990. For-

mer Secretary of Defense James R. Schlesinger predicted casualties running into several tens of thousands in a direct assault, 116. Lt. General William E. Odom predicted ten thousand or more allied casualties, 477.

44. The author is indebted to conversations with Motō Shiina, Cambridge, Mass., spring 1991, and Professor Satō Seizaburō, Tokyo, summer 1992. See also Tanaka Akihito and Satō Seizaburō, "Fukenshoku na Seifu Musekinin na Seiron," *Chūōkōron* (March 1991), esp. 66–67. See also *Far Eastern Economic Review* (July 18, 1991), 18–21; and *Japan Economic Journal,* March 23, 1991. On the German side see Kielinger, "The Gulf War and Consequences"; Günther Giellesen, "Der Isolationsimus der Deutschen," *Frankfurter Allgemeine Zeitung,* July 4, 1991; and interview with Wolfgang Schäuble, *Der Spiegel,* January 25, 1993; *Der Spiegel,* March 11, 1991.

45. See Kosaka Masataka, "Wangansensō no Kyōkun to Reisengo no Sekai," *Shinbōeironshu* 19, no. 2 (February 1991); Tanaka and Satō, "Fukenshoku na Seifu Musekinin na Seiron," 60; Sassa Atsuyuki, "Posuto Maruta ni Okeru Nihon no Chii," 58–59; and the editorial in *Nikkei,* March 15, 1991.

46. *Die Frankfurter Allgemeine,* March 15, 1991; *Der Spiegel,* March 25, 1991; *Boston Globe,* March 14, 1991, 1.

47. *Asahi,* April 24 and April 25, 1991; Purrington, "Tokyo's Policy Responses during the Gulf War," 172; *Japan Economic Journal,* April 20, 1991.

48. After reunification, East Germans were initially more ambivalent toward the Bundeswehr and the NATO alliance than most West Germans. Ronald Asmus, *German Perceptions of the United States at Unification,* R-4069 (Santa Monica, Calif.: Rand, 1991), esp. 20; and Hans-Joachim Veen, "Die Westbindung der Deutschen in einer Phase der Neuorientierung," *Europa Archiv* 46, no. 2 (1991), 38–40. By 1995 there was hardly any difference between them. See Renate Köcher, "Unerwartete Wende," *Frankfurter Allgemeine Zeitung,* June 14, 1995, 5.

49. Wolfgang Schlör, *German Security Policy,* Adelphi Paper no. 277 (London: IISS-Brassey's, June 1993), 32. Earlier studies showed more concern on this point. See Asmus, *German Perceptions of the United States,* 21–28.

50. *Aktuell,* January and June, 1993.

51. Legloannec, "The Implications of German Unification for Western Europe," 262.

52. *Frankfurter Allgemeine Zeitung,* February 11, 1993.

53. *Süddeutsche Zeitung,* April 22, 1992.

54. EMNID polling data in *Der Spiegel,* April 26, 1993.

55. *Der Spiegel,* July 27, 1993.

56. See *New York Times,* December 3, 1991, A16; Kathryn Tolbert, "Pacific Grim," *Boston Globe Magazine,* March 29, 1992; and Bill Powell and Bradley Martin, "What Japan Thinks of America," *Newsweek,* April 2, 1990, 16–22.

57. Eugene Brown, "The Debate over Japan's Strategic Future: Bilaterialism vs. Multilateralism," *Asian Survey* 33, no. 6 (June 1993), 557.

58. See *Bōei Handobukku* (Tokyo: Asagumo Shimbunsha, 1993), 535.

59. In a poll taken one year after passage of the peacekeeping operation legislation, 56 percent approved of Japanese participation in the peacekeeping operation, and 38.9 percent had a negative opinion. *Yomiuri,* July 3, 1993. See also *Yomiuri,* April 30, 1993.

60. *Yomiuri,* July 7, 1993.

61. *Yomiuri,* April 30, 1993.

62. *New York Times,* December 3, 1991, A16.

63. See, for example, *Frankfurter Allgemeine Zeitung,* July 2 and July 16, 1993.

64. Author's interview with Gert Krell, Frankfurt, November 1993.

65. See, for example, Wolfram Wette, "Der Wunsch nach Weltmacht," *Die Zeit,* July 30, 1993, 4.

66. Chalmers Johnson, *Japan in Search of a 'Normal' Role,* Policy Paper no. 3 (San Diego, Calif.: Institute on Global Conflict and Cooperation, University of California, July 1992), 21–22. On Japanese technonationalism, see Richard J. Samuels, "Reinventing Security: Japan since Meiji," *Daedalus* 120, no. 4 (1991).

67. On Rengō's role in recent Japanese politics, see Lonny E. Carlile, "Party Politics and the Japanese Labor Movement: Rengō's 'New Political Force,'" *Asian Survey* 34, no. 7 (July 1994).

68. See Müller, "German Foreign Policy after Unification," 132–35; and Schlör, *German Security Policy,* 10.

69. *Der Spiegel,* May 7, 1993.

70. See *Frankfurter Allgemeine Zeitung,* July 10 and July 17, 1993. For a contrasting view, see *Der Spiegel,* May 7, 1993.

71. See Heidemarie Wiezorek-Zeul, "Eine neue Architektur für Europa," in Schmidt-Eenboom and Angerer, *Siegermacht NATO,* esp. 237–40.

72. See *Frankfurter Allgemeine Zeitung,* August 9 and September 9, 1993.

73. On the maneuvering between the political parties up to 1992, see Müller, "German Foreign Policy after Unification," 139–42.

74. *Frankfurter Allgemeine Zeitung,* October 28, 1992, 5.

75. *Frankfurter Allgemeine Zeitung,* July 15, 1995, 1–2.

76. The Japanese Socialist Party has renamed itself the Social Democratic Party of Japan, but uses the term only in English. In Japanese it continued to refer itself by the old name (Nihon Shakaitō) until 1996. Since the party personnel have remained much the same, for reasons of clarity I have chosen to use the old English name here.

77. For events leading up to the reorganization of Japanese politics, see Purnendra C. Jain, "The New Political Era in Japan: The 1993 Election," *Asian Survey* 32, no. 11 (1993).

78. See *Yomiuri,* July 3, 1993; and *Nikkei,* July 15, 1993 and August 10, 1993.

79. See *Yomiuri,* July 3, 1993.

80. *Asahi,* August 10, 1993. See also the interview with the new director general of the Defense Agency, Nakanishi Keisuke, *Asahi,* August 22, 1993.

81. See *Yomiuri,* July 9, 1994, 1–2.

82. See *Asahi* and *Nikkei,* December 3, 1993; and interview with Nakanishi Keisuke, "Haigun no Sho, Kempō o Katarō," *Voice,* February 1994.

83. Müller, "German Foreign Policy after Unification," 154–55.

84. Bundespresseamt, *Bulletin* no. 68 (June 23, 1992), 649–53, and no. 144 (December 11, 1992), 1513–14. For an analysis of French thinking regarding these issues, see Peter Schmidt, "French Security Policy Ambitions," *Aussenpolitik* 44, no. 4 (1993).

85. See Presse—und Informationsamt der Bundesrepublik, *Stichwörter zur Sicherheit-*

spolitik (May 1992), 7–8; and comments made by inspector general of the Bundeswehr, General Klaus Naumann, in *Frankfurter Allgemeine Zeitung*, May 13, 1992.

86. Thomas Durrell-Young, *Franco-German Security Accommodation: Illusion of Agreement* (Carlisle, Pa.: U.S. Army War College, Strategic Studies Institute, 1993), 11–15.

87. *Frankfurter Allgemeine Zeitung*, December 5, 1992.

88. See Genscher's comments in the *Frankfurter Allgemeine Zeitung*, May 24 and July 22, 1991; and his address at the Evangelical Academy Tützing, *Europa Archiv* 15 (1990), 473–78.

89. Müller, "German Foreign Policy after Unification," 156–58; Rudolf, "Doomed to Lead?," 1; and Schlör, *German Security Policy*, 46–47.

90. Ottfried Nassauer, "Die NATO—Aufbruch zu neuen Ufern?" in Schmidt-Eenboom and Angerer, *Siegermacht NATO*, 46–54; and Schlör, *German Security Policy*, 46–48.

91. Schlör, *German Security Policy*, 30, 58–59.

92. See, for example, *New York Times*, December 15, 1991; *Der Spiegel*, December 23, 1991.

93. Müller, "German Foreign Policy after Unification," 150–54; Beverly Crawford, "German Foreign Policy after the Cold War: The Decision to Recognize Croatia," Working Paper no. 2–21 (Berkeley, Calif.: University of California at Berkeley, Center for German and European Studies, August 1993), 11–18.

94. Brian Bridges, *Japan, the Hesitant Superpower* (London: Research Institute for the Study of Conflict and Terrorism, 1993), 18–19; *Nihon Keizai Shimbun*, March 15, 1991, editorial; *Nihon Keizai Shimbun*, special series on Asia, October 2 and 3, 1991.

95. *Yomiuri*, September 12, 1991; *Asahi*, September 19 and September 28, 1993.

96. See *Asahi*, March 29, 1997, 1.

97. Bridges, *The Hesitant Superpower*, 19–20; *Nikkei Weekly*, July 19, 1993; *New York Times*, July 27, 1992, A7. Kiichi Miyazawa describes the new policy as a two-track approach—the bilateral relationship with the United States plus regional security dialogue. *Japan Times*, July 4, 1992.

98. *Asahi*, May 26, 1993; *Wall Street Journal*, July 12, 1993. On Japanese fears concerning China, see Okazaki Hisahiko, "Chūgoku Mondai Saibo," *Chūōkōron* (February 1992); and Hiramatsu Shigeo, "Chūgokukaigun to 'chūkasekai' no saikō," *Shinbōeironshu* 20, no. 3 (1992). The author would also like to thank Professor Nishihara Masashi for his comments on this issue, spring 1992.

99. These efforts have met with a certain degree of success. *Japan Times*, July 22 and July 25, 1992; *Asahi*, July 23, 1992; *Nikkei*, July 23 and July 27, 1992; *Yomiuri*, March 21, 1994.

100. Schlör, *German Security Policy*, 40–43; and Hilmar Linnenkamp, "The Security Policy of the New Germany," in Stares, *The New Germany and the New Europe*, 95–96, 115–16.

101. See *Frankfurter Allgemeine Zeitung*, February 22, February 23, and February 25, 1994.

102. See *Frankfurter Allgemeine Zeitung*, July 1 and July 2, 1995; *Der Spiegel*, June 26, 1995; *Die Zeit*, July 7, 1995.

103. Cited in Johnson, "Japan in Search of a 'Normal' Role," 23.

104. The complete text of the law can be found in "Kokusaiheiwajikatsudō nado ni tai suru Kyōryoku ni Kan suru Hōritsu," *Shinbōeironshu* 20, no. 2 (1992). Also see Aurelia George, "Japan's Participation in UN Peacekeeping Missions: Radical Departure or Pre-

dictable Response?" *Asian Survey* 33, no. 6 (1993); Naoki Saito, *The Passing of the PKO Co-operation Law* (Tokyo: International Institute of Global Peace, 1992); Purrington, "Tokyo's Policy Responses to the Gulf War," 173–76.

Chapter 7. Conclusions: Culture, Cultural change, and the Future of German and Japanese Defense Policy

1. See Martin van Creveld, *Fighting Power: Germany and U.S. Army Performance, 1939–1945* (Westport, Conn.: Greenwood, 1982).

2. The author is indebted to Professor Victor Cha of Georgetown University for his insights on North Korean–South Korean relations.

3. For a structurally similar argument see Geoffrey Garret and Barry R. Weingast, "Ideas, Interests, and Institutions: Constructing the European Community's Internal Market," in Judith Goldstein and Robert O. Keohane, *Ideas and Foreign Policy: Beliefs, Institutions, and Political Change* (Ithaca, N.Y.: Cornell University Press, 1993).

4. See, for example, Robert O. Keohane, *International Institutions and the State* (Boulder, Colo.: Westview, 1991), 173–74; Jack S. Levy, "Domestic Politics and War," in Robert I. Rotberg and Theodore K. Raab, *The Origins and Prevention of Major Wars* (New York and Cambridge: Cambridge University Press, 1989), 25–27; Joseph S. Nye, Jr., and Sean M. Lynn-Jones, "International Security Studies," *International Security* 12, no. 4 (1988), 25–27.

5. Peter J. Katzenstein, *Between Power and Plenty* (Madison, Wis.: University of Wisconsin Press, 1978); Peter J. Katzenstein, *Small States in World Markets* (Ithaca, N.Y.: Cornell University Press, 1986); Peter Gourevitch, *Politics in Hard Times* (Ithaca, N.Y.: Cornell University Press, 1986); G. John Ikenberry, David A. Lake, and Michael Mastanduno, eds., *The State and American Foreign Policy* (Ithaca, N.Y.: Cornell University Press, 1988).

6. Levy, "Domestic Politics and War"; Jack Snyder, *The Myths of Empire: Domestic Politics and International Ambition* (Ithaca, N.Y.: Cornell University Press, 1991).

7. John Mearsheimer, "Back to the Future: Instability in Europe after the Cold War," *International Security* 15, no. 1 (summer 1990); Christopher Layne, "The Unipolar Illusion: Why New Great Powers Will Rise," *International Security* 17, no. 4 (1993), esp. 41–51; George Friedman and Meredith Lebard, *The Coming War with Japan* (New York: St. Martin's, 1992).

8. For an analysis of the differences between realist and liberal theories in international relations, see Andrew Moravcsik, "Liberalism and International Relations Theory," Working Paper no. 92–6 (Cambridge, Mass.: Harvard University, Center for International Affairs, 1992).

9. Richard Rosecrance, *The Rise of the Trading State* (New York: Basic Books, 1986).

10. Jeffrey J. Anderson and John B. Goodman, "Mars or Minerva?: A United Germany in a Post–Cold War Europe," in Robert O. Keohane, Joseph S. Nye, and Stanley Hoffman, eds., *After the Cold War: International Institutions and State Strategies in Europe, 1989–1991* (Cambridge, Mass.: Harvard University Press, 1993).

11. On the difference between theories regarding foreign policy and theories regarding the state system, see Kenneth N. Waltz, *Theory of International Politics* (New York: McGraw-Hill, 1979), 121–23.

12. See Douglas J. Murray and Paul R. Viotti, *The Defense Policies of Nations: A Comparative Study* (Baltimore, Md.: Johns Hopkins University Press, 1982), introduction, for

a good overview of the comparative defense policy literature. See also Graham T. Allison, *Essence of Decision: Explaining the Cuban Missile Crisis* (Boston: Little Brown, 1971); Patrick McGowan and Howard B. Shapiro, *The Comparative Study of Foreign Policy* (Beverly Hills, Calif.: Sage Publications, 1973); and James Roherty, "Defense Community: A Concept for Comparative Analysis" in James Roherty, ed., *Defense Policy Formation* (Durham, N.C.: Carolina Academic Press, 1980).

13. See Peter Hall, *Governing the Economy: The Politics of State Intervention in Britain and France* (New York: Oxford University Press, 1986); Peter Hall, ed., *The Political Power of Economic Ideas: Keynesianism across Nations* (Princeton, N.J.: Princeton University Press, 1989); and the essays by Peter Hall, Margaret Weir, and Desmond King, in Kathleen Thelen, Sven Steinmo, and Frank Longstreth, eds., *Structuring Politics* (New York and Cambridge: Cambridge University Press, 1988).

14. John S. Odell, *U.S. International Monetary Policy: Markets, Power, and Ideas as Sources of Change* (Princeton, N.J.: Princeton University Press, 1982); Judith Goldstein, "Ideas, Institutions, and American Trade Policy," in Ikenberry et al., *The State and American Foreign Policy;* and Emmanuel Adler and Peter M. Haas, eds., "Epistemic Communities, World Order, and the Creation of a Reflective Research Program," in *International Organization* 46, no. 1 (1992). See also Peter J. Katzenstein and Nobuo Okawara, "Japan's National Security: Structures, Norms, and Policies," *International Security* 17, no. 4 (spring 1993).

15. See, for example, the discussion of culture, institutions, and ideology in Hall, *Governing the Economy*, 8–10, 19, 276–80; and Peter Hall, "The Movement from Keynesianism to Monetarism: Institutional Analysis and British Economic Policy in the 1970s," in Thelen et al., *Structuring Politics*, 91–92.

16. See Ronald Inglehart, *Culture Shift in Advanced Industrial Societies* (Princeton, N.J.: Princeton University Press, 1990); Robert J. Putnam, *Making Democracy Work: Civic Traditions in Modern Italy* (Princeton, N.J.: Princeton University Press, 1993); Mary Douglas and Aaron Wildavsky, *Risk and Culture: An Essay on the Selection of Technical and Environmental Danger* (Berkeley, Calif.: University of California Press, 1982).

17. For a highly sophisticated version of this type of argument, see David D. Laitin, *Hegemony and Culture: Politics and Religious Change among the Yoruba* (Chicago: University of Chicago Press, 1986).

18. This is basically the Weberian position on the problem of generalizability in the social sciences. See Max Weber, *On the Methodology of the Social Sciences* (Glencoe, Ill.: Free Press, 1949).

19. The author is grateful to Professor George Downs of Princeton University for bringing this point to his attention.

20. Snyder, *The Myths of Empire.*

21. See John Mearsheimer, "The False Promise of Institutionalism," *International Security* 19, no. 3 (1994–95).

Index

Index

Business community, Japan, 203–4; and
arms production, 158–59, 181, 236n.115;
and Japanese Socialists, 163; and Mutual
Security Treaty, 45; and rearmament, 35,
44, 76–77; and Sino-Japanese relations,
221n.46. *See also* Weapons exports

Cambodia, and Japanese peacekeeping
forces, 179, 191
Carter, Jimmy, 124
Catholic Church: and *Ostpolitik*, 92; and
rearmament, 35, 74
CDU (Christian Democratic Party), 37, 46,
70–71, 79, 182; and Atlanticism, 166; Atlanticists versus Gaullists, 90–91; détente,
129–30; and dual-track decision, 128; and
NATO, 182; and *Ostpolitik*, 92–93, 123,
129–30, 145, 147–48, 166, 200; and out-of-
area missions, 182, 188. *See also* Adenauer,
Konrad; Kohl, Helmut
Central Europeanists, 61–62, 65–66; and
détente, 89–90, 92; and dual-track deci-
sion, 128; and European integration, 145
Centrists (Japanese), 62–64, 65–66, 98
CGP (Clean Government Party), 121–27,
162–63, 184; and BNDPO (*Taikō*), 103; and
emergency laws, 139; and Gulf War, 174;
and 1 percent barrier, 141
Chévenment, Jean-Pierre, 176
Christian Socialist Union (CSU), 79. *See
also* Strauss, Franz Josef
Chūōkōron, 117
Churchill, Winston, and rearmament, 34
Civil-military relations, Germany, 50, 52–53,
83, 107–9, 142–44, 189–90; and Central
Europeanists, 62. *See also* conscription;
Innere Führung
Civil-military relations, Japan, 50–52, 83,
105–7, 109, 138–42, 190
Clay, Lucius, and the Nuremberg Trials, 29
Collective defense. *See* Alliance policy, Ger-
many; Alliance policy, Japan; NATO;
U.S.-Japanese defense cooperation
Collective guilt: and Central Europeanists,
61; and German Student movement,
93–94, 118; in Germany, 3, 4, 6–7, 27–30;
in Germany compared to Japan, 208–9;
in Japan, 7, 27–30, 140; and *Ostpolitik*, 197;
and Right-idealists, 57; and West Europeanists, 58–59. See also *Historikerstreit*

Collective memory, 7, 12
Collective security: and Central Euro-
peanists, 61–62; and *Ostpolitik*, 93–95.
See also CSCE
Comprehensive security (*Sōgōanzenhoshō*),
147, 200
Conscription: and Bundeswehr, 53; and
civil-military relations, 53, 54; after German reunification, 170; and Japan, 138
Constitutional Court, Germany: and overseas dispatch, 183, 190; and political parties, 80
Constitution of Japan (*Kempō*), 31–32; and
Article 9, 30, 31; and defense, 30–31; and
rearmament, 51; revision of, 32, 44, 184–85
and Right-idealists, 57
Croatia, 187
CSCE (Conference on Security and Cooperation in Europe), 94–95, 168, 186, 197
Cuban missile crisis, 88
Culture, 8–19, 214n.12; anthropological
approach to, 9–10, 205; cultural change,
12–15, 18, 20–22, 110–11, 145, 147–48,
198–201, 206–7; historical approach to,
10–12, 205

Defense spending, Germany, 136–37
Defense spending, Japan, 136–37, 171. *See
also* 1 percent of GNP limit on defense
spending
De Gaulle, Charles, 88–90
Democracy: and attitudes toward defense, 5,
32, 195; and German military, 53, 195 (*see
also Innere Führung*); and Japanese mili-
tary, 50, 185, 196
Détente, 88–95, 103. *See also* CSCE; *Ostpoli-
tik*
DGB (German Trade Union Federation).
See Labor unions, German
Dibelius, Otto, 74
DIHT (German Chamber of Trade and
Commerce), 78
DKP (German Communist Party), 80
Domei (Confederation of Japanese Labor
Unions), 158
Dregger, Alfred, 130, 166
DSP (Democratic Socialist Party) 72, 79,
120–21, 122, 162, 184; and BNDPO (*Taikō*),
103; Emergency Laws, 139; and 1 percent
limit, 139

Index

Index

Index

Japan; 1 percent of GNP limit on defense spending; Overseas dispatch of the SDF; Three non-nuclear principles; Weapons exports

Rheinischer Merkur, 75

Richter, Hans Werner, 72

Right-idealists, 56–58, 65–66, 146–47

Right-wing radicals, Germany, 178–79

Right-wing radicals, Japan, 30, 38, 45–46

Rosecrance, Richard, 202

Rühe, Volker, 3, 166, 174

Russian-German relations, 169. *See also* Soviet-German relations

Sakamoto Yoshikazu, 117, 157

Sakisaka Itsurō, 81

Sankei, 75, 172, 181

Sasaki Ryosaku, 139

Satō Eisaku: and civil-military relations, 105–6; and intellectuals, 117; and *Jishubōei*, 98; and Okinawa, 95–97; and three non-nuclear principles, 102

Satō Seizaburō, 157

Scharping, Rudolf, 182

Scheel, Walter, 123

Schmidt, Helmut, 95, 164; and Atlanticism, 64; and dual-track decision, 127–28, 133, 198; and neutron bomb, 127

Schnez, Albert, 108–9

Schröder, Gerhard, 64, 90, 92

Schumacher, Kurt, 26, 46, 61

Schwarz, Hans-Peter, 158

SDF (Self Defense Forces of Japan, *Jieitai*), and rearmament, 34, 60, 138–39, 189

SDI (Strategic Defense Initiative), 132, 134

Sea-lanes, defense of, 131–32, 135–36, 197

Sekai, 117, 181

Senghaas, Dieter, 157

Sethe, Paul, 75

Shigemitsu Mamoru, 74

Shimizu Ikutaro, 73, 146, 156

Singapore, 5

Sino-Japanese relations, 40, 41, 189; and Centrists, 63; and Left-idealists, 60

Slovenia, 187

Snyder, Jack, 15, 208

Social Democratic League (*Shaminren*), 189

Socialization, 10, 13

Sohyō (General Council of Japanese Trade Unions), 75–76, 158. *See also* Labor unions, Japan

Sokka Gakkai, 60. *See also* CGP

Soviet-German relations, 61–62, 63, 94–95, 169

SPD (Social Democratic Party), 29, 82, 70–72, 182; Bad Godesberg, 89, 91–92, 119, 200; and Central Europeanists, 122–23, 164–65, 181–82; and defense, 119, 120, 164–65, 200; and détente, 91–92; and dual-track decision, 127–28; and NATO, 43, 92, 120, 200; and out-of-area missions, 182; and peace movement, 49; views of the USSR, 37, 164–65

Spiegel, Der, 48

Spratley Islands, 189

Springer, Axel, 75

Stern, 157

Strategic culture, 15

Strauss, Franz Josef, 58, 76, 79–80, 88–89

Students, German, 93, 118–19

Students, Japanese, 74

Stürmer, Michael, 158

Sugita Ichiji, 106, 227n.65

Suzuki Zengo: and defense of sea-lanes, 131, 135–36, 197–98; and 1 percent limit on defense spending, 141

Sweden, 5

Switzerland, 5

Taishō democracy, 9

Takemura Masayoshi, 184

Territorial boundaries, Germany, 23, 36, 43; and *Ostpolitik*, 94; and reunification, 169

Territorial boundaries, Japan, 23–24

Textbooks (Japan), 30, 58, 95, 96

Thatcher, Margaret, 168

"Third Way" neutralism, 61, 72

Thompson, Michael, 14–15

Three Arrows Plan, 105–6, 138, 194

Three non-nuclear principles, 97–98, 102, 106, 226n.51. *See also* Nuclear Weapons, Japan

Todenhöfer, Jürgen, 130, 166

Tokyo trials. *See* War Crimes trials.

Tomioka Sadatoshi, 33

Treaty of San Francisco, 39

United States: and Gulf War, 2, 6, 171, 173, 176–77; and security environment, 4, 5

U.S.-German relations, 6, 40, 124, 175, 186–87, 199; and détente, 89–92, 99–100; and *Ostpolitik*, 95, 129. *See also* Alliance

Index

.

Printed in the United States
1036700003B

9 780801 872389

You, Me and Coffee

Our lives, your journal …
and so much to talk about

DIANNE PARSONS

LION

Text copyright © 2018 Dianne Parsons

This edition copyright © 2018 Lion Hudson IP Limited

The right of Dianne Parsons to be identified as the author of this work has been asserted by her in accordance with the Copyright, Designs and Patents Act 1988.

Published by
Lion Hudson Limited
Wilkinson House, Jordan Hill Business Park
Banbury Road, Oxford OX2 8DR, England
www.lionhudson.com

ISBN 978 0 7459 8057 7

First edition 2018

Text acknowledgments
The scripture quotation on page 63 is taken from the Holy Bible, New Living Translation, copyright © 1996, 2004, 2015 by Tyndale House Foundation. Used by permission of Tyndale House Publishers, Inc., Carol Stream, Illinois 60188. All rights reserved. All the other scripture quotations are taken from the Holy Bible, New International Version Anglicised. Copyright © 1979, 1984, 2011 Biblica, formerly International Bible Society. Used by permission of Hodder & Stoughton Ltd, an Hachette UK company. All rights reserved. "NIV" is a registered trademark of Biblica. UK trademark number 1448790.

Every effort has been made to trace copyright holders and to obtain permission for the use of copyright material. The publisher apologizes for any errors or omissions and would be grateful to be notified of any corrections that should be incorporated in future reprints of this book.

Extract p.27 'There is freedom waiting for you' from *Voyage: The Poetic Underground 2*. Copyright © 2016 Erin Hanson.

Extract pp.54–55 from *Let Me Tell You A Story: The Best of Rob Parsons*. Copyright © 2017 Rob Parsons. Reproduced by permission of Hodder & Stoughton Limited.

Image acknowledgments
pp.11, 20, 21, 55, 69, 73, 75, 105, 125 © Dianne Parsons
Alamy Stock Photo: p.123 © Everett Collection Inc/Alamy Stock Photo
iStock: p.17 © franviser/istockphoto.com; p.24 © KristinaGreke/istockphoto.com; p.51 © photoBeard/istockphoto.com; p.64 © SumikoPhoto/istockphoto.com; p.71 © kjekol/istockphoto.com; p.101 © zlikovec/istockphoto.com; p.113 © Andrew_Howe/istockphoto.com; p.115 © dejankrsmanovic/istockphoto.com; p.119 © omgimages/istockphoto.com
Unsplash: p.116 Luc van Loon/Unsplash

A catalogue record for this book is available from the British Library

Printed and bound in Serbia, August 2018, LH55.

*To Rob, Katie, Paul, Lloyd, Becky
and all my gorgeous grandchildren –
Harry, Lily, Evie, Jackson, and Freddie.*

You're all so special to me.

*And to my amazing girlfriends who have
shared many a coffee with me down the years.*

Contents

Acknowledgments

It's been my dream to one day write a book and I am so grateful to all those who helped to make that happen. To Stephen Hayes, I want to say a huge thank you – I really couldn't have done it without you. Thanks for the dedication, expertise, fun and the way you would so often arrive for meetings equipped with two skinny lattes.

Thanks also to Suzanne Wilson-Higgins, Deborah Lock and the whole team at Lion Hudson – your creativity, energy and encouragement have been brilliant!

And to the team at Care for the Family and to my husband Rob, who basically said to me one day "Di – Stop dreaming and start writing!"

Thank you all.

Introduction

Dianne and I have been married for over forty years. In all that time there is a scene that I have watched play out time and time again. The setting could be a café, a restaurant, a park, at the gates of a school, in a hospital waiting room – the truth is that it has occurred in hundreds of places. And in the scene Dianne has started talking with a woman – it could be a teacher, a waitress, somebody queuing at an airport check-in. In the early years of our marriage, I would assume that the conversation would be brief, but I have learned now not to rely on that. It is true that the interactions normally end with a simple, "Lovely to talk with you" but often, phone numbers are exchanged and it would not be at all unusual that in a few months' time Dianne would say to me, "Oh you remember Jacquie that I met at that quiz night last year [I don't!] well, she's in the area and she's coming around.''

And so it will begin – the next stage of a chance encounter. But it's not just with strangers – friends, friends of friends – more people than I can remember have been welcomed into our home to talk... and drink coffee. I can honestly say I have rarely known the content of the conversations that took place in front of the fire, but I have often heard raucous laughter and sometimes seen Dianne scurry out of the room to find some tissues.

And now you too, like many others are about to sit down for coffee with Dianne. I hope with all my heart you have a wonderful time together!

Rob Parsons, OBE
Founder and Chairman, Care for the Family

Take a Seat

I love to talk. I have had the privilege of speaking all around the world – sometimes in prestigious venues like the Royal Albert Hall or the Birmingham Symphony Hall. I have loved those occasions but they're not what energize me most. No, if you really want to see me come alive, then come into my front room... I can't promise you that it will look like something you would see on Pinterest, but the fire will be lit and the armchairs are deep. And when we are sitting comfortably and the coffee is brewing, we can begin the kind of talking that I really love. Two of us. Face to face. One minute outrageous laughter – the next, mascara running as our hearts are moved.

So why would someone who loves to talk decide to put pen to paper? Well, I suppose this book was in some ways born out of a sunny October morning many years ago when I woke up and whispered to Rob, "Darling, I don't think I can cope any more..." The events and experiences that flowed from those words were very hard, but they weren't all negative. I learned lessons of faith and hope that I wouldn't have grasped if the sun had kept shining... I will share more about that day later on...

A lot of water has gone under the proverbial bridge since then and I have found that lessons of life can be born out of laughter as well as through tears.

I can't promise you that everything I share will be orderly – but I do promise that it will be from the heart.

So... here are stories, quotes, odd bits from the family scrapbook and of course memories and snippets from my thirty years with the national charity, Care for the Family. I share most of them with you not because they are special but because they are ordinary – and in the ordinariness of it all, I pray that at least on one page you will discover something, however small, that will enrich your life. I realize that you may not share my faith and I understand that. But whatever you do or don't believe, my heart is that you might identify with some of my hopes, fears, joys... and struggles.

You'll see that every so often, there are some journal pages. They are for you. I am so grateful to Deborah Lock for writing some questions – use them if they help prompt your writing.

So... come on in, put your feet up; the fire's lit and the coffee is brewing...

> *Oh the comfort, the inexpressible comfort of feeling safe with a person; having neither to weigh thoughts nor measure words but to pour them all out, just as it is, chaff and grain together, knowing that a faithful hand will take and sift them, keeping what is worth keeping, and then, with the breath of kindness blow the rest away.*
>
> Dinah Craik

I love this quote. Don't you think she's put her finger on the quality we all crave from a good friend? The willingness to listen, knowing full well that much of what we say won't be judged, allowing us to share our heart, and that every word spoken doesn't have to be profound or carefully crafted. If we can find a friend like that, although we may look back on our conversation and think, "Oh she must have thought me silly/shallow/dim for saying that," we will realize that actually it didn't really matter. Our good friend allowed us to pour it all out – "chaff and grain" – and we trust that they will sift our words, "keep what is worth keeping", and then, most wonderfully, "with the breath of kindness blow the rest away."

Friendship is a sheltering tree.

-Samuel Taylor Coleridge-

This is a canvas that we have in our home, and for me, it sums up everything about what true friendship should be. There have been times when I have been so grateful for that shelter.

The Talk Salon

"I'd like Dianne to curl my hair."

Those words were said by an elderly lady over half a century ago and yet they are still in my mind. At that time, I saw myself as just a "Saturday girl" in a local hairdresser's, so for me those words gave me dignity and value. I believe, when our self-esteem is low however seemingly insignificant, words of encouragement are like rain in the desert.

Growing up, I didn't "get" school. I loved the social aspect of it, but apart from some sports and one particular art project that I was proud of, nothing ever really felt like "my thing". I left when I was sixteen and I was suddenly faced with the question, "What am I going to do with my life?" Children in schools all over the world ask this, and while it is necessary, it almost seems premature. So there I was, a teenager asking this of myself. But before I could really find an answer, a friend told me about a hair salon that needed a part-timer. Although I can't say I had any aspirations to go into this world, I thought, *There's not much else going so, heck, why not?*

I managed to get an interview. I went along, trying to keep any nerves under wraps, and then... the questions started – actually, just one question! They asked me if I could work between 9 a.m. and 12 noon, I said I could, and... that was it. I was given the job. It was comfortably the least extensive interview process I have ever had. I agreed to start the very next day, and it didn't take long for me to realize that this would suit me down to the ground – not so much because I got to wash people's hair and sweep up, but because I got to chat to customers. Even though I was not yet the seasoned conversationalist that I am today, I could still talk for Britain.

As the weeks went by, I started figuring out different aspects of what the job entailed – I believe today they call that "upskilling". One thing I was particularly good at was curling! Sometimes, I would be halfway through making a cup of tea out the back or cleaning the equipment when I would hear the bell on the door, followed by a shaky voice asking, "I'd like Dianne to curl my hair." I can remember feeling like a million pounds! Honestly, you would not believe what this did for my confidence; one minute I was scraping hair out of a hair-washing station, and the next I was "Dianne, Hair Curler Extraordinaire". As I curled her hair, we would just chat non-stop as she would tell me of the things concerning her, from the extortionate price of stamps to the struggle of missing her kids who had all moved away. It was in that setting, as I chatted with this dear lady, that I realized I had a heart for people. Even then I wanted to say things to her that would speak life into the difficulties she faced. I wanted to give her hope and reassurance.

It was standing behind that chair as I curled that I began to discover not only the thing that would become my greatest gift, but also my greatest love – talking.

The Visit

Isn't it incredible how memories of childhood can come back to you as clear as the day they happened, yet you can't remember where you left your phone? As I look back on my childhood, there are some memories that I'll carry until the day I die.

One day I was at home on my own. My dad was at work and my mum had probably popped to the shops. There was a knock on the door. I opened it and there stood a little old lady. She looked about 200 but was probably in her eighties. She was wearing a thick grey jacket that appeared to have once been a feasting ground for a family of moths. Her hair was white and wiry and she was hunched over a walking stick. She peered up at me through her cloudy spectacles and said, "Oh my dear, I wonder if you can help me... I desperately need to use the toilet; do you think I could come in and use yours?" I didn't even hesitate and welcomed the lady in. I helped her up the stairs to our little bathroom. She came down, thanked me profusely, gave me a little kiss on the cheek, and then she was gone.

The next day I was in the house alone again and I heard the letter box open and close. I ran out to see what it was and a little card was waiting for me on our welcome mat. By the time I opened the door to see who was there, the street was empty.

On the card was a verse from the New Testament in the Bible. It was Hebrews 13:2:

> *Do not forget to show hospitality to strangers,*
> *for by doing so some people have shown hospitality*
> *to angels without knowing it.*

Well, was she? I don't know, but whenever I think back to that day, I can't help but wonder.

Seeing Further

A small boy said to his mother, "Mum – have you ever seen God?"

"No, darling," she said, "nobody has ever seen God."

He asked his father, "Dad – have you ever seen God?"

His father was busy, and shouted over his shoulder as he repaired a leaking tap, "No son – nobody has ever seen God."

The little boy ambled into the front garden of his house. A priest was passing on the road outside. The little boy's face lit up. Surely here would be some success!

"Sir – have you ever seen God?"

The priest screwed up his eyes, "Well, not in the way you think, sonny. Of course He is everywhere, at once, at all times, but… no, I have never seen Him."

The boy was sad and ambled down to the riverbank. It was a beautiful summer's day and the river sparkled as the sun's rays hit it. An old man sat fishing, his face and hands gnarled with time. The boy thought it worth one last try. "Old man," he said, "have you ever seen God?"

The old man looked up and saw a dragonfly blazoned with colour hovering over the water. He saw what seemed like a million diamonds dancing in the sun on the surface of the river, and suddenly a fish jumped, the sun catching its back as it shimmered in the sunshine.

"Son," said the old man, "sometimes I think I see nothing else."

Have you ever seen God?
Sometimes I see nothing else...

The Proposal

These days, the lengths that some men go to in their proposals is off the scale. I know of a lad who used a flying drone to deliver the big question! I remember a friend of mine drinking champagne only to find a rather large diamond ring at the bottom of her glass. Wow... what wonderful romance!

Rob's proposal to me however was slightly different...

We started our relationship when I was sixteen but by the time I was twenty-one, I was already dreaming of a wedding and it seemed that Rob was not quite so keen. In fact, one rainy Tuesday night in November I decided, if he found it so hard to even talk about getting married, I was going to find somebody who didn't. That was that. I "finished" with him.

Apparently Rob was heartbroken – so forlorn that a kindly gent in our church who owned a men's clothing shop took pity and decided to lift his spirits by giving him a new sand-coloured suit with matching shirt and tie. The only problem was Rob didn't have shoes to match so he painted his black ones a light brown colour.

Anyway, Rob must have thought he looked pretty good in this outfit because a few weeks later, he decided to "accidentally" bump into me getting off my bus after work while wearing the whole set! To be honest, by then I was having a few second thoughts about the new guy I had started dating, and when I saw Rob dolled up to the nines I thought "best hedge my bets". I finished with the other guy and invited Rob to join me and my parents on the second week of a caravan holiday in Cornwall.

The day for Rob to join us finally came and my brother-in-law, Rog, kindly drove him down. I glanced out of the caravan window to see if there was any sight of Rob. There certainly was. He was trudging across the muddy field, in the pouring rain, dressed in his brand-new suit, shirt, and tie! Years later, he told me that I had obviously been so impressed when he met me at the bus, he thought wearing his new attire was vital to winning my heart back.

I opened the door to him. He stood there looking like a drowned rat on the way to a Buckingham Palace garden party! He seemed a little agitated and asked if we could go for a walk immediately. Off we went together across a very boggy caravan park and it wasn't long before he stopped, turned to me, and proposed. To say I was taken aback would be an understatement. And while my mind was reeling I looked down and couldn't believe what I saw. The paint was coming off his shoes!

If a heart can smile, mine did at that moment and I knew I had to say yes. You see, many women expect to meet a man who is the complete package from the off – rugged good looks, physically and mentally strong, and yet, a conflicted poetic type under the surface. It's not reality. Sometimes you have to look past the proverbial shoe paint to see what's really in front of you.

So... it wasn't quite as romantic as the diamond ring in a champagne glass, but I wouldn't have had it any other way!

I'm glad Rob *hasn't* got his "painted shoes" on here!

Dear Rob.

After what seemed an endless journey we arrived here safely. The Caravan is great. The address is below Caravan 11. Rog said he'd call in on his way home so if you 'phone him he'll ma the arrangements. Hope you ca come down it'll be great. i soon if you have time

THE SWIMMING POOL   lots of [

POST
PRINTED IN
CORRESPONDENCE
NEWQUAY
12.15PM
20 JLY
1970

iteacres Holiday Park,
iitecross, Newquay, Cornwall.

Just the other day I discovered the actual postcard I sent Rob giving the address to the caravan park.

You Can't Have Everything

When Rob and I got married, I knew he wasn't very good at DIY. He wasn't then, and to be honest with you, he isn't now. But I would nag him a bit when things needed doing. I suppose I felt it was a "husband thing" that he should be able to do.

I remember somebody gave us a towel rail for our wedding present. After about a year, I said to him, "Are you going to put this towel rail up in the bathroom or not?"

He said, "OK, I'll give it a go."

Somebody told him he had to drill a hole and add something called a "rawlplug". The only problem was, it was a hollow door and when he put the plug in, it just fell down inside! He looked at it with the same confusion as a dog who catches their reflection in a window. So... he put another one in, and another. I was counting. I think at twenty-four he realized it was going to take him a long time to build up sufficient depth of rawlplug. He sat down in exasperation on the toilet but, unfortunately, the top seat was down and he cracked it. I just watched thinking, "This is my husband!"

I remember another occasion when we had a new carpet fitted and they had to take the door off to fit it. It was off for about a month, and I asked when he was going to reattach it to the hinges. He told me some wood needed to be shaved off the bottom. I said in no uncertain terms, "It's not going to happen miraculously. Either you've got to do it, or we leave the door off forever."

He got the message and borrowed an electric saw. I

remember the day now. It is seared into my memory. He put the door in between his legs and sat there with the electric saw in hand. It's fair to say he looked a touch apprehensive. He positioned the saw close to the bottom of the door and shouted to me, "Turn it on."

I turned it on at the plug. It leapt into life in his hands – this thing was flying everywhere. It wasn't too long before I heard him shouting, "Turn it off, turn it off!"

He eventually got the "thing" to work. He went part of the way along the bottom right of the door and then started on the left side. The problem was, the door still wasn't level and had a big lump in the middle that needed to be chiselled off. We didn't actually have a chisel but Rob, being the great DIY man improvised with a big screwdriver. Phew! He was on a roll! The door was eventually back where it should be but there was a substantial gap at the bottom. In fact, the cat could get under without too much difficulty and we did think about taking up limbo dancing. But at least the door was up.

My dream of a husband who was great at DIY was shattered but I learned to appreciate Rob for the things he *could* do. In fact, in my heart I vowed to see the wisdom of the first part of a very old saying about marriage – as long as Rob would accept the wisdom of the second part. It says, "Women marry men with the foolish notion they can change them."

And the second part? "Men marry women with the silly idea that they will be the same forever."

A dream catcher

The Dream Catcher

When you were a child, what did you want to be? For some it may have been a firefighter or an airline pilot, but for me it was a princess or a ballerina in one of those gorgeous net tutus, dancing on the stage and receiving the applause and the bouquets. How many of us practised that little routine in front of the bedroom mirror? Nowadays, I *avoid* full-length mirrors and the tutus are just a memory. I have different dreams now – perhaps a little more realistic!

Some Native American cultures have something called a dream catcher. It's a small hoop with a net attached to it and feathers hanging from it. Apparently, all the bad dreams are supposed to fall through the larger holes in the net, but the good dreams are caught in the central net where they cannot escape. Of course the dreams we have in our sleep are often lost forever, but the other dreams – our aspirations – *can* be caught.

We need dreams, something we can work towards outside the everyday routine of our lives. However small we think it is, it's our dream and we can strive towards it. I am inspired as I think of some who have pursued their dreams. The other day I was watching Tanni Grey-Thompson on television, who against all the odds, has seen so many of her dreams come true in the sporting world. In spite of her confinement to her wheelchair, this young lady had dreams to win gold medals – and she did, eleven of them! When she was asked, "What is the greatest barrier you have had to face?" she replied, "People who make assumptions about what I *can't* do."

Now our dreams may not be as adventurous as those of Tanni, but they are still as valid. I wonder what so often stops us fulfilling them? Do you think that we're afraid we might fail? That probably has a big part to play. I know it has for me. I think I am a "what if" person. *What if this happens? What if I fail? What will people think of me?* But as I get older, I see life speeding by so very quickly and I am now thinking, *So what?* So what if I fail while trying to achieve my aspirations? At least I've given it a try.

Rob loves poetry and he has a favourite: it is very short but it moves me to at least try for my dreams. It's the one on the facing page.

*There is freedom
waiting for you,
on the breezes of
the sky,
and you ask,
"What if I fall?"
Oh but my darling,
What if you fly?*

Erin Hanson

The Rainbow Through the Rain

Over thirty years ago, Rob was preparing to speak to a group of about 300 doctors and social workers on some family issues.

At that time, I was feeling frustrated that I'd never had the opportunity to share things that I strongly felt people would benefit from. As Rob was at his desk preparing I said, "I think I might have something to say that's worth listening to."

Rob said, "But you've never spoken in public, not even to ten people. How would you do it?"

I replied, "I think I'd be fine – why don't you ask them?"

To his credit, he did, but he didn't tell the organizers that I had never given a speech in my life. They agreed!

I will never forget the look on his face as he stood in front of the audience that day and said, "And now would you welcome my wife Dianne…" I suppose he was very brave really. Since that day I have spoken to thousands of people and have used the words that I began that talk with in auditoriums across the world. They are etched in my memory. (And I am sure in Rob's as well!)

"It was in so many ways a perfect autumn day. The sun was streaming through the curtains and across the bed. I had a little girl of three years old and a brand-new baby boy. We had a lovely home and I was lying next to my husband who loved me. The only problem was I had just whispered to Rob, "I don't think I can cope any more. Could you take Katie to nursery today?"

Rob said, "Yes – sure."

But neither of us knew that those words of mine would usher in a period in our family life that was very dark. And if we thought that time would be over in a week, a month or even a year, we were wrong. Even now I don't really know what went on in my body. Yes, I am sure that post-natal depression was part of it, but it seemed also that my immune system just crashed. I was later told I had ME.

For quite a long time I couldn't even look after my own children. I still look back at that time and feel guilty. You have every right to ask me why I felt guilty for being ill, but I was young, and to be honest, the Christian community of which I was part was pretty good if you broke a leg (they would bake a cake!), but anything from the neck up and they weren't quite so sure. I had people tell me I was lazy, selfish, and should just "pull myself together". Oh, how I would have loved to have pulled myself together, but when your body and your mind feel so weary, it is hard to pull.

There is a lovely old hymn by George Matheson, "O Love That Will Not Let Me Go". It has a remarkable line in it: "I trace the rainbow through the rain."

Do I wish that time of my life had never happened? Yes, with all my heart. But without doubt I am a different and a softer – even a little wiser – person because of it and I can say that now, looking back, I can trace the rainbow through the rain. Since that day all those years ago I have had conversations with hundreds of women who have told me of times when they weren't sure they could go on in life. I have been able to whisper those wonderfully healing and liberating words – "*Me too.*"

During those dark times Rob was great and some friends were wonderful, but over and above that, I had to believe that God cared.

In the next story, I'll tell you about the wonderful "Strugglers' Group" that was born out of that dark experience.

Oh joy that seekest me through pain,
I cannot close my heart to thee;
I trace the rainbow through the rain,
And feel the promise is not vain
That morn shall tearless be.

from
"O Love That Will Not Let Me Go",
by George Matheson

The Strugglers' Group

One day, a couple of years after I first became ill and was beginning to see the light of day, I said to Rob, "Do you know what I would love to do?" He raised an eyebrow. I said, "No, not that! I'd love to start a little group in our home, perhaps once a month, where people who are going through really hard times can share how they are feeling – really honestly – and see if we can help each other." In fairness to Rob, he's normally up for a challenge and he said, "Let's do it." And then he said, "I think I know just the name for it." And so we put the word out that on a certain day there would be the inaugural meeting of the "Strugglers' Group"!

People flocked to it – all kinds of people. All different and yet in some ways all a bit broken. Rob and I were honest. We admitted on the first night that we weren't in a brilliant place ourselves, so not to expect any great or easy answers from us. But we also said that we believed that together we could help, encourage, and sustain each other. They were remarkable evenings. Atheists came and sat quietly as those with faith prayed for the group, doctors who spent their lives advising others shared their own fears and worries, and some hardly said a word and yet never missed a meeting.

I remember one evening opening the door to a man I thought exceedingly capable, a high-flyer in his field. I can recall him now standing there on my doorstep. I was so shocked to see him I hadn't even invited him in. He simply said, "I have come for the Strugglers' Group."

One couple, Steve and Gill, started coming at the very beginning. Steve was a good friend that Rob and I had known for many years. He had once had a very real faith but because of doubts and circumstances, that was no longer the case. He was married to Gill, a very bright social worker. Gill had no particular religious beliefs, but whereas Steve would often sit and listen quietly, she was very vocal and let us know quite clearly that she had *lots* of questions.

I remember Rob saying to the group once (but I'm sure he was particularly speaking to Gill), "I'm sorry that you don't have better examples of Christians to look at right now. As you know Di and I are struggling a bit at the moment."

Gill said, "Oh – you're fine!"

Nevertheless, as we did the dishes that evening after everybody had left, we talked and Rob said, "You know I don't think Gill will ever find faith in Christ; she is so very cynical."

We went to bed.

At midnight the phone beside our bed rang. It was Gill. She blurted out, "I'm so sorry to ring you so late. We brought two cars tonight and I was driving home across the mountain alone when suddenly I was filled with an incredible sense of forgiveness. I have met *Him*. I felt His love flood the car. My heart is physically hurting." She paused. "Will it always be like this?"

I remember Rob saying, rather sleepily, "I'm not sure. It's never happened to me. You're very fortunate."

That incident was over thirty-five years ago. Shortly after that, Steve rediscovered his faith. Since that evening, Gill and Steve have been constantly up to their necks in serving God. I can't think of another couple who have touched more lives – and they are doing that even as I write. The Strugglers' Group ran for years. No clever answers, no judgement, just people being community to each other. Sometimes as I watched them talking and sharing and remembered the autumn morning that began it all, I thought of the sheer power of weakness. I marvelled at the ways and the wisdom of God.

Your Journal

"I began to discover the one thing that would become my greatest gift."

What do you consider to be your gifts and how can you best use them? (The Talk Salon)

Do you have any memorable
moments from your childhood
that still impact you today?
(The Visit)

"Sometimes you have to look past the proverbial shoe paint to see what's in front of you."

Who have you had a special relationship with? What do you value about them? (The Proposal)

"*I learned to appreciate Rob for the things he* **could** *do!*"

Are there any lessons you can learn here in your relationship with others? (You Can't Have Everything)

When you were a child, what dreams did you have?

Have you fulfilled them or has something stopped you?
(The Dream Catcher)

42

"I trace the rainbow through the rain."

Who kept you going throug any dark times? How do yo think they helped you? (The Rainbow Through the Rain)

What fears and worries do you have? Is there anyone you can share these with? (The Strugglers' Group)

48

Vulnerability

I don't expect that you and I have met. But can I share with you a quality that I would so love to find in you should you and I become friends? It is simply this: vulnerability. Now I know that is such a scary word – most of us spend our lives trying to prove that we are anything but vulnerable. I can remember for a time playing the game of pretending I was a perfect mother; that I was every bit as capable as *that* lady, who seemed to have it all together and whose sponges for the school fayre did not double up as Frisbees. I pretended not to be bothered when I arrived at the school gate with what at first sight looked like highlights but turned out (on closer inspection) to be bits of Weetabix in my hair, while *she* looked as if she had just stepped straight into the playground from the set of a Special K advert.

Thirty years have passed since I stood at that school gate, and since then I have had more coffees than I can count with my friends – and believe it or not, the "Special K Lady" is one of them. And of course we have discovered in those talks that the key – the essential key to deep relationships – is very simple. In fact, it is one of our three main values in Care for the Family: vulnerability. I wonder why that should be so. I don't think the answer is so hard to find: it is simply that we can face most things in life if we know that we are not alone – that others have trod the painful or difficult path that we are now walking. Of course we want answers to our problems, but even more than that, we want to hear from somebody those blessed words that I've already mentioned: "*Me too.*"

It is hard to understand why such phrases are so potent, and yet time and time again they bring hope, not despair;

they bring encouragement, not despondency. They shoo away loneliness with understanding and comfort. Our brokenness becomes a source of healing for others; it can even be beautiful.

The Japanese have a wonderful skill called Kintsugi. You may have heard of it. When pottery is broken, instead of it being discarded it is repaired using lacquer mixed with liquid gold. The repaired vessel wears its scars both beautifully – and proudly. But what I've learned is that it is based on a Japanese philosophy that teaches about the wisdom of using the flawed and the imperfect together. It all stems from an old fable that goes something like this:

In the Far East, there was an emperor who lived in a palace with untold wealth, and every spring, royalty from other kingdoms would visit him, to see his exhibition of wealth and finery. One year, as the visit was approaching the emperor decided he would show off a new prized possession – a bowl made by master craftsmen out of the most exquisite materials. Days before his guests would arrive, the emperor went to check that the bowl was ready to be displayed, but to his horror, it was smashed into pieces and no one knew how it happened. He went to his chambers and locked himself away in distress.

The next morning, things got even worse. A thief had broken into the palace and not only stolen the fragments of pottery, but also a gold crown.

The morning of the royal visit came and the emperor was awoken by a great uproar. He ran to his cabinet expecting further treasures to be missing but, to his wonder, the bowl was back in its place in one piece – only now it had gold veins running through; its beauty was even greater than before. Next to the bowl was the crown – now half the size. It had given of itself to the glory of another and it too was somehow more stunning because of it.

The bowl wears its scars
both beautifully – and proudly.

Flawed but Fruitful

Kintsugi is amazing. Of course sometimes the cracks don't heal in a beautiful way, but God can still use them.

Let's stay on the theme of pottery.

There is a lovely old story of a farmer who had two water pots – one red, one blue. Each day, he would carry the pots to the well. The little path that he trod at least twice a day was well-worn, beaten-down earth. When he had filled them, he would heave them on to his shoulders – the blue one on the left and the red one on the right. He never varied which side. Then he would walk the little path again back to the farmhouse.

At night, he kept them outside the door of the farmhouse but he had to be careful in the winter months to be sure they were completely empty, lest any water freeze and crack the clay. One winter's night he didn't empty the blue pot completely. There were a few inches of water left in the bottom. That night was one of the coldest of the year and the water in that pot froze, expanded, and cracked the pot – just a hairline – but nevertheless flawed from now on. When he picked the pots up the next day, the farmer didn't notice the crack, not even when he filled them and lifted them both, as normal, onto his shoulders. When he set them down he noticed that the blue pot he had carried on his left shoulder seemed to have a little less water in it than the other, yet he was sure he had filled them equally.

As the days went by the farmer realized what had happened but kept using both pots – after all, the loss of water was negligible. That night, after the farmer had gone to bed, the red pot said to the blue, "You are flawed. You can't even carry water properly. We are water jugs and if we can't do that then we are good for nothing." As the red pot spoke a tiny drop of water rolled down the outside of the damaged jar, but it was not water from the well.

Each night, the perfect red pot would say similar things to the blue one, and started talking even as the farmer was carrying them back from the well, saying things like, "Look at the water seeping out of you – what use are you?" Day by day, month by month, and all through winter and into spring this went on.

But the pots did not know that the farmer could understand their language, and one day as the perfect pot was taunting the other, the farmer stopped, took both jars off his shoulders, and set them down, one on the right and the other on the left. The pots wondered what was going on but soon the farmer spoke. "I have been listening each day as I have carried you and I want to show you something." He turned to the red pot, "You are right – you are perfect. No water is ever lost from you, but look at the path under where you are carried. The ground is dry, hard, and bare of life. It received nothing to soften the soil as I walked along it."

Then he turned to the blue pot. "It is true that you are flawed; that was not your fault – but mine. It is also true that you do not carry water as well as your companion. But look at the ground under where you pass. Day by day, as a little water has seeped from your wound, it has fallen on the ground. In the darkness of winter, it was hardly noticed, but little by little it softened the soil and seeped deep into the ground, where it found seeds desperate for a little refreshment and encouragement. And look – the ground under where you pass is filled with the colour and life of the new spring flowers."

The Tears of a Clown

National treasure, Roy Castle was famous for presenting Record Breakers, as well as being an outstanding dancer, singer, comedian and actor. Just before Roy died, Rob and I got to know him and his lovely wife Fiona. Sometime after Roy's death, she and I were talking about the tremendous pressure that many people had shared with us about having to keep up appearances even when our hearts were breaking. We decided we would try to address that issue and the result of that conversation was an event called 'The Tears of a Clown'. Thousands of people came to it. The heart of it is summed up by this little story:

A man went to visit a doctor. He sat hunched in his seat, his dark-ringed eyes set deep in one of the saddest faces the general practitioner had ever seen. He told the doctor that he was tired of life, that although once a positive man, he now felt a deep sadness daily – but he didn't know why. The doctor listened for a while and then reached into his desk drawer and took out a brochure advertising a circus. On the front of the flyer was a clown with a massive smile painted onto his face and next to him the words, "The Great Grimaldi! The funniest clown in the world!" The doctor handed him two tickets. "Somebody gave me these," he said. "I think if you go to the circus Grimaldi will lift your spirits – at least for a while." The patient slowly handed the tickets back. "Sir," he said, "I am Grimaldi."

This man had used his clownish make-up as a type of mask for so long, but underneath there was sadness. During The Tears of a Clown event, we urged each other to find somebody with whom we could take the mask off and we used a little poem that we wrote for the occasion.

I have played the part for so long
Worn the make-up and the smile
Took the bow and the applause
Said, "Oh fine, oh yes, of course...
I'm fine."

Donned the costume, trod the boards
Learned the lines and sung the song
Made you laugh and made you cry
I have done it all so long.

I have done it all so long
That I don't expect you see
That to get this leading role
The real cost was... me.

We managed to dig the front cover of the brochure out of the attic. Perhaps we should put it back up there before it scares the grandkids!

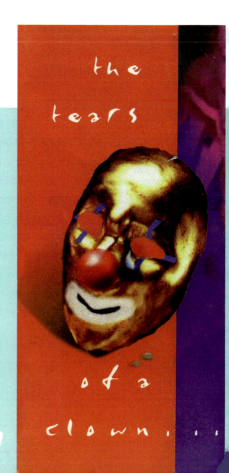

the

tears

of a

clown...

A Really Big Job

When Rob was in the law practice, we were once invited to a business dinner. I had given birth to Lloyd just a few weeks before and struggled to get into the dress that I was convinced a week before would be just fine. I knew there would be some pretty high-powered women there and my confidence level was low.

When we got to the restaurant I said to Rob, "This would be a good night to stay close to me. Don't go wandering off!"

To be honest, as the evening unfolded I thought it was going better than I had expected, until suddenly a very attractive and, to my eye, "altogether" woman said to me across the table, "So Dianne, do you work?"

I have worked full-time and part-time but just then I was a stay-at-home mum. Isn't it strange how so much can go through your brain in milliseconds? I remember thinking, *Do I work? Well, I know that two young lives are totally dependent on me. I know that I start very early and finish late every day. I know that it's the toughest job I have ever had in my life*. But the words that came out of my mouth reflected none of that. I whispered, "No, I'm just a mum at home with small children." She smiled and turned to the seemingly far more interesting woman on her left.

Sometime after that I came across a brilliant reply given by another mother to that same question. I learned it by heart and spent the next ten years hoping that somebody would ask me the question again. Here is the answer she gave:

> *Yes, I do work.*
> *I'm in a programme of social development.*
> *At present, I'm working with three age groups.*
> *First, with babies and toddlers. That involves a basic*
> *grasp of medicine and child psychology. Next, I'm*
> *working with teenagers. I confess the programme is*
> *not going too well in that area. Finally, at evenings*
> *and weekends I work with a man aged thirty-nine*
> *who's exhibiting all the classic symptoms of a mid-life*
> *crisis. That's mainly psychiatric work. The whole job*
> *involves planning, a "make it happen" attitude,*
> *and the ability to crisis-manage. I used to be*
> *an international fashion model,*
> *but I got bored.*

Nailed it! If only I could meet the lady who
asked me the question now!

Losing Weight

Loads of my friends have been helped by slimming clubs... and I have to say that although I have joined almost every one, I haven't been very successful. (I wonder if it's because I ate too much!)

Some years ago I went to one and, after three weeks, I had lost just one pound. I think the leader of this class thought I was getting discouraged – and she was right, *I was*. A few days later a little postcard landed on the mat in the hall. It read like this:

> *Just a pound I hear you say*
> > *I've lost so little weight today*
> > *Here encouragement is found*
> > *You'll gain that victory pound by pound*

I think she must have caught me on a bad day. I wrote this little reply, but I can't quite remember if I had the courage to send it.

> *Thank you for your lovely card*
> > *Although I found it rather hard*
> > *That glorious pound I lost that day*
> > *I put back on by Saturday!*

A Mother Remembers

Over two decades ago, Rob and I worked together on *The Sixty Minute Mother* book. In one of the chapters I wrote, "When a mother remembers", and as I reflected on the words written by my younger self, I realized that they were still valid for so many mums today. I decided to share them with you here:

I often have to drive past the infants' school that my children attended. They are both grown with children of their own now, and yet I only have to glance at the gates at the end of the playground for a hundred memories to come flooding back. Suddenly it is a crisp September morning and it is my daughter's first day at school. We walk from our home together, her hand tightly gripping mine. The excitement and bravado of this step into the world of the "big children" seem to desert her the moment we close the front door, and now she looks white and worried and I catch her nibbling her bottom lip – a sure sign that tears are close at hand.

I edge her down the road towards the school and talk of anything except this special day. She mumbles replies but I catch her watching the other children to whom this is all old-hat; the kids who jostle us are seven-year-old veterans. She begins to slow her step and I begin to fear the worst when suddenly an angel appears, or so it seems to me. Actually it is her best friend for whom this is also the first day. Suddenly Katie leaves my side and runs towards Rhian. I am left standing, watching as these two little girls walk solemnly up the school drive together, holding hands and each clutching a My Little Pony lunch-box. I feel my eyes fill up and then Katie turns and shouts, "See you later, Mum!" Against all the predictions, my shy, careful child has done it. She has entered the big wide world of academia.

And then my mind fast-forwards three years. It is Lloyd's first day. The parenting gurus tell us that if your first child is shy, careful, and compliant, your second will be different. Lloyd was desperate not to disappoint those experts. In fact, he dedicated most of his young life to proving them correct in every detail. I knew that his first day of school would be quite different. I just didn't have any idea *how* different. In an event never to be repeated he was up and dressed before me and hammering on my bedroom door yelling, "Come on, I want to get there early!"

As I had with Katie, I took his hand as we walked down the road together, but whereas Katie had found this comforting, Lloyd looked as though somebody had tethered him to a walking embarrassment. He dragged me towards the place of learning, firing off threatening glances at children twice his size and, with a burst of impatience, finally broke loose and ran ahead. I turned a corner and saw he was almost at the gate. And then it happened. He took one look into the playground, grimaced at a teacher, then slowly walked back to me and said, "I'm not going", and grabbed a nearby lamp post.

I immediately clicked into my, "no-pain-no-gain", "you'll-be-sorry-when-you're-thirty", and "superman-went-to-school" routine. He looked up with that little jaw set in the now familiar look of defiance and repeated, "I'm *not* going." And so the battle began.

There were moments over the following ten minutes when it seemed possible that with the aid of other mothers I would loosen his grip on the lamp post. But he held firm. The prospect of Lloyd beginning his formal education linked to twenty feet of vertical concrete with a light on top was rushing through my brain when the Deputy Head appeared. I have never managed to work out whether her concern was for me, Lloyd, or the property of the County Council, but she ordered me to leave. I will never forget Lloyd's face. He was torn between running after me – which meant giving up his hold on the lamp post, and remaining within the influence of a woman who looked decidedly less sympathetic to the plight of small boys than his mother.

He hesitated and I went, not willingly, but propelled along by Sheila Harrison, who had done all this four times already. As she whisked me away she said, "He'll be better off without you."

I have since wondered whether she meant just at that moment or in life generally.

But on that morning, at least, she was right and I had finally ushered my two children into the "real" world. How was I to know that motherhood involves a million school-gate experiences at every age and that the process was only just starting? Why didn't somebody tell me? I'll tell you the reason – because if they had, you'd have never got *me* off that lamp post!

Candles

I love candles. I love to watch a flame flickering in the darkness; I find it mesmerizing. I take any opportunity at parties, meals, and of course at Christmas, to fill our home with their light. In fact, one of the things I most love about people coming for a meal is decorating the table and lighting the candles. I sometimes wish that could be just my part instead of sweating over the cooking and all those dishes!

Some years ago Rob and I were in South Africa and some friends took us into the bush. It had been a long day and it was just getting dark as we neared the compound where we were staying. Suddenly we turned a corner and there was an incredible sight that I will never forget. In a clearing there was a table set out for a meal and a roaring fire waiting for us. I must admit my first thought was, *I hope there are no lions lurking; otherwise we might be on the menu!* Anyway, once I'd assured myself that no big cats were prowling, my attention was drawn to something different. Along a path that led into the trees, there were dozens of small lights glowing. Somebody had taken some simple brown paper bags and sunk a lighted candle into a little sand in the bottom of them. The amazing thing is that the bag doesn't burn and you have this wonderful lantern flickering in the darkness. It was simply magical. A few years ago (quite a few years ago actually) I had a "special" birthday and we tried to recreate that scene in our garden for a party. It was the talk of the evening; it looked like fairyland!

Candles are special in so many different settings. The other day I was visiting a friend and went into the cathedral in a nearby city. I sat quietly and watched as people walked towards the altar and lit the wicks – in memory, in thanks, in hope, in prayer. It struck me that candles evoke such different feelings in people, at different times of their lives.

I sometimes wonder what it is about them that appeals to me so much. After all, candles are definitely not as efficient as electric lights, and certainly more messy, but the truth is, their light is soft, enchanting, and in some way vulnerable. The candle often looks as though it is only just managing to stay alight – and in that sense, frail. I suppose I have spent some of my life feeling a little like that. It might be that I have felt my faith weak, my body tired, or even doubted my ability to go on trying in some small way to bring light. But I am encouraged by that lovely verse in the Bible: "He will not crush the weakest reed or put out a flickering candle" (Isaiah 42:3).

It is true that the candle may sometimes appear weak, and yet in another way, it is so powerful. When I was a little girl we used to sing a song in Sunday school, "This little light of mine, I'm going to let it shine". As an adult I have learned not to despise the ability of the smallest light to make an incredible difference.

There is a lovely quote attributed to St Francis of Assisi: "All the darkness in the world cannot extinguish the light of a single candle."

"He will not... put out a flickering candle."

With Friends Like This

I've said it many times: women are under a lot of pressure to look a certain way. Sometimes this isn't just through the media; the people close to us can be just as bad. I have a friend – let's call her Hannah. She is a remarkable woman, with a fantastic sense of humour and she's great company. Hannah once told me a story about someone she was really close to when she was younger – let's call her Louisa. Louisa was Italian, beautiful, very tall, and very leggy, with dazzling eyes and hair.

Louisa went back to Italy for twenty-five years, but one day Hannah received a note from her saying that she was coming back to Cardiff and would like to meet up. Hannah was conscious that she had put on a few pounds down the years and she suspected that Louisa might be as striking as ever. So, the race was on… She had a month to prepare to see her long-lost friend. Hannah went on a crash diet, got her hair done, dolled herself up, but even then she didn't feel tremendously confident.

The big day finally came and Hannah waited on the platform for her friend to arrive. People began billowing off the train and Hannah spotted Louisa. All of Hannah's fears were realized. Louisa looked incredible.

Much to Hannah's dismay, Louisa walked straight past her. Apprehensively, Hannah called after her and Louisa turned. They both smiled and hugged. Then this Italian beauty looked at Hannah with shock and in her thick Sicilian accent said, "It's so good to see you. Gosh, when I left you had a little face and big eyes; now you've got a big face and little eyes."

Have you ever had a friend like that? They probably don't mean to – but somehow they bring you down pretty regularly. Sometimes people excuse negative comments by saying, "Oh, it's just having a bit of a laugh. They know I don't mean it." And of course, there has to be room in friendship for a bit of banter. Nevertheless, we all do well to remember the incredible power of words – both to build up and to tear down. When I was a child we used to recite a little ditty in the playground: "Sticks and stones will break my bones but words will never hurt me."

If only it were true...

My Lesson from the Car Boot Sale

My niece Jenny and I decided that it would be good fun to set up a table in the local car boot sale with the odds and ends that had been in my attic for years. I just hoped Auntie Peg wouldn't walk by and see her "unusual" choice of vase sat on top of our stall! Jenny and I set off early in the morning with our box of goodies and a red-and-white checked cloth for our table. Thankfully the weather was looking great for our venture into the world of high finance.

We were shown to our pitch by a man with a physique like Arnold Schwarzenegger, so we didn't disagree with his decision! We set out our table and Jenny put her final touches to it to help persuade our customers to part with their pounds – or should I say pennies. We started the day well, but by midday the sales were flagging a little, so I decided to take a break and browse around the other stalls. I was hoping to see something that was selling for a pound or two that, when valued, would be worth thousands. I have obviously watched too much daytime television!

I eventually saw something I really liked and after much haggling bought an old picture frame. In it was a picture of a First World War soldier, but I thought I could replace that and use the frame for something else. We arrived home, still with some of our unsold goods and armed with my new purchase. (I think it ate up much of my "profits"!) Rob's face was a study. It was then that I realized that he doesn't have an eye for the finer things of life and neither does he recognize a good bargain. I explained that he needed to understand that I had probably saved him a lot of money. He didn't seem convinced. I can't imagine why!

It was later that evening that I decided to look at my purchase properly. It was an old wooden frame made all the more attractive by its oval shape. But as I was examining it, the picture in it really caught my attention. The young man in uniform appeared to be confident and his half smile seemed to say that he could handle all that may come his way. To me, he looked handsome, with kind eyes... and then I realized how very young he was.

My mind drifted for some time, thinking, *Who was this man who had hardly left his childhood before going off to war? Had he survived? Even as he smiled out of the photograph, was his stomach churning inside him? How did his mother and father feel as they waved him goodbye?* And suddenly it was as if it wasn't a snapshot in my home – but a person.

I have never replaced his photograph and he still smiles out of the old oval frame. Almost every time my eye catches him, I am reminded of the brevity of life, and I sometimes wonder, as people gaze at photographs of me long after I am gone, what will I be remembered for. Will I leave a mark on this world for some good that I have done? Will my children be able to say, "She taught us right from wrong but she was also fun to be around?" Will they remember that I tried to tell them that relationships are the most important things in life? Will they recall that time and time again, I reminded them that God loves them unconditionally?

Even as I write he stands there now – young, proud – my dear soldier.

And he teaches me.

My young soldier.

The Battle Within

I love being a grandmother. Most of all I love it when the grandkids *cwtch* (a Welsh word that means "cuddle") into me and say, "Tell me a story Nandi." Evie, aged six, has a perennial favourite: "Let's have the one about the big bad wolf!" she says.

Of course I squeeze her in close and tell the old tale of a young girl in red who has a nasty shock visiting her grandmother. But when Evie is a little older I will tell her of another wolf. It is an old Cherokee story.

The Chief was talking with his grandson. He said, "Inside me are two wolves and they are always fighting: the one is good and the other bad. The one is full of bitterness, anger, resentment, regret, impatience, and greed; the other is filled with kindness, patience, faithfulness, and hope. All day long they battle against each other and at times the fight is furious."

The little boy's eyes were wide. "But Granddad," he said, "which one wins?"

The old man pulled the boy close and whispered in his ear, "The one I feed."

"Which one wins?"

Ice Cream

Some years ago I spoke at a Care for the Family event called Issues Women Face. The theme of the evening was on pressures that women have to deal with today – not least the pressure to look amazing and always be in control. During the evening I used to tell the following story. To be honest I can't vouch that it's true but I promise you that every woman I spoke to wanted it to be.

A very glamorous and "got-it-all-together" business executive was driving along the freeway in America in her bright red convertible. The roof was down and, although pretending not to notice, she was enjoying the looks from men in the cars that pulled up alongside her at traffic lights. It was a hot day and she decided to pull into an ice-cream parlour.

As she walked into the shop, she noticed a very good-looking man sat at a corner table and thought that he looked familiar. He really was very attractive. Not only that, but he smiled at her. She gave him a nervous smile back, went to the counter, and bought her ice cream. Her stomach was churning. The young man behind the counter took her money, handed her the change, and stood her cone in the little container on the counter. As she turned, the man in the corner smiled again. She was almost sure she recognized him from somewhere. She showed him some perfectly capped teeth and left the shop – she was weak at the knees.

When she got into her car she realized that she didn't have her ice cream. She must have left it in the little container on the counter. At that moment, she thought, *Oh I can't go back in; it would just be too embarrassing, especially with him there*. And then she thought, *No! I'm a successful business executive and I can do this*.

She got out of the car and with great purpose stalked into

the ice-cream parlour and made her way to the counter. To her horror her ice cream was not on the counter. She felt completely flustered – then she heard a voice just behind her... "You're right – you do recognize me. I'm George Clooney. And your ice cream is in your handbag."

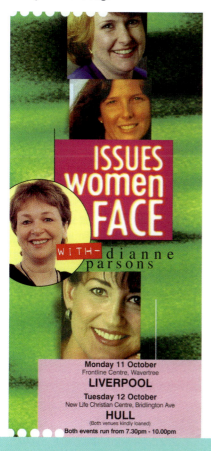

Issues Women Face

with Dianne Parsons

Monday 11th October
Frontline Centre, Wavertree
LIVERPOOL

Tuesday 12 October
New Life Christian Centre,
Bridlington Ave
HULL
(Both venues kindly loaned)

Both events run from 7.30pm - 10.00pm

I assure you, there was a time when grainy green backgrounds were all the rage... I think...

God's Reward

Someone once said, "Grandchildren are God's reward for putting up with your kids." We have five of them now – would I be biased if I said they are the best grandchildren ever? I love seeing how different they all are – and spotting their individual talents.

I have taken Lily to her ballet lessons on occasion and it warms my heart to sit and watch her using her arms so elegantly while doing her *plié*. She has such poise, even at this young age. Then there's her younger sister Evie. She will have a go at just about anything and she especially loves the challenge of swimming. She's taken to the water like a duck to… well, you get the idea. Even now I can hear her in my mind shouting, "Watch me do a dive-bomb Nandi!" Then comes the youngest of the trio, Freddie. He is four years old and he's a great little footballer. I think the Manchester United scouts will be *begging* for his signature within weeks! Their cousins are Harry and Jackson. Jackson is almost five years old and he's a Lego buff – I think the world of architecture could be radically transformed when he grows up. Lastly, there's Harry, who is eight years old. Harry does karate along with his dad and Jackson, but as fearsome as his karate chops are, under it all, he's as gentle and kind natured as can be.

Now, I'm a proud grandparent, but my love and delight in the grandkids isn't based on how cute they are or on their aforementioned gifts and talents. I just love them for who they are. In the society in which we live that is not just a nice idea – it is absolutely vital. There has never been a generation of children who are told in a thousand ways, "We will love you if you are beautiful or handsome, we will love you if you achieve, and we will love you if you are successful." So deeply do children grasp this that many, when asked what they want most in life, do not say, "To be happy", but "To be famous". I want to encourage those little ones to make the most of their gifts and talents, but even more so I want to let them know time and time again that they are loved – *anyway*. A friend said to me many years ago, "There is no freedom like having nothing to prove."

When I consider this, I'm reminded of how God thinks of us. In the book of 1 Samuel it says: "People look at the outward appearance, but the Lord looks at the heart." (16:7)

My grandkids are great, but deep down, I know there are moments when they are challenging. Of course, every family situation is unique and carries different challenges, but if we can capture the sentiment of this verse, to not look at the outward appearance, achievements, and strengths but see the heart, wouldn't the world be a better place?

I know that Lily may not become a dancer, Evie might not swim professionally, the football contract for Freddie may never come, Jackson could have no interest in architecture, and there's a possibility that Harry won't be practising his karate moves in adulthood, but does that matter? Not really. I love them for *them*.

Some of us spend a lifetime looking for somebody to love

us like that, without realizing that is how God loves us... unconditionally.

Oh, how I wish they would stay this age!

Spider-Man Trick

I love this story!

A little boy of six said to his mother, "Mummy when is Granny coming to stay?"

His mother was puzzled – her son wasn't usually keen on his grandmother visiting. "Why do you ask?" she said.

The little boy replied, "Because I want to see Daddy do his Spider-Man trick."

"What's that?" asked his mother.

"I'm not sure," the little boy replied, "but I heard Dad say to his friends, 'The next time my wife's mother comes to visit, I'm going to climb up the wall.'"

And we fool ourselves that children never listen!

I Remember...

As I look back on my kids' lives so many recollections come flooding back. I feel that the illness I've told you about robbed me of quite a lot of Lloyd's young life, but I still have some wonderful memories. One is of him giggling. He had such an infectious giggle; sometimes I would be so angry with him, but against all my will he'd make me laugh.

I remember the joy of him when he was so very tactile; even up until he was twelve he would lie with me on the settee and put his arm in mine. And I remember the feeling almost of grief in his teenage years when that suddenly stopped and it appeared he didn't want to be seen out with me unless I had a brown paper bag over my head.

And I remember when, in his later teen years, I saw the first signs of a thaw after such a long winter – and how it warmed my heart. I remember Lloyd telling me when he was little that he would never marry anybody else except me, and *both* my kids telling me that they would never leave home. And I remember, when they were teenagers, worrying in case they meant it.

I remember being jealous if they went through times when they communicated with Rob more than me. I remember being desperately hurt if they didn't want to eat the meals I'd prepared. And I remember that no matter what they had done to me during the day, and no matter how old they were, it was impossible not to feel tremendous love for them when they were asleep.

And I remember times of helpless laughter. I remember the day I got my little family around me and said, "I have some important information to impart – listen well."

Rob said, "Does this include me?"

I said, "Especially you." Without pausing for breath I went

on, "It appears that there are some things in this house that only I can do. In case I get hit by a bus I want to pass on the wisdom of the years to you." They stood there open-mouthed. "Today's lesson is how to replace a used toilet roll. The first part is to notice the empty roll on the holder. You have to remove it – it will not self-destruct. Push the spindle gently and remove the empty roll.

"Put it in the bin, not on the windowsill. We've stopped collecting them to make *Blue Peter* castles. Now, here's the really hard part: push the spindle again and put a new roll on. There! Now you can try it on your own next time."

I am a mother. I am not a perfect mother. I learned a long time ago that "perfect" is too great a burden to carry. Nor am I "just" a mother. I am a woman with gifts, hopes, and desires that are unconnected to my two kids. But I know, without a doubt, it is the most important job that *I* will ever do.

The Silent Age

I was taking part in a radio programme and I shared on air an encounter I'd had with a nurse a few years before. The nurse in this story said something so profound that I've never forgotten it. It was around Christmastime, the nights were getting colder, the shops were brimming with decorations, and for once I actually felt Christmassy.

Then, out of nowhere, I received a phone call. My brother had just had a massive heart attack. The festive sense of harmony suddenly departed as I rushed to the hospital with my sister-in-law. When we arrived, the medical staff still weren't able to let us see him, so we lingered in the corridor of the ward, and waited. After about ten minutes, a nurse appeared, and she was amazing. She took us into the family room, made us a cup of tea, sat down with us, and encouraged us to try not to worry. I have to confess: usually, if people tell me not to worry at a moment like that, I don't necessarily accept it.

On this occasion, however, her manner did actually give me a sense of calm. At this time of year, the hospital too was filled with tinsel, ornaments, and fairy lights, and rather than sitting in silence, I asked this nurse what she was doing for Christmas. I expected her response to be something about having family over, or about the weight of the turkey she needed to buy, but it wasn't. She simply said, "I don't know what I'm going to do with my life and I don't know if I'm going to stay with my husband." It was 2 a.m. and here was this lady that I hadn't met before, or since, sharing her deepest feelings.

To say I was taken aback would be an understatement, but I didn't have time to think of my response, because she continued, "I'm very gregarious but my husband isn't. He's retired and never wants to do anything. I go out with my daughter sometimes and all the men look at her because she's stunning and I can't even get my own husband to pay me attention." Then came the words, "I feel like I'm living in the silent age!"

Well, after I told this story on the radio, the phone lines were jammed with women for whom this story resonated in a big way. But I shouldn't have been surprised. I meet so many people in middle or later years who feel as if life is passing them by. They use phrases such as "It's a young person's world." Yet older people often have so much to give. I think it is generally true that in our society we do not honour the elderly. Of course this is not just an issue for society but for those of us who are a little older ourselves and how we view life and the part that we can still play. There is no doubt that as life goes on for us we may get side-lined by society – even made to feel as if we have little worth. But that is not how God sees us, and it's not how we should view ourselves. I'm always inspired when I meet older people who, in big or small ways, are making a difference in the lives of others. And of course, we can sometimes see a lifelong dream fulfilled in the latest years of our lives.

Bertha Wood had her first book, *Fresh Air and Fun: The Story of a Blackpool Holiday Camp*, published on her 100th birthday on 20 June 2005. She started writing it at the age of ninety!

Now there's a lady I'd like to have had coffee with!

"Me too!" When have
you felt vulnerable? Was
there a friend who gave you
hope and encouragement?
(Vulnerability)

"This man had used his clownish make up as a type of mask for so long..."

Do you feel you sometimes wear a mask? What steps can you take to strive to be yourself? (The Tears of a Clown)

What "school gate experiences" can you remember from your childhood or, if you're a parent, with your children? (A Mother Remembers)

Light a candle and
watch it flicker. What
thoughts and feelings go
through your mind?
(Candles)

> *"Words will never hurt me... If only that were true."*

Has anyone said something harsh that stayed with you? How might you lay down this hurt?
(With Friends Like This)

What item that cost you little
has great sentimental value?
(My Lesson from the
Car Boot Sale)

What pressures do you
feel society puts on you?
(Ice Cream)

If you can, take a moment
to recall some times of
laughter in your family.
What comes to mind?
(I Remember...)

95

Are you or do you know
others who may feel that
they are in "the silent age"?
(The Silent Age)

Alone

Sometimes I feel that loneliness is an unspoken epidemic in the UK and I'm sure that's true for other countries. It's easy to look back at past generations with rose-tinted glasses, but I'm sure we used to be so much more aware of our neighbours. As a child I knew that, in our street, if someone was in trouble, people would have been there to help.

Not long ago we had snow unlike anything we have seen for decades, and on the news there were so many heart-warming stories where people stuck in traffic for hours were brought food, water, and blankets by complete strangers. Those severe weather conditions brought the best out in people – it's just a shame that it's not always the case.

One evening, Rob and I were watching television when the phone rang. I'd like to say we were engrossed in something highbrow, but it was probably a detective drama or, more likely, *Strictly*! Rob paused the TV and I took the call. The voice on the other end of the line obviously belonged to an elderly woman and I realized she had dialled incorrectly. I said, "Oh, I'm sorry – there's no 'Mary' here – you must have the wrong number." There was a long pause, but something stopped my saying goodbye and hanging up immediately. Then she said, "Oh, please don't go. You're the first person I've spoken to all day." We chatted. By the time we'd finished, Rob was asleep on the sofa but I don't think he minded. I got her to write my number down and told her to call me anytime.

Loneliness is a terrible scourge in our society. I remember saying to an elderly lady, "Where are you going tonight, Doris?" She said, "I'm going ballroom dancing." I smiled. "I didn't know you liked dancing!" She replied, "Oh, I don't really, my dear.

But since my husband died it's the only time of the week when anybody touches me."

Psalm 68:6 says, "God sets the lonely in families." I am challenged by that verse – challenged to make sure that the door of my family is secure – but not so tightly shut that we don't allow others into our lives.

Sand and Stone

Two elderly women walked on a beach together. As they walked, Emily gave Florence a beautiful book that she knew her friend had wanted for months. Florence bent down, took a large pebble, and scratched on it, "Today my friend Emily blessed me." But a little later, as they talked, Emily said something that hurt Florence deeply. After a while Florence stooped and wrote in the sand, "Today my best friend hurt me."

Later that day, as they ate together, Emily said, "When I gave you the book you wrote of it in stone, but when I hurt you, you wrote in the sand. Why?"

Florence replied, "When someone hurts us, we should write it down in sand, where the winds of forgiveness can erase it, but when someone does something good for us, we must engrave it in stone, so it is kept forever."

As much as possible write your hurts in the sand and carve your blessings in stone.

What I Learned from a Coffee Mug

There is nothing like a cup of coffee and a natter with a good friend. To sit for a while and catch up on all our news usually involves laughter and a little seriousness. I have a very special friend, Claire, who has a kitchen with a farmhouse table, and when I visit that is where I love to sit. Somehow the kitchen seems a secure place to share our stories with each other.

Behind the table is an old dresser and Claire has an unusual collection of crockery displayed there, including an interesting assortment of mugs. There are mugs from across the world. There are some with cartoons on, and others with pictures of family members printed on them. Some are unusual shapes and the colours on a few of them are incredibly eye-catching. On my last visit to Claire's home, I noticed that she had acquired a new addition to her collection. It wasn't the colour that caught my eye, but rather the sentiment written on it. It read, "You can't turn the clock back, but you can wind it up again."

I asked her where she'd bought the mug. She told me it had been given to her by a friend, who had been through a very traumatic experience the previous year. Apparently, her mum had died suddenly and she had also discovered her husband was having an affair, which subsequently ended in divorce. This dear lady told Claire that for many months she had grieved both the losses and thought that her life would never hold any laughter or normality again.

She went on to tell Claire that one day she woke and made the decision that she needed to change the course of her thinking, so she decided to join a local book club, which one of her friends organized. It was there she met a woman who had gone through similar circumstances herself. From there they would meet for coffee occasionally and just look out for each other. Over the months, Claire's friend began to realize she was feeling much more positive about life and decided that she too could help others who have felt just as she did. She had decided just as the mug read: "You can't turn the clock back, but you can wind it up again."

This also reminded me of a story about an eastern monarch who sent his wise men into the world to find a phrase that would fit every circumstance of life. They were gone for seven years. When they finally came back to the palace they said, "Oh king, we have scoured the earth and found the phrase you wanted. You can write these words over people, buildings, organizations, and circumstances: 'This too will pass away.'"

I felt so inspired by the mug in my friend's kitchen I decided to get one of my own, to remind myself that whatever I'm going through, hopefully I can manage, with good friends and God's help, to take a few tentative steps towards a new tomorrow.

You can't turn the clock back, but you can wind it up again.

To Change the Future

> *It is true that if we do not learn from history we may have to relive it. But if we do not change the future we may have to endure it – and that could be worse.*
>
> Alvin Toffler

Some years ago, I was challenged by this quote of Alvin Toffler. The phrase "change the future" caught my imagination, particularly the idea that we could take actions now – even small ones – that would lead to a better world tomorrow. I was inspired to sound a call to action that wherever we are and *whoever* we are, we can make a difference. We decided to hold a Saturday event for women in the Royal Albert Hall called To Change the Future.

I'm not sure how it happened (and I can assure you that when we signed the contract for the Royal Albert Hall I began to wonder whether this was the greatest idea I'd ever had). I will never forget walking onto the stage and gazing out at an audience of thousands of women – of all ages. I watched as elderly people were being helped up the stairs and young women in skinny jeans rushed in late to their seats.

Of course I felt nervous, but I tried to imagine that this

was not a vast auditorium but my living room. It was filled with all kinds of women: those who were confident and those who felt they had nothing to give, those who felt loved and those desperate for a touch of affirmation.

The other day I looked up my notes from that occasion. This is how I began my talk that day.

"Just about 2,000 years ago, two very different women met in the Temple at Jerusalem. One was called Mary and was probably only about fifteen or sixteen years of age; the other woman, Anna, was in her eighties. When they met, Mary was holding a new-born baby boy and Anna was holding on to a hope – that one day she would see the messiah. The second Anna set eyes on this little child cradled in Mary's arms she knew that her long years of waiting were over.

"These were ordinary women and yet, in so many ways, they were very special. Mary was young but she was willing to do whatever God asked of her. She had said, 'I am your servant. Be it unto me as you have said.' Anna was old – eighty-four and still counting – and had devoted her life to prayer that the messiah would come. Both of them would have had good reason to be unwilling to play their part. Mary had known shame and pain even in her young life, and Anna had lost her husband after just seven years of marriage. Here were two women, years apart, probably worlds apart, but both allowing God to use them not only despite their difficult circumstances but perhaps *because* of their difficult circumstances.

"I'm so glad that there are no age limits with God. There may be some of us who are older in years, and we have some empathy with Anna. Hey, I have some empathy with Anna! But you know, it may be that the most fruitful years of our lives are still ahead. That's part of the message of To Change the Future – young or old, single or married, rich or poor, God can use us to make a difference."

Some years after that event a woman wrote to me. Here is part of what she said:

Dear Dianne,

I meant to write sooner (much sooner!), I wanted to tell you what an incredible effect To Change the Future at the Royal Albert Hall had on us. I came with six friends and we all went away challenged to begin to do something – however small – that would make a difference. One lady started a parent and toddler group at her church, another began helping in a pregnancy advice centre – but all six of us did something. Thank you for the inspiration of that day. I wanted you to know that however much effort it took – it was worth it.

As I turned that letter over and over in my hand I mused on six women – I had no idea how old they were or what they had been through in life. But I knew this: whatever their age and circumstances God was using them to change somebody's future.

Sometimes I still have to pinch myself – the talking that began in the salon ended up here!

On Ageing

It was my daughter Katie's college ball and I remember being in London with her; she wanted to buy a little black dress for a special occasion. We pounded the pavements of Oxford Street not just once, but until I was about to drop. She must have seen the look of sheer exhaustion on my face when she promised me the next shop would be the last one. It was a large store which had shops within the shop. We looked once more at the little black dresses and she eventually picked out two or three to try on.

As I looked for the nearest seat to collapse on and revive myself, she handed me a dress that looked suitable for the older woman! She requested my company in the changing rooms, so I could give my opinion on the ones she wanted to try. As I walked into the inner sanctum, I was confronted by women of various shapes and sizes. Some looked a little uncomfortable being exposed to the public domain as they tried on their hopeful purchases, while others cast care to the wind and really didn't mind who was looking. There were those who slid graciously into their chosen clothes, and those who fought tooth and nail with sheer determination.

Luckily, I found a cubicle that had just been vacated. I went in and drew the curtain. It was then that I realized my head was thumping, the music was thumping, and my bunions were thumping. As soon as I closed the curtain I found myself sliding down the wall and wishing this could all be a dream that would soon end.

Suddenly a conversation between two girls who were talking about their plans for that evening stirred me back to reality, and I pulled myself up and began to try on the dress that had been chosen for me. I was halfway through fighting to get this dress (which was supposed to be my size) down over my hips, when the curtain flew back and there stood my daughter – my size eight daughter – looking stunning, saying, "Mum, do you think my bum looks big in this?" At that moment I wanted to scream at the injustice of life and middle-age spread. I only just stopped myself yelling at the top of my voice, "Yes, it looks massive!"

What is it, though, that makes us so aware of the way we look – especially for those of us who feel that all the muscle (and fat) that surrounds our skeletal frame is migrating south? Or that the wrinkles on our face, when pulled taut, twang back at great speed when we let go? And so often the kids don't help. I remember when Lloyd was about thirteen (blessed age!) he said to me, "Mum – you've got something on your chin." When I went to wipe it off he said, "No – not that one." The fact of the matter is I do have something on my chin – I have hairs growing there! And I feel very vulnerable at times about them. A few years after that, he told me that he had read that as people get older they shrink (not inwards unfortunately). Even now I am only just over five feet one inch tall. It seems to me that, pretty soon, I am going to look like a garden gnome with a beard!

It's quite a pressure when you live in a world dominated by Hollywood films. But hey, if Lloyd is right, perhaps I can get a part in one of them. Anybody know if Snow White needs a little helper?

One Busy Mum's Story

I was speaking at a women's conference, and for some reason, Rob was there that evening, hovering at the back trying not to look too out of place. The first half seemed to be difficult and I felt the audience needed lifting. I said to Rob in the interval, "I think we need to bring a bit of laughter to this event. I'm going to tell the smear test story." Rob's face fell so much he resembled Droopy! He said, "You can't!" I said, "What do you mean 'I can't'?" "Well," he spluttered, "you just can't!" I didn't argue. What was the point when I knew that I was going to do it anyway? All I can say is the moment I had finished telling it the audience started laughing, the atmosphere was different, and we had a wonderful evening. So here it is.

A woman had an appointment for a smear test. It was for 9.15 a.m. and she was rushing around the house trying to get there on time. But by the time she had made the kids' sandwiches and finished off a bit of maths homework for her eldest, she was late – very late. She didn't have time to shower so she rushed into the bathroom, grabbed a flannel, gave herself a quick wash, threw the flannel in the wash, and shot out of the door.

She didn't have to wait long at the hospital and an elderly doctor called her into the consulting room. She lay back as he began the procedure and then he said, "My, my, Mrs Tomkins – we have made an effort today!" She had no idea what he was talking about and didn't reply.

Later that day her ten-year-old daughter came running upstairs, shouting, "Mum, where's the red flannel from the bathroom?" She replied, "Oh it's in the wash, darling. Use another one."

Her child yelled back, "But it's got all my silver glitter in it for my school project."

P.S. Any complaints about including this story, please write to Rob.

The Woman Who Was Afraid to Go Out

When I read a book, I often imagine I am in the scene. If it's a novel I picture the setting of the room, the colour of the furniture perhaps, the fire crackling, and the conversations that the people are having. I especially love to do that when I read the Bible. I put myself in the picture and imagine hearing the lapping of the water on the shore of Galilee and the chatter of the fishermen as they haul their nets and, maybe in Jerusalem, the hustle and bustle and haggling in the narrow, cobbled streets.

One of my favourite stories is the one told in Mark's Gospel about the woman who had suffered a blood disorder for twelve years. This was an illness that, according to the law, alienated her from people. If she touched someone while out and about and they knew her problem, they had to go home and wash themselves completely and change their clothes. I often wonder how that would have made her feel: ashamed, dirty, devastated – and that had been going on for twelve years. Her loneliness must have been unbearable. In our day it would have meant nobody asking us to a party or out for a coffee.

This woman had trawled around all the doctors and had spent all her money in the process but without getting any better. One day she heard that Jesus was coming to her town – the one they called the "Miracle Man" – and she knew that this was not her only hope but her last hope. And with that belief in her heart she got the courage to go out among people again and made her way to the village. Did she cover most of her face so that no one would recognize her? I wonder. In the distance she could hear a cacophony of voices, and suddenly He was there. But He was surrounded by crowds of people – all trying to get near

Him. It was no use. She couldn't get anywhere near enough and then suddenly she stretched her hand through the crowd and managed to touch the very edge of His cloak.

Suddenly it's as if the scene was frozen. Jesus stopped walking and asked, "Who touched me?" I can imagine the disciples looking at Him and then at the crowd and scratching their heads in disbelief at those words! But Jesus knew this was something different to the push and shove of the crowd; He felt power go from Him.

Then this extremely brave woman stepped forward to admit it was she who touched Him. From here on I love to imagine that Jesus looked at her with utter compassion, and I would love to think that He reached out and touched her arm, something she had not experienced for all those years. What a wonderful experience. I don't know whether any of that happened or not, but I know the next part definitely did. He said, "Daughter, your faith has healed you" (Mark 5:34).

The woman that nobody wanted to touch was *His* daughter. And in that moment everything changed – not just in the healing of her body, but her *heart*.

Just a Nobody

I was invited to have coffee with a woman I had met while on a speaking tour in Canada a few years back. Coffee was brewing and as we sat and chatted my eyes wandered around the room; it was filled with memorabilia from all over the world. As I gazed at these treasures my eyes fixed on a shelf in a glass cabinet. It housed three of the strangest dolls I have ever seen. They were made of cloth and each had a different expression but all were haunting. They each raised a hand, as if in supplication to the onlooker. My friend told me that they were collectors' items and very valuable. I was intrigued by them. The more I looked at them the more they caught my imagination.

I asked my friend what each doll was called. She said, "Oh, all the same – Little Miss No Name."

We finished chatting and I made my way home, but as I drove, I couldn't get those dolls out of my mind. They seemed to symbolize how so many people feel: they almost have no identity of their own. Perhaps through circumstances or upbringing, any vestige of self-esteem has been wrung from them. Or maybe they have tried so hard to please others they have forgotten who they are themselves.

There have been times in my life when I have felt like that.

It's not just that sometimes people try to label us in unhelpful ways; it's that once in a while I feel like one of those old dolls – a nobody. I like it that Jesus gave his disciple Simon a new name – Peter. Peter means "rock", and although he often felt a failure, I'm sure the name that Jesus gave him helped sustain him and convince him that he had not only potential, but also value.

The Bible says that God will give us "a new name" (Revelation 2:17).

Singing in the Dark

I've had some remarkable gifts for my birthdays, but one of my favourites was a bird table my children bought me, which we duly erected outside the living room window. It is amazing the number of different birds that visit me each day.

My favourite bird is the robin. It seems to me to be the most faithful of friends. Unlike many other birds that migrate to warmer climates in the winter, the robin stays with us all year. And it simply cannot stop singing. It's the robin that so often begins the dawn chorus, and it is one of the few birds that sing at night – a little joy piercing the darkness.

Not so long ago I was going through a particularly difficult time, which was affecting me deeply. My heart was consumed with worry. One morning I had scattered the bird table with seeds and nuts and sat down to watch my new-found friends through the window. As I sipped my coffee, I gazed with wonder as these little birds scurried back and forth for sustenance, taking titbits back to the nest for their young. I felt God say to me, "This is what I want from you Dianne – I want you to come and feed from me." Without any warning I felt the warmth of tears rolling down my face.

The words from the Sermon on the Mount came back to me: "Look at the birds of the air; they do not sow or reap or store away in barns and yet your heavenly Father feeds them. Are you not much more valuable than they?" (Matthew 6:26).

I felt as though God was speaking to me personally, saying, "Dianne, I want you to keep coming back to me, so that I can sustain you each day. Not next week, or next month, but day by day."

If I can grasp the truth of that I think maybe even *I* could learn to sing in the dark.

Maybe even I could learn
to sing in the dark.

The Empty Chair

I often find it hard to pray. I wonder why that is. It's not that I don't love God, it's not that I don't believe in the power of prayer, and it's certainly not that I don't feel the need for it. I sometimes wonder whether part of the difficulty is the simple problem of speaking to somebody I can't see.

My friend Paul Francis tells a story in his book *A little Book on Soul Care* that has been a big help to me in that area.

Jack was elderly (well into his nineties) and almost bedridden. Each day a young friend, Tom (just eighty-two!) would visit him and they would talk. One day Jack shared with his friend how he found it so hard to pray. Tom said, "I was the same, Jack – until one day a friend gave me a little idea. I put an empty chair facing me and I imagine Jesus sat there. I talk to the chair. I'm not sure why it helps so much and if my kids ever caught me doing it they'd have me hauled off for treatment. But it works for me. You should try it someday."

And Jack did. In fact, the empty chair stayed in the same position facing the bed for the next three years. Sometimes visitors who thought they heard somebody talking would pause at the door, only to discover that apart from Jack the room was empty.

Jack died in his sleep in the early hours of the morning one winter's day. When his daughter found him, he was lying half out of the bed with his head resting in the seat of the chair.

I put an empty chair facing me
and I imagine...

Being Me

I was watching one of those old James Bond films with Rob. One scene was set in a place like Switzerland (anyway very snowy!). One minute all was pretty calm; the next Roger Moore was hammering down a mountain pass on skis, chased by four men with machine guns, and a helicopter. Perhaps I'd seen it before, or maybe my life with Rob is so like being with 007 that I lost interest, but I found my mind wandering. Suddenly the years were rolled back and instead of James on the slopes, it was me. Only I wasn't hurtling down them; I was learning – and it was a nightmare.

I recall with stunning clarity my efforts to master the art of trying to move with those cumbersome additions to my feet, wishing I could sense the wind on my face. The only problem was that my face was constantly in the snow. I remember particularly how hard it was to do the simplest things, like manoeuvre my body off the nursery slope pulley – that ungainly contraption that sat between one's legs. Those around me seemed to alight this gadget so gracefully, but for some reason, even though I was sporty at school, I could not release my body from the thing with anything approaching dignity. I found myself falling on my face, my bottom or my back. Those around, who had to step over me while my skis were flailing around above my head somewhere, seemed a little irate. I very much wished I could have done it properly – just once.

I can recall lying awake at night practising the move in my mind, and I got it right every time. I remember standing at the end of the queue the next day, watching all these talented learners get on and then off without any difficulty at all. I even prayed about it, but to no avail – except for one time. I wished someone had taken a video just to remind me in my older years that I had achieved it – just that once. But I digress. I felt so good at that moment – and so proud of myself. I had extricated my bottom from the toggle and I was actually moving down the slope. But what was it my mother used to say to me? "Pride comes before a fall." I really should have listened to her more. I took off slowly at first, but soon, I gained speed...

And then I realized there was a group of men standing half-way down the slope being taught the basics of skiing by their instructor. They were all lined up end-to-end and I was heading straight for them! The first one looked surprised as I hit him but not as surprised as the man at the very end of the line. They all went over like dominoes.

I know you are meant to stop after accidents and exchange names and addresses, but I didn't for two reasons. Firstly, I didn't want anybody on that slope to have the slightest inkling of who I was and where I lived, and secondly, I couldn't have stopped even if I'd wanted to. I heard somebody shout something rude as I disappeared down the slope. I was wearing a muffler around my face each time I went into the coffee shop after that in case one of them recognized me.

I never did learn to ski. Do I feel inadequate as I look back on those efforts, knowing that so many of my friends mastered it all with such ease (and aplomb)? No, not any more. As I have become older I have come to realize that it is better to have tried and failed than not to have tried at all, as the saying goes. It doesn't hurt to be a little adventurous at times.

But far more important than even that is to understand that it is counterproductive to spend time worrying that we cannot be good at those things which others can achieve. I have come to realize that I have some gifts that those around me do not have. That doesn't make me a better person than they are; it just makes me different. I believe each of us has something that we are good at. Some would call this a gift. It may be baking a cake for someone; it may be we're a good listener. There are a variety of gifts within us all, and we can all make a difference even in the smallest of ways.

I found skiing tiring, but nothing like as tiring as the endless pursuit of trying to be somebody I was not made to be.

The Power of One

One of my favourite stories of all time is of a little boy walking along a beach. A freak tide had stranded thousands of starfish and they were struggling for life. The water had receded and they were trapped on the sand. The boy decided he wanted to help, so he started working his way along the shore, throwing them back into the water, one by one.

An old man came along and asked the boy what he was doing. The boy replied, "Sir, I'm throwing the starfish back into the sea."

The old man laughed and said, "Son, there are so many of them, it won't make any difference."

The boy looked up at the old man and smiled. "Sir," he said, "for the ones I throw back, it makes all the difference in the world."

The Falls and the Drought

How many times a day do most of us turn on a tap and take it for granted that water will flow? Water is something that we cannot live without, yet most of us have the luxury of going through life without really giving it a second thought. In the western world, we may occasionally come across hosepipe bans, but in the grand scheme of things, we don't really know anything of real drought.

Some years ago Rob and I went to Canada. While visiting, we were taken to Niagara Falls, and what an experience that was! We climbed into a boat with a group of other people donned in bright yellow plastic capes. We looked like an opera of canaries setting off on a trip! The boat bobbed up and down from the impact of the Falls. The sheer immensity of it all filled me with excitement but also an awestruck respect. We found our boat taking us behind the Falls and the noise was thunderous. We eventually headed back to the docking point, and when I looked around the boat, I saw that most of the women, including me, had massive black rings around their eyes as our mascara had run.

After this, imagine the contrast that Rob experienced when he was taken into the Sinai desert years later. While there, the guide showed him a plant that had learned to survive in times of drought. It would close down sections at a time until the last section was left holding on, waiting for the rains to come. If the rain did come, there was a seed pod on the end of the stalks that would burst into life and explode, sending seeds into the desert, bringing new plant life into being.

The Bible talks often of water and drought, but a verse that is a particular favourite of mine is Isaiah 43:19: "See, I am doing a new thing! Now it springs up; do you not perceive it? I am making a way in the wilderness and streams in the wasteland."

Through some of my "wilderness experiences", most of which you'll probably be familiar with by now, that verse was unendingly helpful. There are times of course when our lives feel like those falls in Canada – when God just seems to be pouring His goodness into our lives, but there are also seasons which feel like that dry season in the desert. Truthfully, I often feel like that plant waiting for the refreshing rains of God to fall on me, but I have learned to wait patiently and to remind myself that He specializes in making streams in the wasteland.

Heroes

I recently saw a giant billboard for the new, rebooted version of *Wonder Woman* advertised on the side of a building. As I looked at it, my mind started to wander. I imagined it wasn't Gal Godot's face above the glamorous Amazonian outfit but my own. In my mind's eye, I saw myself jumping as high as a house, running at speed and fighting off villains from every angle. Then suddenly, I snapped back to reality. At five feet one inch, I'm nowhere near tall enough.

As I went about my day, I started thinking, *What do real heroes look like?* If we believe much of what we see in films, then they look like Wonder Woman. But of course, heroes come in all shapes and sizes, and that is because heroism is usually not about looks, age or even ability. Some time ago I read the story of Christopher Reeve who played Superman in the original film series. He was left quadriplegic following a riding accident, and when asked to comment on the nature of heroism Christopher said, "I think a hero is an ordinary individual who finds strength to persevere and endure in spite of overwhelming obstacles."

Some women who are heroes don't fit the Hollywood profile for success. In fact, their heroism is based on something much deeper than body shape and even height. Let me mention two that come to mind.

The first became famous while taking a bus ride. It was a cold December evening in 1955 in Montgomery, Alabama, and Rosa Parks (same height as me!) was returning home after a shift as a seamstress. Rosa, an African American woman, took her seat on the bus and she chose the front row of the section designated for "coloured" passengers. A few stops further on and a number of white passengers got on the bus but had to stand. The now infamous moment came when the bus driver, James Blake, asked Rosa's row to give up their seats. Three black passengers complied but Rosa refused and was ultimately arrested.

I don't think anybody, least of all Rosa, could have imagined what would result from that simple "no". The events that flowed from that incident eventually led to the Supreme Court ruling that segregation was unconstitutional. Many say what happened that day was the true beginning of the Civil Rights Movement. I am in awe of the courage Rosa showed that day. She said, "I did not want to be mistreated, I did not want to be deprived of a seat that I had paid for. It was just time... I had not planned to get arrested. I had plenty to do without having to end up in jail. But when I had to face that decision, I didn't hesitate to do so." Rosa was asked what made her take her stand that day. I can't get her reply out of my mind: "People always said that I didn't give up my seat because I was tired... No, the only tired I was, was tired of giving in."

Rosa Parks

My second hero is Gladys Aylward. She was so short her biography was called *The Small Woman*. I immediately liked her but for the wrong reason. At just four feet ten inches tall, she made me feel positively leggy! But if Christopher Reeve was right about the nature of heroism, then Gladys had the necessary qualities – "perseverance" and "endurance" in bucket loads. She was a housemaid but desperately wanted to go to China as a missionary. She failed her exams with the mission board and was told she was not suitable. But Gladys didn't give up. She wrote directly to an elderly missionary in China, Jenny Lawson, who said that she could join her in her work in Yang Seng – if she could get herself to China. Gladys couldn't afford to travel by ship but she bought a one-way ticket on the Trans-Siberian Railway, and in October 1930 she set off for China with a suitcase, a Bible, and two pounds nine pence.

The story of what Gladys achieved has become the material of books and the film *The Inn of the Sixth Happiness*, from quelling riots in prisons, to being used by the Mandarin to help eradicate the shameful practice of binding the feet of baby girls (it left most disabled for life), to leading a hundred children to safety across the mountains and the Yangtze River during the war with Japan. This tiny woman affected the lives of millions.

Don't get me wrong: I'd like to have the beauty, strength, and agility of Wonder Woman. But the older I get the more I crave the kind of heroes that go to China with two pounds and nine pence in their pocket and who have the courage to say "no" when the easiest thing in the world is to whisper, "Yes, of course you can have this seat – right away."

The Lady in the Photograph

A legacy of love

I think this is simply one of my favourite photographs in the whole world! It was taken on the day of my daughter Katie's wedding to Paul. My dear mother had Alzheimer's and was very frail. She just couldn't attend the wedding, and so straight afterwards, Paul and

Katie called in on her. Why do I love this snap so much? Oh, for many reasons, but mostly because of the sheer happiness and joy on my mother's face.

But of course, that is not the only photograph I have of her. In my living room I have one when she was a teenager. The face that looks out at me each day is that of a very attractive young woman with eyes sparkling with fun and love. That is exactly how I remember her as a mother. She died some years ago, but as I look back and remember my days as a child, the words I would use to describe my memories of my mother are "patience" and "gentleness".

We weren't a wealthy family. We lived in a small terraced house. There was no central heating in those days and the toilet was outside in the garden. We didn't have a bathroom installed until I was about nine years old, but I do remember a tin bath in the kitchen that was covered with a wooden board and used for storage. On Sundays, the board would be taken off and all the stuff hauled out of the bath to enable the weekly "before school on Monday" bath routine to begin.

I remember our small black-and-white television in the cosy living room – the only room with heating, which came from a coal fire. Drying my hair when it had been washed was interesting. I would lie on the floor on my back with my head resting on the fireplace, with a towel behind my neck for comfort. The top and left-hand side of my hair dried quickly as I would lie with my head turned to one side watching the TV! They were happy days for me. My parents filled my life with security. As a teenager, there were no pressures put on me to achieve, and looking back I realize that I was loved whatever.

I had two older sisters and a younger brother. My mother had another daughter who would have been older than me, but she died at the age of four. We never talked much about my mother's feelings of loss, but being a mother myself now I can only think of how that must have been for her and my dad. I have come to realize that life takes us on all sorts of journeys – some exciting, some unusual, some tragic. It's how we deal with them, I have learned, that so often governs how our life is moulded.

That experience for my mother could have made her so bitter, but that didn't happen to her. I do know she felt angry at first and grieved, which is normal. I also know that each Easter, the time of my sister's death, her thoughts drifted back to the daughter she'd lost, but it seems to me she chose, and I really do mean that – she chose to be the gentle lady that I knew. How grateful I will always be to her for the things she taught me in my life. Oh, that I could be like her: generous, sacrificial, always available, and loving unconditionally. If I could be like that to my children, what a mother I would be.

In the last months of her life, when I visited her, I would often find myself laughing out loud with her. She loved to laugh, and she would still, even through the Alzheimer's, in her own way reassure me of her love for me. And I never left her room without telling her that I loved her too, and that Jesus loved her. Without any hesitation and in a clear voice she would reply and say, "Yes, and that's the best."

When she died, my share of her estate was 800 pounds. She didn't leave much, did she? Oh, but she did. The lady in the photograph left love and security, she bequeathed laughter and memories, and she passed on values that even now I pray will seep into the lives of my grandchildren.

A legacy of love. I pray my children will inherit such richness.

Thanks for Coming

I can hardly believe it but I guess our time together has come to an end.

Thanks for taking the time to journey through the highs and lows, and for allowing me to be *real* with you. Even though I may never see what you've written on *your* pages, I genuinely, with all my heart hope that it has been helpful and cathartic to have a place to jot down your dreams, fears, struggles, and joys.

I said in the beginning that I know my stories are not remarkable – but with all my heart, I believe there is power in sharing the ordinary stories of our lives with each other.

Your stories matter and I have no doubt there are those who would be blessed by hearing them.

I think that sense of journeying together is at the heart of genuine friendship. C. S. Lewis put it like this: "Friendship... is born at that moment when one... says to another, 'What! You too?'"

So, until next time...

Love,

Dianne x .

Is there some way you
can help someone in
your life who is lonely?
(Alone)

Do you have
friendships you value?
Do you tell those people?
(Sand and Stone)

"You can't turn the clock back but you can wind it up again."

Are there any steps you can take towards a new tomorrow? (What I Learned from a Coffee Mug)

Is there any way that you could change someone's future for the better? (To Change the Future)

"It's quite a pressure when you live in a world dominated by Hollywood films."

What could we do to lessen the pressures on ourselves (and our teenagers!) to match the looks of people in the movies? (On Ageing)

Have you or a friend
had an embarrassing
moment that you can laugh
about afterwards?
(One Busy Mum's Story)

"In that moment everything changed."

Try to imagine yourself in that scene – the crowd, the fear, the noise. What emotions do you think the woman felt? (The Woman Who Was Afraid to Go Out)

"Perhaps... they have tried so hard to please others they have forgotten who they are themselves."

Who speaks positivity into your life? Is there anyone *you* can encourage with your words? (Just a Nobody)

What song or sound brings
you peace or comfort
when things are tough?
(Singing in the Dark)

> *"I put an empty chair facing me and I imagine."*

Do you like the idea of the empty chair? (The Empty Chair)

"I believe each one of us has something we are good at."

What gifts do you think you may have? Are there steps you could take to develop them? (Being Me)

Have you or a friend
made a difference to
someone's life? If so, how?
(The Power of One)

*"He specializes in
making streams in
the wasteland."*

Are there any wilderness
experiences you have come
through in your life? What
have they taught you?
(The Falls and the Drought)

152

Who are your
heroes and why?
(Heroes)

"The lady in the photo left love and security."

Who in your life has made an impact that will stay with you forever? (The Lady in the Photograph)

A final word from Dianne...

When the idea of *You, Me and Coffee* came into my mind, I knew of course that we wouldn't *literally* be having coffee together – nevertheless I did believe that at least at some level, the stories I shared, and perhaps even a little of the hard times might touch your life. If you ever see me at a Care for the Family event, please come and say hello and if we both have time, lets *actually* have coffee!

Love, Dianne

Care for the Family is the national charity Dianne
has worked with for over thirty years. They aim to
promote strong family life and to help those who face
family difficulties. A snapshot of their work includes
events, networks, and resources to support:

• Parents • Couples
• Families with additional needs
• Bereaved parents • Young widows/widowers
• Single Parents

Care for the Family
mail@cff.org.uk

If you would like to support the work of
Care for the Family,
visit cff.org.uk/donate
for further information.

You can also keep in touch by following them on
Facebook, Twitter, and Instagram.